D1757342

NEOCLASSICAL HISTORY AND ENGLISH CULTURE

Studies in Modern History

General Editor: J. C. D. Clark, *Joyce and Elizabeth Hall Distinguished Professor of British History, University of Kansas*

Published titles include:

Neoclassical History and English Culture

From Clarendon to Hume

Philip Hicks
Saint Mary's College
Notre Dame
Indiana

First published in Great Britain 1996 by
MACMILLAN PRESS LTD
Houndmills, Basingstoke, Hampshire RG21 6XS
and London
Companies and representatives
throughout the world

A catalogue record for this book is available
from the British Library.

ISBN 0–333–65940–6

First published in the United States of America 1996 by
ST. MARTIN'S PRESS, INC.,
Scholarly and Reference Division,
175 Fifth Avenue,
New York, N.Y. 10010

ISBN 0–312–16091–7

Library of Congress Cataloging-in-Publication Data
Hicks, Philip Stephen, 1958–
Neoclassical history and English culture : from Clarendon to Hume
/ Philip Hicks.
p.   cm. — (Studies in modern history)
Includes bibliographical references and index.
ISBN 0–312–16091–7 (cloth)
1. Historiography—Great Britain—History—17th century.
2. Historiography—Great Britain—History—18th century.
3. Clarendon, Edward Hyde, Earl of, 1609–1674.   4. England–
–Civilization—Classical influences.   5. England—Civilization—17th
century.   6. England—Civilization—18th century.   7. Great Britain–
–Historiography.   8. Classicism—England.   9. Hume, David,
1711–1776.   I. Title.   II. Series: Studies in modern history
(Macmillan Press)
DA1.H53   1996
941.06'007202—dc20   96–25840
                                                                                    CIP

10   9   8   7   6   5   4   3   2   1
05   04   03   02   01   00   99   98   97   96

Printed in Great Britain by
The Ipswich Book Company Ltd, Ipswich, Suffolk

Contents

Acknowledgements

It is a pleasure to acknowledge the gracious permission of Her Majesty Queen Elizabeth II for use of the Stuart Papers. I also have to thank Lord Egremont for making the Wyndham family papers available, and the Oxford University Press Archives for permission to use the Minute Books of the Delegates of the Press. Quotations from the work of the 1st Earl of Clarendon have been made by permission of Oxford University Press.

I thank the staff of the Cushwa-Leighton Library (Jill Hobgood, in particular), the Milton S. Eisenhower Library, the Cambridge University Library, the Bodleian Library, and the British Library for their assistance.

For their many kindnesses over the years, I am grateful to Tommaso Astarita, Jean H. Baker, Pauline Bieringa, Thomas Blantz, DeAnn DeLuna, John Garrigus, Lisa Graham, William Kuhn, David Leitch, Dennis Moran, John Morrill, Katherine Penovich, and Wyger Velema.

At Saint Mary's College I have benefited from the unceasing generosity of my colleagues, Tom Bonnell, Gail Mandell, John Shinners, and Bruno Schlesinger.

For their advice at key stages in the history of my manuscript, I thank Jonathan Clark, Jack Cope, Mark Phillips, Nicholas Phillipson, Orest Ranum, and Nancy Struever. I am particularly grateful to Professor J. G. A. Pocock, who supervised my graduate studies in historiography and has continued to be a source of inspiration, encouragement, and counsel.

Closer to home, I owe an enormous debt of gratitude to my parents. Closer still, to Joyce, Stephen, and Reilly.

A Note on Abbreviations, Quotations, and Dates

The following abbreviations have been used:

BL	British Library
Bodl.	Bodleian Library
Bolingbroke, *Letters*	Henry St John, 1st Viscount Bolingbroke, *Letters on the Study and Use of History*, 2 vols (London, 1752). In citations, roman numerals will refer to individual letters, I-VIII.
Clarendon State Papers	*State Papers Collected by Edward, Earl of Clarendon . . .* , 3 vols (Oxford, 1767–86)
DNB	*Dictionary of National Biography*
Greig	*The Letters of David Hume*, ed. J. Y. T. Greig, 2 vols (Oxford: Clarendon Press, 1932)
HMC	Historical Manuscripts Commission
Pope Corr.	*The Correspondence of Alexander Pope*, ed. George Sherburn, 5 vols (Oxford: Clarendon Press, 1956)
Swift Corr.	*The Correspondence of Jonathan Swift*, ed. Harold Williams, 5 vols (Oxford: Clarendon Press, 1963)
TLS	*Times Literary Supplement*
Walpole Corr.	*The Yale Edition of Horace Walpole's Correspondence*, ed. W. S. Lewis, *et al*, 48 vols (New Haven, Conn.: Yale Univ. Press, 1937–83)

In quotations, the capitalization, spelling, and punctuation have not been modernized, except in cases of block capitals, which have been put in lower case, and abbreviations for words such as 'the' and 'that,' which are spelled out. Misprints have not been corrected. All italics have been omitted except those used for special emphasis by their authors.

Dates are 'Old Style,' except that the New Year will be taken to have begun on 1 January.

viii

1

The Weakness in English Historical Writing

By the middle of the eighteenth century, Englishmen had complained for over two centuries about the quality of their historical writing.[1] They cared passionately about their past and were almost overwhelmed by the quantity and variety of historical works they produced, and yet the English elite insisted that it had almost no history worthy of the name, no narrative history of England written to the Olympian standards of the inventors of 'history,' the ancient historians of Greece and Rome – Herodotus, Thucydides, Xenophon, Polybius, Sallust, Livy, and Tacitus.[2] While France and Italy possessed historians comparable to those of antiquity, it was 'a general observation among learned men,' according to the Earl of Orrery, that England 'still remains defective in excellent historians . . . [W]e have had a Locke, a Newton, and a Dryden; but we cannot boast a Livy, a Thucydides, or a Tacitus.'[3] Whatever twentieth-century assessments of English historiography may be, leading men of letters and political figures of the day, native as well as foreign, perceived a chronic defect in English historical writing. Bacon, Milton, Clarendon, Dryden, Addison, Bolingbroke, Voltaire, Montesquieu, Hume, and a host of lesser lights reiterated this commonplace disparagement of English histories.[4] During the sixteenth and seventeenth century, a number of continental historians had gained acclaim as peers of the ancient historians – Machiavelli, Guicciardini, Commynes, Mariana, Davila, de Thou, Mézeray, Sarpi, and others.[5] These 'neoclassical'[6] historians had written something Englishmen had failed to write: history in the grand manner, a majestic, authoritative narrative of political and military deeds often containing the character sketches, political maxims, and invented speeches for which the classical historians were famous. These celebrated neoclassical historians did not write histories of the classical period but did

1

write in imitation of the classical historians, sometimes in Latin, more often in the vernacular, on a modern subject, usually the modern history of their native country. The lack of an English neoclassical masterpiece, a history of England written according to the conventions of the ancient historians, constituted a weakness in early-modern English culture.

More, Hayward, Raleigh, Bacon, Camden, Cherbury, Daniel, and Milton stood out as noteworthy English historians.[7] However, none of them ever quite captivated the canonical status of continental historians. Although English writers could boast of achievement in a variety of genres, and had made successful translations of ancient literature and composed Latin poetry,[8] some critics, especially in France, argued that Englishmen had failed in the most exalted prose genre, history, as well as the most prestigious poetic genre, epic. Not even Milton had been un-animously accepted as the poet of a national epic comparable to Homer or Virgil. Although *Paradise Lost* was considered a work of genius and a source of national honor, it had its detractors who said that Milton's poem lacked the proper language and decorum,[9] that its theme was so Christian it could be made to appear to mock the pagan literary form it was presumed to embrace. Dryden and Pope struggled to answer the call for epic, but they only managed to compose translations of their classical exemplars, the Homeric and Virgilian epics.[10] Milton actually tried his hand at history but enjoyed considerably greater success with *Paradise Lost* than with his truncated *History of Britain*. In general, the parallel neoclassical projects shared a record of failure, as both epic poets and historians failed to attain a classical standard for their work.

Despite mounting dissatisfaction with native historiography, Englishmen continued to pursue the neoclassical ideal for history-writing. They wished to demonstrate that the vernacular language, the literary skill, and the subject matter of an English historian could compete with continental or even ancient Greek and Roman historiography. The social prestige and political utility of neoclassical history, together with the strength of humanist educational ideals, also sustained this quixotic quest for a perfect national history. After many failed entries in what would become an international literary competition, England at last gained what appeared to be a prizewinner in the Earl of Clarendon's *History of the Rebellion*, published between 1702 and 1704. As a young man Clarendon had been reading a biography of Thucydides, and in his commonplace book, next to the passage he had copied out describing Thucydides' decision to imitate Herodotus, Clarendon scrawled the words 'noble ambition.' It was this Englishman's ambition, in turn, to emulate Thucydides, who himself had possessed the noble ambition to make perhaps the most important imitation in the history of Western historiography by trying to model his work after that of Herodotus, the 'father of history.' Clarendon recognized both the literary and the social nobility of Thucydides', as well as his own, ambition. In Clarendon's time history was the most respected form of prose literature, and in fact Clarendon as well as Thucydides were 'noble' – the one became an earl, the other was descended from Thracian kings. Each possessed an ambition appropriate to his class: history-writing was a noble way to occupy one's leisure, a worthy ambition for noblemen. However, Clarendon's noble *History* did not entirely end the complaints about English historical writing. Clarendon had triumphed as a neoclassical historian of one particular episode in English history, the Civil War of the 1640s, but English critics still called for a neoclassical history of England's entire past. In the 1750s and '60s the Scottish philosopher David Hume met this challenge by writing his *History of England*: an outsider finally solved the problem in historical writing to the satisfaction of the English cultural elite.

This book presents an analysis of the content and the culture of English historiography from the point of view of this problem. The weakness in historiography may represent a relatively minor episode in literary history, but examining it helps us to reassess several aspects of English cultural history. At a time when recent scholarship has called into question the applicability of classical models to eighteenth-century political and literary culture,[11] it may be appropriate to question just how viable an option neoclassicism was for English historical culture. By taking the problem of English historiography as seriously as contemporaries did, we re-discover not only the centrality of classical models for historical writing and the stubbornness of humanist ideals of behavior and thought well into the eighteenth century, but also the intractable difficulties of the neoclassical project. We shall see that aspirant neoclassical historians kept bumping up against the modern world and that most came to grief trying to sustain an ancient literary genre in a modernizing society. One reason for the generally mediocre quality of historical narratives in this period has to do with the way in which certain modern phenomena such as Christianity, print, party politics, and antiquarian erudition compromised historians' ability to fulfill their lofty ambition. Early modernity nearly extinguished the neoclassical project. On the other hand, study of this problem raises the question of just how 'modern' the 'early-modern' period was, when two historians could sustain an antique genre created in very different social circumstances two millennia before. It is for the very reason that Clarendon and Hume somehow triumphed over the impediments of modern life that our study takes as its focus the last century in the history of this problem, roughly from the year 1660 to the year 1760, from Clarendon to Hume, when English life was becoming less and less like that of antiquity and yet two historians could still write like a Greek general banished to a distant isle or a Roman senator enjoying retirement at his country villa.

Early-modern English historians were not bent on inventing modern academic historical methods, as some scholars today seem to suggest, but rather they were grappling with the difficulties inherent in composing history in a manner two thousand years old. Contemporaries conceived of their historical writing as suffering from a chronic weakness because it failed to live up to classical standards, and yet modern scholarship has paid scant attention to such concerns.[12] Studies of English historiography, for all their richness of detail and interpretation, have not given the early-modern encounter with classical historiography its just due.[13] Although it is a commonplace that early-modern culture was remarkably indebted to the ancient world for its inspiration, and that the classical historians were held in high regard, the effects of classical imitation on English historical writing have never been traced. Many of the most important studies of historical writing instead focus on the origins of modern historiography,[14] identifying the early-modern period – roughly the fifteenth to the eighteenth century – as the seed time of the modern historical profession. Originating during the Italian Renaissance, these studies argue, and spreading through the rest of Europe in succeeding centuries, the modern method of historical writing and research was born: the emphasis on the critical use of original sources, the historicist understanding that discrete historical epochs deserve study on their own terms, the scholarly panoply of footnote, appendix, and index, the determination to study all of the human past – not simply politics and war – and to study it in a secular and 'scientific' way. Various students of historiography locate and celebrate these strands of modern historical consciousness and technique. However, the heroes in their story are usually antiquarians, philologists, or essayists, not proper 'historians' as contemporaries understood the term, so they are exploring early-modern attitudes to the past generally but not early-modern 'history' specifically. Contemporaries applied the term 'history' to a narrative art form handed down from ancient times. Once we investigate this art, we find in fact that the moderns never vanquished the ancients as swiftly or completely as these studies of the subject may imply. Indeed, we are invited to consider the extent to which the classical strain in historiography extends, albeit with many breaks and modifications, from Herodotus to the present day; to consider also whether the classical statesman – the amateur – or the modern academician – the professional – is best suited to writing history.

Such issues come into view once we focus on the readers and writers, not simply the texts, of history. Indeed, contemporaries identified the historian's social role as an important part of the problem of historiography; aspirant historians failed because they lacked the social and political stature advantageous to writing neoclassical history. Historians had to possess sufficient social standing to procure historical sources that were not open to the public but guarded by the jealous keepers of aristocratic muniment rooms and private archives. Success or failure as a historian could depend on the historian's reputation for integrity and on his social role, whether as statesman, man of letters, bishop, or country gentleman. However, scholars have generally overlooked this crucial dimension of historiography, perhaps assuming that the activity of writing novels or poems was identical to that of composing histories. Surely, that both John Milton and Jonathan Swift tried but failed to solve the weakness in historiography suggests that more than simply literary genius was required for the task. A social history of historians will reveal that most historians lacked the requisite political and social clout to become masters of neoclassical historical narrative.

By examining these historians and their readers, we can increase the chances of recovering some of the original meaning texts of history had for contemporaries, thus offering a counterweight to correct scholarly studies that tend instead to privilege twentieth-century responses to the texts. Indeed, the historical writing of this period becomes more intelligible once it is treated as a communication between author and reader. Seen in such a light, the Battle of the Books, for example, a contest between proponents of ancient and modern learning, takes on less the appearance of a theoretical dispute among literary critics, and more that of a culture war waged between political partisans using neoclassical history to score polemical points. Since the historical works under discussion purportedly answered a challenge to produce neoclassical history, a challenge posed by the English elite,[15] our project is, in part, a history of that elite, and it thereby helps to redress another balance. Herbert Butterfield observed the inclination of historians to focus on the 'winners' in history and not to pursue dead-ends, social and intellectual movements without a future.[16] The study of early-modern historical culture, on the other hand, entails an examination of 'losers' – of writers usually failing to write history successfully, of classical genres now often forgotten in the hierarchy of genres, of a ruling class that no longer rules as it once did. Our study contributes to the revisionist efforts of historians to consider anew the English elite,[17] here defined as the male members of the 4 to 5 per cent of adult Englishmen comprising the gentry and the titled nobility,[18] the principal social group possessing the leisure, money, and interest for such a monumental, expensive, and political form of literature, for grand folios recounting the deeds of their families, the makers of history. As Chapters 3 through 7 of this book should demonstrate, the cultural history of 'history' illuminates the elite ethos, its notion of privacy, its leisure pursuits, its modes of communication, its intellectual temper.

The elite attempted to monopolize neoclassical historiography, and valued its exclusivity and its tendency to enforce social deference. However, certain individuals lacking the prescribed social status, gender, or nationality also had a part to play in our story, either as readers or writers, even though they generally adhered to elite notions regarding the form, purpose, and nature of history. Women, especially at the end of this period, stepped forward to play a role in historiography. Men who lacked gentle birth also assisted in the elite's cultural expression. Various Scottish, Irish, French, and American writers tried to present the English elite with a neoclassical history of England. We shall be focusing on historians the English elite appears to have taken most serious notice of, whether foreign or native, common or noble: Clarendon, Brady, Tyrrell, Kennett, Echard, Burnet, Rapin-Thoyras, Oldmixon, North, Guthrie, Ralph, Carte, and Hume.[19]

HISTORY: A DEFINITION

These historians and their readers did not simply define 'history' as any study of the past claiming somehow to be 'true,' as it may very casually be defined today. In fact, many early-modern writers composed works about the past but only a few were 'historians.' The English, like the ancients before them, realized that history was only one of a number of literary genres treating the past. Observers of the past who felt confined by history's exacting rules had to express themselves in other ways. For example, King Charles I's *Eikon Basilike*, which, along with Clarendon's *History of the Rebellion*, functioned as an important historical prop of tory ideology, was a political testament, not a proper history. In his influential propaganda tracts, *Oldcastle's Remarks on the History of England*, Lord Bolingbroke used epistolary form and the title *Remarks on . . .* (not *The History of . . .*) to attack the ministry of Sir Robert Walpole. Much of what, to us, may be the most interesting historical thought or scholarship of the period did not always appear in the form of a 'history.'

History was a specific literary genre, invented in antiquity, rediscovered during the Renaissance, and still alive in the seventeenth and eighteenth century. *Artes historicae*, manuals on how to read and write history – themselves with ancient precedents – helped to guide Englishmen in their understanding of historical theory and practice. Relying heavily upon classical authorities, these books defined history, then evaluated ancient and modern attempts to meet classical criteria for it.[20] The most influential of the *artes historicae* were French,[21] which is hardly surprising, given the intensity of cultural exchange between France and England, particularly in the century after the year 1660. From about 1660, when the Stuart court returned from exile in France, Englishmen deferred to French critics on many literary matters, not just historiographic ones. The extent and duration of French neoclassicism in England remains a matter of scholarly dispute;[22] however, Pierre Le Moyne, the late seventeenth-century author of a French *ars historica* well-known to Englishmen, furnished one of the most concise and commonplace definitions of history, a definition no early-modern English gentleman would have quarreled with: 'History is a continued Narration of things True, Great and Publick, writ with Spirit, Eloquence and Judgment; for Instruction to Particulars and Princes, and Good of Civil Society.' In other words, history was a continuous, truthful story about important and public events. It was written with intelligence, in a noble style that would be pleasing and memorable while consistent with its dignified subject. The historian was also a judge, deciding the cause of events rather than just describing occurrences, and distinguishing between good and bad events and persons rather than suspending judgment. The function of history was to instruct political society by these judgments, and so its primary audience was the prince and other important political individuals.[23] Rounding out this definition, other commentators added that history's subject matter was war and politics; its style was polite, not polemical; speeches, character sketches, and maxims or 'reflections' enhanced its instructive power;[24] its scale was formidable – a history could not be read in just one or two sittings.[25]

History was the literature of an elite, ideally suited for a princely audience. It enjoyed a privileged place in the prince's curriculum because it offered him impartial counsel as an alternative to corrupting flatterers, and the prospect of his being included in a future history was supposed to inspire him to do good and avoid evil in the present.[26] The criterion of public benefit dictated the historian's choice of subject and selection of details: his task was to select and preserve the most important, instructive events of the past for a political class with the power to act on such instruction for the public good. The classical commonplace that history was intended for the education of political leaders, and the Renaissance conception of history fitting in a mirror-of-princes genre, were both reiterated for good reason in the early-modern period. More, Raleigh, Bacon, Camden, Cherbury, Daniel, and Clarendon had royal audiences in mind for their historical works.[27] Princes actually read histories, and tutors of princes actually wrote them. The Earl of Clarendon, Gilbert Burnet, and Abel Boyer, to name only three historians, served as royal tutors. Courtiers wrote historical works for, and dedicated to, William, Duke of Gloucester (1689–1700), sole surviving heir of Princess (later Queen) Anne.[28] The appointment of royal governors and preceptors could be of great political moment, and lavish attention was paid to an education in which history was thought to play a decisive part.[29] The readers who were perhaps most receptive to the lessons of history were actually future, not reigning, occupants of the throne or members of the court or assembly. The contemporary prince or statesman commonly could not bear to hear the hard truths about the past, especially if they cast shadows upon his regime, so historians learned to settle for a posthumous audience.

History taught public men political policy as well as personal morality. Historical knowledge 'teaches us to conduct Armies, secure Conquests, invent necessary Laws, restrain the intemperate Rule of Princes, and acquire Power and Happiness,' according to James Hampton. It was a 'Science' used to 'take notice of good and evil, to imitate the one, and avoid the other,' an *ars historica* stated. David Hume declared history the best teacher of moral virtue, better even than poetry – which was so entirely directed at 'the passions' that it often led readers to vice – or philosophy – which could be too subtle and speculative. In general terms, examples proved to be more effective teachers than abstract precepts; the examples of history proved to be the best teacher of morality, history being 'philosophy teaching by examples,' according to Bolingbroke, quoting Dionysius of Halicarnassus.[30]

As serious as the historian's project was, his tale could not be dull or it would find no audience. It had to meet the dual criteria of 'Entertainment and Instruction.' As Hume wrote, 'The first Quality of an Historian is to be true & impartial; the next to be interesting.' The historian had to sustain interest in, but not compromise, the inherent dignity of his noble subject. René de Rapin advised:

> You must then resolve to write nobly, if you design to write History. For, from the moment you speak to all the world, and to all Ages, you are endued with a Character which gives you authority to raise your voice, because then you speak to Kings, Princes, and to the Grandees of all Countries and of all Ages ... [A]dorn your discourse with a lofty strain ... [A]n Historian quits the low and common Language, that so by the dignity of his Expression, he may answer the merit of those things he has to say.

Abel Boyer agreed: 'The Gravity and Dignity of History excludes all low and vulgar Expressions, mean Jests, clenching Witticisms, trivial Proverbs, and such like Trash.'[31] The historian's proper tone was one of lofty impartiality. He kept enough distance from events and from his own self-interest or vanity that he could gain the correct perspective for telling the truth and rendering wise judgments. He avoided speaking in the first person, because that would call his objectivity into question and draw undignified attention to himself. Instead, he used the third person to describe his own part in events, as Thucydides had done. Although he had his own political program to put forward, he tried to be fair-minded while doing so and preferred making oblique references to historians espousing opposing historical interpretations.[32] Since history was 'merely narrative,'[33] the historian simply told his own story, rarely digressing to argue over disputed interpretations or adding self-justifying transcriptions of supporting documents. To describe many of these literary protocols, Englishmen sometimes used the word 'polite,' by which they meant that which was polished, tasteful, refined, pleasing, aesthetically excellent.[34] Politeness was defined in opposition to controversy, whether the wrangling of the cleric, the scholar, or the partisan. Addison saw the 'Hatred and Violence of Parties' as 'destructive of all Politeness.'[35] Various 'polite' moments in the world's history, including Addison's own age, had existed. The ancient historians, especially the Romans, also produced polite literature, and therein lay part of their appeal.[36]

A narrative of worthy deeds, polite and dignified, written to instruct the political elite with moral and political lessons: this is how the English elite conceived of history. Englishmen still defined history, with some help from French neoclassical critics, essentially as it had been understood in antiquity and by explicit reference to the ancient historians. Contemporaries were careful to define history in precise terms to distinguish it from related but lesser forms in the literary hierarchy, and so should we. They believed that certain forms of literature had greater prestige than others. Since history was the most prestigious prose genre, political partisans fought over its literary cachet, trying to appropriate it to their cause by arguing that writings supporting their partisan vision of the past constituted 'history,' while opposing visions belonged to less reputable literary genres. Because history was highly regarded for being 'true,' readers disagreeing with the political import of a historical work often responded with a generic attack, denying that the work was actually history because it had violated history's defining quality of truthfulness. The title page was deemed fraudulent, renamed libel or satire if it criticized one's political friends, panegyric if it overrated one's political enemies.[37] Thus, the border between history and its encroaching neighbors and near relations was worth fighting for. Much generic warfare was waged not on aesthetic grounds by detached critics, but on political grounds by polemical adversaries attempting any means, including generic ones, to devalue an opposing political interpretation. If a historical work was well received and the audience accepted the respected denomination 'history,' then the work's credibility was enhanced and its influence extended. But if one wished to denigrate a historical work, one's strategy was to name it something else, the further down the generic hierarchy the better – at least down to memoir, if not biography or, even better, political pamphlet or romance.

The memoir was inferior to, often only preparation for, full-scale, authentic history. The memoirist was an actor in important historical events or an eyewitness to them, but unlike the historian, the writer of memoirs wrote from a patently personal perspective, often in the first person, and was not held to such high standards of impartiality as the historian. Like the historian of one's own times, the memoirist based his account primarily on his own observations and interviews with other participants in events, rather than on research into public records or the accounts of other historians. However, he was not as ambitious as the historian: he told only a limited part of the story; he was not expected to explore the deeper causes of events; he was allowed a less formal prose style.[38] Caesar's *Commentaries* offered the classical precedent and sometime model for memoirs.[39] Closer at hand for the English, however, were French examples. Indeed, the French were credited both with having revived the form and with debasing it. Works by Philippe de Commynes (1447–1511) and Cardinal de Retz (1613–79) provided influential models for English memoirists, but subsequent French memoirists earned the genre a reputation as egotistical and untruthful.[40] Ever since antiquity both history and memoir had been highly esteemed because each relied on eyewitness testimony.[41] The difficulty was in determining whether an account of the immediate past possessed sufficient range and objectivity to warrant promotion from the status of memoir to that of history. In the cases of Caesar[42] and Commynes especially, contemporaries could not decide whether their exemplary works were histories or memoirs, so much did the genres have in common. Jean Le Clerc judged Caesar to be a memoirist and criticized Clarendon's *History* for its resemblance to the *Commentaries*. '[T]his History,' he declared, 'has sometimes rather the Air of *Memoirs* than that of History; because the Author is too particular in the detail of things of little Importance, and which concern himself or some other private Men.'[43]

Biography, like memoir, shared many attributes with history, sometimes bore the title 'history,' and on account of its more limited scope lacked the prestige of history proper. One finds historians apologizing for having 'descended from the Dignity of an Historian, and . . . fallen into the lower Class of Biographers,' and remarking that Plutarch and Suetonius had 'only' been biographers, not historians.[44] Since history itself was in one sense just the story of great individuals, biography, the account of a single great man or woman, commanded respect in the literary hierarchy.[45] Plutarch, Tacitus, and Suetonius furnished important classical precedents. However, biography could be so preoccupied with seemingly trivial details concerning an individual's life that it could lose its focus. Biography, Abel Boyer explained, cannot omit the subject's

> Descent, Character, various Fortunes and Adventures, Intrigues . . . nothing, in short, that may serve to delineate his Picture in full Length. [But in history] the Dignity of the Subject forbids an Historian to bestow the least Attention on minute Particulars, that relate to private Men. For the principal Object of the History of a Nation, Kingdom, or Reign, being the Prince and State, this is the Point of View, in which all the Historical Passages ought to center.[46]

The distinction was a classical one, and just as in antiquity Lucian had noticed that the degeneration of historiography was accompanied by the growing popularity of biography,[47] so in eighteenth-century England did this genre come to challenge unsatisfactory historiography. By the 1740s, well-received biographies by Roger North and by Samuel Johnson's circle increased the genre's prestige, perhaps invalidating Clarendon's complaint that Christians had not written exemplary lives as well as Greek and Roman pagans had.[48]

Despite the growing respect for biography, history retained

pride of place in the hierarchy of prose genres. However, history was never quite so monolithic an entity as the preceding account might suggest. Other forms of 'history,' besides the 'civil' history we have been describing, also existed – natural history, universal history,[49] and ecclesiastical history, for example, each with its own rules for composition and often its own precedents in antiquity. But with the exception of ecclesiastical history, to be discussed in Chapter 2, these had little if any part to play in the fate of neoclassical historiography in early-modern England. The distinction between particular history and general history, on the other hand, proves to be germane to our story. Englishmen noticed that ancient histories could differ markedly one from the next. The classical historians' scope of inquiry could vary so widely that divergent notions of evidence, of objectivity, and of politeness served to bifurcate civil history. The English saw in antiquity as well as contemporary England two distinct kinds of history, two different genres. On the one hand, they identified what they often designated 'particular' history, usually the history of one's own times, and on the other hand 'general,' or 'complete' history, as it was sometimes called. A history of the world, a kingdom, or an empire was general history. The history of a monarch's reign, a war, or a family was particular history. Hugh Blair, a Scottish rhetorician writing in the second half of the eighteenth century, explained:

> Such a work ['a regular and legitimate work of History'] is chiefly of two kinds. Either the entire History of some state or kingdom through its different revolutions, such as Livy's Roman History; or the History of some one great event, or some portion or period of time which may be considered as making a whole by itself; such as, Thucydides's History of the Peloponnesian war, Davila's History of the Civil Wars of France, or Clarendon's of those of England.[50]

Different standards of impartiality applied to each genre. Required to narrate several centuries of history, the general historian obviously could not witness firsthand the entirety of his massive subject matter. He had to weigh conflicting pieces of evidence and present as balanced and detached an interpretation as he could. However, the particular historian often narrated the history of his own times, so he had actually seen the events he described and did not have the luxury of abstaining from controversy. He therefore tended to write with more assuredness and less politeness than the general historian.[51] He was expected to be less impartial than the general historian, because as a participant in events he naturally narrated from his own point of view and could not be expected to empathize completely with his enemy's viewpoint. Different perspectives on the past, in turn, generated different styles of narrative. Horace Walpole observed:

> They who write of their own times love or hate the actors and draw you to their party, but with the fear of the *laws* of history before his eyes, a compiler affects you no more than a chancery suit about the entail of an estate with whose owners you was not acquainted.[52]

The qualifications required for compiling general history also differed from those for writing contemporary history, as we shall see presently. In fact, these two forms of historiography were different enough from one another that they warrant separate investigations. Chapters 3 and 5 treat particular histories, Chapters 4, 6, and 7 general histories.

THE ROLES OF HISTORIAN

A participant in the great events of history, either a warrior or a statesman, wrote the particular history of his own times, while the author of general history did not have to be such a public figure and, practically speaking, could only witness several decades of his story at most, the period of his own lifetime, only a small segment of the epoch covered by his general history. Among Englishmen, there was no clear consensus regarding either the pre-eminent general historian or particular historian. According to editors of the *Complete History of England* (1706),

> Livy among the Ancients, and Mariana among the Moderns, are plac'd in the highest Rank ['of General Historians'], tho' others have their Parties and Favourers, and are allow'd many Beauties, which every one magnifies or lessens, according to his particular Relish.[53]

Rather than seize upon a single favorite author for imitation, Englishmen more often chose a variety of historians to serve as models for their historical thinking, their style, their career: 1) they might imitate the ancient historians directly; 2) less straight-forwardly, they might imitate the greatest continental 'modern' imitators of those ancient historians; 3) they might also find inspiration in the native English historians who came closest to, but never fully succeeded in, imitating either the ancients (1) or the neoclassical continentals (2); 4) they might choose to reject the neoclassical project entirely.

Englishmen did not take on classical roles uncritically. Thomas Hobbes saw classical posturing as disastrous idealism, unsuited to real politics, which ought instead to be grounded in a hard science of human affairs. Cicero, Seneca, Cato, Aristotle were to blame, in part, for the English Civil War. According to Hobbes, Presbyterian power had fatally grown through recruitment of gentlemen inspired by 'the glorious histories and sententious politics of the ancient popular governments of the Greeks and Romans, amongst whom kings were hated . . . and popular government . . . passed by the name of liberty.' James Hampton thought Englishmen had read too much into the experience of the early Romans, whose society was so different from his own. Little political wisdom could be extracted from the history of 'this savage and illiterate People, a troop of Herdsmen, and obscure Adventurers, in the very Infancy of their Society.' How, he asked, could the English learn about peace and justice from a history filled with 'Disorder and Anarchy,' 'Tumult,' and 'Faction?' Even Bolingbroke, an accomplished classical role-player, admitted that servile imitation of great men was foolish, even absurd: 'if a general should act the same part now [as Codrus and the Decii in antiquity, acting on superstition], and, in order to secure his victory, get killed as fast as he could; he might pass for a hero, but I am sure he would pass for a madman.'[54] Nor were the classical historians above reproach. Thucydides' subject was not so worthy of remembrance as events of the modern age, some argued. Sallust, Thucydides, and Polybius did not compose introductions preparing readers for what was to follow as artfully as Machiavelli had.[55]

Such criticisms constituted specific indictments of particular aspects of classical historiography. However, many times when an English historian cited a classical or neoclassical historian as a guide or a reader referred to one as a means of comparison, it is difficult to pinpoint exactly what in that historian was being praised or criticized. The classical or neoclassical historian might be admired for his prose style, his literary devices, his politics, his historical interpretations. He often had a variegated career or one that was barely known. When Gibbon likened Hume to Livy, did he mean Hume's career was Livian, his theme, his philosophy, his narrative pace? Lacking sufficient context, it is hard to make any definitive judgment in the case of this as well as other classical references. Because the English encounter with classical and neoclassical historians was so allusive and the choice of exemplars so eclectic, it would be more fruitful for us to examine two classical genres broadly defined, rather than to study only those historians expressly claiming, say, Livy or Thucydides as their models. For purposes of convenience, the terms 'Livian role' or 'Livian genre' will henceforth designate the genre or role of general historian writing according to classical protocols, even in cases when Livy was not explicitly invoked. The terms 'Thucydidean role' or 'Thucydidean genre' will designate the genre or role of historian of one's own times writing according to classical protocols, even in cases when Thucydides was not explicitly invoked.

Let us now look in some detail at these exemplary ancient historians. According to John Oldmixon,

> Those of the Ancients, who . . . wrote of their own Times, and of Things within their own Knowledge, or that of their Friends, were always held in the highest Esteem, as being both most useful and entertaining; such as Thucydides, Xenophon, Polybius, Salust, Tacitus, Lactantius, Marcellinus. Among the Moderns the most famous are Philip de Comines, Guicciardin, Davila, Monsieur de Thou . . .[56]

Oldmixon was not alone in putting Thucydides' name at the top of his list. An influential, but by no means the only, career model for the historian of one's own times belonged to Thucydides, an Athenian nobleman and one-time general, who had written the *History of the Peloponnesian War*. Thomas Hobbes praised Thucydides:

> He overtasked not himself by undertaking an history of things done long before his time, and of which he was not able to

inform himself. He was a man that had as much means, in regard both of his dignity and wealth, to find the truth of what he relateth, as was needful for a man to have. He used as much diligence in search of the truth (noting every thing whilst it was fresh in memory, and laying out his wealth upon intelligence) as was possible for a man to use. He affected least of any man the acclamations of popular auditories, and wrote not his history to win present applause, as was the use of that age: but for a monument to instruct the ages to come ... He was far from the necessity of servile writers, either to fear or flatter.

In other words, Thucydides had the wealth, the respect, the contacts, the independence, the physical mobility necessary for uncovering the requisite sources, for being taken seriously, and for writing the truth. He possessed the social, political, and financial standing necessary for maintaining his intellectual independence and for discovering the truth of events in which he had participated, or which he himself had witnessed, or for which he had obtained other eyewitness accounts. As Hobbes noticed, banishment for a failed naval campaign provided Thucydides the leisure to write this great history. Historical composition, in turn, dignified political retirement.[57]

While this pattern of the man of action in retirement or enforced leisure might prove advantageous for anyone wishing to write the history of his own times, it was not a prerequisite for becoming a general historian.[58] Livy's career illustrated this point. Livy's public life was less well known than that of Thucydides; there was less to know. He 'was of an Honourable Family'[59] and spent most of his time isolated, engaged in literary pursuits. He recited his *History of Rome* to the Emperor Augustus, who was so impressed that he named Livy tutor to his son Claudius. Livy recorded contemporary history, and perfected it by giving deep background, making it part of a massive general history. Although he indeed wrote the history of his own times, he was better known to Englishmen as the general historian who narrated more than seven centuries of Roman history. This sort of history could be written from archival sources and other histories rather than requiring firsthand experience as a 'great man.' Livy did not have a political career of his own but he earned canonical status as a general historian by virtue of his insight into the workings of contemporary public life, his understanding of human nature, his erudition, and his considerable literary gifts. Neither a senator nor a general, Livy showed that a teacher of rhetoric, buoyed by imperial patronage, could write an exemplary history. There was, then, a role in historiography for men not of the highest public rank, those who were suitably educated in the skills and culture of rank without themselves holding the highest social and political position.

One did not have to imitate Livy's unique career mechanically in order to acquire the political acumen, literary prowess, and leisure for undertaking a monumental general history. On the other hand, to write the history of one's own times appeared to require, more narrowly, that the historian be a prominent statesman or warrior with a period of enforced or voluntary leisure at hand. In the case of both sources and audiences, the historian's social and political standing was more crucial in assuming the Thucydidean role than the Livian role. Thucydides relied on his own high standing to tease out recent, closely held historical documents and interviews. He had to be an actor in the events he was relating, if his eyewitness account was to be taken seriously. Livy relied on older, less sensitive sources, and was not expected to witness events himself. There would always be fewer candidates for writing contemporary history than for writing general history, because the qualifications for the former were more stringent than those for the latter.

A man of Thucydidean political standing was qualified to write both general and particular history. Tacitus was qualified to do both and did both; he could serve as the model general historian or the model contemporary historian.[60] Like Thucydides, he had a public career, in fact, as senator and consul, a much more impressive one. He described many events occurring 40 years before he was born and so, like Livy, he was not always an eyewitness to history but only a second-hand researcher. Early humanists were much enamored of Livy's eloquence, moralism, and republicanism, but in the late sixteenth century Tacitus came into vogue throughout much of Europe. In an age of absolute monarchy, political corruption, and civil war, the Tacitean virtues of fortitude and prudence appeared more relevant than Livian rhetoric and idealism. In England, neo-Tacitean historiography was featured in the opposition literature sponsored by the Earl of Essex in the 1590s, ideally suiting a mood of political disillusionment. Tacitus taught one how to live in a monarchy, unravel hidden causes, and explain secret court dealings. His laconic style cut to the heart of political dynamics more quickly and surely than copious Livian narratives.[61] Clarendon and Bolingbroke admired Tacitus extravagantly, and their histories were Tacitean at those moments when they exposed corruption at court, or unmasked secret motives, or inserted terse philosophical maxims – all features for which Tacitus was famous. From a Tacitean perspective, Bolingbroke might have seen his rival, Sir Robert Walpole, as Sejanus or Tiberius;[62] Clarendon, too, might have seen his ungrateful royal master, Charles II, who forced him into exile, as a Tiberian figure. But both historians found themselves less in the Tacitean mode of an officeholder suffering under a corrupt despotism than in the Thucydidean predicament of an exile needing to vindicate a once prominent but now languishing career.

Career patterns, ancient and modern, played a fundamental part in contemporary perceptions of historiography. The English elite understood that producing a great neoclassical work meant finding a historian with social standing, leisure, and at least some acquaintance with public affairs. The failure of English historians to satisfy these criteria greatly contributed to the weakness in historiography. Clarendon explained the miserable quality of English histories in terms of 'the want of encouragement of fit persons' – 'men of action and experience.'[63] He observed:

> For the historians, I think a man may very warrantably say, that there never was yet a good history written but by men conversant in business, and of the best and most liberal education. Polybius was a counsellor, and an officer in a part of the wars which he writ. Livy was in the court of Augustus, well known to the emperor, and in great grace and conversation with the favourite, and so acquainted with all the transactions of the world. Tacitus, besides his noble extraction, had his education in the near trust of two gr[e]at emperors, Vespasian and Titus, underwent several great employments and offices in the commonwealth, and was afterwards consul in the time of Nerva, after whose death he began to write his history.[64]

The great modern historians likewise usually possessed firsthand knowledge of public life. They were either born into the nobility and hence expected to do some sort of public service, or they were of humble birth and by dint of employment at lower echelons of government worked their way up to positions of influence and trust. Machiavelli, a Florentine administrator, exemplified the latter route to political experience, while Guicciardini, who came from a patrician family and served the Florentine state in several capacities, and Commynes, who had a noble lineage and a varied career as diplomat, soldier, and royal counsellor in France, epitomized the former. All three employed their enforced leisure to write history once their public careers suffered reversals. Davila, a professional soldier, could brag that he had 'spent many years in the chambers of kings and in the front line of armies.' De Thou had been a counsellor to Henri IV. The least conspicuous public careers of these continental historians belonged to Sarpi, a priest, and Mézeray, a man of letters. Yet neither lived in complete isolation from public business. Sarpi served as advisor to the Venetian senate, and Mézeray once held a minor post in the French army as supplier.[65]

Some of the Englishmen coming closest to imitating these exemplary modern historians also possessed public experience and social standing at the time they became historians. Thomas More, the son of a knight, served as MP, diplomat, and member of the privy council before or during his writing of *The History of King Richard III*. Sir Walter Raleigh was the consummate 'man of action' – warrior, explorer, courtier. Francis Bacon had a distinguished public career culminating in the lord chancellorship and a viscountcy. Edward Herbert had experience as a soldier and diplomat, before becoming Baron of Cherbury and sitting on the council of war. On the other hand, John Hayward did not have a public career to speak of, and was knighted only after publishing his history. William Camden was essentially a professional scholar and spent over two decades as a master at Westminster School. Samuel Daniel, the son of a music master, had no public service to his credit either. John Milton, the son of a prosperous scrivener, enjoyed more financial independence than Daniel but never belonged to the ruling class, although during the Interregnum he served as Latin Secretary to the council of state, translating foreign despatches and writing propaganda.[66]

Could it be that the lack of public experience on the part of Milton, Daniel, Camden, and Hayward diminished their capacity as historians? Contemporaries certainly believed that English historiography suffered because candidates unfit for the role of historian had been writing it. Joseph Addison argued that to write on a plane with the classical historians, Englishmen had to be worldly-wise and socially elevated:

> Those who have succeeded best in Works of this kind, are such, who, beside their natural Good Sense and Learning, have themselves been versed in publick Business, and thereby acquired a thorough Knowledge of Men and Things. It was the Advice of the great Duke of Schomberg, to an eminent Historian of his Acquaintance, who was an Ecclesiastick [Gilbert Burnet], That he should avoid being too particular in the drawing up of an Army, and other Circumstances of the Day of Battle; for that he had always observed most notorious Blunders and Absurdities committed on that Occasion, by such writers as were not conversant in the Art of War. We may reasonably expect the like Mistakes in every other kind of Publick Matters, recorded by those who have only a distant Theory of such Affairs. Besides; it is not very probable, that Men, who have passed all their Time in low and vulgar Life, should have a suitable Idea of the several Beauties and Blemishes in the Actions or Characters of Great Men. For this Reason I find an old Law quoted by the famous Monsieur Bayle, that no Person below the Dignity of a Roman Knight should presume to write an History.[67]

Only a gentle or noble man was truly worthy of the noble subjects found in history. The moderns had never equalled the ancients in historical writing, according to Joseph Warton, owing to 'this single consideration, that the [modern histories] are commonly compiled by recluse scholars, unpracticed in business, war, and politics; whilst the [ancient histories] are many of them written by ministers, commanders, and princes themselves.'[68] To historians the message was clear enough: the examples of the ancient historians remained relevant to modern historical projects; historical composition went hand in hand with social and political eminence.

As revered an activity as history-writing was, however, it was still beneath the dignity of kings. In antiquity history had been a leisure activity of generals and senators rather than kings and emperors.[69] The king judges and legislates; he does not compile or justify. Charles I might have contributed memoirs to a history, and commissioned his trusted servant Clarendon to write it, but he had to worry more about preserving his kingdom in the first instance than preserving a record of that kingdom's history. His son, Charles II, perused and approved histories for publication, and like his father had contributed to Clarendon's *History*, but he never wrote his own. His brother, before becoming King James II, wrote some memoirs of his military campaigns in the 1650s,[70] but took them no further. After the Glorious Revolution, James spent the first seven years of his exile in war and intrigue trying to recover his crown. From 1695 to 1701, the last six years of his life, he did not recast his memoirs into a history of the loss of his crown, because the attractions of prayer and meditation outweighed those of historical composition.

Just as anyone beneath the rank of gentleman or nobleman was unfit for the role of neoclassical historian, so, apparently, was anyone *above* those ranks unfit. During the sixteenth, seventeenth, and eighteenth century, no one above the rank of earl ever wrote an exemplary history: Clarendon was an earl, Bacon a viscount, Cherbury and Lyttelton barons, More, Hayward, and Raleigh knights.[71] Responsibility for writing history belonged to these servants of the crown, not to the monarch. And yet, qualified as they might be, these historians inhabited a modern world that seriously threatened the neoclassical project, a world that remains to be explored.

2
Neoclassical History and the Modern World

In 1716, writing in *The Freeholder*, Joseph Addison restated the commonplace complaint against English historical writing:

> The Misfortune is, that there are more Instances of Men who deserve ... Immortality, than of Authors who are able to bestow it. Our Country, which has produced Writers of the first Figure in every other kind of Work, has been very barren in good Historians. We have had several who have been able to compile Matters of Fact, but very few who have been able to digest them with that Purity and Elegance of Stile, that Nicety and Strength of Reflection, that Subtilty and Discernment in the Unravelling of a Character, and that Choice of Circumstances for enlivening the whole Narration, which we so justly admire in the antient Historians of Greece and Rome, and in some Authors of our neighbouring Nations.[1]

This criticism dated from the sixteenth century and lasted until the mid-eighteenth century.[2] Before the sixteenth century, Englishmen had fundamentally different conceptions of what history was and how it should be written; they saw no need to write their history along classical lines. In that century, however, the Italian Renaissance made its belated arrival, and English humanists, like their continental counterparts, rediscovered the historians of antiquity and began to model themselves after them. But what was it, precisely, that constituted a modern 'imitation' of ancient historical writing? How closely did Renaissance historians actually come to resuscitating classical historiography? What was the standard by which Englishmen judged the attainment of neoclassical ideals? This Chapter attempts to answer these questions by examining the continental historians Englishmen deemed most successful as neoclassical historians, by looking at what went wrong in the earliest English attempts to compose neoclassical history, and finally by evaluating the modern impediments to classical imitation facing all early-modern historians, English ones in particular.

In the middle ages history did not enjoy the prestige that it had in antiquity or that it would later acquire during the Renaissance. Theology reigned queen of the curriculum, relegating history to a very modest position as a subset of rhetoric. Scholastic philosophy focused on eternal and divine truths rather than the ebb and flow of mere human contingency with which history concerned itself. Medieval chroniclers provided materials useful in teaching personal morality and in showing the ways of divine providence. In constructing these tales the monks did not see differences between fact and fiction as very important. As a consequence, chronicles contained a mix of legends and forgeries, as well as more factual accounts. And because so little a sense of anachronism existed, no attempt was made to explain how past events contributed to the making of the present – the past and the present were frequently indistinguishable. Alexander the Great was depicted as a knight, Roman ruins as just another piece of the contemporary landscape not requiring an act of historical imagination to understand on their own terms as the product of an alien and remote epoch. Because chroniclers aimed primarily to build up a storehouse of happenings that might teach humans the ways of God, they made little effort to connect those events in a cause-and-effect narrative. Chroniclers often showed more concern for the quantity of their materials and for their chronological arrangement, than for editing or critically analyzing them in the form of a story. Hence, the chronicler's typical transition was not 'therefore' or 'because' but 'meanwhile.'[3]

To humanists the chronicle, as a genre, appeared to be a useless jumble of disconnected facts and fictions, written in bad Latin by superstitious monks.[4] Not appreciated on its own terms, medieval historical writing came off rather badly in comparison with the pagan historiography of antiquity rediscovered by humanists during the Renaissance. The classical purpose and form of history held great appeal for Renaissance men of affairs more interested in history's lessons of statecraft than its spiritual edification. The humanist historian focused single-mindedly on war and politics, constructing a narrative explaining the causes of great events so that the ruler might thereby learn how to gain or to maintain political power. Chancellors and secretaries served as official historians, garnering the lessons of the past for the ruling dynasty, as well as glorifying its achievements.[5] The devices of the ancient historians – the invented speeches, the character sketches, the political aphorisms – often proved useful to these ends, and the elevated style seemed appropriate to the new and prestigious purpose and audience for history. The humanist resurrection of ancient historiography did not sweep away the medieval chronicle in one mighty blow, however. In the 1670s the most popular account of the English past remained Sir Richard Baker's *Chronicle of the Kings of England*, then in its seventh edition. But neoclassical critics discredited the chronicle. 'A String of meer Facts,' wrote Thomas Burnet, 'may compose a good honest and dry Chronicle; but it is the account of the Springs and Motives of important Transactions, that constitutes a History.'[6] A collection of facts grimly arranged in chronological order, the chronicle lacked explanatory power. According to Lord Bolingbroke, 'monkish annalists, and other ancient chroniclers . . . [cannot] be called historians, nor can enable others to write history in that fulness in which it must be written to become a lesson of ethics and politics.'[7] History was only history if it lived up to its didactic, humanist purpose. Of course, the annals form had been perfected in antiquity by Bolingbroke's hero, Tacitus, but no imitator matched the Tacitean artistry in composing a flowing narrative of motives and causes within the confines of an annual account. Consequently, annals had lost prestige by the seventeenth century, although William Camden made a famous attempt to revive the form, and both annalists and chroniclers survived into the eighteenth century.[8]

RENAISSANCE HISTORIOGRAPHY

For the father of humanist historiography it was this concern for the causes of events that most distinguished classical historical writing from the medieval chronicle. Leonardo Bruni (1370–1444) wrote the *Historiae Florentini populi* (1449) in Latin for Florentine merchant bankers. Moved by communal patriotism, Bruni came to believe that Florentine history was as worthy of analysis as the story of Greece or Rome, and that the methods of classical historiography could be applied to the history of his own postclassical society.[9] Bruni employed the language and style of the Roman historians; at the same time, however, he established by his example a principle that was to prove fundamental to his successors, whether Italian, French, or English: the historian does not have to worship his models as sacred and beyond reproach. Indeed, a pervasive humanist conception of imitation held that classical models ought to inspire their imitator, not impede him. The act of imitation was intended to initiate a dialogue with the dead whereby the imitator criticized his exemplar, even while holding up his own work to the criticism of that exemplar. A broad range of authorities was to be tested in this way so as to create in the imitator an individual style of his own. After all, reasoned critics such as Erasmus, Pico della Mirandola, and Juan Luis Vives, we live in an age distinct from that of antiquity, so it would be foolish to expect ancient literary forms to meet our needs exactly. Indeed, a hallmark of Renaissance historical thought was the appreciation of anachronism, the historicist sense that historically distinct societies existed and needed to be understood in their own right. This being so, there was little reason to expect that a classical author, product of a unique era, could or should be copied exactly by an author inhabiting a different era.[10] The question for Florentine neoclassical historians, as for their English counterparts, was: how closely could or should a model be imitated? Conversely, how far from the model could the historian deviate while still reaping the benefits of an 'imitation?'

For his part, Bruni found Livy to be an especially useful model. Still, Bruni pointed out the lessons of his history in a more heavy-handed way than his classical exemplars did, and he subjected his documentary sources to more criticism. As we shall see, Bruni's successors likewise departed from their models in one way or another, and chose different models for their histories depending on their peculiar circumstances. Machiavelli mocked the classical set-piece description of battles, and shortened classical character sketches and invented speeches. Intent upon understanding events in all their complexity, he also questioned the classical focus on worthy deeds and avoidance of trivial detail.[11] Both he and Guicciardini actually incorporated chronicle material into their narratives. Although he produced an exemplary specimen of neoclassical historiography admired for its political acumen, Guicciardini rejected the classical subject matter of the city-state, being convinced Italy's collapse could be understood only by studying all of Italy, not just Florence.[12] In his *Memoirs* Commynes wrote compellingly enough that his recollections were elevated to the rank of a modern classic, even though he was not fluent in Latin and did not write a polished history, only a preparatory aid for the Archbishop of Vienne's projected history of Louis XI. De Thou modelled himself after Tacitus and Livy, but he did not care to imitate their practice of inserting moral exempla. However, his work was accepted as a scintillating piece of neoclassical historiography, accepted all the more readily in England because he blamed the Wars of Religion on Catholics, not Protestants. Mézeray successfully exploited the possibilities of print to an extent unprecedented in the moderns and, of course, the ancients. In his bid for as large an audience as possible, he inserted lavish engravings of coins, medals, and royal portraits, and deliberately eschewed the pure, polished French of his fellow Academicians in favor of a more popular, Rabelaisian style.[13]

Mézeray's work once again demonstrated that a modern history did not have to imitate ancient historiography exactly in order to please English critics. What those critics admired in the moderns, what reminded them of the ancient historians, was a constellation of esteemed attributes – penetrating analysis, important subject matter, powerful eloquence, cogent evidence, and artful story-telling, all in the form of an instructive narrative of deeds. These qualities, appearing in various proportions depending on the historian, constituted the core of neoclassical history, the *sine qua non* of this genre. As we have already seen, the canonical modern historians occasionally dispensed with a number of devices in the repertoire of the ancient historian – the invented speeches, for example, or the moral lessons. Moreover, certain postclassical phenomena such as the printing press made it difficult to write sixteenth- and seventeenth-century European history in a mechanically antique fashion – even if historians had wished to write that way, which they did not.

Mézeray had written in response to calls for a 'complete,' 'general,' or 'perfect' national history in humanist form. Juan de Mariana had composed such a work for Spain, but England lacked a neoclassical masterpiece enshrining its entire history. In the early sixteenth century Polydore Vergil became the first of a long and distinguished line of men attempting to write a general history of England to classical standards. An Italian humanist, Polydore arrived in England as a papal civil servant in 1502. Shortly thereafter he began writing for Henry VII and for continental readers, in Latin, a complete history of England to the present day. Intending to legitimize the Tudor regime in the eyes of European monarchs, Polydore wrote his apologia according to the prestigious conventions of Italian humanism. The *Anglica historia* (1534–55) won over many foreign readers, who accepted his work as the definitive English history, an advance over chronicles by virtue of its focus on causation. However, Englishmen complained that it was too brief. Besides, argued Reformation Anglicans, Polydore was not just an Italian and a Catholic but an agent of the Bishop of Rome.[14] Native English writers found their greatest success writing the history of a single reign, rather than the entire history of the nation. In the 1510s, More wrote *The History of King Richard III*, a Tacitean portrait of a tyrant. Its coherence, its stunning language, its invented speeches earned it praise as a work of neoclassical historiography, even if it was, properly speaking, only a biography. Hayward's *First Part of the Life and Raigne of King Henrie the IIII* (1599), replete with invented speeches and political lessons, indebted to Tacitus, Guicciardini, and Machiavelli, inspired several other 'particular' histories that also ranked among the most competent works of modern English historiography. Camden published a history of his own times, in Latin, *Annales rerum Anglicarum et Hibernicarum regnante Elizabetha*. Tacitus, Polybius and de Thou figured in Camden's design, although he put ecclesiastical affairs at the heart of his story rather than martial and political ones.[15] If Camden was admired for his tenacious rooting out of causes and for his scholarship, Bacon's *Historie of the Raign of King Henry the Seventh* wor. acclaim for its literary style. Bacon offered a work brimming with maxims, invented speeches, and translucent prose, but met criticism for having lost control over his subject. And like More, Bacon had composed biography rather than full-dress history.[16] Herbert of Cherbury wrote a history of Henry VIII that, on account of its invented speeches and understanding of diplomatic affairs, was sometimes also compared to the best of ancient and modern historiography.[17] Like More, Hayward, Camden, and Bacon, Cherbury seized upon a single reign of English history as relevant to the present, and constructed a particular history or a biography more or less to humanist standards. However, no English historian completely mastered the genres of particular or general history, strict neoclassicists argued.

Camden and Raleigh entertained thoughts of embarking on a complete history of England but for different reasons chose to pursue other projects. Although never getting beyond the year 130 BC, Raleigh's *History of the World* (1614) did reap praise for, among other things, its beautiful language and its political usefulness as a weapon against Stuart monarchy. Two humanist poets wrote general histories, but neither John Milton nor Samuel Daniel fulfilled Englishmen's highest hopes for the genre. Daniel's *A Collection of the History of England* was instructive and eloquent but unfinished. Convinced that the sources for early English history were untrustworthy, he began his story with the Norman Conquest but never succeeded in bringing it beyond Edward III's reign.[18] Like Daniel, Milton sought to write a national history along humanist lines, to answer the complaint about the impoverished condition of English historiography. Milton's appointment as Latin Secretary to the council of state interrupted composition of the *History of Britain*, which Milton resumed, only to abandon, in the mid-1650s. He became fed up with his source materials, which he found incomplete and inaccurate. He lost interest in medieval history and finally gave up his survey of ancient Britain at the Norman Conquest, turning instead to more appealing and pressing projects – *De Doctrina Christiana* and later *Paradise Lost*. In the event, history had passed Milton by: with the monarchy restored in 1660, a republican history such as his faced poor prospects; cautiously and belatedly, therefore, he published his abortive work in 1670, a smooth narrative of early British history, modelled after Sallust, somber, didactic, filled with political maxims. Readers applauded his style but found him wanting as a general historian. Like Daniel's *History*, Milton's was interpreted as an abridgement only, not a full history. It conspicuously lacked the legal and ecclesiastical history Englishmen expected in a 'complete' history of England.[19]

Having briefly examined the English histories that laid claim to the prestige of classical history, we can see that they had pretensions to noble history because of their antique prose and their literary devices, their periods and their invented speeches, their high tone. That Englishmen sometimes ignored classical literary conceits or made compromises with the modern world might easily be forgiven because the continental historians they emulated also strayed from their classical models on occasion. What could not be forgiven was the limited scale of the best English histories: general histories were not complete enough, particular histories more nearly resembled mere biographies. Despite flashes of genius, they failed to match up to the moderns whose works had somehow captured the essence of classical historical writing by virtue of their scope and comprehensiveness, their insight into men and events, their political utility and importance, their compelling style. What, then, might be preventing English historians from reaching the summit of Parnassus?

CLASSICISM AND MODERNITY

During the two millennia separating the invention of 'history' in classical times and the English attempts to imitate it in the early-modern period, many technological, religious, social, scholarly, and political developments called into question the relevance of classical history. Englishmen took note of several such phenomena which were without precedent in antiquity and thus capable of modifying, even revolutionizing, the way history had to be written: the mariner's compass, modern commerce, Christianity, gunpowder, the printing press, political parties, a middle rank of citizens, modern antiquarian scholarship.[20] In 1759, Horace Walpole contemplated the effect of these modern agents on a proposed history of ancient Greece by William Robertson:

> The very terms *ways and means* imprints ideas that never occur in Greek and Roman story. Add, banks, premiums, bank notes, remittances, and the whole visionary fabric of jobbing; what a new world! How all the mystery of money would have barbarized Livy and Sallust! how it would enliven and make interesting a new history of the ancients, by showing how far they used the same resources, how far not! . . . There are many other magazines of ideas opened to modern men, on the existence of which half their transactions depend, which were absolutely unknown to the ancients – and yet as I said, the course of things produced much the same events, though by agents so unlike.[21]

Hume explained how the invention of artillery altered the whole nature of war and politics by making battles less bloody and politics more stable.[22] However, as Walpole suggested, in practice only certain features of modern life elicited significant comment from, or appeared to affect, historians trying to sustain neoclassical history. Christianity, the printing press, political parties, and antiquarianism each in its own way served to transform the subject, the form, the sources of history, and appeared to call for a new kind of history to take account of them; they could not be ignored. Was it still appropriate for a retired statesman or warrior to record the noble political and military deeds – and words – of other great men, when one lived in a society where propaganda campaigns conducted in print could be more important than speeches delivered in the public assembly, where clergymen could play a decisive role in public affairs, where erudition in the history of law, language, or custom was required for a thorough understanding of politics, or where the profusion of printed documents as well as unpublished archival materials could overwhelm even the most diligent and expert researcher? In fact, had the genre of history outlived its usefulness in a society so different from the ones which had produced it in the first place? Or was there enough continuity between ancient and early-modern societies, or enough elasticity in the role and genre of ancient history, to allow Englishmen to play at being Livy or Thucydides?

Antiquarianism

Although some precedents for it existed in antiquity, antiquarianism came of age in the hands of Renaissance humanists attempting to unlock the secrets of the ancient world. They read the ancient historians as teachers of statecraft and rhetoric, and sometimes dared to imitate them as models for writing the history of their own society. However, they never dared to write the history of Greece or Rome, because they believed the ancient historians had written those narratives once and for all. Thucydides and Livy might be imitated but not replaced. Much humanist scholarship devoted itself to understanding ancient texts more thoroughly or even supplementing them, and humanists ended up developing a new manner of studying the past that, ironically, looked nothing like the classical histories antiquarianism was invented to appreciate. Non-literary remnants of antiquity – inscriptions, coins, topography, ruins – helped to clarify and correct literary remains, and the general field of antiquarianism eventually came to have specialized sub-disciplines such as chorography, numismatics, archeology, and epigraphy. As imperfect ancient manuscripts came to light, specialized textual study also became necessary for understanding them. Grammatical criticism became a useful tool to trace the different meanings of words within or between texts, and the science of philology came into being.[23]

In England the antiquarian movement began to flower in the second half of the sixteenth century. John Leland sought to apply the methods of Italian humanists not only to classical but also to medieval antiquities in Britain. He planned to make an inventory of those historic remains, to do a topography of Britain, and to learn whatever ancient British languages that could assist him in these enterprises. Generations of antiquarians toiled along the lines marked out by Leland, most notably William Camden. Camden's *Britannia* (1586) surveyed British topography and antiquities, partly in order to demonstrate the importance of Britain in the Roman Empire, partly to show foreign scholars that antiquarian scholarship in England could match continental achievements.[24] As an international showpiece for English antiquarianism, the *Britannia* succeeded, at the same time as Camden's compatriots were failing to meet the continental challenge to produce neoclassical historical narratives.

While Camden's triumph as a chorographer won him an international reputation, English legal antiquarianism, like English neoclassical historiography, continued to lag behind continental efforts in these very different investigations of the past. In fifteenth-century Italy, Valla and Politian had founded legal humanism. By the collective philological efforts of their French successors, scholars such as Guillaume Budé, François Hotman, and Jacques Cujas, a historical basis for law was established. Placed into the historical context of the society that produced it, law, whether Roman or barbarian, was seen to have originated in such an alien society that its relevance to sixteenth-century France came seriously into question. By tracing the history of evolving laws, the French antiquarians began to uncover the social arrangements and institutions of ancient, medieval, and modern France, and to see them as distinct from one another. In England, however, despite some acquaintance with the new French legal scholarship, the immemorial and virtually unchanging quality of English law continued to be emphasized by common lawyers, who believed that the common law was the only law ever known to England. Not forced to compare civil and customary law as the French had been, many Englishmen clung to the myth of the ancient constitution until crises in Stuart monarchy led John Selden and Sir Henry Spelman to chip away at the insular common-law mind. Selden's opposition to the crown fueled his research into the history of legal, political, social, and ecclesiastical institutions and customs. Importing the most modern French philological techniques, Selden demonstrated that such institutions had real human histories and did not originate mysteriously in the primeval mists of time. Spelman pointed out that the English constitution, far from being unchanging and dating from time out of mind, had in fact been greatly transformed by the Norman Conquest.[25] Such discoveries by early seventeenth-century legal antiquarians suggested that the constitution had a history, and that that history was important to gaining an understanding of past and even present politics. It remained to be seen, however, whether general historians would accept that such a history should or could be incorporated into a neoclassical history of worthy deeds centering on war and politics. The question of how the genre of antiquarian treatise, replete with the scholarly paraphernalia of index, glossary, and footnote, could be molded into a polished narrative conforming to humanist standards of style, also troubled neoclassicists. The classical historians, after all, never had to deal with the findings or the form of this sort of antiquarian scholarship.

Antiquarians had always been engaged in an activity distinct from that of historians. Manners, art, trade – unworthy subjects in their own right cut off from politics, according to the classical historians – had always been at the core of antiquarian activity. The antiquarian focused on the remains of historical events, great and small alike, not the causes of those events. His work emphasized the collection of things which he had found rather than an interpretation or a narrative concerning what brought those artifacts into existence. The Renaissance legal antiquarians wrote philological treatises and commentaries, not narratives. Issues of genre, subject matter, and purpose thus separated the antiquarian from the historian. While Florentine antiquarians once shared with historians humanist ideals about pursuing a program of moral and political edification and participation in public life, some antiquarians, perhaps beginning with Politian, began to study antiquity for its own sake, not for its possible civic benefits. Antiquarianism as he practiced it became so specialized and all-consuming that it did not allow for a public life of one's own. So completely did he put the ancient objects of his inquiry into historical context that they seemed immaterial to any other time or place, including his own.[26] In seventeenth-century England the reputation of antiquarians to study things irrelevant to public life and themselves not to have a role in public life became well entrenched. Selden and Spelman were motivated by a practical desire to settle public issues by means of scholarly research and they even held public office. However, polite society justifiably ridiculed many antiquarians as pedantic and frivolous, purveyors of mere 'curiosities' of little value or interest to the rest of society. The study of antiquities had a modest part to play in the formation of an English gentleman but could never be a full-time occupation for a man of the world,[27] because a life devoted to scholarship prevented the gentleman from putting into action the political lessons learned in real histories.[28] Historical study was only a means to the reader's performance of deeds themselves worthy of a place in future histories.

At many points during the sixteenth and even seventeenth century the English elite might have been satisfied with a political education based on classical and neoclassical histories presented as advice literature for princes and centered on the acts of individual great men as praiseworthy or blameworthy. But this classical conception of history was appearing rather narrow under the pressure of modern events, for narratives of civil history in the antique manner could not satisfy many English political controversies; only the less prestigious activity of antiquarianism could. This realization of the importance of what we today call social and cultural history, or even just a more broadly defined political history, has been called a 'historical revolution,' an unbinding of Clio.[29] When Englishmen turned to the past to settle such issues as the respective powers of crown and parliament, or the proper relations of church and state, or indeed whether the reformed or the Catholic Church was the true church, they turned to antiquarianism in addition to traditional history as an aid. It turned out that composing a civil history based on the most recent antiquarian findings proved impossible for the first man to attempt it. When Leland, in the mid-sixteenth century, tried combining political narrative with antiquarian research, he lost his sanity. Leland provided succeeding generations with a cautionary tale about the difficulty – the madness – of harnessing modern scholarship to traditional historical narrative.[30]

To their critics it was bad enough that antiquarians studied classical remains in the manner they did; it was even worse that they dug up an entire culture many considered repulsive. Many gentlemen had an almost physical distaste for the middle ages. Historical records of the middle ages were written by socially inferior monks, in the form of chronicles, about events so uncivilized or incomprehensible as to lack instructive value. David Hume braced himself to the chore of narrating two volumes of medieval history in his *History of England*; simultaneously, he put readers on their guard:

> The Monks, who were the only annalists during those ages, lived remote from public affairs, considered the civil transactions as entirely subordinate to the ecclesiastical, and besides partaking of the ignorance and barbarity, which were then universal, were strongly infected with credulity, with the love of wonder, and with a propensity to imposture; vices almost inseparable from their profession, and manner of life. The history of that period abounds in names, but is extremely barren of events; or the events are related so much without circumstances and causes, that the most profound or most eloquent writer must despair of rendering them either instructive or entertaining to the reader. Even the great learning and vigorous imagination of Milton sunk under the weight; and this author scruples not to declare, that the skirmishes of kites or crows as much merited a particular narrative, as the confused transactions and battles of the Saxon Heptarchy.[31]

The monks, in sum, had perverted the classical conception of history. The problem for Hume, as for other historians, was that he had to deal with feudal society as left to him by the monks and as interpreted by the antiquarians, if he was to write a general history of England, one that told the whole story, medieval warts and all. But could the middle ages be written about classically?

Could the neoclassical historian, a polite gentleman or noble-man, master the erudition necessary to narrate the history of medieval times or would he be overwhelmed by it or refuse to do it on social grounds as interfering with a balanced life of leisure and public service? Would a nobleman soil his hands with records in the Tower of London discovered by the antiquarians and demonstrated to be vital to an understanding of medieval legal and political institutions? Historians were left to ponder these questions.

Christianity

All of Christianity, not just medieval Catholicism, presented neo-classicists with a formidable challenge. Did the new religion that had transformed European society explode the pagan historical categories of the classical historians? Christians found the pagan genre of history an inadequate tool for framing their own past, so they conceived of a new historical genre and a new role of historian, each at odds with its pagan predecessor. Classical historiography placed an emphasis on secular wisdom and in-vented speeches, not on proselytizing or on transcribing sacred documents. But in the year 312, Eusebius had founded ecclesias-tical history as a supplement to the Gospels, and reversed this proportion between speech and document, downplaying the former while emphasizing the latter. Whereas the classical historian preferred contemporary or near-contemporary history, and oral to written testimony, the ecclesiastical historian looked to the remote Christian past and connected it to the present through the explication of sacred documents, whether scriptural or patristic. Other differences also marked Christian from pagan historiography. The story of a Christian nation, unlike a pagan one, had at its center the continuing purity of doctrine in the face of persecution and heresy. It also had new actors, new 'great men,' not classical heroes but ordinary men and women living exemplary lives, bearing witness to the Christian truth through martyrdom.[32]

Because church affairs became so mixed up with secular mat-ters, ecclesiastical history, especially since the time of the Refor-mation, had a decisive role in any history of England, thus calling into doubt the relevance of classical historical writing as a model for English Christians. Theorists of historiography neatly divided political from church history, but civil history and ecclesiastical history were frequently in fact indistinguishable, and neither was accorded any special esteem over the other. This blurring of distinctions between ecclesiastical and civil was nothing new, of course: by the sixth century the church was so involved in affairs of state that ecclesiastical history lost much of the distinctiveness it had possessed in Eusebius' day.[33] While Reformation Anglicans writing church history confidently detected the hand of God in the creation and sustenance of the Church of England, Fuller, Heylyn, Burnet, Collier, and Strype also incorporated civil history into their work. The Church of England had been established by civil law, and the events church historians recounted were so entwined with national politics that it was impossible to write church history without civil history. Alternatively, civil historians writing Tudor history could not write 'secular' political history without deep engagement in ecclesiastical affairs. Writers of general histories commonly used the subtitle 'Ecclesiastical and Civil,' because this was the only kind of political history that could be written. In an effort to be more comprehensive, authors of church history often promised to take account of civil affairs; ostensibly civil or general historians promised to include church affairs. Instead of saying that during the seventeenth century 'ecclesiastical history was gradually being absorbed into civil history,'[34] we may as easily see civil history being absorbed into ecclesiastical. Civil history and ecclesiastical history proved far easier to separate in theory than in practice.

Devoted to the salvation of readers' souls, the ecclesiastical historian was supposed to impart spiritual wisdom, not the secular political knowledge of the pagan historians. Naturally, the individual best suited to playing this role was a clergyman skilled in spiritual exhortation, accomplished in scriptural exegesis, learned in church history. A divine of considerable stature, who had risen far enough in the hierarchy to observe and play ecclesiastical politics of the sort he would be called upon to narrate, clearly had a leg up on other claimants to the role. But what happened when an ecclesiastical historian decided to compose church history from a secular point of view? A Venetian priest, Paolo Sarpi, wrote *The History of the Council of Trent* (1619), proving that a clergyman actually could write a masterpiece of neoclassical historiography, however incongruous such a feat appeared to be. The council had been convened to reform and unite the church, but ended up doing the opposite, according to Sarpi, who wished to preserve a record of the reforms it had rejected. His Tacitean delineation of character and motive showed prelates engaged in simple political controversy, not the work of the Holy Ghost. Sarpi defied not only the council but also the protocols for writing history. He was a priest writing about the ignoble deeds of other priests, not a warrior or statesman writing about the worthy deeds of his peers. He believed the importance of his subject allowed him to pursue his topic in more detail than historians were usually allowed. Rather than compose a connected narrative, he inserted his diary as a record of conciliar sessions and wrote 'by way of Annals' for other periods. However, many Englishmen overlooked these aspects of the *History* to see in Sarpi's ruthless exposure of papal hypocrisy a history whose significance and analytic power rivalled that of the ancient historians.[35] English Protestants, as well as infidels, found Sarpi's analysis so delicious, so politically satisfying, they sometimes forgot he was writing a kind of history that departed from many classical ideals. They affectionately referred to him as 'Fra Paolo.'

Sarpi demonstrated that a secular treatment of what was supposed to be a sacred subject could earn the respect of an English audience. However, William Temple, comparing his achievement with that of the ancient historians, complained that Sarpi's subject was only negotiation, not great actions. William Wotton responded that Sarpi's topic was the war between Protestants and 'a mighty Empire' – the Roman Church – which was larger than 'any of the Four Ancient [Empires].' Moreover, the political intrigue at the council rivalled anything in the political history of antiquity.[36] Wotton's reading of Sarpi made the point that a historical project could acquire prestige so long as the subject was of great import but regardless of its religiosity *per se*. The new subject matter furnished by Christianity did not trouble Englishmen, who merely added religious motives to their repertoire of explanation, and influential holy men and women to their cast of characters. Neoclassical critics sometimes reproached historians for an overactive providence in their accounts, but Christian providence did not function so differently from the way 'Fortune' did in classical histories.[37]

What most bothered neoclassicists about ecclesiastical history was the polemical stance of the author and the disruptions to his narrative caused by the inclusion of documents. The partisanship and the documentary quality of ecclesiastical histories could be traced back to Eusebius, but for seventeenth- and eighteenth-century Englishmen the more relevant models belonged to Reformation controversialists.[38] The reformers wanted to overturn the Eusebian view of early church history, a story of salutary growth and development, and to show instead how the Catholic Church had corrupted the pristine, apostolic church. In their destruction of the Eusebian interpretation of history, however, Protestant historians clung to the Eusebian emphasis on documents, while subjoining a vituperative zeal and a humanist's philological sophistication lacking in the father of church history. Modern ecclesiastical historiography, in the age of Reformation, thus became even more unlike pagan historiography than Eusebius' *History* had been. In the case of England, the task of Anglican apologists was to demonstrate that the creation of the Church of England by an act of state did not constitute a new church but a return to the original church of Christ and the apostles, before the Bishops of Rome had transformed it into a false church. John Foxe's *Acts and Monuments* (1563) was the most influential work to argue that the Church of England was in fact the true church, and the English a chosen people. Both a martyrology and an ecclesiastical history of England, the *Acts and Monuments* bore little resemblance to a polite, neoclassical narrative. Locked in battle with his Catholic opponents, Foxe interrupted his story-line to insert dissertations employing humanist source criticism to dismantle the evidence adduced by adversaries. Foxe also found it necessary to retrieve the earliest historical sources and to transcribe entire documents for dozens of pages at a time to ensure that he could not be accused of taking quotations out of context.[39] In the 1560s and '70s the Archbishop of Canterbury, Matthew Parker, took Anglican antiquarian apologetics a step further. He scoured the kingdom for manuscripts that could demonstrate the connections between the church he shepherded and the earliest Christian church on the island. According to Parker, the English church had always taken a position different from Rome on such issues as the Eucharist and the marriage of priests, and not only had he the documents to prove it, he published a collection of them. By publicizing his defense of the Anglican settlement, Parker made medieval antiquities, especially those relating to the Anglo-Saxon church, more accessible. Reformation controversy did not single-handedly uncover the medieval world – laymen such as William Lambarde simultaneously tried to establish a native and Anglo-Saxon ancestry for English law[40] – but confessional disputation did nourish antiquarian research.

Modern erudition, civil as well as ecclesiastical, had the capacity to crush the neoclassical historian by its sheer volume. In an age of controversy, a battle for souls, modern scholarly paraphernalia and contested documents appeared to be so necessary to convince readers of a historian's truthfulness that audiences began to demand them of their historians, despite their lack of classical precedents. Polydore Vergil had not noticed ancient historians citing their sources or their Renaissance imitators doing it either, so he declined to do so as well. A half century later, however, Foxe upbraided Polydore for this omission.[41] Two centuries later, David Hume admitted that the neoclassical battle against the footnote, or at least against marginal notes, had been lost. In 1758 Horace Walpole wrote to Hume criticizing the lack of supporting references in an early volume of his *History of England*. Hume wrote back:

> it wou'd have been easy for me, after I had noted and markd all the passages, on which I founded my narration, to write the references on the margin. But I was seduc'd by the example of all the best historians even among the moderns, such as Matchiavel, Fra paolo, Davila, Bentivoglio; without considering that that practice was more modern than their time, and having been once introduc'd, ought to be follow'd by every writer. And tho' it be easy for the falsest and most partial historian to load his margin with quotations, nor is there any other certain method of assuring ones self of the fidelity of an author than to read most of the original writers of any period; yet the reader has reason to expect that the most material facts, at least all such as are any way new, shou'd be supported by the proper authorities.[42]

Hume promised to cite his sources in the future, admitting that slavish imitation had to give way to common sense, that scholarly citations, a rather recent development in historical writing, had become a necessity in even a polite narrative history such as he was composing.

Print

Hume realized he lived not only in an erudite culture but also a print culture. He noticed how the advent of printing had forever changed the social composition of authors, historical or otherwise, as well as audiences. He blamed the corruption of literary taste on 'the invention of printing; which has rendered books so common, that even men of slender fortunes can have access to them.' Hume also saw that 'the greater part of the classic writers [in antiquity], whose works remain, were men of the highest quality,'[43] but he did not go on to make a connection he might have made and one that turned out to explain a great deal about the weakness in English historiography – namely, the printing press had created a commercial market for history which encouraged unqualified historians to write for money rather than for the edification of princes and posterity. In the seventeenth and eighteenth century a substantial, if not mass, readership for history patronized less prestigious historical works such as chapbooks, chronicles, epitomes, histories of natural disasters, and secret histories.[44] That readership gave financial support to a class of professional writers who occasionally tried to write with pretensions to noble history, even though neoclassicists denied their right to do so.

Although the invention of movable type created numerous readerships for history undreamt of in antiquity, aspirant neoclassical historians perforce wrote on a grand scale, a scale that usually kept it out of common hands, because the greatest single expense in book production was the cost of paper. While a mere political pamphlet might cost six pence or a shilling or two, and could be read in one sitting, a single part of James Tyrrell's *General History of England* cost 30 shillings and took dozens of hours to read. The minimum annual income a gentleman required to maintain his status was £300, so the outlay for the complete set of the *History* represented about 1.5 per cent of this income. The same expenditure for a shopkeeper making £45 was 10 per cent. Less than half the families in England made this much, and those that did rarely had anything left over after covering the cost of subsistence.[45] Ingenious publishers devised means of reaching common folk with extracts of mammoth histories, but these represented mere morsels of exclusive fare.[46]

Perhaps more striking than its effect on issues of audience and authorship was print's impact on the discursive makeup of histories. In the early-modern period, printed propaganda became such an important weapon in the battle for souls as well as territory that it acquired an undisputed place in the history of modern war and politics. Many historians, Davila, for example, promoted the printed declaration or treaty to the status of a new 'worthy deed,' one as legitimate as any speech delivered in the Roman Senate. The only way to tell the whole story of modern events was to insert transcriptions of these vital agents, regardless of the violence such insertions did to narratives. Archbishop Parker certainly saw the value of the printing press in his struggle to secure the Elizabethan settlement; roundheads and cavaliers relied upon it in the English Civil War; tories and whigs deployed it to sway public opinion during the War of Spanish Succession. Polite historians now faced the challenge of incorporating the contents of propaganda into their story without themselves being relegated to the role of transcriber, collector, or editor. Print had in fact become a two-edged sword: in the hands of publishers such as Parker it made obscure historical documents more accessible; but the dissemination of antiquarian works as well as documentary collections could also inundate historians, who, failing to digest them, might revert to copying them into their own work, thereby unraveling their narrative.

Party Politics

With hindsight, we can certainly appreciate the various threats to neoclassical history the printing press presented. However, contemporaries more frequently blamed the English party system for the chronic weakness in historiography. Many seventeenth- and eighteenth-century historians traced the origins of that system to the reign of James I or to the Civil War.[47] Recent scholarship acknowledges that the roots of party conflict can be located in the Civil War period but points to the Restoration as the era in which constitutional and religious issues fought over in the war erupted and eventually gave birth to 'tory' and 'whig' parties.[48] One crucial moment in the development of these parties came at the Exclusion Crisis (1678–81), when these labels attained common usage. The political nation was divided over the prospect of a Roman Catholic, James, Duke of York, succeeding his brother, King Charles II, on the throne, and the whig party was born in an attempt to exclude James from the succession. Tories and whigs alike exploited widespread fears of 'popery and arbitrary government.' Whigs argued that a Catholic ruler would not protect English Protestantism, and would necessarily model his government after that of Louis XIV of France, crushing parliament and ruling arbitrarily by means of a standing army. Tories replied that dethroning kings, such as the whigs' parliamentary bill of exclusion proposed to do, was actually a popish activity associated with jesuit theorists, and that the 'arbitrary' government England had to fear would come at the hands of the whigs, whose model of government was the Commonwealth of the 1650s when Cromwell ruled through a standing army. After skillfully moving, dissolving, and proroguing parliament, and keeping James out of mischief, Charles II defeated the whigs and preserved for the time being the principle of hereditary succession. Even after the Glorious Revolution of 1688–9 placed William and Mary on the throne, vindicated the whigs' policy of exclusion, and secured legislative sovereignty for parliament, England remained divided over constitutional and religious issues into the next century. Party strife continued to tear at the political fabric of England because the Glorious Revolution, like the Restoration, had not solved constitutional questions concerning the executive powers of the crown or religious questions about whether tolerance should be granted to Protestant dissenters. The 'rage of party' reached a crescendo during the reign of Queen Anne (1702–14), and then cooled off under Hanoverian rule after 1714, when whigs ushered in single-party government. Although a full-fledged two-party system did not develop until the nineteenth century, the period 1680-1750 has been dubbed 'the first age of party.'[49]

Hume denounced the party system as contrary to good government, and considered it a very modern development which he blamed in part on Christianity.

> Parties from *principle*, especially abstract speculative principle, are known only to modern times, and are, perhaps, the most extraordinary and unaccountable *phenomenon*, that has yet appeared in human affairs.... [The] principles of priestly government... have engendered a spirit of persecution, which has ever since been the poison of human society, and the source of the most inveterate factions in every government.[50]

Whatever its effects on English government, the party system had a devastating effect on English historical writing. Adam Smith claimed that historical argument was so fundamental to modern political and religious life that modern historians abandoned narration and took up partisan proofs in their works, thereby destroying the genre invented by the ancients:

> Long demonstrations as they are no part of the historians province are seldom made use of by the ancients. The modern authors have often brought them in. Historicall truths are now in much greater request than they ever were in the ancient times. One thing that has contributed to the increase of this curiosity is that there are now severall sects in Religion and politicall disputes which are greatly dependent on the truth of certain facts. This it is that has induced almost all historians for some time past to be at great pains in the proof of those facts on which the claims of the parties they favoured depended. These proofs however besides that they are inconsistent with the historicall stile, are likewise of bad consequence as they interrupt the thread of the narration, and that most commonly in the parts that are most interesting. They withdraw our attention from the main facts, and before we can get thro them they have so far weakened our concern for the issue of the affair that was broke off that we are never again so much interested in them.
>
> The Dissertations which are everywhere interwoven into Modern Histories contribute among other things and that not a little to render them less interesting than those wrote by the Antients.[51]

As history became more important to modern life, it became less compelling, less artistic, less true to its ancient foundations.

Modern Englishmen enjoyed an extraordinary degree of political liberty, but it was, paradoxically, too much liberty for historiography to bear, Montesquieu argued in the *Spirit of the Laws*:

> In monarchies extremely absolute, historians betray the truth, because they are not at liberty to speak it; in states remarkably free, they betray the truth, because of their liberty itself; which always produces divisions, everyone becoming as great a slave to the prejudices of his faction as he could be in a despotic state.[52]

The ancient historians themselves wrote as partisans, according to James Hampton's analysis. However, they favored the interests of their own country, and doing so 'at least proceeded from an honest Cause. But in later Times, private Interests, and Animosities, have perverted the Truth of History; Patriotism gives place to Faction.'[53] The classical historians could not claim to be completely impartial, but they managed to refrain from abusive, small-minded partisanship. In the 'age of party,' however, we shall see that English historians became pettifoggers in the name of one party or another. To the MP, the lawyer, the landowner, the bishop, the authority of the past was so great that employing history for political ends could rarely be resisted. History became the tool of party.

Politics, print, Christianity, and antiquarianism all seemed inescapable aspects of modern life, and each offered a stumbling block to the successful composition of neoclassical historiography. Yet in 1671 a fat, aging, exiled nobleman began collating two manuscripts into a work that would show to what degree an English historian could vanquish the obstacles modernity strew before him. Now we must turn to the man whose ambition it was to become the English Thucydides.

3

Clarendon as the English Thucydides

Visiting Moulins, France, in 1671, Laurence Hyde brought his father Edward, Earl of Clarendon, the trunk containing an unfinished history of the English Civil War. As advisor to King Charles I, Clarendon began the history in 1646, after a series of military defeats forced him to go to Scilly, then Jersey, a last royalist stronghold. Composition was interrupted in 1648, when the queen summoned him from Jersey to the Paris headquarters of the royalist camp. For the next dozen years he worked to restore the monarchy, which parliament had abolished, and the Prince of Wales, whose father King Charles had been executed. Both were restored in 1660, and Hyde served as chief royal counselor. After seven years of government, however, Clarendon ran afoul of both court and parliament, blamed for naval defeats at the hands of the Dutch. He was banished in 1667 and spent the next two years writing his life's story to vindicate himself from articles of impeachment.[1] He completed his *History* by adding passages from his autobiographical *Life*, written 1667–9, to the earlier *History*, written 1646–8 and delivered to him by Laurence in 1671.

Clarendon proved that the victors do not always write history. Defeated in 1648, when parliament's triumph over the king was complete, and again in 1667, when he was disgraced, Clarendon created the most famous work of history to emerge from and about the turbulent age in which he lived. *The History of the Rebellion and Civil Wars in England* was a massive narrative describing one of the greatest events in the nation's history, written by one of the tragedy's chief actors, from a lofty, impersonal perspective, in rolling, archaic periods. Clarendon was the first Englishman to be so widely acclaimed a peer of the classical historians. Thomas Sprat had prophesied his coming. In 1667 Sprat observed that the Civil War had devastated the English language, not just the body politic. In the peace of Restoration he saw an opportunity to take stock of his native tongue, to purify and polish it with help from an English academy modeled after the French Academy. Sprat saw the language maturing rapidly and he took pride in it but concluded the English language could only gain influence if an exemplary work of it were to be composed. Needed first was a great history, which his proposed academy could use as an exhibition piece for the new language. It would be a history of the Civil War, written after classical models, polished to a French lustre.

> Of all the labors of mens Wit, and Industry, I scarce know any, that can be more useful to the World, then Civil History: if it were written, with that sincerity, and majesty, as it ought to be, as a faithful Idea of humane Actions. And it is observable, that almost in all civiliz'd Countries, it has been the last thing, that has come to perfection. I may now say, that the English can already shew many industrious, and worthy Pieces in this kind: But yet, I have some Prophetical imagination in my thoughts, that there is still behind, something Greater, then any we have yet seen, reserv'd for the Glory of this Age. One Reason of this my strong persuasion, is a comparison, that I make, between the condition of our State, and that of the Romans. They at first writ, in this way, not much better then our Moncks: onely Registring in an undigested manner, some few naked Breviaries of their Wars, and Leagues, and Acts, of their City Magistrates. And indeed they advanc'd forward by very low degrees: For I remember, that Tully somewhere complains, in these Words: *Historia nondum latinis literis illustrata.* But it was in the peaceful reign of Augustus, after the conclusion of their long Civil Wars, that most of their perfect Historians appear'd. And it seems to me, that we may expect the same progress amongst us. There lye now ready in Bank, the most memorable Actions of Twenty years: a Subject of as great Dignity, and Variety, as ever pass'd under any Mans hands: the peace which we injoy, gives leisure and incouragement enough: The effects of such a Work would be wonderfully advantageous, to the safety of our Country, and to His Majesties Interest: for there can be no better means to preserve his Subjects in obedience for the future, than to give them a full view of the miseries, that attended rebellion.[2]

Before dying in 1674, the Earl of Clarendon completed such a work, and Sprat himself put the polite touches on it before its publication for royalist purposes between 1702 and 1704.

From its inception in the 1640s to its reception in the eighteenth century, Clarendon's *History* faced numerous obstacles. Like other retired statesmen, Clarendon had political ambitions and family obligations that jeopardized his single-minded pursuit of the truth about the past. Chronicling a war waged in large measure through printed propaganda, Clarendon felt obliged to reprint massive documents in his *History*, thus departing from classical protocols for historical writing. He refused to insert invented speeches into the narrative, and so he appeared to deviate still further from the Thucydidean model he apparently chose for himself. He died before the 'age of party' was born, but party politics posed a posthumous threat to his manuscript, as Clarendon's politically committed sons appropriated his text on behalf of the tory party, transforming his stately work into a shrill, partisan document. And yet the *History* survived these editorial emendations and the many traps modern society set for it, to enter the canon of neoclassical historiography and become, in turn, a model for other moderns wishing to write Thucydidean history.

LEISURE AND THE NOBLE HISTORIAN

Like any other English gentleman, Clarendon had studied the classical historians as a young man. When he came to write his own history, he returned to them. During both of his exiles Clarendon transcribed passages from their works, along with those of modern historians, into his commonplace book. He recognized that modern philology and criticism had corrected factual and textual errors in the work of ancient authors, particularly the church fathers, and that important consequences followed: 'it is an extraordinary improvement that divine and humane learning hath attained to,' Clarendon wrote in his *Essays*, 'since men have looked upon the ancients as fallible writers, and not as upon those *ne plus ultra*, that could not be exceeded.'[3] Clarendon for his part appears to have believed he could write a history matching or surpassing those of the ancients. He was aware of the weakness in English historiography,[4] respectful though not uncritical of the ancient historians, and intent on filling the Thucydidean role. How did Clarendon succeed in becoming the English Thucydides? Why were there no other noble historians able to take advantage of so promising a subject as the Civil War? Only by examining elite notions of leisure and public service can we appreciate the rare combination of circumstances that helped Clarendon prosper as a historian.

It is worth recalling that those at the apex of English society, including Clarendon, were set apart by virtue of the fact that they did not have to work for a living. Their independent income, usually from land, gave them the leisure and freedom to pursue their own interests – political, social, familial, intellectual, and artistic. In his *Essays*, Clarendon described how attractive these pursuits were, especially to a political retiree:

> He is as active as he was before, with less trouble of body and mind, and finds new pleasures in the place of those with which he was before enough satiated; a garden and a park supplies him with greater variety and more innocent divertisement, than the city and the court used to do. He was hitherto so much perplexed with what related to the public, that he had never a full joy in his own domestics, nor those a sufficient protection and providence from him: now he is in possession of the company and conversation of his own wife, which he seldom had before; he is acquainted with his own children, who were before strangers to him, and whom he makes wise by his instruction . . .[5]

Many activities held great appeal for the English nobleman or gentleman. He spent his leisure running a household and raising a family, managing and improving his estates, tending and rebuilding houses and gardens, visiting and entertaining friends, creating, patronizing, or collecting works of art and literature.[6] Reading and writing were favorite pursuits, but even when composition turned to historical subjects these projects were often of a local, even private nature, not public and national or international. The country gentleman's daily activities and interest in immediate surroundings could inspire him to study genealogy, antiquarianism, and family biography. Antiquarian studies commonly originated as legal histories of the estate, village, or church over which the gentleman presided. Curiosity about everyday

life and scenery might lead him to legal and architectural research into nearby buildings. Family pride and the quest for self-
knowledge moved him to construct genealogies and family
histories. Legal exigencies were also involved: a fertility crisis
among the elite from 1650 to 1740 meant that family continuity
could depend upon the preservation of family documents pointing to a distant relative who could inherit the estate intact. Passing on the family estate, the house, and the name required keeping
an archive.[7] This abiding interest in family history helps to explain why some men, even if they retired, even if they used that
retirement to reflect on the past, might not lift their pen to write
a neoclassical history.[8] Clarendon, on the other hand, at least in
his final retirement, never had to choose between his family and
his history. The terms of his banishment proscribed contact with
his family, so from 1667 until his death – with rare exceptions
such as Laurence's visit in 1671 – there was nothing the patri-
arch of the Hydes could do for his own family, even write to it.
Since family matters could distract aspirant historians from their
task, Clarendon, who was legally prohibited from such concerns,
thus enjoyed an advantage in his role as historian.

To many of Clarendon's social equals, the quiet enjoyment of
private life might prove more attractive than historical composition; the hurly-burly of political life might also prove more en-
ticing than the pursuit of Thucydidean history. Membership in
the elite was defined by one's freedom from toiling for subsistence, but with that freedom came serious responsibilities, chief
among which was public service, whether as justice of the peace
or member of parliament. Since Tudor times, a system of local
self-government had promoted a sense of responsibility and co-
operation among the gentry. Public service was a duty, even if
it sometimes brought little if any reward in terms of prestige or
money, especially at lower levels of administration.[9] The gentlemanly and especially aristocratic ideal was activist, not contemplative, and emphasized generosity, not hedonism. Retiring from
public life for any reason was difficult, because it required renouncing these norms of civic responsibility. Even in the aftermath of political defeat, retirees felt not only humiliation but
also guilt about their newfound leisure:[10] they wrote to friends
justifying their productive and hence virtuous use of retirement,
and friends wrote back reassuring them of their noble and continuing public service in trying, even wicked times.

The retiree's sense of shame was a significant theme in the historical culture of early-modern England, because one source of redemption for him was to make himself useful to the public by writing history. Retirement was meant for meditation, philosophy, study, but also for literary composition, and the literary endeavor which best dignified political defeat was history. History returned a man in private life to a public role – reflecting on public affairs and communicating those reflections to a future public. Clarendon, for example, wrote a friend that 'even this retirement [of 1646] is not absolutely unprofitable to the publick.'[11] By 'preparing the story of your sufferings' for posterity, Clarendon wrote to reassure the king (and possibly himself) a few weeks later, he was still serving the crown.[12] Continuing and finishing that history proved to be Clarendon's overriding ambition during his banishment 21 years later. Only returning to England mattered more to him. In his autobiography Clarendon claimed that during his various retirements he had 'served God and his country with more devotion, and he hoped more effectually, than in all the other more active part of his life.'[13] Whether Clarendon was correct or not, whether he had convinced himself this was so, he was borrowing a rhetorical commonplace from classical antiquity that was useful for defeated statesmen imploring those in power to return them to favor. The political exile argued that the historical and philosophical meditations of the contemplative life were as valuable to the state as the political or military service of the active life had been, that writing and thinking prepared him for state service, indeed justified his return to it.

This is not the place to trace the origins of these values, but it is safe to say they were largely commonplace by Clarendon's time, an admixture of Christian and classical sources, Cicero and Seneca in particular. Clarendon's essays encapsulated many themes of retirement rhetoric that would last at least through the eighteenth century. In his essay 'On an Active and on a Contemplative Life,' Clarendon evaluated political activity and inactivity on the basis of their respective contributions to men's 'service of God, to the benefit of their country, and to their own salvation; which are the three peculiar ends of man's creation.' Public life was more valuable than private, contended Clarendon, because publicity for one's 'wisdom' and 'piety' affected more individuals than one's deeds in the private sphere did. Men were called to set examples for 'the great benefit of the church and state.' They retired on account of their own stupidity or incompetence, their sloth, cowardice, or selfishness. They were not supposed to retire even when public life had been corrupted, since they were morally enjoined not simply to avoid evil but actively to 'propagate virtue.'[14]

In this essay, in his autobiography, and in his correspondence, Clarendon showed himself to be torn by two conflicting visions of retirement. On the one hand, he depicted retirement as an abdication of duty; one did not choose it but only accepted it when forced to do so. This explained his second retirement in 1667, when Clarendon fled at the last possible moment, staying at court long after he was not wanted. On the other hand, Clarendon advocated voluntary retirements from public life, such as the one he took in 1646, when he might have attended the Prince of Wales but instead stayed behind on Jersey and began to write his *History*. Clarendon emphasized this second, more positive vision of retirement, and in his essays dwelt on the long and worthy tradition of using leisured retreat for reflecting on the past. History was in fact best written in voluntary retirement, a state of calm which conduced to impartial observations and reflections.[15] The best historians were 'men of action and experience,'[16] great men, but they needed a respite from public life to be effective. According to Clarendon, the statesman in general, and the statesman-historian in particular, required voluntary retirement in order to refresh himself, to study, and to contemplate so as to act wisely upon returning to public life. The solitary life of pure contemplation was selfish and, because it did not include the experience of dealing with other men, it did not even result in true wisdom;[17] the hermit was not fit for statesmanship. 'The wise man,' argued Clarendon, 'must compound his life both out of action and contemplation, and they must as it were succeed each other, *alternis vicibus*.'[18] This salutary career pattern was rare in England, however, Clarendon admitted. The scheme better suited republican forms of government, 'where an inferior officer this year is superior the next, and so the other in vicissitude,' where servants of the state were deemed more or less equal and so took turns in office. In England, on the other hand, monarchy was predicated upon 'the difference and distinction of persons' and so the pool of chief ministers was smaller than in a republic. Politicians remained secure and effective only if the prince gave them longer tenures of office, in which case the royal servant would not step down voluntarily for fear his enemies might gang up on him in his retirement.[19] Clarendon almost, but not quite, linked his portrait of the ideal historian with his analysis of retirement to conclude that England was not producing the sort of history which the classical republics produced because its form of government differed; that England's great men spent too much time performing great deeds and not enough preparing for them through analysis of the past.

Clarendon's formula for a political career leading to voluntary leisure and historical composition found few takers. As the 5th Earl of Orrery, writing in 1742, noticed, England's greatest historians had only come upon the leisure for history when compelled to do so:

> The only histories, from which our nation may claim any degree of reputable honour, have arisen from the leisure of those misfortunes, wherein the historians themselves were unjustly, and in every other respect unhappily, involved; I mean those of Sir Walter Raleigh, and the earl of Clarendon. To the long imprisonment of the former we are indebted for his history of the world; and to the unjust exile of the latter we owe his account of the civil wars.[20]

Was English political culture constructed so perversely that terms of imprisonment or exile offered the only solution to the weakness in historiography? The careers of Restoration politicians certainly revealed how difficult political practice made living up to Clarendon's high ideals about using voluntary retirement to write history. George Savile, 1st Marquis of Halifax, succeeded in alternating between business and leisure, office and retirement, in the 1680s and '90s, but he wrote political pamphlets and essays instead of history. Though prominent, he was not a politician of the highest rank. Some men tried and failed to achieve such a rank, while others declined to make the attempt. For example, Bulstrode Whitelocke sat in the Long Parliament and served the Cromwells. Upon exclusion from office in 1660, he used his retirement for historical composition. Although he had the best sources for narrating Civil War history from the parliamentary perspective, as Clarendon had the best for the royalist, he never played a role in events comparable to Clarendon's and so never attained the highest political offices in the realm. The diplomat Sir William Temple was on his way to joining the top tier of public men; he might have played a role in 1688 similar to the one Clarendon had played in 1660. Yet he lacked Clarendon's sense of public duty. He preferred a secluded life of gardening and writing, and apparently felt little guilt about turning down public office and choosing periodic retirement. He engaged in various historical projects, and wrote his memoirs, the choice of genre a man makes who either does not have high enough position to write a Thucydidean history, or who has the stature but does not make the time for the necessary research. Temple could not fill the Thucydidean role because he decided not to assume higher office and because he found other things to do in his leisure. Perhaps Clarendon had men like Temple in mind when he recommended that a prince improve the quality of his servants 'by compelling men who have been very conspicuous in action, to come again into the light out of this beloved retreat.' There was, however, little chance of princely intervention from Charles II, who wanted to enjoy his hard-won throne rather than take charge of government the way Clarendon advocated.[21]

This was an age of political adventurism in which the higher one rose, the higher the stakes, and the price of defeat was great. High-ranking losers in the political game usually did not have the luxury of a safe, leisurely retreat from which to write history. Clarendon had been able to escape in time and move to a secure distance, but the 1st Duke of Ormonde, busy fighting for the royalists, helping the Prince of Wales in exile (1651–60), then holding office, had little time to imitate Thucydides, even if he had possessed the inclination or aptitude. The 1st Earl of Danby spent nearly five years in the Tower preoccupied with legal battles to save his own skin. From 1681 until his death in 1683 as a fugitive in Amsterdam, the 1st Earl of Shaftesbury was either imprisoned or running for his life or ill. Ensconced in the Tower he began writing his memoirs, but, once outside, the lure of politics proved too powerful and he did not play the retirement card to finish them.[22]

The Thucydidean historian needed to be cut off from politics decisively enough so that he had no future in politics, only a posthumous future as historian of public deeds. However, Restoration politics was so fluid that its players were often tempted to re-enter the fray, as Shaftesbury was. When the high political temperatures of the 1640s, '50s, and '60s finally fell, the motives for writing Clarendon's sort of history also declined. Seldom were disgraced politicians irrevocably severed from the state and given the pariah's leisure to become a historian as Clarendon had been. In fact, from the late seventeenth century into the eighteenth, the vengeance visited upon defeated politicians was decreasing,[23] as 'outs' were given the opportunity if not to become 'ins' again, then at least to retire quietly to the country with a modicum of dignity. Political defeat rarely landed them in the Tower, so they had less need to exonerate themselves by composing a history of evil times.

The biographies of leading politicians illustrate the changing rules for political apostasy. The 1st Earl of Arlington survived impeachment proceedings in 1674 and was able to engage in diplomacy for four years before seeing that this failed to win him favor. He grudgingly retired. The 2nd Earl of Nottingham played a waiting game during his retirement from 1693 to 1702, alternating between rural retirement and political maneuvering that fell short of outright opposition. The 2nd Earl of Sunderland, a cynical, ruthless turncoat, was at least tolerated, if not respected. For him 1688 was a disaster, but he managed to cheat ignominy and assume a modest role as elder statesman. Side-switching, deceit, and lack of principle were not peculiar to him but characteristic enough of the politics of his time that contemporaries despaired of finding the requisite level of integrity in their statesmen-historians.[24] Clarendon might never have finished his *History* had he been given a chance to return to the world of Restoration politics, or even if he had been sent packing to his own English estate, where domestic and familial responsibilities might have occupied his attention. The unusual circumstances attending his second retirement gave him an advantage over rival historians. As we have observed, the political scene of the late seventeenth century snuffed out many opportunities for other statesmen to write Thucydidean history.

CLARENDON AND THUCYDIDES

Clarendon's encounter with classical historiography was so multi-faceted that one would be hard pressed to argue that any one ancient historian, even Thucydides, claimed a special hold on Clarendon as a writer. The *History* appeared to echo a whole range of classical authors – Plutarch, Caesar, Polybius, Livy, Thucydides, Tacitus, and Sallust – as his readers, both in the eighteenth and succeeding centuries, would testify. Besides, there was no reason to expect him to choose a single author and imitate him mechanically; the modern historians Clarendon admired never did so.[25] And yet, in terms of genre and role, the example of Thucydides proved to be particularly relevant to Clarendon's enterprise. A public man who decided to investigate a civil war his side would lose, Clarendon could identify with the Thucydidean role. In the 1630s, or at least sometime before his enforced leisure of 1646, he copied into his commonplace book passages from Thomas Hobbes' translation of Thucydides.[26] In the introduction to that work, Clarendon read Hobbes' biography of Thucydides. Of noble and even royal blood, Thucydides was a prominent figure on the Thracian coast, owner of a gold-mining concession. Sickened by the demagoguery of the public assembly, he retired from public life and, recalling the example of Herodotus, turned to historical composition, embarking on an account of the war between Athens and Sparta soon after its outbreak. Work on his 'commentary or plain register' of events was interrupted when the action came too near his retreat on the isle of Thasos. Thucydides raised and led a detachment of troops to rescue nearby Amphipolis but arrived late, only to find the city in enemy hands. For his tardiness, Thucydides was banished (unjustly, in Hobbes' view), and he used his enforced leisure travelling to witness and research later stages of the war, and polishing earlier drafts of the history.[27]

Hobbes described how the young Thucydides, upon hearing Herodotus recite his history, wept in hopes of emulating him. Next to this passage, Clarendon wrote the words 'Noble ambition.'[28] Clarendon in turn followed Thucydides' example so precisely that, like Thucydides, he began writing a plain narrative in the midst of a great war as it unfolded, in circumstances of voluntary retirement, and then in a second period of composition perfected the work, writing as a disgraced man. Clarendon played a much greater part in the war he was commemorating than Thucydides had in his, though his social origins were less impressive than Thucydides'. Clarendon recognized it was somewhat presumptuous to justify parts of his modest 'memorials' by referring to precedents in the ancient historians. In 1646 and 1647, with self-mocking irony he compared his own work-in-progress to that of mere chroniclers and criticized his own social position – he was then merely Sir Edward Hyde, a member of the landed gentry. 'I am contented,' he wrote a friend, 'you should laugh at me for a sop in talking of Livy and Tacitus; when all I can hope for is to side with Hollingshead, and Stow, or (because he is a poor Knight too, and worse than either of them) Sir Richard Baker.'[29] By 1661 King Charles II had lavished gifts and honors on his faithful servant, turning the 'poor Knight' into a wealthy earl. Like Thucydides, Clarendon returned to public service a second time (1660–7), then polished and finished his history in a later period of involuntary leisure, a banishment abroad where he died (1667–74). As Thucydides and also Cicero had shown Clarendon, the defeated politician could make retirement honorable by showing how past political mistakes could prevent future errors in statecraft.[30]

Aspects of Clarendon's career and his subject thus bore a striking resemblance to those of Thucydides. Clarendon's *History of the Rebellion* can be considered a Thucydidean history insofar as it was a participant's account of a civil war, and it adhered to many protocols of classical historiography. The case can be made that beyond the specific similarities between the two historians, Clarendon's work also more generally shared the characteristics of ancient historical writing. The political and military events he recounted were comparable in significance to those featured in classical histories. Clarendon drew political lessons from the story, evaluated the policies and performances of enemies and friends alike, and set down examples of men and events for future states-men to imitate or avoid.[31] Obsessed with posterity, with mem-orializing his generation and preserving forever a record of good and bad men 'That posterity may not be deceived' (opening words of the *History*),[32] Clarendon had his work published posthumously, honoring history's ancient function of preserving important events from oblivion. The 'characters' of these men, the set-piece charac-ter sketches, were classical, heavily indebted to Tacitean and Plutarchan models.[33] They were magnanimous, just as the rest of the *History* generally was. Compared with his contemporar-ies, Clarendon gave a rather balanced picture of events, one even criticizing his royal masters, Charles I and Charles II.[34] Instead of arguing with his adversaries throughout the narrative, he simply told the story from his own perspective. He kept the vitriolic language of the polemicist to a minimum and kept himself in the background, often referring to his own role in affairs obscurely, and only then in the third person. If his prose was baroque and English rather than Ciceronian and Latin, it approached the 'middle style' of the classical historian, not excessively oratorical, never pedestrian. His dignity and politeness contributed to the detached, impartial effect of the *History*.[35]

Like Thucydides, like other neoclassical historians and their classical exemplars, Clarendon wrote a solemn narrative of worthy deeds, a didactic analysis of men and events meant to instruct future generations of warriors and statesmen. He appeared to be as fair-minded as one could be in his circumstances. And yet Clarendon's achievement might be called into question for a variety of reasons. Why did he fill his book with page after page of documents that broke his narrative into pieces? Was he not, moreover, simply a historiographer royal, a court historian doing his masters' bidding, an agent of Stuart despotism? Where were the invented speeches for which Thucydides was celebrated? The answers to these questions remind us that even exemplary works of modern history were not beyond criticism, and that readers gave Clarendon some latitude in his adaptation of classical historiography to modern times.

It is true that invented speeches, re-creations of what might have been or should have been said in debate, had a major and undoubted role in ancient historiography. However, they did not appear in every work of ancient historiography, nor, indeed, in every work of modern, neoclassical historiography. In early-modern England there was in fact no consensus regarding speeches. Many of those deemed the greatest English historians did not invent speeches, while some, most notably Bacon and Cherbury, did imitate the practice.[36] English notions of truth harmed the case for speeches, which were rejected as 'improbable,' therefore untruthful, and it could be construed as presumptuous for historians to be speaking in the name of an English king. Although generally divided over the issue of speeches, Englishmen appear to have been more taken with them in the second quarter of the eighteenth century, when something like them was revived as a device for demonstrating the historian's impartiality. In the wake of the Civil War, however, Englishmen were decidedly hostile to them,[37] so Clarendon was very much a man of his time when he chose to dispense with invented speeches. Although the appearance of an invented speech in a modern history signalled to readers that a historian had neo-classical pretensions, it did not ensure that his work would be judged a neoclassical triumph. On the other hand, refusing to invent speeches did not seriously harm a historian's bid for ac-ceptance as a peer of the ancient historians.

While the Civil War had its share of dramatic speeches on the battlefield and in parliament, it was also a struggle for men's allegiances conducted in a larger theater, by means of print. Clarendon recognized that post-Gutenberg warriors fought with the pen as well as the sword. Accordingly, he reprinted wartime declarations, petitions, propositions, and answers,[38] and these transcriptions constituted his chief departure from classical form. He transcribed for pages at a time the declarations made by both parties, so that his readers could judge both sides for themselves.[39] His model for this innovation was the famous modern history written by E. C. Davila, who, according to Clarendon, 'may worthily stand by the sides of the best of the ancients.' Davila's *History of the Civil Wars of France* also recounted a propaganda war,[40] and Davila's verbatim account of that propaganda appar-ently did not violate classical protocols for history-writing, ac-cording to Clarendon and other approving readers in England and on the continent. In fact, Davila's subject, a war of religion, appeared so to resemble the one in which Charles I found him-self embroiled, that the king ordered Clarendon's brother-in-law to translate it for the use of royalist strategists.[41]

Clarendon walked a tight rope. He believed his veracity and completeness as a historian depended on insertion of documents; at the same time, those very documents, if not held in check, could transform his noble narrative into a collection of civil war papers. As he struggled to strike a balance between documents and actions, evidence and narrative, Clarendon explained to the Earl of Bristol the criterion he was employing:

[T]here is a great deal of difference between troubling the series of grave and weighty actions and counsels with tedious rela-tions of formal despatches (though of notable moment), and the relating solemn acts and consultations, from which all the matter of action is raised and continued.

The mainsprings of events, the most vital documents of the war, had a place in the story, but any other transcriptions had to be kept to a minimum in order to preserve the worthy character of the history. One need look no further than Davila for a precedent, Clarendon continued:

> And therefore you will find D'Avila (who I think hath written as our's should be written, and from whence no question our Gamesters learnt much of their play) insert the declarations of both sides in the main body of the story, as the foundations upon which all that was after done, was built.

Clarendon then cited an illustration from his own work that demonstrated the importance of counsel in printed form, its propaganda value, its historical significance.

> The fourth book contains all the passages from the King's going to York to the setting up the standard; which time being wholly spent in talk, and all that followed of action proceeding from that talk, I have been obliged to set down (which I had a great mind to have avoided) many declarations even *in terminis* . . .[42]

Clarendon quoted printed manifestos from the 'paper war' because these were themselves 'events' in the drama, new postclassical agents as important as the speeches, battles, and intrigues which merited a place in ancient historiography. Besides, Clarendon himself had written many of the royal manifestoes he was now copying into the *History*. Because the printing press had provided the possibility of a new sort of worthy deed, even Clarendon could not remain untouched by his age's predilection for inserting documents into histories. And yet with the exception of these insertions, Clarendon wrote his own version of events in his own words without making extensive quotations. He used all kinds of histories, memoirs, and oral accounts of the war but instead of quoting them directly, he silently judged among them.

In general terms, Clarendon's sense of history as literature helped him to avoid the dangers of excessive documentation as well as legal antiquarianism, even though his own background would seem to make him susceptible to both: Clarendon was trained as a lawyer and a close friend of Selden. He was aware of many of the latest antiquarian works and commended the science of philology for its accurate rendering of ancient texts. However, he also recognized the literary shortcomings of modern scholars, and made a point of criticizing Selden's style.[43] Although he collected and integrated a vast collection of evidence into his *History*, and wished his associates had lent him even more papers, he believed the key to a historian's greatness lay not in his erudition and his scavenging for sources, but in his judgment as an experienced statesman able to plumb the depths of human conduct.[44] He clung to the moral and rhetorical tradition of classical historiography, analyzing the Civil War in terms of individual men, wicked and virtuous, and what they did to preserve or to ruin the kingdom. He did not require the philological studies of the antiquarians to accomplish this task. Indeed, as a historian of his own times, he did not have to bother with ancient records to make his case. Famously, he did not even look beyond the reign of Charles I to account for its disintegration.

Rather than erudition and print, it was Clarendon's association with Charles and his son that most endangered his standing as a neoclassical historian, because his political ties to them called his impartiality into question. Clarendon could make a case that he brought a comparatively neutral perspective to his task, in the following terms: he never intended to whitewash the king, or, indeed, all the king's men. His *History* was originally meant not only as an attack upon parliamentary extremists but also as a criticism of the counsel Charles I received from men such as Laud and Buckingham, and as a defense of the moderate, constitutionalist advice Clarendon offered but Charles rejected. After all, until the summer of 1641 Clarendon had actually been in the forefront of parliamentary opposition to the king. At the Restoration he helped restore the monarchy to its reformed constitutional position early in the Long Parliament, a monarchy stripped of the courts of Star Chamber and High Commission, for example.[45] Even as a committed royalist he was never uncritical of his monarch, never an ultra-royalist with nostalgia for the 1630s.

However, a very strong case could also be made that Clarendon's *History* was simply a court history. It was Charles who had first asked Clarendon to write a work that would refute the parliamentarian history being written by Thomas May. The king supplied him with his own 'memorials' of the Civil War and urged other royalists to help in the project.[46] Later, in its final period of composition, self-interested political motives drove the *History* along. From 1667, after his banishment, until his death seven years later, Clarendon tried to ingratiate himself with the court to win a pardon, and the *History* played a part in this ultimately futile campaign to return to England to die surrounded by his children. Clarendon reminded Charles II that both he and his martyred father had encouraged and read the earliest parts of the *History*, and that Clarendon's exilic literary works were all written out of loyalty to the crown. He portrayed the *History* as a last public service done by a faithful servant, 'one of the oldest Servants that is now living, to your Father and your Self.'[47]

Begun for the benefit of one king, and completed in hopes of pleasing another, Clarendon's *History* seemed incapable of escaping the orbit of the court. Clarendon entrusted his manuscript to his family, but it, too, had strong links to the court. Clarendon had been unwillingly connected to the royal family since 1660, when Charles' brother James, Duke of York, secretly married Anne Hyde, Clarendon's daughter. Clarendon was embarrassed at the inequality of the alliance and saw the marriage as a further blow to crumbling royal dignity.[48] Even if he wished to steer his *History* clear of the court, he could not, since writing for his own family meant writing for his son-in-law, heir to the throne. His daughter's daughter, Anne, born in 1665, was also in the royal line of succession. In 1702, Clarendon's sons, the uncles of this Queen Anne, would publish the *History* for partisan gain, capitalizing on its author's authority as royal grandfather. Those eighteenth-century readers of the *History* would have to decide whether Clarendon's government service under Charles I and Charles II and his awkward membership in the Stuart family destroyed his credibility as a Thucydidean historian, whether a work of personal exculpation published amidst ferocious party warfare could claim to be the truth for all time.

THE POLITICS OF PUBLICATION

At Clarendon's death in 1674, his manuscript was not simply handed over to London compositors for commercial publication. Clarendon had written for a posthumous audience of princes, statesmen, family members, and others who could benefit from the political lessons contained in the *History*. Twice during the war Clarendon refused to publish his history for partisan advantage. His own view was that the *History* should not be made public until Civil War passions cooled and a more appreciative public arrived on the scene.[49] In an early will Clarendon gave Charles I 'absolute direction' over all his papers, but after the king's death, he left his own two sons the authority to suppress or publish his works. Clarendon envisioned the editing and publishing of his *History* as a cooperative venture involving not just his sons but a half dozen friends and prelates.[50]

He correctly sensed that so long as the Civil War continued to matter to Englishmen, his work, the work of a royalist with an unsurpassed insider's vantage point, would have political consequences. Sharing this belief that the *History* was a potentially explosive weapon, his sons handled it with care. They circulated the manuscript selectively round the English elite in the 1680s and '90s, especially its episcopal and nonjuring segment. They let their niece, William III's Queen Mary, read her maternal grandfather's work, though her response, if any, is not known. Clarendon's eldest son, Henry, 2nd Earl of Clarendon, had responsibility for the manuscript until the late 1690s, when his brother Laurence, Earl of Rochester, took charge of it.[51] From the family seat at Cornbury Park in Oxfordshire the brothers made frequent visits to Christ Church, Oxford. The Hyde family had close connections to the University, for Clarendon had served as Chancellor, and Rochester as MP. Oxford was the tory party's emotional center, staunchly royalist during the Civil War, a safe haven during the Exclusion Crisis, when the king convoked parliament here and defused opposition. The Hydes, one of the most distinguished and royalist of families, had close associations with the most distinguished and royalist of colleges, Christ Church. In its deanery they prepared the *History of the Rebellion* for the press.[52]

Christ Church was a champion of 'politeness,' a prominent discursive strategy in English political culture and, as we saw in Chapter 1, an attribute of neoclassical history. Most commonly, politeness was spread over the entire elite rather than institutionalized and was featured in a whig rather than a tory cultural program.[53] In Christ Church, however, politeness found an institutional focus and a tory employment. John Fell, Dean of Christ Church (1660–86), together with another dean, Henry

Aldrich (1689–1710), campaigned to strengthen the bonds between the political class and the church. They formed alliances between the college and important Anglican political families such as the Hydes, and attracted and trained the sons of the most prominent tory families. Wary of clerical education, the gentry and aristocracy often bypassed the universities altogether, instead opting for a legal training at the Inns of Court. Fell understood that the elite had to be catered to, and so to meet the competition he created a new curriculum for those not interested in clerical careers. It placed heavier emphasis on traditional political education, the classics and other polite learning, thereby dovetailing with the same fashionable education to which prize recruits from Westminster School had already been exposed.[54]

A famous episode in the Battle of the Books took place at Christ Church in the 1690s, illustrating the social and scholarly dimensions of politeness. Dr Richard Bentley, the king's librarian, had attacked Sir William Temple's choice of Phalaris as an ancient master of epistolary style. One of the 'Christ Church wits,' Charles Boyle, supported Temple's case with an edition of Phalaris' letters. Bentley's *Dissertation on the Epistles of Phalaris* alleged that the letters were forgeries, an accusation which was received as an affront to the whole college. Christ Church had difficulty refuting the *Dissertation* on scholarly grounds, so it launched an attack on social grounds: Bentley's uncouth style, his pedantry, his occupation as a librarian all betrayed his modest social origins and lack of politeness.[55] According to elite canons of behavior, anyone who spent so much time buried in books, even ancient ones, was deprived of the social intercourse and political experience necessary to forming a true gentleman. Pursuit of scholarship for its own sake violated polite codes of behavior,[56] codes Christ Church proved willing to exploit in defense of its good name.

Christ Church's most notorious deployment of politeness for partisan purposes came not in the 1690s but in 1702. In that year, the combination of eased press restrictions and favorable political circumstances finally allowed the college to publish Clarendon's history. Tories must have appreciated the potential usefulness of the manuscript for some time, but the crown's regulation of the press and its desire to build a new political consensus in the wake of the Civil War helped to prevent that war from becoming a subject of historical controversy, in printed form at least. Royal control of the press, lost in the Civil War and Interregnum, was restored in 1660 with a system of pre-publication censorship lasting until the late 1670s. Charles II took an active interest in granting royal licenses for publication, and read in manuscript such historical works as Gilbert Burnet's *Memoires of the Lives of the Dukes of Hamilton* and Thomas Hobbes' *Behemoth*. No history of the Civil War would be published so long as architects of the Restoration settlement believed healing the nation's wounds required blotting out memories of the war. The Act of Indemnity and Oblivion (1660) meted out fines for anything uttered 'tending to revive the memory of the late differences' between king and parliament. To the extent that any official version of the Civil War was propagated it came from the pulpit, not the press; Charles' bishops used the 30 January commemoration of his father's martyrdom to blame the Civil War on a conspiracy of evil men. In the hands of the Restoration episcopate and high church clergy well into the eighteenth century, the annual sermon was used to defend the royal prerogative and the need for civil obedience. However, in 1679 political disturbances allowed the Licensing Act to lapse. During the Exclusion Crisis (1678–81) the number of printed pamphlets and books soared, including memoirs and political documents which had been secretly circulating in manuscript and which their owners could only now safely make public. A pandora's box, the Exclusion Crisis liberated the press, set historical polemicists loose, and put sources for the Civil War in open view.[57]

A decade later, these sources still had political ramifications. The controversy over allegiance to William III's regime placed the Civil War firmly on the political and historical agenda. At, and in the wake of, the Glorious Revolution, the treatment of James II was compared to his father's tragedy; if Charles' execution could be defended, so could the Revolution, the reasoning went, although this was a treacherous, less traveled path. Every variety of whig was burdened with the responsibility for regicide, and whigs defended themselves by distinguishing between regicides in the army, whom they deplored, and parliamentary leaders of 1628–41, whom they portrayed as defenders of the ancient constitution upon which Charles I had trampled.[58] Even after parliament's triumph in 1688–9, parliamentary interpretations of the Civil War were tentative compared to robust royalist accounts. Tipping the balance decisively against them was Charles' own political testament, the *Eikon Basilike*, 'The Portraiture of His Sacred Majesty in His Solitude and Sufferings,' which preserved in the popular imagination the image of a pious martyr and wise king. It had gone through dozens of editions since 1649. In *Eikonoklastes* (1649) Milton had questioned its authorship, and in 1690 the so-called Anglesey Memorandum put forward the case for Bishop Gauden's having written it, the king's chaplain not the king. By 1692 a fierce paper war challenged this mightiest weapon in the tories' arsenal.[59]

The controversy over the authenticity of the *Eikon Basilike* prompted publication of further Civil War histories and memoirs, royalist and parliamentary alike, especially after the Licensing Act lapsed in 1695. In 1698 the *Memoirs* of the regicide Edmund Ludlow began to be printed, and in the following year other memoirs, by Berkeley, Holles, and Fairfax, were also printed for whig purposes. John Toland edited Holles' work and rewrote Ludlow's as part of a radical whig campaign to publish inspirational Civil War republican works by Milton, Sidney, and Harrington. In 1701 the tories answered with their own memoirs, those by Sir Philip Warwick, a loyal Stuart officeholder who wrote a measured defense of Charles.[60] Clarendon's son, Rochester, thought that including his father's work in this response might help to resurrect the tory party. At the Christ Church inner sanctum he had it edited for such a purpose with the aid of Thomas Sprat, Bishop of Rochester and former Christ Church student – who thus put the finishing touches on the neoclassical history which he had prophesied over 30 years before – and Henry Aldrich, Dean of 'the House.'[61] Christ Church attached a preface to volume one of Clarendon's *History*, and dedications to Queen Anne in volumes two and three, all written anonymously, if not by Aldrich alone, then certainly by close associates such as Rochester.[62] The manuscript was ready for the printers as early as 1699, but it was only in May 1702, two months after King William's death, that Rochester struck. With Oxford abuzz in expectation of a rejuvenated university, tory party, and church, and of Rochester's heading the new government with none other than his niece, Queen Anne, Clarendon's granddaughter, on the throne, Clarendon's *History* was published as the manifesto of the new tory party and as counsel to the queen.[63]

News that the *History* was in the press traveled fast. On the eve of publication it was keenly anticipated: would Clarendon settle once and for all the contentious political issues of past and present? Typesetting and printing at the Sheldonian Theater were conducted with the utmost secrecy lest pirate editions of the *History* should appear. In fact, one London publisher used the inside information of the jacobite antiquarian Thomas Hearne, who was indexing the *History*, to beat competitors to an octavo abridgement. The abridger of Richard Baxter's *Life*, Edmund Calamy, trying to make certain the *Life* was not contradicted and thus devalued by the noble historian, paid off a worker in the press, whose family was in dire financial straits, to see the proofs as they came off the press fresh from the corrections of Aldrich and Rochester.[64] The rest of the world, outside the Hyde manuscript network, had to wait.

Because there was, in England, no precedent for a work of modern history so vast, so grave, and so classical as Clarendon's, there was no way to know precisely what sort of an audience, if any, existed for such a work. Between 1702 and 1704, Rochester printed 2500 three-volume folio sets. In 1705 2500 six-volume octavo sets were printed. During the next 30 years Oxford would publish 1400 more copies in folio and 9550 more of the smaller volumes, bringing to roughly 16 000 the number of copies published.[65] Clarendon's editors employed Christ Church's well-worn high church distribution network to disseminate the *History*. Rochester took 101 copies, Aldrich 20, and the Delegates of the Press and the University Library 11. Later there were special sales for Heads of Houses, Proctors, and their friends. It does not appear that the editors took a serious interest in the financial or political gain to be had by a vast commercial sale. They lavished immense effort on the first folio edition and its distribution, but afterwards the initiative for new editions came from London booksellers.[66] Christ Church looked after the tiny political elite for whom the work was originally intended, simply monitoring further printing to ensure that it remained commensurate with the dignity of the press and the Hyde family. Anyone not connected to Christ Church had to get his copy through the college's agent in the publishing world, Thomas Bennet, whose firm dominated London retail sales and acted as wholesaler to 78 other, mainly London, booksellers. An audience beyond Christ Church's horizon indeed existed – the country gentlemen and clerical activists who would be key players in the tory renaissance of 1702. Of course, there were also whigs who wished to read this controversial work. At a price of 30 shillings, however, even the octavo edition did not turn up in many non-gentle households.[67]

Convinced that neoclassical historiography could serve as a political weapon, the editors accentuated the *History*'s classicality. They printed the work on huge sheets with large, elegant type, generous margins, and handsome ornaments. Aldrich took the opportunity to show what the press was capable of under his direction and he designed the decorative headpieces and initials himself.[68] Aldrich's edition of Clarendon resembled his editions of classical texts, which were polite, not cluttered with scholarly marginalia.[69] The *History* was manufactured with the same attention to quality and detail as if it were already indeed one of the treasures of antiquity, another of Aldrich's classical texts. Considered as an artistic object, the folio edition of Clarendon's *History* was easily the most splendid of English historical works in this period, perhaps any period. This edition overwhelmed the reader by its sheer size and beauty as a book, underscoring the editors' ambition to make the *History* an imperishable monument to Clarendon's vision of the war. It could be read and reread with unhurried ease by its first reader and eventually by his descendants, a tory icon that would survive as a valued heirloom to distant posterity.

To increase the likelihood that Clarendon would be read as a polite, neoclassical historian, the editors decided to alter Clarendon's original manuscript. On occasion they softened characterizations of men whose descendants might be offended by Clarendon's depiction of them, but otherwise their intervention was confined to clarifying and simplifying some of Clarendon's involved syntax.[70] Their changes rendered Clarendon's text even more polite than it already was, by smoothening the prose and taking the bite out of some of its judgments. They did not rework the entire manuscript, as some critics were later to charge However, they did invent a title page for the *History* that furthered their neoclassical aspirations for the work. They affixed two well-known classical tags about history, one from Cicero, the other from Thucydides. Cicero's injunction, his first law of history, about not daring to speak anything but the truth – 'Ne quid Falsi dicere audeat, ne quid Veri non audeat'[71] – enjoyed a special currency in this age of party, when partisan historians – or, in this case, their editors – tried reassuring readers of their works' truthfulness. The choice of Cicero might have had a particular relevance to Clarendon's *History*, since Christ Church could, with reason, portray the noble historian in a Ciceronian vein. Like Cicero, Clarendon was trained as a lawyer, rose to the highest political offices in the land, adhered rather old-fashionly to an ancient constitution, suffered unjustly for his political principles, and used retirement to reflect upon statecraft for the benefit of present and future political actors. Readers might well infer that Clarendon had put into practice the high ideals for history propounded by the most eloquent writer in the ancient world, especially as they concerned integrity. The title page now also bore the Greek characters Thucydides had used to describe his own work, 'a possession for all time.' Just as Thucydides had promised not to be popular, not to curry favor with contemporaries but instead to create an everlasting monument to truth, so could Clarendon be portrayed, with some justification, as a man whose contemporaries could not bear to hear his truths but whose posterity, perhaps as early as the year 1702, might be ready to listen to him. Each man participated in the civil war he chronicled, and neither allowed political defeat or even banishment to halt his inquiry into the causes and consequences of political and military catastrophes. Clarendon himself quoted a wide range of classical writers in the body of his *History* – including Thucydides and Cicero – and so his debts to classical models should have been apparent enough, and yet his editors still perceived the need to add two more citations that highlighted further connections between Clarendon and classical historiography. Hoping to appropriate the prestige of Thucydides and Cicero, to introduce the *History* as a worthy peer of ancient historical writing, the editors made explicit what Clarendon's modesty, and the modesty of most of his classical models, forbade him from doing himself: the *History* conformed to the highest standards of its genre, possessing the authority, the integrity, the wisdom, the eloquence associated with Cicero and Thucydides; it was 'a possession for all time.'

After carefully packaging Clarendon's work as a polite and classical history, the editors nearly ruined the whole effect by adding prefatory material that was clearly impolite and modern. A piece of tory propaganda, the preface to volume one deplored the recent publication of memoirs and histories hostile to the monarchy. Clarendon's *History*, the editors proclaimed, offered a useful corrective, providing as it did examples of a time when obedience and respect to duly constituted authority could be counted on as part of the national character. They hoped the *History* could 'awaken men to that honesty, justice, loyalty, and piety, which formerly Englishmen have been valuable for, and without which it is impossible any government, discipline, or authority can be long maintained' (1:xix). In this passage readers were being rather gently reminded that tories, true Englishmen, supported church and crown against whig revolution principles. Aldrich proceeded to make his case for a tory government more pointed, when he advocated the use of naval, not land, forces in the war against France (xxv), a policy most closely identified with the Earl of Rochester.

To compose this preface was a rhetorically difficult task. On the one hand, Aldrich wished to sing the praises of tory doctrine; on the other, he was concerned to give the *History* the appearance of impartiality. Clarendon's manuscript was potent for the very reason that it was more neutral than other accounts of the Civil War, and that quality, the hallmark of an authentic specimen of neoclassical historiography, gave it, ironically, more cogency as a political document. Aldrich wished to draw out the partisan lessons of the *History* for the year 1702, just in case readers could not draw them out of Clarendon's allusive and massive work for themselves, but he could not afford to make the lessons so explicit that readers dismissed the entire *History* as a heavily edited, perhaps even fabricated, concoction of tory propaganda. Throughout Aldrich's prefaces, therefore, politeness competed with partisanship. He inserted classical citations and commonplaces about history being noble, polite, and truthful, an everlasting lesson in morality.[72] At the same time, in the same prefaces, Aldrich violated many of these same *topoi*, by making comments many readers found misleading, polemical, and untruthful. His party politics threatened to destroy this neoclassical history.

Aldrich's second balancing act involved resolving the apparent conflicts between two kings and their historian. As a tory Aldrich wanted to defend the institution of monarchy and its representatives, Charles I and Charles II. As an editor, he wanted to defend the integrity and wisdom of his author, a man who had not always seen eye-to-eye with his royal masters, and who was the grandfather of the reigning monarch. Aldrich admitted that Charles I 'had some infirmities, and imperfections; and might thereby be misled into some mistakes in government' (xix), that indeed mistakes had been committed on both sides in the struggle between crown and parliament. Having thus prepared readers for the criticisms of the king they would find in Clarendon's *History*, Aldrich took pains to praise both Charles and Clarendon and to portray any differences between Clarendon and the king's party as stemming from Clarendon's efforts to preserve the constitution (xxvii–xxix). As for Charles II, he could not be blamed for exiling his minister; the fall of the faithful Clarendon resulted from conspiracies, factions, and backstabbing at court (xxxii–xxxvii).

Aldrich concluded the preface by paying tribute to Clarendon for withstanding the buffeting of cruel fortune. Clarendon's stoical resolve passed from father to son (xxxviii–xxxix), Aldrich implied: Rochester and the 2nd Earl of Clarendon shared the same heroic qualities as their father and like him never deserved to slip from royal favor. In the prefaces to all three volumes Aldrich in fact used the relationships within the Hyde family to drive home his political points. Clarendon's loyal service to the crown vouched for a second generation of Hydes serving in the present government of their niece, Queen Anne. Aldrich relied upon classical commonplaces about history to reinforce these family connections. History was indeed written for posterity and for princes, which was why Aldrich could present Clarendon's *History* as the wisdom of a retired statesman writing the truth for all time and doing posthumous service to the public by advising the reigning queen (xl–xliv). Adopting the mirror-of-princes genre, Aldrich used the *topos* of the historian as royal counsellor to put his own words in Clarendon's mouth as advice to the queen. He reminded Anne that monarchs were liable to receive poor counsel from a court of flatterers, and would do better to heed the lessons of history, of the 'faithful counsellor,' her grandfather (xxvi–xxviii, xliv). Attributing his advice to Clarendon and not to himself, Aldrich could use even braver words with the queen. In a condescending tone, he made party demands on his sovereign, implying that unless she followed his advice and that of her grandfather, church and crown could again be in ruins. Aldrich rudely implored, 'For God's sake, Madam, and your own, be pleased to read him with attention, and serious and frequent reflections' (xliv).

Aldrich used these words in the introduction to the second volume, where he began to turn up the heat on Anne, because she had refused to play the political part written for her in volume one. On her accession, Anne had dismissed whigs from office, replaced them with tories, confirmed Rochester's position as Lord Lieutenant of Ireland. That same spring, the electorate had given the tories a firm majority in the House of Commons. However, relations with the queen quickly soured, largely over the issue of how and when to fight the French. The queen removed her uncle from office in February 1703. Part of Rochester's response involved dedicating to her volumes two and three, published in 1703 and 1704, in hopes she would come round to his way of thinking, after listening to more of her grandfather's history lessons. In strident tones he lectured her about the perilous state of the Church of England, thereby stoking the coals of a high church movement set afire in the late 1690s and now furiously fanned by the brilliant preaching of Henry Sacheverell. Because Anne was still inexperienced and hence susceptible to poor counsel, she urgently needed to mind the advice of her grandfather, Aldrich advised (xli). In the *History*

> your majesty will find the true constitution of your government, both in Church and State, plainly laid before you, as well as the mistakes that were committed in the management of both. Here your majesty will see how both those interests are inseparable, and ought to be preserved so, and how fatal it hath proved to both, whenever, by the artifice and malice of wicked and self-designing men, they have happened to be divided. And though your majesty will see here, how a great King lost his kingdoms, and at last his life, in the defence of this Church, you will discern, too, that it was by men who were no better friends to monarchy than to true religion that his calamities were brought upon him; and as it was the method of those men to take exceptions first to the ceremonies and outward order of the Church, that they might attack her the more surely in her very being and foundation, so they could not destroy the State, which they chiefly designed, till they had first overturned the Church. And a truth it is which cannot be controverted, that the Monarchy of England is not now capable of being supported but upon the principles of the Church of England; from whence it will be very natural to conclude, that the preserving them both firmly united together is the likeliest way for your majesty to reign happily over your subjects (xlii).

This was no longer the conciliatory account of the Civil War found in the preface to volume one, but the more extreme account located in the *Eikon Basilike* portraying Charles as martyr for the

Church of England. The rebellion began as a takeover of the church and inevitably destroyed the state, too, so naturally joined were church and crown. The pity of it was, Aldrich added, that many Englishmen had still not learned this terrible moral from Clarendon's history. How else could one explain the proliferation of so many dissenting academies whose teachings were anathema to both monarchy and episcopacy, or the gleeful, sacrilegious celebrations of the anniversary of Charles' martyrdom (xliii)? Only by the queen's vigorous use of her royal prerogative could such libertines and republicans be disciplined. The queen had to be on her guard at all times, or impiety and atheism would triumph. Already, true supporters of the Church of England were falsely accused of jacobitism (liv–lv). The church truly was 'in danger,' the world turned upside down for a second time, only capable of being righted by Anne's wise action on the basis of the high church principles articulated in the dedications to Clarendon's *History*.

THE *HISTORY* AND ITS READERS

Thus was the *History* introduced to the world, by editors in the vanguard of a high tory movement putting neoclassical histori-ography to their own ends. The *History* became the talk of the *cognoscenti* and the obsession of some readers. Pepys spent the summer of 1702 reading volume one three times. Swift read the *History* four times and annotated it more carefully than any work he owned.[73] The principal reader to whom the work was directed, Queen Anne, actually read the *History*, but made slow headway, not finishing volume one before volume two arrived. She sniffed at the impertinence of her uncles' project, offended by Rochester's manipulation of her grandfather's literary legacy, by the lack of 'sense' in beginning the dedication to her in the second volume as a way of increasing pressure on her after tory ministers had fallen from favor, and by the 'vanity' and ridiculousness in prof-fering such advice to her in the first place.[74] Quite clearly, although royal personages constituted the primary theoretical audience for history, monarchs had the option of ignoring the counsel of his-tory. Little evidence exists regarding royal receptivity to this sort of advice literature, but the glimpses into court life that we do have suggest that history did not always get a favorable hearing. In fact the general histories of England that did receive official royal approbation in the later Stuart and early Hanoverian periods were decidedly clerical, not neoclassical in character,[75] and the entire tradition of giving royal counsel in the form of history, hallowed though it was, appeared somewhat fruitless. From Thomas More to Samuel Daniel, historians had written for princes but with little appreciable effect, at least upon specific royal policies,[76] insofar as such effects could ever be measured. Charles II's rowdy court was no place for such ministrations. Charles, with the English Thucydides at his side, ended up abandoning Clarendon altogether, as well as his advice. Dismissing or refusing to read historians was well within the royal prerogative.

Although Anne put her grandfather's volumes aside, perhaps on account of her chronic eye troubles as much as anything else, tories embraced them, and even whigs appreciated them as a formidable political and artistic achievement. One tory, Henry St John, called the royal dedication to volume two 'a very long and politic epistle to the Queen, full of temper, and the calmest counsels.' Volume one had appeared during preparations for the first general election of the reign, and Oxford dons saw the preface as the intellectual foundation of the next tory ministry. As for the *History* itself, many tories took it as a lesson in the need to obey higher authorities. Clarendon's *History* was 'an antidote against rebellion,' according to one anonymous pamphleteer, who warned that jacobites or Catholics could overthrow church and state using the same means Presbyterians had employed to subvert the constitution in Clarendon's diagnosis of the 1640s. Political fanaticism and conspiracies of evil men had brought about one rebellion and could just as easily bring about a second.[77]

Whig readers saw through the Christ Church appropriation of the text for party purposes[78] and they attacked Aldrich's editorializing. They also criticized the substance of Clarendon's *History*, especially its bias. To allege that his royalist commitments prevented Clarendon from finding the truth about his subject matter was a serious charge, for truthfulness was deemed to be the soul of history. In this age of party, however, it was difficult for any piece of political writing, which history always was, to be universally accepted as the truth so long as political life remained so bitterly polarized. No work of history would earn accolades from the entire political establishment because the political interpretations, the 'truths,' so essential to such a work would always be disputed by political adversaries. In these circumstances, Clarendon's *History* came perhaps as close to being acclaimed a Thucydidean history as any work in England could be at the time.

Because of who Clarendon was – a respected nobleman as well as a participant in, and eyewitness of, the events he described – and because of how he wrote his history – in imitation of the ancient historians and their modern-day peers – criticism of the *History*, even by political opponents of its editors, was muted. That royalist accounts of the Civil War already held the field when Clarendon's *History* was published, that his work reconfirmed and strengthened the force of royalist arguments, and that it was more impartial than any royalist history yet to appear, the most scrupulous royalist study of royalist error, all created an air of untouchability surrounding the *History*. Critics such as Jean Le Clerc made their point about Clarendon's being too 'Zealous for the King's Party,'[79] while taking care not to question Clarendon's personal integrity. Le Clerc faulted Clarendon for his unsympathetic portrayal of parliament, but he went out of his way to make clear that Clarendon had no 'settled Design of betraying the Truth.' In the same breath that Le Clerc criticized him for omitting to discuss the Catholicism of Charles II and the Duke of York because Clarendon was a member of their family, Le Clerc stressed that 'at bottom' Clarendon was both 'honest' and 'sincere.'[80] Le Clerc explained how someone of Clarendon's unimpeachable character could have been led astray:

> Self-love, from which no Person is exempt, does so imperceptibly deceive, that we imagine sometimes we are only writing a History, when we are in effect pleading our own Cause before Posterity. There is ever a great deal of Difference between a Plea and a disinterested Narration; 'tis with Difficulty a Man is brought to accuse himself, and we insensibly give an Advantageous turn to every thing we do . . .; of which a great Example is seen in the Commentary of Caesar, and in most Memoirs which Great Men have left of their Lives.[81]

By putting Clarendon in the company of 'Great Men,' by comparing his work to Caesar's, and by discussing the inherent partisanship in his chosen genre, Le Clerc tried easing the consciences of readers like himself who wished to chip away at the political capital tories were making of the *History*, but who wished not to attack a good man, the Earl of Clarendon, or to defend bad men, the regicides. By labeling the work a memoir rather than a history, Le Clerc meant to deprive the *History* of its literary cachet and thus some of its political power.

There were those who wanted to attack the tories by indicting the party's adopted historian but who feared a backlash. Even Le Clerc's rather empathetic criticisms had originally been published abroad, in Amsterdam, in French, and not translated and published in English until 1710. John Oldmixon, a whig publicist, had to wait 25 years before attempting a full-scale assault on this stronghold of tory orthodoxy. 'The Prepossession, in Favour of his Lordship's Book, was so Strong, for several Years,' Oldmixon wrote, 'that no Body would have given a Hearing to any one, who should have said a Word against it.'[82] Even in 1727, when he published his *Clarendon and Whitlock Compar'd*, Oldmixon handled Clarendon's volumes rather gingerly. Like Le Clerc, he used classical precedents to justify his assertion that even the great Clarendon was not immune from partisanship. '[N]o Name in History,' not even Clarendon's, Oldmixon implied, is 'privileg'd against Remark. Caesar was blam'd by Suetonius, for Partiality in his Commentaries.'[83] Whigs were chagrined to find that the literary repute of the *History* enhanced its authority and utility as a political document. Oldmixon wanted to sever this link between aesthetic and political excellence, arguing that Clarendon's story should not be believed just because it was so finely told, but he acknowledged, in frustration, the failure to break this connection in men's minds: 'the Reputation it acquir'd by its beautiful Imagination and florid Stile . . . render'd all Animadversion vain: The Attempt would have been look'd upon as Insolent and Desperate.'[84]

Indeed, Clarendon's narrative had the elevated language, the discerning political instruction, and the well-drawn characters critics had been waiting to find in an English historian. Henry Felton declared: 'I have met with none that may compare with him in the Weight and Solemnity of his Style, in the Strength and Clearness of Diction, in the Beauty and Majesty of Expression . . .'[85] John Evelyn praised Clarendon's 'masculine' style and his introduction, which was 'so like that of the noble Polybius.'[86] The drawing of moral and political lessons from history was a key task of classical historians, and Clarendon followed their example. Le Clerc approved:

Such [critics] as wou'd have History to be a plain Recounting of passages, which the Historian shou'd leave the Reader to Judge of, will not relish the Method of our [Lord] Chancellor [Clarendon], who frequently makes long Lessons to the Kings, and to the People of Great Britain. For my part, I confess I am of his Taste, and that his Political Remarks please me no less than his Narration. This seems to me to be the true use of History, and that the Historian ought to assist his Readers to do it.[87]

Pepys likewise approved, telling the 2nd Earl of Clarendon that his father's *History* was 'such a lecture of Government for an English Prince.'[88] While some readers criticized Clarendon's style as long-winded and overly complicated, or disagreed with the lessons he drew from his story, they applauded the character sketches as perhaps Clarendon's greatest success. Oldmixon saw discrepancies between the historical actors as they appeared in Clarendon's narrative of events and as they appeared in the character portraits Clarendon sketched of them elsewhere in the *History*. Yet Oldmixon had to admit 'a hundred to one of all Readers of the *Grand Rebellion* admire it most for those very Characters.'[89] Evelyn praised them for being 'so just and tempered, without the least ingredient of passion or tincture of revenge . . . [Clarendon] treats the most obnoxious . . . with a becoming generosity and freedom.'[90] Although James Tyrrell was a devoted whig, he nonetheless recommended the *History* to his friend John Locke, 'it being full of lively (and I believe for the most part) true Characters of the chief persons concerned in the public affairs of that time besides many curious particulars of secret History not before published.'[91] The characters, indeed many sections of the *History*, were so well-received that enterprising publishers sold extended extracts of the *History* in the guise of histories of the Civil War or reviews of Clarendon's *History*. Mr. Le Clerc's *Account of the Earl of Clarendon's History of the Civil Wars* was one such book. In it Le Clerc justified the transcribing of Clarendon's characters by explaining their popularity in terms of their classicism: 'Salust has not much better succeeded in the Characters so cry'd up.'[92]

The reputation and impact of Clarendon's *History* owed something not only to its arrival on the scene with debate over the *Eikon Basilike* boiling over, with royalist historiography already dominant, and with a powerful political coterie championing it, or to its moderation, or even to its fulfillment of expectations that a

royalist insider would come forward to recount the Civil War. Its
fame also owed something to the artistry Clarendon brought to
it and the form he gave it, not just its discursive content. His work
was history, the noblest of prose genres, and he executed his design
so convincingly that many readers put Clarendon on a plane with
the historians of antiquity. Clarendon joined the company of
Thucydides, Livy, Polybius, and Tacitus, and the moderns Mariana,
Davila, and Sarpi.[93] William Wotton gave perhaps the most extended analysis of Clarendon as a neoclassical historian. An apolo-
gist for the moderns, Wotton had been sparring with Sir William
Temple in the Battle of the Books. Temple compared Davila,
Sleidan, and Strada with Herodotus, Caesar, and Livy, and found
the moderns sadly lacking. Wotton agreed that the eloquence of
the ancients surpassed that of the moderns, but argued that these
modern historians held their own in terms of their power to instruct.[94] Publication of Clarendon's *History* served to rescue
Wotton's case and just possibly to win the argument with Temple,
who had died in 1699. Wotton concurred with Clarendon's publishers, who used Thucydides' words to boast that this history was
'a possession for all time.' Wotton then described how Clarendon's
History measured up to the Thucydidean standards for history, even
as Wotton gently poked fun at some of those criteria:

> The Subject is every way as Great, the Events as Surprizing, and
> the Conclusion as Miraculous, as Sir W. Temple himself could
> have desired. Here is Fighting enough (too much in Truth) for
> those that love it, and Negotiations [in] abundance . . . Great
> Examples of true Virtue . . . wonderful Fortitude shewn by Great
> Men under the greatest Sufferings; Mankind described under so
> many different Characters of Good and Evil Men, that one would
> hardly think it possible the Mind of Man should be capable of
> so much Variety, are every where to be met with in that Work;
> and all this with so much strength of Stile, and such a rich Copia
> of Words, that when the Prejudices of the present Age shall be
> worn off, and the Faction then raised be quite extinguished, I
> doubt not but Dispassionate Posterity . . . will oppose it for
> Matter and Elocution, to the most Celebrated Performances of
> all Antiquity.[95]

Whether explicitly compared to Thucydides, to Sallust, or to
Caesar, Clarendon in fact filled the Thucydidean role. The *History*

of the Rebellion was a Thucydidean history in the sense that it was a grave, searching, moralistic analysis of a civil war in which the author himself had taken part and witnessed, a gripping narrative of the most worthy deeds of the war intended to instruct future statesmen. But Clarendon did not extensively model his work stylistically or thematically after Thucydides' *History*. To Clarendon's contemporaries it was always more important that an aspirant neoclassical historian write like *a* classical historian rather than like any *one* classical historian in particular. Clarendon's was not a slavish imitation, but readers recognized in Clarendon's prose, his characters, and his political insights the earmarks of classical history. Even readers who criticized the work for its partisanship, and especially for the political use being made of it 30 years after Clarendon had written it, had to acknowledge that it was a formidable literary and political achievement, that its one-sidedness was inherent in the genre Clarendon had selected, that Clarendon's own character and qualifications for writing history were difficult to impugn. The Earl of Clarendon was deemed to have been 'honest,' 'sincere,' 'noble,' 'great.' He and his work became so famous that if someone wrote 'the noble historian,' everyone understood that the allusion was to Clarendon. Instead of referring to Clarendon by name, contemporaries simply spoke of 'the noble historian,' ambiguously alluding to both his legal and aesthetic capacity, his titles both as nobleman and as author of noble history.[96] To one reader Clarendon was in fact 'the noblest, and most impartial Historian this Nation hath produced.'[97] To another it was clear 'how truly that great Man deserves the Character of a Perfect Historian.'[98] Clarendon had met the impossibly high standards for the 'perfect' historian, one who rivalled the ancients and the continental moderns.

But just how effective was neoclassical history as a political vehicle? In the *History* Clarendon had set himself two political tasks: first, to justify the moderate royalist policy he had pursued during the Civil War; second, to remind Charles II of the services Clarendon had rendered the crown, in hopes a grateful monarch would lift Clarendon's banishment. The latter objective was never realized, but posthumous publication of the *History* did succeed in securing his interpretation of the Civil War firmly in eighteenth-century historical and political thought. At a time when political debate relied heavily on historical arguments, and when the Civil War supplied the most controversial subject matter in English history, Clarendon's *History* proved to be a boon for tory propaganda, a rich vein that was mined for several decades. However, the greatest beneficiaries of Clarendon's moderate royalism were moderate tories, not the high church movement which had attempted to re-cast Clarendon's interpretation to suit its own ends. Although the *History* undoubtedly invigorated high-flying tories, in the short-run their strategic use of Clarendon backfired: Rochester lost office, the tory majority was reduced in the House of Commons in 1705, and parliament emphatically rebuffed the charge that the church was in danger. The Christ Church manipulation of Clarendon's text revealed just how politically powerful neoclassical historiography was perceived to be. The editors wrote introductions to the *History* and timed its publication for patently political purposes, and the way they edited it showed that they perceived a more explicitly classicized Clarendon to be more useful to them than the diffuse imitation of classical and neoclassical historiography found in the original manuscript. By making the text even more polite, by publishing such a luxurious edition, by introducing it with even more classical citations than its author had used, the editors believed they were increasing the chances the *History* would be accepted as a neoclassical masterpiece sturdy enough to carry the burden of their polemical program.

Whatever effect these ploys actually had on readers, the *History* survived the high tory tracts appended to it, survived as well the fact Clarendon had close, even familial, ties to the Stuart family whose devastation he chronicled. Clarendon managed to evade many of the obstacles which the modern world presented to aspirant neoclassical historians. His contemporary subject matter and keen literary sense helped him to avoid the snares of legal antiquarianism. Readers judged his transcriptions of printed manifestoes to be so important to telling his story that they accepted this comparatively new development in historiography; besides, the depth of Clarendon's analysis and the brilliance of his characters prevented the *History* from becoming simply a documentary compilation. Clarendon succeeded as a historian, in part because his political career furnished him with extended periods of enforced leisure conducive to historical composition, episodes usually lacking in other candidates for the title of English Thucydides. His probity and independence helped him to fill the role of Thucydidean historian so ably, and his eloquence, evidence, and insight proved to be so compelling, that the *History* became inoculated against debilitating criticism. A national treasure, it proved that neoclassical historiography was incompatible neither with English literary genius nor with late seventeenth-century modernity. And yet no Englishman had succeeded in the even more ambitious and very different neoclassical project of composing a general history of England.

4

Dr Brady and the History of England

The Earl of Clarendon's *History of the Rebellion* appeared to have answered neoclassical critics once and for all by repairing the weakness in English historiography. However, Englishmen recognized that only two or three decades of their history – and to many the Civil War represented perhaps the most disgraceful part of it – had been narrated in the manner of the greatest historians of ancient and modern times. As long ago as the early sixteenth century, Polydore Vergil had written a general history of England, and during Clarendon's own lifetime both Samuel Daniel and John Milton attempted to write, according to humanist protocols, the history of England, from earliest times to modern ones.[1] This Chapter will examine the general histories of England written in the half century following Clarendon's death, roughly from the year 1675 to about 1725. In the second quarter of the eighteenth century, the expansion of audiences for history and the emergence of foreign-born historians would present different challenges to the writing of Livian history, to be considered separately in Chapter 6.

We have already seen how the royal court and party politics called into doubt Clarendon's success as a historian. They likewise posed threats to Livian historians of the late seventeenth and early eighteenth century. But general historians faced another potential foe in antiquarian erudition, which appeared to be a necessary tool to uncover the whole of English history but which was in many ways at odds with neoclassical historiography. Moreover, the sources for medieval history were so imperfect and the subject so barbaric to polite readers that the Livian historian faced yet another stumbling block which Clarendon never encountered. Although the qualifications for writing the history of one's own times were more stringent than those for writing general history, one of the problems of Livian history concerned the historian's role: the wrong sorts of individuals tried to become historians, an odd assortment of courtiers, country gentlemen, and minor clergymen too easily swayed by political forces or financial inducements to maintain the credibility required of neoclassical historians. So monumental a task did the composition of Livian history appear to be that most general historians in this period entertained no high ambition to write it, only a wish to prepare the way for a future Livy. Dr Robert Brady produced a hybrid of legal antiquarianism and medieval chronicle that proved to be an influential model for general historians of England throughout much of the eighteenth century. However, Brady recognized the difference between 'history' and the 'introductions' to history such as he was writing. His contemporaries, James Tyrrell, Jonathan Swift, and Laurence Echard, also understood this distinction, but they could not or would not translate the whole of the English past into a neoclassical idiom.

ROBERT BRADY AND THE STUART COURT

Robert Brady (1627–1700), like the 1st Earl of Clarendon, came from a respectable family, suffered for his support of the Stuarts during the Civil War, and even took refuge at the same royal garrison on the Scilly Isles where Clarendon had begun writing the *History of the Rebellion*. Brady had nothing of the Lord Chancellor's political experience and responsibility, however. Nor did he succeed in escaping the gravitational pull of the court to achieve the critical detachment from his royal masters which made Clarendon famous and which could have helped Brady write a balanced history of England.

Brady's loyalty to Charles I and the Prince of Wales had resulted in sequestration of his goods, exile, and imprisonment. At the Restoration Charles II admitted him by special patent to the MD, which his political allegiances during the Interregnum had hitherto prevented, and in 1660 also appointed him Master of Caius College, Cambridge, a position Brady held until his death in 1700. For reasons that are still unclear, Brady, Professor of Physic, began to take an interest in historical studies as early as 1675. By the 1680s he emerged as the principal historical writer at court. From 1682, when Charles appointed him a royal physician, he spent long periods attending the royal family, and he attested the birth of

James II's son in 1688. Brady also sat in the House of Commons and looked after records in the Tower of London. In December 1688 he failed to convince James not to flee the country. The loss of James' throne ended Brady's career as court physician and historian; he pursued his studies cautiously under the new regime in the last years of his life,[2] but his greatest contributions to English historiography lay behind him. Brady produced pathbreaking works of legal antiquarianism, but his partisanship on behalf of the Stuarts prevented him from ever composing a magnanimous history in the grand manner.

The crown encouraged a clerical style of historical propaganda rather than a neoclassical style, and did not use historical works to fight its political battles to the extent it might have. We have already seen how Charles II played deaf to the Earl of Clarendon's pleas for clemency, thus missing the opportunity to co-opt *The History of the Rebellion* to royalist advantage. In general, the Restoration court was not an aggressive player in English historical culture. Despite the strength of the restored monarchy, and the exemplar it found in Louis XIV, neither Charles II nor James II employed literature and the arts as systematically or extensively as the French king or as their father Charles I had. The English court had no scheme to classicize political culture, no program to sponsor the composition of neoclassical histories. The Royal Society did not create a uniform, centralized court culture such as existed in France, where a system of royal patronage glorified divine right monarchy through sponsorship of official histories.[3] Charles II lacked both the determination and the money to construct an elaborate court-based cultural program. Early in his reign Charles revitalized the court as a leader in artistic patronage, but in his final years financial difficulties impinged upon that sponsorship, and a decline in court culture was discernable in the reign of James II, whose frugality and moralism had a stunting effect upon the court as a social center.[4] Opponents of both regimes accused them of 'popery and arbitrary government' and feared Charles and James wished to re-model English society along French lines; perhaps it was best not to adopt the state-sponsored neoclassical historiography associated with Louis XIV.

Charles II did bring to his court the French office of historiographer royal, but used it somewhat differently from the way Louis employed his official court historians. The exact origins of the institution of historiographer royal are unknown, but Clarendon, serving as Charles II's chief minister and director of publicity, seems to have played a part in establishing it as an organ to justify government policies. In 1661 the king appointed as the first historiographer royal one of Clarendon's clients, James Howell, but the office was apparently not a significant post.[5] Obviously, Clarendon did not need or use it to write his own historical masterpiece. Accomplished writers such as John Dryden served in the office, although their main interests and training were not historical. Dryden held the office from 1670 to 1688 as a way to supplement his income as poet laureate, but wrote nothing in his capacity as historiographer until the 1680s, and even then very little.[6] There is no evidence that anyone at court ever asked him to write a neoclassical history. Instead, he translated Maimbourg's *History of the Catholic League* as a royalist polemic suggesting a parallel between the traitorous Duke of Guise and the king's enemy, the Earl of Shaftesbury.[7] Insofar as the court supported historical studies, it tended to sponsor books and pamphlets in specific, immediate political controversies. When Dr Brady of Cambridge approached the court about writing a general history of England, the Stuart court was financing short-term, topical, polemical historical projects, not long, diffuse, polite neoclassical narratives that could take years to write but might bring international literary and dynastic prestige such as Clarendon's *History* eventually brought to Stuart monarchy.

ANTIQUARIANISM AND THE ANCIENT CONSTITUTION

During the Exclusion Crisis the court argued that King Charles II ruled by divine right, and that the hereditary succession must be preserved against whigs wishing to exclude Charles' brother, James, Duke of York, a Catholic, from the throne. Since neither Charles nor James had broken the law, royalists contended, each was owed obedience, Charles now and James when he succeeded his brother as king in due course.[8] Since court publicists relied so heavily on legalist arguments such as this one, it was natural that they should turn to legal antiquarians to establish that parliament was subordinate to the crown and not permitted to alter the rules of succession. In a series of polemical tracts, Brady took up the cause of the king. He set about refuting whig controversialists William Petyt, William Atwood, and James Tyrrell, who were making effective use of a historical thesis about the English constitution expounded by Sir Edward Coke and Sir Matthew Hale. According to this view, the common law was the only law ever known to England. Hale saw the law being refined almost imperceptibly, making it impossible to date constitutional change precisely. Petyt and Atwood asserted that whatever date might be fixed to an innovation, that constitutional adjustment was already ancient. In either case, exclusionist whigs wished to avoid assigning an exact date to the origin of any component of the ancient constitution, fearing that part could then be subjected to a sovereign. The Norman Conquest, in the view of Petyt and Atwood, did not represent a break in the continuity of the law. They concluded that since William the Conqueror had not ruled absolutely, Charles II did not have the absolute power to revoke the laws and liberties granted by English kings since the eleventh century.[9]

Rather than criticize the immemorial character of the constitution, royalists such as Clarendon instead emphasized the important place the royal prerogative had within the immemorial law. Sir Robert Filmer took a different royalist tack, demonstrating that the king's absolute sovereignty had descended from Adam, the first man and the first sovereign. Filmer made this argument for the prerogative in his *Patriarcha*, published posthumously by the court in 1680. John Locke wrote his *Treatises of Government* in response to this work and to the more historical case for absolute power put forward anonymously by either Filmer or Sir Robert Holbourne in the *Freeholders Grand Inquest* (1648), which was reprinted in 1679. There the antiquity of the House of Commons was denied and its origins fixed in Henry III's reign. According to the *Inquest*, the Lords alone, not the Commons, had originally been summoned to give the king counsel, so whatever functions and privileges the Commons possessed originated in the command, and by the grace, of the king, who is and was sole judge and legislator.[10]

Dr Brady took this assault on the immemorial constitution a step further, demonstrating the profound disjunction between Anglo-Saxon, feudal, and Restoration constitutions, showing how land-holding practices introduced by William the Conqueror had first specified the duty of lords to offer counsel. The common law regulated the tenure of land, and Brady pointed out how the rules for tenure had been imported by the Normans. Parliament had originally been simply a court of tenants performing feudal services for their lord, the king.[11] The people's privileges and liberties were not provisions of any pact made between the monarch and the people, but free gifts of the king, who relaxed the feudal law, which, in any case, had never constituted onerous servitude but 'the most Free and Noble Service.' In the 1680s, Brady argued, a distinct but nonetheless glorious constitution, the cumulative result of these royal concessions, provided Englishmen with more freedom than any people in the world; giving them more would only lead to anarchy. Petyt and his associates portrayed political authority as resting in the people, who were entitled to bestow it on, or remove it from, the monarch at will. To depict the past in this way, according to Brady, was to 'infuse Dangerous Notions of Soveraingty and Power into the Peoples Heads, which they never had.'[12] Brady demythologized the ancient constitution in an attempt to break its spell over his contemporaries. Relying on decades of philological scholarship, especially the work of Sir Henry Spelman, he built up a glossary of medieval words, showing their meaning in the context of feudal society, and pointing out how different their meaning was from the anachronistic seventeenth-century definitions supplied by Petyt and other whigs.

The preceding account of Brady's historical thought has been well known for the past four decades. However, Brady's work has never been fully situated in the context of the neoclassical criticism of English historiography or the various genres of history available to him. Let us look then at how Brady struggled to increase the repute and authority of his historical interpretation, to transform partisan pamphlets into proper history. Brady publicized his findings in three stages. His historical analysis first appeared in a series of pamphlets in the early 1680s defending the royalist cause in the Exclusion Crisis. In 1684, with the exclusionists defeated and the court in an elated, less frantic mood, he gave these antiquarian discourses more permanent form, entitling them *An Introduction to the Old English History, Comprehended in Three Several Tracts*, in a more considered work containing a preface describing the controversy, an enlarged version of his tracts, an appendix of vital documents, a glossary, and an index. However, as Brady himself realized, this was not, properly speaking, history, but only an introduction to the issues, methods, and sources of history: '*Introductions* I know are Written after another manner.'[13] Brady wanted to go further, to ascend the hierarchy of literary genres, to write history. In a third period of publication, he tried enshrining his discoveries in a more prestigious genre than mere pamphlet or collection. He wrote *The Complete History of England* in two volumes appearing in 1685 and 1700.

As early as 1675 Brady had envisioned writing a general history. In that year he made an unsuccessful application to the court for support of a work he foresaw strengthening the people's allegiance to the crown. Now, a decade later, having proven his usefulness as a polemicist, Brady was receiving royal aid, handsome salaries derived from his official post as royal physician and his unofficial duties as keeper of the Tower records. By James II's reign (1685–8), he was involved in coordinating the composition and publication of works of feudal history buttressing royalist political theory, including his own *Complete History*,[14] dedicated to James and bearing the royal portrait in the frontispiece, a work Brady described as 'an Impregnable Rock against the pretended Soveraignty and Power of the People in this Nation, which the Republicans can never climb over.'[15] Brady never gave any indication of aiming to remedy the weakness in English historiography or to write a humanist history as Milton had done. Instead, he sought to correct what he saw as grievous political error and to defend Stuart monarchy. By entitling his work a 'history' he betrayed some pretension to writing in the noble genre of antiquity, but in fact he failed to get beyond the lesser historical forms of chronicle and antiquarian tract. He composed his history by interspersing reworked versions of his pamphlets with compilations of medieval chronicles.

After presenting a series of contentious prefaces setting out his view of constitutional history, Brady embarks upon his general history. This history, however, is made up of very different components: first, a narrative of great deeds virtually transcribed from his sources – the medieval chroniclers – without any real connection to his constitutional interpretations; second, a series of digressions or discourses about the changing state of the law in a given king's reign. Brady assumes that his narrative of deeds has been written once and for all; it is a sacred text he does not feel free to alter and he rarely criticizes. His footnotes add a commentary on the text, but even when he repudiates his source for an episode in the narrative, he still feels obliged to transcribe the discounted story into his history.[16] Sometimes digressions make it out of the footnotes into the text itself, but they bring the storyline to an abrupt halt, and then, once the digression comes to an end, the narrative begins just as suddenly as it stopped, without transitions.[17] Brady may as well have produced two separate works: 1) a chronicle of English history such as Sir Richard Baker had written; 2) a polemical discourse of legal antiquarianism such as Brady had formulated in the *Introduction to the Old English History*. Instead, Brady appears to have tried dignifying his partisan constitutional arguments by embedding them in a bland narrative of worthy deeds, numbing the sting of his argument by placing it among so much inoffensive matter, thereby appropriating the prestige of 'history' to his antiquarian tracts.

In various 'Prefaces' he worked out his theses showing the differences between Saxon and Norman constitutions, yet he could not connect static analyses of medieval institutions to the working of those institutions over time and their relations to the great deeds of men.[18] The monastic sources for those deeds presented a problem for Brady, who attacked them with a venom worthy of Hume: 'the Monks [were] the only Historians of those times, and they Wrote the Actions of Kings and Great Men, and rendered them good or bad, as they were more or less Kind and Beneficient to the Church, Churchmen, and themselves; and Extolled or Defamed them, as they appeared for, and favoured their Ecclesiastic Liberty.'[19] The chroniclers told 'ridiculous,' 'incredible,' and 'vain' stories.[20] False and incomplete, the surviving sources for medieval history were 'wholly confin'd to the Descriptions of the Customs of some particular places, and the Lives and Actions of particular Persons, and those so blended with the Fabulous Hyperbolies, and Metaphors of Ignorant Writers (such as the Age they lived in afforded) that the brightest Rayes of Truth, could scarce penetrate and appear through those thick clouds of darkness, and Ignorance.'[21] Yet these were the records Brady had to work with, and he followed them so closely that he never could tame them into a neoclassical narrative. The problem of digesting and gaining control over the sources for medieval history was to plague general historians of England for the next 70 years until the polite man of letters David Hume succeeded where the royal physician and antiquarian had not.[22]

Although he employed as sources a methodologically diverse set of ancient, medieval, and modern historians (Tacitus, William of Malmesbury, and Camden, for example), Brady did not acknowledge any of them to justify his intermingling of antiquarian discourse and medieval chronicle. Although Brady was self-conscious about the innovative nature of his historical interpretations, he was tight-lipped about what models, if any, he had for the form of the *Complete History*. He showed no interest in this matter of genre, only a resolve to beat back his political adversaries. In the *Complete History* his only programmatic statements came as Brady tried to distinguish his method from that of his opponents:

> this History [was] not Written according to the Ordinary Method, by which the Readers are Bound to Depend upon the Integrity and Faith of the Author, for the Truth of the Things Related, but proved by Authentic Testimony. 'Tis not my own Invention, but Matter of Fact laid down, and warranted by. . . sufficient Record [by either chronicle or document].[23]

> Through the whole Course of the History, I have not Laboured after an Exact and Even Style . . .[24]

> Nor have I made any Reflections or Politic Observations upon what I have written from the Relations of others, which some are so much in Love with, as they Esteem nothing to be History without them; Let these Men injoy their Opinions, it may be others will think, that they serve only to Pervert and Disguise Matter of Fact, and make History Romantic . . .[25]

Brady was snubbing classical protocols regarding the drawing of political and moral lessons, the primacy of narrative, and the polite and elevated style of history. In denigrating his opponents and creating his own persona as an honest and impartial historian, Brady claimed to muzzle himself so that the all-powerful documentary source might speak for itself. Far from being a neoclassical historian whose reputation for integrity, wisdom, and diligence, and whose literary skills convinced readers of the truth, Brady, according to this scheme, appeared to be a rather anonymous collector of documents. This re-definition of history and the historian might have pleased Brady's fellow partisans, but in the eyes of eighteenth-century critics, Brady was discredited by his manifest prejudice, the fact he was in the pay of James II and writing 'on the Side of Arbitrary Power.'[26] Neoclassicists remained dissatisfied with English history.[27]

A CLERICAL STYLE OF HISTORY

It was certainly not the first or the last time an antiquarian challenged the neoclassical conception of history, but it was the first serious bid by an antiquarian to write the general history of England since John Leland tried over a century before.[28] The strange form of Brady's *Complete History* owed much to the lawyerly and clerical historical writers of an earlier age. For example, Brady's attempt to mix polemical discourses with narrative and then pass it off as 'history' resembled Selden's maneuver in composing and entitling *The Historie of Tithes* (1618), a patently philological and partisan piece of scholarship, not a neoclassical history. The form and style of Selden's legal antiquarianism, in turn, owed much to Selden's clerical opponents,[29] and there is a sense in which both Selden and Brady employed a mode of discourse invented by Reformation controversialists such as John Foxe in the sixteenth century[30] and alive and well in Brady's own day.

Brady's *Complete History* bears comparison with a contemporaneous work of ecclesiastical history, another product of the Exclusion Crisis, Gilbert Burnet's *History of the Reformation of the Church of England*. Fearing the growing power of France and the increasing likelihood of a Catholic on the English throne, Burnet aimed to put popery and reformed religion in a true light so that the church might be united enough to stave off both threats. In content, form, and inspiration there was little that was neoclassical about Burnet's *History*. His purpose was polemical and spiritual – to direct readers to heaven, to convert Catholics, 'to compleat and perpetuate' the Reformation. A hastily written tract for the moment, the second of his three volumes was composed in just six weeks. Burnet interrupted his narrative with documents and attacked opponents with angry words and 'low' details.[31] Brady's *Complete History* actually resembled this ecclesiastical history rather than neoclassical history. Each author stitched together religious and secular affairs in a highly documentary political account. Each preferred to cover his pages with scholarly paraphernalia rather than conceal his erudition in the seams of a flowing narrative. Each depended on highly-placed patrons for access to state papers and neither did very much to hide his partisanship. Their projects only parted ways insofar as the *Complete History*, unlike *The History of the Reformation*, contained long digressions on constitutional matters and spent less time on church affairs. Brady issued erastian rebukes of power-hungry clerics,[32] and providence, which had such a prominent place in Burnet's work, had none in Brady's.

It is little wonder Brady wrote like a bishop and not like a Roman senator, for he inhabited a remarkably clerical culture located at university and court. In fact, the Church of England had been the most important institutional patron of historical research since at least the Restoration and it enjoyed a powerful presence in the historical culture of the English elite well into the eighteenth century. Clerical antiquarianism flourished at both the university and the court, Brady's two bases of operation. The Restoration church, legally defined by a series of statutes, ancient judicial judgments, canons, and customs, sponsored research out of necessity. Only by mastering arcane points of ecclesiastical and legal history could the church be administered. To advance through the ranks of ecclesiastical preferment, therefore, historical erudition was highly advantageous to possess. In Charles II's time the chief patrons of medieval learning were his bishops. The church rewarded those within its ranks skilled in antiquarian study and historical controversy, because historical research proved useful for fighting the church's political battles, helping, for example, to justify the restored episcopal order and the alliance of church and state.[33]

Since 1660 the greatest concentration of philological and historical study had been at Oxford and Cambridge. At Oxford in the 1670s Lincoln and then Queen's College led the revival of Anglo-Saxon studies with their compilations of glossaries and editions of old texts. However, in the historical culture of this period the universities did not act as independent institutions with a program distinct from that of the church. Oxford and Cambridge were veritable seminaries. The vast majority of collegiate fellows were clerics not intending to make academic life a career but only using it as a source of visibility to attract lay and ecclesiastical patrons who could further their careers in the church.[34] From this perspective, the universities constituted just another set of benefices allowing the church to work on its own agendas. Not only was the church paying writers to produce historical works that departed from neoclassical ideals, but these same clergymen were also educating a large segment of the English elite, whether in university or gentle household or even the royal court. And just as the universities, under ecclesiastical direction, generated no uniquely academic, non-clerical historical culture, so the court had little to offer in its own right, instead allowing prelates to manage royalist uses of history. Archbishop Sancroft appears in fact to have been chief court supervisor of historical polemics for party gain. He had a role in the republication of Filmer. He and Bishop Turner saw Clarendon's *History* in manuscript and had close ties to Dr Brady.

Brady never completed the *Complete History*. When royalist fortunes were reversed in 1688, Brady returned to Cambridge, managing, without much enthusiasm, to continue the *History* through Richard II's reign, in a second volume published in 1700, the year of his death. By his literary clumsiness, his partisanship, his willful neglect of conventions for history-writing, or his susceptibility to clerical example, Brady's sweeping indictment of the common-law view of history created a novel historical form, a compound of antiquarian disputations and compiled narratives closely resembling ecclesiastical history. Some of Brady's successors, especially clergymen, took a keener interest in church affairs and divine providence than Brady, and most improved upon the literary quality of his narrative, dovetailing constitutional interpretations with men's deeds. However, they continued in Brady's footsteps. Far into the eighteenth century Englishmen defined history in neoclassical terms, but practicing historians, variously mired in political partisanship and antiquarian erudition, continued to write in the manner of Brady.

THE WHIG RESPONSE: JAMES TYRRELL

If no one had imitated, thereby helping in some sense to legitimize, Brady's genre, the *Complete History* might have descended to us simply as a one-of-a-kind hodge-podge, a failed attempt to turn discourses into history, polemics into story. However, the English political class found his constitutional disputations useful in political controversy, and Brady's political adversaries determined that Brady had to be answered. As distasteful to literary sensibilities as Brady's *Complete History* was, the only way for whigs to refute him was to adopt much of his genre in the process. Brady's opponents felt compelled to respond in kind, to offer a point-by-point refutation with philology and documents, to write like legal scholars rather than become neoclassical historians. They did not begin their counter-offensive with history, just as Brady had not begun with history but with polemical tracts. Appearing between 1692 and 1704 in a series of pamphlets, James Tyrrell's *Bibliotheca Politica* rehearsed the arguments of Petyt and Atwood against Brady over the antiquity of parliament.[35] Since these dialogues failed to demolish Brady's thesis, Tyrrell decided he had to meet Brady on his own ground with a general history.[36] Tyrrell's *General History of England* appeared in three volumes between 1696 and 1704. The whig response to Brady's *Complete History*, it resurrected the issues of the Exclusion Crisis and his own *Bibliotheca Politica*, resurrected as well the complaints about the state of English historiography.

Tyrrell accused 'the Doctor' of attempting 'to reduce our mixed and limited Monarchy into the like absolute and despotick Tyranny that is now exercised in France.' Tyrrell wished 'to shew that the ancient Government of this Nation was not an absolute, but a limited Monarchy, from its very Institution.'[37] Brady had argued that the Norman Conquest fundamentally changed the constitution by establishing the feudal law, while Tyrrell stressed the continuity of the English constitution from its 'Gothick' origins to the present. Tyrrell contended that Danish and Norman invasions were not actually 'Conquests, but rather Acquisitions gained by those Princes upon certain Compacts between them and the People of England; both Parties standing obliged in solemn Oaths, mutually to perform their parts of the Agreement.'[38] Far from providing a basis for absolutism, these so-called conquests actually illustrated the contractarian nature of the constitution as an agreement between the prince and the people. Alleging that 'Friends to the Arbitrary Power of Kings' employed the conquest thesis in order 'to confer on the Prince an absolute Power to break all our Laws' and enslave the people,[39] Tyrrell instead interpreted the ancient constitution as preserving the liberties of Englishmen by limiting the power of kings, who shared sovereignty with parliament. Tyrrell focused his study upon those historical issues bearing on the Exclusion Crisis and the Glorious Revolution. He claimed parliament had never been subordinate to the crown but had co-existed with it in Saxon times, when laws 'were all enacted by the joint and unanimous Consent of the King and his Great Council.' In fact, Tyrrell argued, as he justified exclusionist whigs as well as revolution principles, this council of wise men actually elected the monarch and could depose him if he became tyrannical.[40] The practice of deposing kings had been part of the 'Original Constitution' and based upon an 'Original Compact' between the people and the king, renewed in his coronation oath on the accession of every king.[41] Far from being absolute, the Saxon kings enjoyed even fewer prerogatives than modern English kings, unable to dispose of crown lands without the council's consent, for example.[42] Constitutional history taught that the English monarchy was limited and mixed, whatever might be asserted to the contrary by frenchified supporters of Stuart absolutism.

However much Tyrrell detested Stuart loyalists, he accepted their mode of argument. Both Tyrrell and Brady turned to the clerical, antiquarian style of their contemporaries. Tyrrell had a background in legal antiquarianism, as the grandson of James Ussher, Archbishop of Armagh, the curator of that eminent scholar's manuscripts, and a student of law himself at Lincoln College, Oxford. He praised the modern antiquarian specialties of numismatics and chronology, and inserted antiquarian details in the body of his *History*.[43] He portrayed himself as an antiquarian, a historian, and a philosopher but not as a 'Casuitical Divine,' which he accused Brady and Filmer of being;[44] yet Tyrrell wrote history much as a divine might. Providence had a role in his history, and Tyrrell uttered pious oaths about telling the truth and hoping God would let him live long enough to complete his work.[45] He found ecclesiastical and legal history to be more important than military history,[46] so abbreviated this mainstay of classical historiography to attend to church affairs and constitutional questions. The documents so prevalent in clerical histories and in Brady's *Complete History* Tyrrell employed also. Like Brady, Tyrrell's extensive use of quotations and digressions served to break his narrative and his argument to bits.[47] Like Brady, Tyrrell criticized the superstition of the middle ages, the barbaric, misinformed, credulous monks on whom he was forced to rely for his sources,[48] but then he followed those same sources very closely, simply compiling or epitomizing them.[49] Captive to these sources, Tyrrell wrote down almost whatever they said, even if they made for a disjointed narrative, or in some cases just an annalistic collection of trivia serving no argument or story.[50] Tyrrell's entry for the year 802 was a single sentence: 'This Year the Moon was eclipsed . . . and Beormond was Consecrated Bishop of Rochester.'[51]

It must be admitted, however, that Tyrrell's *History* did have some neoclassical characteristics. His avowed purpose was to instruct and entertain posterity with the truth about the past.[52] He inserted maxims of state and characters of great men.[53] He claimed the events he depicted were important, dignified, and public,[54] which indeed many of them were. These declarations were so expected and so familiar to his readers that Tyrrell rarely bothered to cite the classical tags justifying them.[55] For Tyrrell three modern historians stood out as exemplary: Bacon, de Thou, and Mézeray,[56] and yet Tyrrell never came as close as they to filling the role of neoclassical historian. His critics exploited the fact that, in Tyrrell's own words,

> I being a private Man, not famed for much Reading, or deep Learning, should, almost unassisted with Materials from the present Historians and Antiquaries of the Nation, attempt to write a General History of England, out of my own private Readings and Collections.[57]

Tyrrell did not offer much of a defense against these charges that he had not done enough research, was not a public figure, and enjoyed no repute for erudition, except to argue that such theorists as Le Moyne and Nicolson had listed impossibly high qualifications for historians.[58] Tyrrell was indeed a private man, little known to contemporaries but known to us as John Locke's friend. Tyrrell possessed the leisure and the social standing to satisfy requirements for the role of Livy, but he lacked the preferred involvement in public affairs, and apparently did not even join in Locke's secret political intrigues against the Stuarts in the 1680s. Aside from the work incumbent on him as a country gentleman – serving as justice of the peace and deputy lieutenant for his county – his main public performances involved publishing pamphlets against Brady and Filmer.[59] For these King William awarded him a modest sinecure, the ceremonial court post of cupbearer.[60]

Although Brady and Tyrrell, or their publishers, each entitled his work a 'history' and Tyrrell even implied he would solve the chronic weakness in English historiography,[61] each retreated from such claims in the body of his work. Tyrrell cast doubt upon his own title as historian, his own work as 'General History.' Awed by the high standards for history, Tyrrell shied away from claiming the mantle of Livian historian.

> I will not affirm this to be an Exact History according to the strict Rules of Art ... But if the not Writing any thing which I did not believe to be true, nor the concealing any thing useful to the

World, that is so, might qualify me for an Historian, perhaps then I may have some pretence to that Title.[62]

He wrote these words to introduce his first volume. Like Brady, he argued that truth and utility, not literary presentation and historical form, made a work of history valuable. Tyrrell became more modest still in his second volume:

> I hope these Collections (for I will not presume to give them the Title of a Complete History) being Register'd in a due and exact Order of time, may at least deserve the name of Annals. And as such may prove useful in time to some abler Pen to compile out of them a complete Body of English History . . .[63]

Out of the 'Collections' he and Brady had written, a true history would one day be composed that would reduce their work to 'little better than waste Paper.'[64]

Tyrrell and some of his successors adopted this meek persona because they did not wish their work to be evaluated by the exacting standards of neoclassical history. More interested in polemics than the title of English Livy, both Brady and Tyrrell recognized that their own work was only preparatory to a 'true,' 'perfect,' or 'complete' general history. However, there was a market for their histories among political partisans and gentlemen antiquarians indifferent to or contemptuous of neoclassical criticism. As late as 1746 James Hampton remarked upon the disjunction between the high-minded purpose of history and the appetite English readers instead had for petty antiquarian details.

> The grand Design of History, which is to instruct Men in civil Prudence, though universally acknowledged, is not often regarded with that Diligence it deserves. Many Readers are content, if they can satisfy a present, indolent curiosity: some labour in the Discovery of insignificant Modes and Customs: while others direct their whole Attention to the Greatness and Variety of Facts.[65]

Englishmen complained about general histories but sometimes bought them nonetheless, for they helped to satisfy certain needs of English society. In a history such as Tyrrell's, the sheer volume of historical facts was helpful to gentlemen pursuing antiquarian study or family history. Large blocks of ecclesiastical history and characters of holy men increased the store of Christian knowledge. The digest of laws constituted a legal history of England.[66] Historical data, regardless of the literary form it might take, fueled political debate.

Tyrrell once entertained grandiose plans for extending his compilations beyond the medieval period in future volumes, abridging the entire work, then having it translated into Latin or modern languages for foreigners. Behind these schemes lay the self-criticism that his 'bulky Volumes' had grown so large and become so difficult to read that he had failed to make his work accessible to any but the most erudite reader.[67] In fact, he stopped the project where Brady had, at Richard II's reign, his polemical ambition spent, his work already too drawn out and expensive for the vast majority of readers.

THE BATTLE OF THE BOOKS: TEMPLE AND SWIFT

Neither Brady nor Tyrrell enjoyed second editions, although Tyrrell wrote at a time when public interest in a new general history of England had been roused by the Battle of the Books. As would be the case so often in the ongoing despair over the state of English historiography, much of the hand-wringing came from abroad. It was an outbreak of the French *querelle* between the ancients and the moderns that prompted another round of soul-searching on the part of English men of letters concerned with the fate of their history. Literary events like this one, not just more purely political ones such as the Civil War, could raise expectations about the appearance of an English Livy or Thucydides. The Battle of the Books compounded the historiographical inferiority complex and broached once again the issue of writing a neoclassical history of England.

The debate over the respective merits of ancient and modern learning was an old one, old in France as well as in England, a debate which originated in antiquity itself. Should writers imitate classical authors or should they press on to employ modern literary forms more befitting a postclassical world? Once the French resumed this long-simmering dispute in the 1680s, Sir William Temple brought it to a boil in England as well. In 1690 Temple responded indignantly to a French tract that had sided with the moderns. He published an essay championing the ancients and found a worthy English opponent in a boy wonder of erudition, William Wotton. Temple and Wotton battled each other until the turn of the century, by which time they had been joined by several other combatants.[68] At stake was the reputation of the ancients as the ultimate standard of values. Had natural philosophy, literature, and art, indeed all the arts and sciences, been perfected for all time in the golden age of classical antiquity, or was Western civilization capable of setting new standards of attainment that put classical ones in the shade? The 'ancients' did not see such improvement, only decadence, especially as regarded imitative arts such as oratory and literature. More optimistic about the possibility of equalling or eclipsing such achievements, the 'moderns' took special pride in science and philosophy, which were perceived to be more susceptible to improvement than imitative arts because they benefited from the accumulation of knowledge and experience in a way poetry or history did not.

Wotton and Temple fought several skirmishes over history. Temple introduced his team of ancient historians to face off against the greatest modern historians. In the ensuing war of words Wotton largely acquiesced in Temple's apologia for classical historiography, except to assert that Commynes and Sarpi could hold their own against Polybius in terms of their power to instruct. In the realm of historiography, interestingly enough, what thus distinguished ancients from moderns was the question of whether the moderns had already matched or would someday match the ancients, not whether the moderns had invented or would invent new and better ways of doing history. They disagreed in their assessment of modern attempts to meet classical standards, not in what those standards should be – both sides agreed upon the primacy of classical standards. So far as history was concerned, both sides thus found much common ground. A difference between the two camps only really emerged when some of the moderns, Wotton included, dared to assert that certain modern investigations of the past such as philology and antiquarianism had rendered modern scholars superior to ancient historians in terms of accuracy. Wotton agreed that the ancient historians provided the only models for eloquent narratives but not the only models for every historical inquiry. Generations of classical scholarship had enabled modern men to know more about antiquity than the inhabitants of the ancient world themselves. While Wotton lauded the modern techniques of textual criticism that revealed this insight, Temple rejected them as a pedantic waste of time, denying any claim they might have to being real 'history.' For a man of the world, the ancient historians remained the only measure of historiographical achievement, the only source of instructive historical knowledge; neither tedious glossaries nor antiquarian trivia did he find in them. Temple nipped Wotton's impudent modernism in the bud, firmly rejecting the notion that modern scholarship furnished a valuable and legitimate supplement to history.

If Englishmen had discarded classical historians as exemplars in favor, say, of these modern approaches to history celebrated by Wotton, then the whole issue of a weakness in historiography would never have surfaced during the Battle of the Books, for there would have been no reason to try emulating a rejected literary form. Moreover, in the seventeenth century Englishmen had in fact matched continental accomplishments in the sort of scholarship Wotton described; there was now no hue and cry about the inferiority of Camden and Selden compared with their counterparts across the English Channel. In the event, however, the English elite did *not* adopt modern scholarship as a replacement for narrative history modelled after the classical historians. Both the ancients and the moderns – with the exception of the position of modern scholarship just examined – upheld the classical standard for history and hoped to remedy the weakness in English historical writing. The most insistent cry for improvement came from the moderns, whose hearts quickened at the idea of actually matching or vanquishing the classical historians at their own game. But even the ancients, though they never expected modern Englishmen to equal or best the ancient historians, believed that they certainly could do a better job of writing like them.

In 1694 one such ancient, Temple himself, sounded the call for a new general history of England, a history more nearly approaching classical ideals. Temple tried his own hand at the task, or claimed to have tried, disingenuously citing higher duty to public service as an excuse for not persevering as a historian. He urged friends to attempt it, but they also declined, 'pretending modesty' or 'too much valuing ease.'[69] To show what he had in mind, Temple published his own *Introduction to the History of England* (1694), a polite if scanty narrative history from the earliest times through the reign of William the Conqueror. Temple took the narrative no further but he did inspire what was to be perhaps the best-known history of England ever *not* written. His secretary, Jonathan Swift, picked up the gauntlet next, starting where Temple had left off and taking the story as far as the 1150s before aborting it.[70] Swift later contemplated publishing his fragmentary history, and explained his false start in a dedicatory epistle to the Count de Gyllenborg:

> I was diverted from pursuing this history, partly by the extreme difficulty, but chiefly by the indignation I conceived at the proceedings of a faction, which then prevailed [in 1701]. . . . I publish [it] now . . . for an encouragement to those who have more youth, and leisure, and good temper than I, towards pursuing the work as far as it was intended by me, or as much further as they please . . .[71]

Just as Temple gave up on Livian history and published his *Introduction* to inspire Swift or others to carry it forward, so now did Swift consider publishing his fragment as a fillip to better candidates. Swift seems to have arrived at the belated conclusion that he was not the best man for the job, that the project was too difficult and time-consuming for him, and that whoever might tackle it could not be drawn into factious party politics as he had been or lack gentlemanly leisure as he did.

To any aspirant historian the project must have seemed daunting: years, not months, of work lay ahead; no one had ever succeeded in doing it; few, if any, short-term benefits could be expected from it, although the potential long-range pay off in terms of prestige and even finances was enormous. Clearly, an extended period of leisure was required, supplied either by one's own income or that of a patient patron. Yet without the time or the quiet that would seem necessary for accomplishing such a feat, Swift foundered in the role of Livian historian. Young Swift had nestled himself under Temple's wing in 1689 and served the retired diplomat for ten years as secretary, amanuensis, and literary editor, while Swift was not scrounging for more lucrative, exalted posts to which he believed his talents entitled him. After Temple's death in 1699, Swift joined the household of the Earl of Berkeley as chaplain and continued to work on the history he had begun two years before. A frustrated Swift was finding English history as difficult to crack as English society. In 1701 he arrived in London with Berkeley, just in time to see the political furor over the impeachment of Lords Somers, Halifax, Orford, and Portland. The scene 'diverted' Swift from his manuscript history, as he later told Gyllenborg, and inspired him to write his first political pamphlet, the success of which finally provided Swift with an entrée into whig high society.[72] Ironically, *A Discourse of the Contests and Dissensions between the Nobles and Commons in Athens and Rome, with the Consequences they had upon both those States* employed analogies from classical history, even as Swift was renouncing his own role as a neoclassical historian. He apparently concluded that partisan political pieces would advance him more quickly than his monumental historical work-in-progress would. During the next 13 years, when he came as close to the center of great events as he ever would, Swift did enjoy the company of 'great men,' tory and whig alike. However, he never stood on equal footing with them: he wrote useful party pamphlets on their behalf but did not enjoy the ease, comfort, or leisure that marked them as gentle or noble. Swift had a tendency to idolize the 'great' and to write things in order to gain their favor.

After setting aside his Livian project, born of a desire to please Temple, Swift did not return to history-writing until 1712, when he started a Thucydidean history for another hero, the Earl of Oxford, to be discussed in Chapter 5. Swift was ambitious enough to flirt with both neoclassical roles but too distracted by political and ecclesiastical clientage networks to embrace either of them completely. These histories represented two of Swift's longest unfinished works; neither was published in his lifetime. That a writer of Swift's gifts came to grief twice over history suggests that much more was required of a great historian than simply a pen of genius and a grounding in classical literature. Swift had the means – the literary virtuosity and book learning – but not the motive or the opportunity for writing Livian history. He lacked the leisure to master this genre, and took a greater interest in the immediate favor of parties and patrons able to offer him position and place than in the eventual literary fame that would accrue to whomever took care of the chronic problem in English historical culture.

MODEST AMBITION: LAURENCE ECHARD

Clergymen lacking independent means were by training and circumstance not the best candidates for writing neoclassical history, as Swift amply demonstrated. And yet Temple's grand plans for

English history inspired another Church of England man, less prominent than Swift, to follow through on a general history that arguably came closer to satisfying neoclassicists than Brady or Tyrrell had.[73] Laurence Echard (1670?–1730) wrote *The History of England*, published between 1707 and 1718. Echard was a country priest who, from an early age, had written works of travel, geography, history, translation. He delved into a variety of historical forms, composing *The Roman History* (1695) and a *General Ecclesiastical History* of the primitive church (1702), and helping prepare an edition of Camden's antiquarian classic, *Britannia* (1695). These projects revealed Echard's interest in church history and antiquarianism, interests that also colored his *History of England*.

Like his predecessor Tyrrell, Echard adopted a modest persona, acknowledged the neoclassical criteria for history, alluded to the weakness in historiography, cited the high qualifications for the historian who would solve it, then confessed to failure, admitting his work was neither 'perfect' nor 'finished' nor 'complete.'[74] He claimed to wish that someone else would render his work obsolete:

> I have so little Regard to Fame or Applause, but so much Love for the Publick, that I heartily desire that not only my History of England, but all my other Books, may have their Memory utterly extinguish'd by better and more useful [works written] upon the same Subjects.[75]

While this exaggerated stance, perhaps an echo of Livy's exordium, might serve as an ironic rhetorical device, many readers in fact took it at face-value and agreed that Echard's work was only a stopgap. An acquaintance observed that Echard meant well but had 'the least knowledge of the world of any man I ever knew, that made so much noise in it.'[76] Working out of his rectory at Louth in Lincolnshire, Echard conceded he lived too far away from libraries and learned men to write the sort of history he had once dreamt of composing. Discouraged by his 'Distance from Books and able Assistants,' he admitted lacking the learning and experience necessary for a 'Work of so great Importance.' He begged readers to send him sources for contemporary history so that he might add a concluding volume to his work.[77]

Without independent means, Echard confessed, 'common Authors' like himself had difficulty maintaining their integrity and telling the truth. Yet, more so than finances, politics was the real culprit. Echard criticized the party system as the enemy of historical truth: 'of the two great Evils that so usually attend common Authors, it is more eligible and less slavish to write for Bread, than for a Party. In the former Case I believe it is possible for a Writer to preserve his Honesty; in the Latter, I will say nothing.'[78] A common man, not a noble historian, Echard relied on Archbishop Wake, whom he had once served as chaplain, to butter his bread. Wake secured permission for Echard to dedicate volumes two and three to George I, and convinced the king to grant Echard £300. After publishing his final two volumes in 1718, Echard, still unsatisfied, felt obliged to travel to London in search of 'gifts' he might receive for his work from 'wealthy persons.'[79]

True to his word, Echard refrained from violent partisanship as he carried out the political program of the Hanoverian dynasty and whig bishops who supported him. Volume one had a surprisingly tory look about it from page one with its dedication to the Duke of Ormonde, but it was not Robert Brady's toryism. Echard saw the origin of English law, government, and language in a Saxon conquest, not a Norman one, and he skirted key issues of medieval history such as the date of the first parliament and the meaning of Magna Carta.[80] By devoting just one of his three 900-page volumes to 1700 years of history, and the other two volumes to just 30 or 40 years apiece, Echard showed that he and his readers were more interested in the recent than the medieval past, the focus of the 'Brady Controversy.' He was in fact a moderate whig whose main concern was to trace and praise the survival of Anglicanism against its multiple foes in the seventeenth century – Catholics, Puritans, dissenters.[81] He might give a largely Clarendonian version of the Civil War, offer a hagiographical account of Charles I, and criticize the first whigs of the Exclusion Crisis, but Echard was a staunch supporter of the Glorious Revolution.[82] He was in effect making the whig point which Tyrrell had made, that the current establishment owed so little to the distant past that historiographical debate should focus on the recent past;[83] such a study made clear the debt Englishmen, and in particular the Church of England, owed William of Orange and parliament for saving England from popery. Echard's modernism helped make him acceptable to George I and other patrons such as the whig churchman Wake.

No writer on the subject of the Civil War could avoid confronting Clarendon's legacy. Echard relied extensively on 'our noble and best Historian, whose Work ought to continue as long as the Name of the English Nation.' Echard recognized that anyone writing about the Civil War after 1704 had to justify recounting a topic on which many thought Clarendon had already written the last word:

> Because I may be thought too much to have trodden upon the Heels of that great Man, I ought to be a little particular, and say something of what I have done with Relation to Him; and rather, because I know it is almost generally expected.[84]

What Echard did was to quote or paraphrase[85] Clarendon to fill out his own work and buttress his interpretation of the Civil War, demonstrating that a moderate whig could find much common ground with a moderate royalist, particularly on the issue of King Charles as guardian of Anglicanism.[86] However, Echard did not write for so select a readership as Clarendon had, and he used this fact to justify his departure from the criterion of great events which had ruled Clarendon's selection of detail. He made allowances for 'the Vulgar,' readers impatient or unconcerned with maxims of state.

> [T]o render the Whole more Complete, and to answer the Expectations of a numerous sort of Readers, curious in some Particulars, I have several times deviated and descended from the Dignity of an Historian, and voluntarily fallen into the lower Class of Biographers, Annalists, &c. more especially in the Catalogues of Men['s] Names, particular Descriptions of publick Solemnities, Processions, Entries, &c. which I have been often assur'd, and am fully satisfy'd, wou'd be acceptable and useful to the Generality of the Nation.[87]

Echard even criticized solemn historians such as Clarendon:

> it has been too usual for Historians of the highest Class, and largest Views, frequently to omit and overlook Things little and trivial in Themselves, only because they are so in Themselves; without considering how necessary, and even ornamental, the poorest Materials are in the noblest Buildings . . .[88]

Echard made little pretence that he, his audience, or his subject could compare with the nobility of Clarendon and his.

To a limited degree, Echard's populist strategy served him well. His concern for the non-specialist reader led him to simplify and smoothen his narrative, giving it a literary quality lacking in Brady and Tyrrell. This quest for readability needs to be seen in the context of the rest of Echard's writings, which were abridgements – of Raleigh's *History of the World*, for example – or translations aimed at less erudite readers. In his other historical works, too, Echard explicitly appealed to the novice.[89] In the *History of England* he fancied himself a polite writer taking English history beyond the most learned segment of a political class grappling with arcane, even insoluble, constitutional questions. By polishing the controversial, disconnected, and crude remnants of the past into a pleasing and instructive story, Echard spared readers the time and labor incumbent on trying it themselves. He saw himself as the literary, though perhaps not the scholarly, superior of Brady and Tyrrell. The documents and chronicles which they reprinted he transformed into a story in modern English prose. He explained, for example: 'These articles [concerning Richard II's deficiencies as king] were very long and aggravating, and may be seen at length in Doctor Brady's and Mr. Tyrrell's Histories, where they take up above eight Pages in Folio.'[90] Their narratives, he argued, were impaired by long digressions on intricate contentious points. Echard pruned these, preferring instead simply to tell the story or to summarize it without dwelling on its contemporary political significance. He put citations in small type in the margins so as not to distract 'the Eyes of the Reader, who in History ought to meet with no Impediments nor Interruptions.'[91]

Despite his passion for continuity, Echard presented yet another instance of an English historian inserting documents to the detriment of narrative. Echard succeeded in distancing himself from events more than a century old and describing them in a well-proportioned story, but as his history approached the present he lost narrative control.[92] He could not resist telling, at great length, the story of Charles II's flight from the Battle of Worcester, even though it crippled his narration and featured 'low' characters incompatible with the dignity of history:

The Manner and Particulars of the King's Escape are so wonderful, and attended with such visible Marks of the immediate Hand of Heaven, that no Circumstances, or Names, how mean soever, ought to be omitted; tho in the Relation we shall be oblig'd sometimes to descend from the Rules of History to the Liberties of Biography.[93]

Echard's depiction of Charles' encounter with loyal country folk often included humorous anecdotes and hagiographic details calculated to be popular. However, sales of the *History* never met Echard's expectations: damaging pamphlet responses and the size of Echard's work harmed his reputation.[94] Echard believed the most serious criticisms came from those protesting the omnipresence of providence in the *History*, and the freedom with which Echard interpreted events as divine punishments for the evil deeds of historical actors. Defending himself, Echard insisted that God gave 'many plain and visible Marks of his Pleasure and Displeasure,'[95] and it was the historian's duty to point out these divine judgments to readers. Charles' escape from Worcester provided just one of many opportunities to fulfill this responsibility. What Echard seemed unable to understand was that readers were objecting to a trait more appropriate to an ecclesiastical history than to a general history of England. It was not the case that Englishmen no longer believed in providence; Clarendon's depiction of it did not generally draw criticism.[96] Rather, Echard had been too partisan and effusive in his account of its operation. Echard's providentialism, like his partiality and his reprinting of documents, betrayed a reliance on ecclesiastical models for historical writing, not neoclassical ones.

However, until Rapin's *History* began to appear seven years later, in 1725, Echard's work held the field among general histories of England.[97] Echard contributed more literary artistry than could be found in his immediate predecessors, but otherwise he remained well within the bounds of what was by 1718, when the last two volumes of his *History of England* appeared, a well-established historical form. Englishmen had never been fully satisfied by the general histories of England written in the sixteenth and seventeenth century and they seemed little nearer their ambitious ideal in the early eighteenth century.[98] General historians writing in the half century after Robert Brady first asked the court to patronize his *Complete History* wrote on a grand scale but not entirely in the grand manner. During the Exclusion Crisis Brady's assault upon the ancient constitution led him to fashion a history that was part antiquarian discourse, part medieval chronicle. The contemporary style of royalist historical propaganda was lawyerly and clerical, not French and neoclassical, and so Brady wrote in a way that closely resembled ecclesiastical history in its open partisanship, its antiquarian methods, its insertion of documents that ran roughshod over the narrative. Brady's whig opponent adopted Brady's manner even as he attacked his substance, knitting together partisan antiquarian tracts with the deeds of medieval kings. Tyrrell's *General History of England* was designed in part to capitalize on renewed expectations about neoclassical historiography spawned by Sir William Temple's entrance into the controversy over ancient and modern learning. In the Battle of the Books radical moderns trumpeted philological and antiquarian studies, which Brady, Tyrrell, and their successors certainly employed. However, these historians used antiquarian techniques out of political expediency, not on any declared principle. They seized upon modern practice as useful in polemics, as the prevailing style of historical controversy, not as an academic demonstration of the virtues of modern scholarship. In fact, they were all aware just how miserable their own productions were compared with neoclassical ideals for narrative history, and they backed away from the title of 'historian,' which they agreed actually belonged to some great man in the future.

Swift and Echard, by their clerical training and meager social position, lacked the status advantageous to writing an impartial, polite history. Even Brady and Tyrrell, both laymen possessing a modicum of independence and political experience, did not elude a clerical style of historical writing at loggerheads with neoclassical historiography. Modern party politics made evenhandedness difficult for them: the royal court in one way or another rewarded Brady, Tyrrell, and Echard for their partisanship, and party strife had a part to play in Swift's decision to stop writing history. Treating the subject of, and sources for, medieval history, which they generally found to be repulsive, presented a challenge to these modern historians the ancient historians never faced. The moderns also found themselves struggling to preserve their narrative from the inclusion of documents partisan readers demanded to see at full length. Disheartened by the gigantic size to which their compilations had grown and by the lukewarm reception which greeted them, or by sundry other discouragements, Brady and Tyrrell quit at the late-medieval period, Echard at 1689, and Swift before he really started. Given the many impediments to writing a general history of England, given how anachronistic classical historiography appeared to be, it is little wonder that no English Livy had emerged to match Clarendon's neoclassical achievement in the role of Thucydides. Clarendon's mantle, in turn, was to slip through the hands of those attempting to don it in the age of Lord Bolingbroke.

5

The Death of Thucydidean History

Henry St John, Viscount Bolingbroke (1678–1751), played a vital part in the politics of the eighteenth century, first as a prominent member of the last tory administration before the onset of whig rule, then briefly as a supporter of the Pretender to the throne, James Francis Stuart, and finally as a leader of the opposition to Sir Robert Walpole in the 1720s and 1730s. Bolingbroke and his circle also played a decisive part in the historiography of the age of party. As we have already seen, English history was largely written along party lines, and so whigs and tories scrutinized the past to score political points with partisan historiography. For their part, Bolingbroke and his associates championed the tory peace, which he had negotiated to end the War of Spanish Succession, and the Church of England, which he had campaigned to preserve from endangerment by dissenters and Catholics. In terms of their historiography, tories took a particular interest in guarding the reputation of Clarendon and his *History of the Rebellion*, whose prestige and political capital they wished to monopolize. They challenged whig initiatives to write the history of their own times, a genre which Clarendon had perfected and which was seemingly reserved for tories alone to pursue.

In the event, several attempts to write Thucydidean history, whether tory or whig, came to naught, or at least could not compare with Clarendon's *History*. In 1706 White Kennett, a whig clergyman, responded to Clarendon's high tory editors by writing his own history of the seventeenth century. In 1712 Jonathan Swift, who had already attempted to write a general history of England, began a history of the negotiations leading to the peace of Utrecht, a partisan piece of journalism aimed at vindicating the tories. Gilbert Burnet, a prominent whig prelate, wrote a damning account of the tories' 'four last years' in his famous *History of His Own Time*. As incensed as high tories were by whig versions of contemporary history, they failed to supply an adequate response, at least not one to rival Burnet's sales or Clarendon's prestige. Although each wrote a great deal about the past, Bolingbroke and Roger North were tongue-tied in terms of launching an attack in the form of a neoclassical narrative. North's reaction to whig rule, indeed to the Glorious Revolution, was to withdraw from public life and lick his family's wounds, to reject historical form itself, irreparably soiled by whigs such as Kennett, and to attack neoclassical historiography as uninstructive. Bolingbroke's psychological inhibitions, his unquenchable political ambition, his refusal to accept his status as political pariah, all prevented him from playing the role of Thucydides, which to his contemporaries Bolingbroke had seemed destined to play, the maker and the writer of history.

Modern party politics frustrated these various essays at contemporary history. The vicissitudes of the political game either deflated the historiographical ambitions of Bolingbroke and North or infected the works of Burnet, Swift, and Kennett with ugly partisanship. We shall see that the clerical status of these last three writers proved detrimental to their self-appointed work as historians. North and Bolingbroke, as well as other lay political figures, might have possessed better qualifications for writing the history of their own times, but their examples illuminated structural peculiarities in English political culture that forestalled the appearance of another Clarendon. In addition, the neoclassical historian of one's own times faced many of the same obstacles confronting the general historians discussed in Chapter 4. Print, political parties, antiquarianism, Christianity all presented challenges to any historian trying to preserve classical values in the face of modernity. In any case, tories would never admit that whigs could approach Clarendonian standards for history, and condemned them for the attempt. However, tories themselves appeared to be so awed by Clarendon's achievement that they hesitated even to write, or at least to publish, their Thucydidean history. Bolingbroke's anguished endeavor finally ground to a halt in the 1730s. His failure, coupled with the perception that Hanoverian England had not produced deeds sufficiently great for a place in history, spelled the death of Thucydidean history, at least for the foreseeable future. We shall see that by mid-century doubts were even raised about the *History* written by Clarendon, the English Thucydides.

IN THE SHADOW OF THE GREAT: KENNETT, SWIFT, BOYER

Clarendon's repute was far different in 1706, when Kennett decided to test the scalding waters of Civil War historiography. Kennett's whig history was part of a far larger project, one long in the works. In the mid-1690s, Sir William Temple's calls for the rewriting of English history to neoclassical standards inspired, in varying degrees, Tyrrell, Echard, and Swift to embark on general histories of England. But realizing the difficulty of such an undertaking, Temple had also proposed another project, a temporary fix. He wanted to construct a composite history of England by reprinting the best available histories of individual reigns. Even if English historians had never equalled the classical historians, it would still be useful to put together an anthology of England's most distinguished historians, those who had most closely approximated classical ideals for history. London booksellers liked the idea. They used histories by Milton, Daniel, More, Bacon, and others to fill two volumes that took the story of Britain from earliest times to the Tudors. White Kennett was asked to cover the seventeenth century in what amounted to a history of his own times and the Civil War, the third volume of *A Complete History of England*, published in 1706.[1]

Kennett (1660–1728) was an obscure country divine until the Convocation Controversy broke out in 1697. By that time most Anglican clergymen were dissatisfied with William III's plans for religious comprehension. Francis Atterbury led a group of highflying tories in a campaign to exploit Convocation, the Church of England's own legislative body, as a means of attacking William's clerical appointments and preventing the spread of heresy. For two decades Convocation inspired a torrent of historical polemics, as Atterbury, Jeremy Collier, and George Hickes squared off against whig defenders of the Revolution settlement, William Wake and Edmund Gibson. The Exclusion Crisis historiography was revived, but the usual roles exchanged. Now circumstances called for whigs to resuscitate Brady and Spelman to defend the present episcopacy, the royal prerogative, and the late emergence of the House of Commons, and tories and nonjurors to adopt whig interpretations of the common law minimizing the rights of king and bishop.[2] Kennett's *Ecclesiastical Synods and Parliamentary Convocations* (1701) denied that the tory-styled alliance of civil and ecclesiastical government had a precedent in Saxon times and established him as one of the most prominent opponents of the high church party.

Kennett was an accomplished clerical scholar, but it is hard to imagine why he should have been chosen to contribute to the *Complete History*, except on partisan political grounds as a whig respondent to Clarendon's *History*. He stood little chance of keeping up the literary standard on display in the first two volumes of the *Complete History*; nothing in his background as clergyman and antiquarian suggested he was fit to vie with Clarendon for the title of English Thucydides. Not a figure of political experience and independent means writing for posterity, Kennett was paid by the page while patrons such as Bishop Gilbert Burnet looked on.[3] Not a prominent public man taking responsibility for his work and gaining authority for it on the basis of a public reputation for political acumen or personal integrity, Kennett instead wrote anonymously because he feared a political backlash.[4] It was only by appropriating the prestige of a genuine neoclassical historian that Kennett could shore up his own credibility. Like Echard before him, he transcribed several serviceable passages from Clarendon,[5] which alone gave Kennett's part of the *Complete History* any claim to a place among the noteworthy histories comprising volumes one and two. Kennett's *History* countered the high church version of the past propounded by Clarendon's editors but did not criticize Clarendon directly. A sermon Kennett delivered in 1704 had already attempted to discredit Christ Church historiography, but failed, because adversaries simply quoted Clarendon back at him. In the *Complete History*, Kennett essentially conceded that tories controlled the Civil War as a political issue, and so he used the Restoration period as a stick to beat them. In order to defend the current Marlborough-Godolphin ministry, the 1688–9 establishment of church and state, and the war against France, Kennett praised Shaftesbury and the Glorious Revolution, condemned Charles II and James II as proponents of popery and arbitrary government, and defended his own position in the Convocation Controversy.[6]

Predictably, nonjurors and tories attacked this interpretation of events. Roger North began compiling a 700-page indictment, which he left to be published posthumously. In the meantime, he issued an anonymous pamphlet in 1711 charging that the work was a 'Libel,' not 'History.' North proceeded to condemn Kennett's method, which was to form and model the Matters of Fact, by paring away, adding, concealing, varnishing, and colouring of them, like Painters, or rather like Romancers, so as to make the Person of that Prince [Charles II], and his Government appear to all Posterity, black, odious, and deformed.

North looked upon Kennett as an ecclesiastical historian, and not a very competent one at that: 'even [Kennett's] Predecessor [the church historian] Tom Fuller was a very Thucydides or Livy [compared] to him.' North insisted that Kennett, a clergyman, was ill-prepared to narrate civil history, just one in a long line of clergymen to prove by his own counter-example that laymen alone were qualified to interpret civil history.[7] Although whigs and tories alike championed neoclassical historiography, North's criticism of Kennett on the grounds of his implausible qualifications for writing like 'Thucydides or Livy' became a conspicuous tory polemical tactic, as the tory indignation at Bishop Burnet's *History of His Own Time* would also later attest. Tories attacked whig facts and interpretations, to be sure, but they also attributed whig historical errors to a casting problem: whig churchmen were unfit to be historians of England. In fact the same strains of clerical historiography that marred Echard's general history prevented Kennett's *History* from conforming to neoclassical protocols: the antiquarianism, the partisanship, the documents, the faulty narrative. Kennett produced a confused jumble of obituary notices, disconnected ecclesiastical information, and polemic. More than one third of the work consisted of someone else's words, quoted by Kennett. He so rarely witnessed important events that he gave too much weight to those events he actually did know firsthand. Kennett became so involved in his account of the Convocation Controversy, to which the very history he was writing made a direct contribution, that he barely mentioned the death of King William.[8]

Kennett failed to elevate the events of the Convocation Controversy to the status of worthy deeds or to describe them with the eloquence of a noble historian. The Controversy produced no Paolo Sarpi, no quasi-classical revelation of ecclesiastical hypocrisy and politicking. Convocation had few pretensions that it was concerned with anything other than simple churchmanship; it lacked the Council of Trent's solemn agenda for general reform of the universal church. Moreover, its proceedings were already highly publicized. Open scandal and petty bickering, not Tacitean exposure of secret dealings, put Convocation in disrepute and helped bring about its collapse in 1717. To contemporaries it was instead the wars of William's and Anne's reigns, the War of the League of Augsburg (1689–97) and the War of Spanish Succession (1702–13), that assumed the appearance of a monumental struggle of classical proportions, a heroic defense of English liberty and Protestantism against Louis XIV's expansionist universal monarchy of absolutism and popery. 'There is hardly any Century in History which began by opening so great a Scene, as the Century wherein we live,' Bolingbroke told Alexander Pope. 'This War foreseen for above half a Century had been during all that time the great and constant object of the councils of Europe. The prize ... was the richest that ever had been Stak'd since those of the Persian and Roman Empires.'[9] And yet it was not Bolingbroke, the Secretary of State who negotiated the end of the War of Spanish Succession, nor the Duke of Marlborough, the General who fought it, but Jonathan Swift, a clergyman who wrote propaganda about it, who first attempted to record that great war for posterity's sake. In 1712 and 1713 Swift wrote *The History of the Four Last Years of the Queen*, although for various reasons this work would not do for the tory ministers of Anne's reign what Clarendon had done for moderate royalists of Charles I's – vindicate and immortalize them in a Thucydidean history.[10]

The *History*, on which Swift would expend more effort than anything except *Gulliver's Travels*,[11] was born as a journalistic piece, begun in the summer of 1712 to convince parliament to approve the peace treaties in its autumn session. To defend the tory negotiations at Utrecht, Swift launched a two-pronged attack: one on the Dutch for their two-faced role in the settlement; another on the whigs for their unpatriotic opposition to it.[12] In a blow-by-blow account, Swift demonstrated how the Dutch had attempted to make a separate peace with France.[13] He also drew the characters of leading whigs so as to reveal their vengefulness, dissimulation, and ambition,[14] then argued that as officeholders they had never acted like true Englishmen but like Dutchmen. When William of Orange took possession of the English throne, it was none other than the tories' bogeyman Gilbert Burnet, landing with William at Torbay, who foisted Dutch schemes of government on England, including the establishment of a national debt to pay for William's wars. Whigs exploited the debt to line their own pockets, impoverish the landed gentry, and promote their own narrow faction. This polemic against the moneyed men allowed Swift to show readers the true colors of the party opposing Utrecht, and to praise Harley and the tories, supported by the people and the church, for heroically stemming the tide of whig corruption.[15] Swift concluded his *History* on a triumphant note. Against all odds and whig subversion especially,

> [t]he firm, steady Conduct of the Queen, the Wisdom and Courage of her Ministry, and the Abilities of those whom she employed in her Negociations abroad, prevailed to have a Peace signed in One Day by every Power concerned, except that of the Emperour, and the Empire.[16]

This was a partisan tract, not a work of neoclassical historiography. A single, slim volume, the *History* was written in a matter of months for immediate use as propaganda, while Clarendon's massive volumes took years to compose and he scrupulously rejected proposals to publish them for such a propose. Living before the age of party, and in circumstances very different from Swift's, Clarendon had written with much greater equanimity. The main point of similarity between the two historians was their common interest in contemporary high politics and in drawing character sketches. In these portraits, however, Swift was less generous to his adversaries than Clarendon had been to his. Swift admitted that 'in an Age like ours I can expect very few impartial Readers.'[17] His readers in effect replied that Swift could scarcely call himself an impartial writer. One called Swift a 'pseudo historian,' a 'biassed party-[writer]' who had libelled Marlborough and whitewashed Oxford.[18] *The Monthly Review* called Swift's book 'an Apology,' and concluded 'a good Apology may be bad History.'[19] Even Swift's friends begged him not to publish the work. Bolingbroke wrote to the 5th Earl of Orrery that he 'thought Swift's Pamphlet unfit to be published for a history.'[20] Orrery decided 'The title of an history is too pompous for such a performance. In the historical style, it wants dignity, and candour: but as a pamphlet, it will appear the best defence of Lord Oxford's administration.'[21] Horace Walpole informed Horace Mann, 'Pope and Bolingbroke always told [Swift] it would disgrace him, and persuaded him to burn it. Disgrace him indeed it does, being a weak libel, ill-written for style, uninformed, and adopting the most errant mob stories.'[22] Most notoriously, Swift swallowed whole a story about Prince Eugene attempting to murder the Earl of Oxford. According to Lord Chesterfield, the author of *Gulliver's Travels* had learned the hard way that writing history was different from writing political journalism and satire:

> As for the History, it will not be half so good a one as that of Lilliput and Brobdingnag, for, to tell you the truth, it is only a compilation of party pamphlets. I have good authority for what I now say, for Lord Bolingbroke, who had seen the original manuscript, told me that it consisted chiefly of the lies of the day, which they had in seeming confidence communicated to the Dean to write *Examiners* and party pamphlets upon, and which the Dean took as authentic materials for history.[23]

If Swift's immersion in party politics prevented the content of the *History* from being polite or even accurate, print culture militated against his construction of an undulating narrative. When Clarendon chronicled a paper war, a battle for public opinion conducted in print, he transcribed documents into his *History* as modern noble deeds, and in so doing marred his narrative and strayed from classical models. Swift likewise made the decision to interrupt his story with documentation.[24] He inserted the 'Representation' to the queen written in 1712 by Swift himself and by Sir Thomas Hanmer.[25] Like Clarendon before him, Swift the drafter of political documents played a sufficiently important role, as propagandist, in the events he described that as a historian he felt justified in reprinting those same documents in the *History*. Before breaking up his story with this digression, which represented 8 per cent of the entire *History*, Swift apologized to his readers:

> I did intend for Brevity sake, to have given the Reader only an Abstract of it, but upon Tryal found myself unequal to such a Task, without injuring so excellent a Piece. And although I think Historical Relations are but ill patched up with long Transcripts already Printed, which upon that account I have hitherto avoided; yet this being the Summ of all Debates and Resolutions of the House of Commons in that great Affair of the War; I conceived it could not well be omitted.[26]

Regardless of Swift's obvious delight in praising and then reprinting his own words, it is clear that he recognized excessive documentation as a common failing in historiography but nonetheless succumbed to the temptation to print a document, to 'injure' his 'Historical Relation' in order to preserve the 'Representation' intact. He reasoned that the 'Representation' 'will be a very useful authentik Record for the Assistance of those who at any time shall undertake to write the History of the present Times.'[27] Arguing in this way, Swift momentarily forgot that *he* was writing the history of his own times, not deferring that task to a greater, future historian using Swift's collection of documents. Like the clerical general historians, an exasperated Swift was backing away from the title of historian and taking on the role of collector.

Obviously, the best candidates for imitating Clarendon and Thucydides were retired warriors or statesmen, yet Bolingbroke, Oxford, and Marlborough did not write such a history, leaving the way open for lesser figures to write it. Just as Swift was not very qualified to write a Livian general history,[28] so was he even less well-suited to the more demanding Thucydidean role. In the *History* Swift boasted about his access to sources and to great men, having 'been daily conversant with the persons then in power; never absent in times of business or conversation, until a few weeks before her Majesty's death; and a witness of almost every step they made in the course of their administration.'[29] Swift did indeed enjoy an interesting vantage point on events, though he was never an independent player in them, only a creature of his patrons, never their social or political equal. He lacked the clout of Clarendon or Thucydides to coax the best historical sources from their owners, even from his own patron, Oxford, who refused to accede to Swift's requests for materials. Swift apparently wrote the *History* in order to get a plum position in the church from Oxford, whom Swift made the volume's hero.[30] The *History* might also have figured in Swift's jockeying for the post of historiographer royal.[31] However, these coveted English posts fell through, so Swift put the *History* in moth balls and settled for the deanery of St Patrick's, Dublin. From his exile in Ireland, Swift urged Bolingbroke to write the history of his own times. Swift had

> been some time providing materials for such a work, only upon
> the strength of having been always amongst you, and used

with more kindness and confidence, that it often happens to men of my trade and level.... But I am sensible that when Caesar describes one of his own battles we conceive a greater idea of him from thence, than from all the praises any other writer can give him.[32]

Notwithstanding Swift's good-natured flattery and self-effacement, it seems clear Swift understood how inferior his qualifications for the Thucydidean role were compared with those of his friend. *The Monthly Review* confirmed this perception in a review of Swift's *History*, lamenting that in 1758 most historians were as unqualified for writing history and as uninformed about state secrets as Swift had shown himself to be 45 years earlier.[33]

As the examples of Swift and Kennett showed, the issue of the historians's role was at the heart of the weakness in English historiography. Contemporaries discussed the matter openly, just as Clarendon had in an earlier generation and in much the same terms. Thomas Sprat had once seen the Civil War as an event of classical proportions requiring a noble historian equal to it, and now Swift's contemporaries looked to the English Caesar, the Duke of Marlborough, to write the history of his own times. '[I]t is the Opinion of some good Judges,' Henry Felton observed, 'that if the Duke of Marlborough would give us his own Memoirs, we should find he could Write, as well as Fight, like Caesar.'[34] Sanguine as some commentators were, others could understand why histories, or even memoirs, were not easily forthcoming. '[L]et it be considered,' reflected Abel Boyer, a Huguenot man of letters living in London, 'how few Favourites, Statesmen, or Commanders, though perhaps excellent in their respective Stations and Capacities, are yet either able, or willing to write:' often they suffered from 'supine Indolence,' lack of leisure, or fear of giving offense. Like Swift, Boyer accepted the classical injunction that the 'great' man ought to write contemporary history, but since no such man was writing it, Boyer felt justified stepping into the breach to do it himself. He had already done prodigious research, compiling printed sources in his *Annals of the Reign of Queen Anne* (1703–13). He had spoken with military men about the war. He had 'liv'd many years in, or on the Skirts of the Court' where he learned 'the Causes of Great Events; the Springs of Political Machines . . .; the Rise and Fall of Favourites and Ministers.' But what for the first time gave an outsider like Boyer the opportunity of writing Thucydidean history was a constitutional shift in power. The causes of great events, argued Boyer, now lay increasingly in parliament, not the court, and parliament was now allowing Boyer access to its proceedings. The making of history was, then, a little more public,[35] not simply the result of backroom intrigue.

Parliament protected its own privacy and freedom of debate, originally from the crown but more and more from the public out-of-doors. In the early eighteenth century the House of Lords forbade publication of accounts of any aspect of its proceedings; the Commons permitted official reports of its votes to be published but not its debates. Boyer made one of the earliest and most successful attempts to defy these parliamentary standing orders, by publishing from 1703 to 1729 a monthly, *The Political State of Great Britain*, which contained accounts of proceedings in both houses. He justified his activity by calling it history rather than news and by postponing publication until each session's end. However, his reports, patched together from the testimony of house messengers and doorkeepers, were thin. Successive periodicals in the 1730s, '40s, and '50s made some improvements in collecting information, but Samuel Johnson's reworking of a few precious notes into parliamentary speeches was hardly the stuff of noble history.[36] 'Invented' speeches of this sort, even the kind found in classical histories, were out of vogue among many critics.

Boyer and Swift numbered among the first journalists on the fringes of power to claim they possessed an adequate standpoint for writing contemporary history. As they readily admitted, however, the only circumstance allowing them to make this gambit was what amounted to a crisis in Thucydidean historiography, the failure of great men to write the history of their own times. Boyer and Swift were not even native Englishmen, and the first half of the eighteenth century witnessed many other foreign-born, politically inexperienced men of modest social origins writing English history, to the embarrassment of the English elite. In Swift's analysis, 'One reason why we have so few memoirs written by principal actors, is because much familiarity with great affairs makes men value them too little; yet such persons will read Tacitus and Commines with wonderful delight.' And when great men finally did pick up their pen, Swift noticed, they wrote memoirs instead of histories out of 'laziness, pride, or incapacity.' It was easier to write about oneself than to do research into the deeper causes of events and supply the contexts that made history intelligible to non-participants. Sheer exhaustion after a strenuous public career commonly led to selfish neglect of higher duty, as Alexander Pope told Swift:

> age, indolence, and contempt of the world grow upon men apace, and may often make the wisest indifferent whether posterity be any wiser than we. To a man in years, Health and Quiet become such rarities, and consequently so valuable, that he is apt to think of nothing more than of enjoying them whenever he can, for the remainder of life; and this I doubt not has caus'd so many great men to die without leaving a scrap to posterity.[37]

For statesmen, episodes of enforced leisure were becoming increasingly rare. They still might land in the Tower but were usually able to rehabilitate themselves and live to fight again. Walpole's confinement there in 1712 was easy and allowed him to play at whig martyr. The 1st Earl of Oxford was so lethargic at the end of his administration that there was little expectation he would use official retirement to inaugurate a project requiring Clarendonian application. His confinement for three years in the Tower produced no history of his own times. He continued amassing his princely collection of books and manuscripts. His colleagues and rivals, their health broken, could not supply a history either. The climb up the greasy pole proved mortal or at least debilitating to them. Rochester died suddenly in 1711, after a brief return to favor. Godolphin was already ill when forced into retirement in 1710. He died in 1712. Marlborough suffered from exhaustion as early as 1711. In 1716 he suffered the first of a series of strokes that was, by 1722, to kill him. Shrewsbury also suffered from poor health, although he made no excuses for refusing to employ his time in public life to become a great man or his time in retirement to become a historian. Like William Temple before him, he showed little remorse for breaking the convention of political culture that required public service of the socially elevated. Failing health plagued Somers' last four years. He was a patron of the arts, a proponent of politeness, a classicist, but too taken with politics to retire in 1710, instead opting for the role of grand old man of the whig party, in which role, in

1716, he died.[38] Thus did the great men of the kingdom miss several opportunities to write the history of their own times.

ROGER NORTH AND FAMILY HISTORY

Roger North (1653–1734) never achieved political greatness because political defeats led him to reject public life altogether, and he found private life and the writing of family history more satisfying than a political career or the composition of public history. His example shows in more detail than the instances just mentioned how and why the would-be historian might fall by the wayside. North was a tory lawyer who had assisted in the prosecution of the whig martyr Algernon Sidney. In 1686 he was made Attorney-General to the queen and a member of her council. North became disillusioned with what he took to be James II's imprudent and illegal Catholic initiatives in the government. He accepted William and Mary as temporary regents, but as a nonjuror he refused to swear allegiance to the new regime or to recognize William and Mary as *de facto* sovereigns. Sickened by public life, and the revenge whigs exacted on his family after 1689, he chose the political wilderness. At first he suffered pangs of guilt for having quit public life and he tried finding solace in classical role models such as Cicero, who had maintained his dignity while in exile. North then discovered that he could compensate for declining political responsibilities by performing worthy deeds of a more private nature. By 1691, with the deaths of his brothers, he alone headed the North family and so he raised nieces and nephews and solved their legal and financial difficulties. He bought an estate, rebuilt it, and laid out gardens, collected paintings and books, conducted agricultural experiments, founded a library, and made an antiquarian study of the village church. He continued to study law, which for him meant the history of law, especially legal etymology.[39]

North's life as a political retiree showed the diversity of serious leisure activities available to men of his class. In the 1700s he found further worthy occupation in the writing of family history, a genre that shared much common ground with Thucydidean history. Tacitus, after all, had composed not only *Annals* and *Histories* but also *Agricola*, a biography of his father-in-law. Like neoclassical history, family history had a moral purpose. 'Family histories, like the *imagines majorum* of the Ancients,' James Boswell declared, 'excite to virtue.' The *topos* ran: we praise illustrious men to reward them for well-lived lives and to instruct their descendants, 'since examples move more than precepts,' as Thomas Carte put it. North explained:

> It was [my three brothers'] good fortune to be surrounded with kindred of the greatest estimation and value, which are a sort of obligation to good behaviour. It is very unfortunate for anyone to stray from the paths of virtue who hath such precautions and sonorous momentoes on all sides of him; and it is almost enough to be educated in a family wherein was no instance of irreligion or immorality . . . [Although there is] no peculiar intrinsic worth, in a particular person, derivable from the honour of his family, because his own value and not his ancestors' must set him off . . . yet there is some good comes from it, which is that the descendants must know that the world expects more from them than from common men, and such a perpetual monitor is an useful companion.[40]

This ancestral monitory companion provided by family history also allowed men to pay debts of honor to deceased kindred, and so offered an acceptable option to those perhaps qualified for writing Thucydidean history but choosing not to do so.

The aristocratic family, the Norths included, provided a fundamental context for Thucydidean history. A neoclassical history of one's own times was written by the member of a great family, written on the subject of other political families (including his own), and written for the benefit of those families, who constituted the elite audience capable of profiting from history's political edification. Since ancestors were the subject of history, descendants often led the way as critics of historical works, trying to set the record straight in pamphlets or even books of their own.[41] The impulse to commemorate and moralize about a family member might find an outlet in Thucydidean history or in the more intimate form of family memoir. North's writings on family history, for example, were born of a desire to vindicate his family name. Kennett and Echard had either misrepresented his brothers or ignored them completely, consigning them to oblivion. From the turn of the century until about 1720, North responded by writing biographies of his brothers Dudley, John, and Francis.

He lashed out against Kennett both with a pamphlet and with the gargantuan *Examen, or an enquiry into the credit and veracity of a pretended complete history.*[42] To North the genre of history had been tainted by whig party writers. North sneered at Echard, the 'late double-column'd Historian in folio.' He ridiculed the 'solemn' and 'pompous' performances of both Kennett and Echard, marveling at their presumption in foisting 'such mighty Works' on the public. Their history wasted the time of the few readers who could afford to buy it.[43] How different their work was from that of the ancient historians, whom North revered and even praised for their invented speeches, and exemplary moderns such as Davila, Commynes, and Clarendon.[44]

In the event, North's links to nonjuring antiquarians such as George Hickes, whose idea it was to write the *Examen,*[45] proved more important to North than his admiration for the high tory neoclassicism of Clarendon's *History*. Disgusted by politics and by formal historians, he decided to attack the very foundations of neoclassical historiography, questioning its polite style, its elite subject matter and audience. North's historical writings were conversational in tone, and he even reproduced the idiosyncratic speech pattern of Lord Sunderland rather than polish him up. North boasted that his own style was 'not polite,' and in the Battle of the Books he took the side of the antiquarians against the men of Christ Church, the 'semi-wits,' as he described them.[46] North denied that 'low history,' the history of private as opposed to public persons, was 'contemptible,' or that 'all actors and events must be of the first magnitude, to rouse the attention and compensate the time' of the reader. After all, Thucydides' repute as a historian was saved only by his 'invincible art and eloquence,' since his subject was a mere feud between two cities not affecting 'the revolution of vaster powers.' Human wisdom was not confined to the lessons learned from 'political cabals, wars, and butcherly sieges,' the essence of 'state history.' Private men received as little instruction from the so-called glories of history as from 'romance.'

[A]re not common men placed as widely distant from the state of kings, generals, or any species of demagogues, and as unfit to conform their actions to any of them, as young men are from the chimeric exploits of knights and giants, or to act and fight as they are represented to do? . . . There is no subdivision of humankind, be it so low as soldiers, pedlars, gypsies, and tinkers, but their actions and behaviour, well related, would be a capital learning to men of the same condition and not amiss to those of a better, nay of the best, education, and highest employment.[47]

So North wrote the history of private life, which was not, properly speaking, history but biography. He admitted that 'this great work,' the life of his brother Francis, 'I would have understood to be rather Instructions, than History.' He believed that by such works one could improve one's conversation, manners, and performance in whatever station in life one found oneself. Knowledge of these things was 'but a tradition or private history of a man's own gathering' enhanced by private histories of persons of similar station. The 'trivial' and 'light Passages' in a person's experience, though not appropriate in a state history, belonged in this kind of work, since the entire truth of an exemplary life had to be given, all the contexts for actions, not just a patchwork of the most virtuous and vicious actions.[48]

In thus criticizing history's narrow focus on public deeds, North's arguments anticipated those used by Henry Fielding to justify the fledgling genre of the novel. Novelists tried distancing themselves from the romance tradition by borrowing titles from more honorable literary forms with classical pedigrees. Novels were commonly 'Adventures' or 'Travels,' later 'Memoirs' or 'Lives,' and finally, in the 1740s and 1750s, 'Histories.'[49] However much novels might resemble histories or memoirs, and incorporate some rather factual episodes, they were still fictional, still fatally tied to romance in the public's mind. Fielding nonetheless marketed his 'private histories' as more relevant to the lives of ordinary readers who had never acted in the political sphere, the realm of neoclassical history. Undeterred by classical prohibitions against ignoble, common subject matter, Fielding argued that his 'histories' gave a full, detailed, and thus superior picture of ethical life. In *Joseph Andrews* (1742) and *Tom Jones* (1749), Fielding claimed that public history was so disreputable and truth so ill-served that his own invented stories rang truer with human experience, provided more authoritative moral instruction.[50] The collapse of public history, the weakness in English historiography, permitted Fielding to promote the novel as an alternative source of moral education and North to refine the art of family biography. Out of disgust with recent essays at aristocratic, 'high' history, North, a tory aristocrat, had turned, ironically, to 'low,' popular history and biography.

Noble history suffered a decline during North's lifetime in part because of the distribution structure for histories of one's own times. North's works shared the common fate of contemporary histories when they were manhandled by a posthumous editor. His son Montagu severely abridged his father's biographies, making them less controversial politically, less personal, and more polite.[51] Clarendon, Burnet, Bolingbroke, Swift, Temple, Whitelocke, and Ludlow also fell victim to editors who either altered, criticized, or prematurely published their texts.[52] These writers often had little choice but to publish posthumously, entrusting their politically sensitive texts to family members or friends for future dissemination. During the sometimes lengthy interval between the composition of a history and its publication, editorial high jinks could result in a corrupted text, placing yet another doubt in the reader's mind about the historian's truthfulness. 'Were these even the historian's own words?' the reader was now accustomed to asking. In fact, one of the most effective ways to discredit a history was to charge the editors with fiddling the text, a ploy used to attack both Clarendon's *History of the Rebellion* and Burnet's *History of His Own Time*.[53] For North, as for Burnet and Clarendon, the family had in some sense betrayed its trust as keeper of literary heirlooms, further damaging the standing of history.

WHIG PROVOCATEUR: BISHOP BURNET

Bishop Burnet died in 1715, bequeathing to his sons a work of contemporary history so explosive that they only published it in 1723 and 1734, and even then reluctantly.[54] Bolingbroke's circle found it just as offensive as North had found the work of Kennett and Echard. Gilbert Burnet was a Scottish clergyman who, by virtue of his *History of the Reformation*, had already succeeded as an ecclesiastical historian. He did not come to national political prominence until the Glorious Revolution, when he served as ecclesiastical advisor to William of Orange. But five years before, as early as 1683, Burnet had begun writing the history of his own times. Originally it was an autobiography, but the publication of Clarendon's exemplary *History* changed his design. Like many whigs, Burnet admired Clarendon as a man and his *History* as art, while disagreeing with his politics. Burnet's own literary ambition and narrative, by comparison with Clarendon's, appeared to be so weak that he was inspired to recast his autobiography into a proper history.[55] An establishment work, Burnet's *History of His Own Time* implored readers 'to form just reflections, and sound principles of religion and virtue, of duty to our princes, and of love to our country, with a sincere and incorruptible zeal to preserve our religion, and to maintain our liberty and property.'[56] It was the new whig, Hanoverian establishment to which he hoped to draw adherents, not the tory, Stuart one that had passed away in 1714. Burnet denounced the Treaty of Utrecht and blamed Queen Anne's caprice for the change of ministry that brought it about.

Burnet's account of the period 1710 to 1713 and, indeed, of the Civil War and Restoration, infuriated a circle of high tories effectively proscribed by a smoothly running political machine tended by Sir Robert Walpole. To dignify retreat and justify political opposition to Walpole, this coterie found inspiration in the golden age of Queen Anne's last four years. One of its replies was Bolingbroke's projected history of his own times, which, Bolingbroke promised, 'should be able to convey severall great Truths to Posterity, so clearly and so Authentically, that the Burnets and the Oldmixons of another Age, might rail, but should not be able to deceive.'[57] The audacious whig publicist John Oldmixon not only compared Burnet to Thucydides but also attacked the tories' Thucydides, Clarendon, questioning his accuracy and alleging that parts of the *History*, including 'Mr. Hambden's' character, had been forged by Atterbury and other Christ Church editors. Tory rebuttals asserted that Atterbury had never even seen the *History* in manuscript, that it was to Clarendon's 'moderate counsels [that] we owe chiefly the preservation of our civil and religious establishments,' and that Oldmixon had himself, 20 years before, defiled Samuel Daniel's contribution to the *Complete History of England.*[58]

Some readers joined Oldmixon in fulsome praise of Burnet, comparing him to Polybius and Commynes. However, others censured Burnet severely.[59] William Stratford, Canon of Christ Church, wrote of volume one:

It is a strange rhapsody of chit-chat and lies, ill tacked together. There is a strong tang of enthusiasm in all accounts he gives of himself. It is plain that in most things he was very ignorant, and very silent in those of which he could have given the best [account] . . .[60]

Swift exploded in a torrent of abuse:

This author is in most particulars the worst qualified for an historian that ever I met with. His style is rough, full of improprieties, in expressions often Scotch . . . His observations are mean and trite, and very often false. His Secret History is generally made up of coffee-house scandals, or at best from reports at the third, fourth, or fifth hand. The account of the Pretender's birth, would only become an old woman in a chimney-corner. His vanity runs intolerably through the whole book, affecting to have been of consequence at nineteen years old, and while he was a little Scotch parson of 40 pounds a year. . . . This work may be properly called, A History of Scotland during the author's time, with some digressions relating to England . . . two thirds . . . relate only to that beggarly nation, and their insignificant brangles and factions. . . . [H]e was a man of generosity and good-nature, and very communicative; but, in his last ten years, was absolute party-mad . . .[61]

Burnet's partisanship, self-importance, poor sources, and unseemly language stemmed from his obscure and Scottish origins, according to Swift. For a whole litany of reasons, political, social, nationalistic, and aesthetic, Burnet was not qualified for the role of noble historian. Nor was Swift himself qualified, as we have already seen.

Swift had many self-interested, political reasons for indicting Burnet, but disinterested critics had to agree that by the neoclassical protocols of the day, Burnet cut a poor figure as a historian. Adam Smith and Hugh Blair, lecturing on the ancient historians in the 1760s, generally concurred with Swift's estimation of Burnet. Scots themselves, and far removed from the partisanship of opposition politics in the 1720s and '30s, they had less reason to belittle Burnet on political or nationalistic grounds. Blair said:

Bishop Burnet is lively and perspicuous; but he has hardly any other historical merit. His style is too careless and familiar for History; his characters are, indeed, marked with a bold and a strong hand; but they are generally light and satirical; and he abounds so much in little stories concerning himself, that he resembles more a Writer of Memoirs than of History.[62]

Smith argued:

His business plainly appears to have been to set the one party in as black a light as he could and justify the other, so that he is to be considered rather as party writer than as a candid historian. His manner is lively and spirited, his Stile very plain, but his language and expression is low and such as we would expect from an old nurse rather than from a gentleman.[63]

Today's scholars may value Burnet's *History* as a historical source, and find its use of vivid, personal details appealing, but Burnet's partisanship, literary awkwardness, and clerical style showed he could not overcome the common pitfalls of contemporary historiography. Burnet's exaggerated sense of importance led him away from public events to personal details of his own life and family. He tipped his hand by describing his own role in events in the first person rather than the third, as a mere memoirist rather than a noble historian would do. His overriding desire to settle political scores and make his peace with God proved to be more important to Burnet than adhering to literary conventions. With a clerical air reminiscent of his *History of the Reformation*, with prayerful addresses to God, pious introspection, superintending providence, and pastoral advice preached as a 'dying speech,' *The History of His Own Time* read like a bishop's spiritual memoir,[64] as indeed it was, in part. Trying to dress up his style in imitation of Clarendon, trying as he had most of his life to gain acceptance from the English elite, Burnet overreached himself. The *History* had some pretensions to noble history on account of its focus on high politics, its construction of characters, its claim that history should describe the truth for the instruction of posterity. However, when readers judged it by the last and only great English history of one's own times, one which covered some of the same ground, they concluded that Burnet's *History* was no match for Clarendon's.[65] Like Clarendon, Burnet took three decades to finish his work, writing history while not making it, alternating between retirement and public service, but Burnet was not suited for the Thucydidean role. He was a key figure in the Glorious Revolution but not in a position to describe authoritatively the politics of preceding and succeeding decades. Debts to superiors limited his freedom to collect materials and to tell the truth: his revisions of the *History* confess as much and explain his less critical treatments of William and Marlborough. At many points Burnet came across as a busybody proffering unwanted advice to higher-ups.[66] He admitted being unqualified to narrate civil history, when he acknowledged omitting martial and foreign affairs because he lacked 'the opportunities that [his sometime model de Thou's higher] station gave him of being informed of these things.' On occasion he skipped over military battles. 'I will not enter farther into the military part: for I remember an advice of Marshal Schomberg's never to meddle in the relation of military matters,' Burnet told readers. In another instance, he explained, 'I will not enter into the particulars of that day's action, but leave that to military men.' Burnet conceded he 'had declared much against clergymen meddling in secular affairs,' but he justified his own political participation by his 'love to my country, and my private friendships,' and his 'hopes of reforming the world, and of making mankind wiser and better.'[67]

To Bolingbroke's circle these high-sounding motives were misdirected. While high tories hoped for a return of the old partnership of church and state, they had no place for clerical pests like Burnet. Bad history, like good, was not produced in a vacuum, according to Bolingbroke's program of political opposition, which was a social and aesthetic program, not just political in some narrow sense. Bolingbroke argued that his coalition of tories and disaffected whigs was incorruptible because its members owned land, which nourished their political independence and civic capacity. Walpole's court whigs, on the other hand, were disqualified from political leadership by their all-consuming, self-interested professionalism, which left them unable to perceive the general good. Professional politicians, professional financiers, professional writers, they were specialists, not citizens. Walpole's men lacked the social standing, public experience, and humanist sensibility that came with membership in the landed elite and that might have made them competent for statesmanship. To Bolingbroke, therefore, Burnet, the upstart Scottish cleric, represented much that was wrong with modern political culture. Who was he, unfit for public service in the first place, to take it upon himself to preserve and glorify for all time the great public events of his generation? And what of the new 'Great Man,' Walpole? He was an assured, self-made man, an administrative genius, coarse and vulgar, possessing an exquisite eye for the visual arts but little interest in literature. He patronized hacks.[68]

OPPOSITION POLITICS AND HISTORY

Of course, Walpole was a durable political figure; he and his so-called 'hacks' could not be taken lightly.[69] Mounting an opposition to him was particularly difficult, given that the very concept of political opposition was considered to be illegitimate at this time. Englishmen were supposed to be loyal to the crown and to the idea of the public interest. They had difficulty reconciling their own integrity with a political enterprise that appeared to represent only a partial, not the national, good.[70] A press campaign would have to win them over, if seasoned politicians in the opposition to Walpole were ever to regain the reins of power they had held in Anne's time. One reason why opposition politicians were especially sensitive to literary transgressions such as Burnet's was that literature was one of the few weapons they had to fight Walpole. They did not have the political patronage or parliamentary votes necessary to upend Walpole. Instead they relied on the considerable power of their pens and the printing press to broadcast journalism, poems, essays, and plays of political defiance. Literary projects and private letters helped to preserve their identity as a group. With Bolingbroke, Ormonde, and Atterbury variously exiled, Swift in Dublin, and Pope secluded at Twickenham, epistles became a necessary means of sustaining morale, one of the few means left to them for participation in civic life.[71] Biding their time, preparing for future power, Bolingbroke's circle of politicians and writers came to look upon the polite genius of the humanist literary inheritance as their own special preserve. The Christ Church distribution network, which had handled Clarendon's *History*, now provided a source of identity to the politically excluded by supporting likeminded literary projects. Oxford's cultural gifts and contacts provided an important component of tory survival between 1714 and 1760.[72]

After the accession of George II in 1727, desperation set in. Tories had once pinned hopes of renewed influence on the new king, but he turned out to dislike them even more than his father had. In response to this dynastic disappointment, Bolingbroke used a French pension to underwrite opposition propaganda and contemplated crowning his career of treasons by replaying the jacobite card. The scions of eminent cavalier families such as the Hydes, Wentworths, and Butlers also had a part to play in opposition politics. In the early 1730s young Lord Cornbury, Clarendon's great-grandson, MP for Oxford University, and new to the treason game, negotiated with Louis XV and the Pretender over the number of French troops that would invade England, and the sorts of peerages that would be dispensed to reward cooperative opposition politicians. For Bolingbroke's circle, therefore, the tory connection to the Hydes and to Christ Church remained strong. Most members of the clique had either attended Christ Church, received honorary doctorates there, or at least considered themselves to be honorary members of the college. They united to defend the honor of the House and its Dean, Atterbury, when Oldmixon impugned the college's editorial work on Clarendon's *History*.[73] Bolingbroke's circle continued to draw strength from the association with Clarendon, whose *History* set forth exemplars of socially and morally upright Englishmen administering government before whigs corrupted the political, economic, and artistic order. In Clarendon they also had a role model, a great and good man beset by evil men, an outcast who dignified exile by writing neoclassical history, a political loser who made a return to power. Might not Bolingbroke and his associates also revisit their former glory? Clarendon's selection of genre certainly seemed appropriate to them, an elite genre the classicality of which meshed with their own humanist literary campaign against the hacks. Clarendon's *History* inspired them to build an immortal neoclassical monument of their own. The Thucydidean genre and role, therefore, not simply the 'history' in the *History of the Rebellion*, the bare discursive content, were what they wished to borrow from Clarendon.

English soil was ripe for an imitation of Clarendon. Here was a set of accomplished, classically educated men who had once been the makers of great events but were now out of power, in need of justification, and with time on their hands. Burnet and Oldmixon provided sufficient provocation, and Clarendon's example reassured them it was possible to do. Atterbury, exiled for his part in the jacobite plot of 1720–2, was an early candidate. Canon Stratford refused to believe rumors Atterbury was writing a history of his own times. Noticing how the genre had suffered at Burnet's hands, he dismissed the project: 'It is now given out that [Atterbury] is retired and writing a history of his own times that is to come out after his death. I believe not a word of this, if there should be any such thing, it will just be of as much credit as old Gibby [Burnet]'s.'[74] The church was important enough to national politics that leaders such as Burnet and Atterbury might qualify as 'noble' men insofar as bishops sat in the House of Lords. Yet many bishops had risen through the ranks by writing polemical works of ecclesiastical history and antiquarianism, modes of discourse antithetical to neoclassical historiography. And as Burnet's compunctions about his worldly political career suggested, to play the part of Thucydides was to masquerade in a layman's role. In his case, Atterbury spent his ostensible retirement from 1716 until his death in 1732 praying, doing pastoral work for other exiles, reading the classics, involving himself in French politics, and directing jacobite activities. According to his biographer, he worked on the synoptic gospels to make amends for an unpriestly political career which he feared might tarnish the church's reputation. Defensive about that career, he wrote to friends saying it was not so, disingenuously protesting to Pope, for example:

> I like you, as I like myself, best, when we have both of us least Buysness. It has been my Fate to be engag'd in it much; and often; by the Stations in which I was plac'd: but God that knows my heart, knows, I never Lov'd it, and am still less in Love with it than ever, as I find less Temptation to Act with any hope of Success.[75]

Atterbury's theory of retirement echoed Clarendon's. He rejected extremes of monkish isolation and worldliness, choosing rather the middle way, Christ's example, 'a Mixture of Contemplation and Action' that allowed voluntary retreat to enhance public attainments. Pope likened Atterbury's plight and opportunity to those of the historians Bacon and Clarendon and the virtuous orator Cicero:

You may more eminently and more effectually serve the Publick, even now, than in the Stations you have so honourably fill'd. Think of Tully, Bacon, and Clarendon; is not the latter, the most disgraced part of their lives, what you must envy, and which you would choose to have lived?

Instead of writing a neoclassical history, which his ordination inhibited, Atterbury's task was to defend his cause at his treason trial in 1723, where, Pope urged him, 'the instruments of your fame to Posterity will be in your own hands.'[76] Pope's arguments mirrored those he and Swift used to prod other associates to write the history of their own times. Posterity, edification, vindication, nobility, eloquence: these were the terms of both Thucydidean history and the law court. The righteous indignation Atterbury might have invested in writing history was instead consumed in legal oratory.

Pope later turned to Charles Mordaunt, 3rd Earl of Peterborough, the next in a series of would-be historians. A *bona fide* candidate for the role of Thucydides, the captor of Barcelona in 1705, he was a tory war hero whose dying wish, in 1735, was 'to give a true account to Posterity of some Parts of History in Queen Anne's reign, which Burnet had scandalously represented; . . . to justify Her . . . [and] her Ministers Oxford & Bolingbroke.' Pope narrated the deathbed scene approvingly: Peterborough 'declaimed with great Spirit against the Meanness of the present Great men & Ministers, & the decay of Public Spirit & Honour.' However, Peterborough was less serious than his friends imagined. His only substantial literary output amounted to three volumes of facetious memoirs, which his scandalized widow burned.[77] Other historical projects also fizzled out in the 1730s. Burnet's *History* agitated the pen of another high tory, the 2nd Earl of Nottingham. Before dying in 1730, Nottingham contributed his recollections to Laurence Echard's abortive history of William III's reign. In addition, he wrote memoirs for his children's sake, although old age cut the effort short.[78] Meanwhile, Bolingbroke was dawdling with his own project, half-suggesting that his friend Lord Cornbury write the history for him. Born in the tory *annus mirabilis* 1710, Cornbury was not one of the great men of Anne's reign, but he sat in on their latter-day counsels and reminiscences. He also preserved Clarendon's papers, including the manuscript history of the years 1660–7 eventually published as Clarendon's *Life*, which

Bolingbroke urged him to use with other histories and interviews to write a history of England since the Restoration. There was a report of Cornbury working on a history,[79] but none ever appeared.

Bolingbroke remained the last best hope for writing the history of his own times. 'It is certainly from him only,' Pope wrote Swift, 'that a valuable History of Europe in these latter times can be expected. Come and quicken him. . . .'[80] Part of Swift's campaign to get Bolingbroke to take up his history involved making a last-ditch effort to publish Swift's own *History of the Four Last Years of the Queen*. Neither Bolingbroke nor Oxford had ever been very helpful in securing the state papers Swift requested for the project.[81] Bolingbroke had always counselled against publishing Swift's *History*, and Oxford's heir, the 2nd Earl, found his father's past dealings embarrassing to his own present prospects. Erasmus Lewis informed Swift that the dust had not settled sufficiently to allow for a favorable reception to the work: 'It is now too late to publish a pamphlet, and too early to publish a history.'[82] Yet Swift insisted on setting the record straight and saw how doing so might fortify the opposition to Walpole. Rather than tone down his manuscript, Swift played up its continuing political relevance in the preface he now wrote for it. There he argued Anne's ministers had been 'blasted as enemies to the present establishment, by the most ignorant and malicious among mankind,'[83] when in fact they 'bound up' the French and the Dutch 'in confirming the present succession; which was in them so much a greater mark of virtue and loyalty, because they perfectly well knew, that they should never receive the least mark of favour, when the succession had taken place.'[84] In thus defending the part played by tories in 1713 and 1714, in the peace and in the Hanoverian succession, Swift implied that the tories of the 1730s were likewise sinless, free from charges of jacobitism levelled against them by whigs. He pointed up the absolute necessity of winning the historiographical battle over Anne's reign. Before finishing this apology, Swift managed to defend the character of his model historian, Clarendon, and to scourge his counter-model, Burnet.[85] Like their politically-charged contemporary histories, Swift's was only published posthumously, in 1758, 13 years after his death, because Swift deferred to the 2nd Earl of Oxford's reservations concerning publication.[86] Swift abandoned his scheme to publish the *History* as opposition propaganda and a goad to Bolingbroke in the 1730s. As the editorial work on the histories written by Clarendon, Burnet and North showed, so the Swift-Oxford confrontation showed that the sons of deceased makers of history controlled publicity of their father's words and deeds. The heir remained gatekeeper of history. Bolingbroke, lacking an heir, would tend his own gate.

BOLINGBROKE, CLARENDON, AND THE DEATH OF THE PAST[87]

After a series of opposition poses, abortions, and missed opportunities, it became clear that Bolingbroke would have to write the opposition its history or it would never be written at all. In response to the nagging of friends, Bolingbroke worked sporadically on his history during the 1720s and '30s.[88] His most concentrated effort came in the winter of 1735–6, in self-imposed exile in France, after the tories' humiliating electoral defeat in 1734. Bolingbroke used an invitation from Cornbury for historical instruction to gather together his ruminations on the nature of ancient and modern history, and to vindicate his career. In this work, which became known as *The Letters on the Study and Use of History*, Bolingbroke did manage to present at least an extended outline of his projected history of his own times. In the seventh and eighth letters he produced a history of Europe between 1659 and 1713, a discursive narrative of the political and diplomatic maneuvering that culminated in the Treaty of Utrecht. He defended the last tory ministry and his own actions in it. He attacked whigs, past and present, for endangering the constitution of church and state, and for committing treason against blessed Queen Anne. He also discussed the current state of English historiography, reminding Cornbury of the chronic weakness of native historical writing:

> Our nation has furnished as ample and as important matter, good and bad, for history, as any nation under the sun: and yet we must yield the palm in writing history most certainly to the Italians and to the French, and I fear even to the Germans. The only two pieces of history we have, in any respect to be compared with the antient, are, the reign of Henry the seventh by my lord Bacon, and the history of our civil wars in the last century by your noble ancestor my lord chancellor

Clarendon. But we have no general history to be compared with some of other countries: neither have we, which I lament much more, particular histories, except the two I have mentioned, nor writers of memorials, nor collectors of monuments and anecdotes, to vie in number or in merit with those that foreign nations can boast; from Commines, Guicciardin, Du Bellay, Paolo, Davila, Thuanus, and a multitude of others, down through the whole period that I propose to your lordship. But altho this be true to our shame; yet it is true likewise that we want no necessary means of information. They lie open to our industry and our discernment.[89]

In 1738 he was still engaged in 'the perfection of such a work,' a history of his own, Bolingbroke told friends.[90] But in 1740, complaining about the loss, destruction, or unavailability of the requisite historical sources, he scaled down the project, confessing it was no longer 'history' he was working at but 'memorials for history' – a mishmash of memoir and historical collection.[91] Just as Swift had found Thucydidean history too difficult to do, and so retreated into the role of collector and editor of historical sources, so now did Bolingbroke do the same. In this age of erudition and party, writing an unbroken as well as impartial narrative of one's own times proved impossible even for leading proponents of neoclassical historiography such as Swift and Bolingbroke. Although Bolingbroke lived until 1751, the modest memoir contained in *The Letters on History,* along with Swift's second-rate *Four Last Years of the Queen,* was the most his circle would ever produce to counter the substantial historical works of Burnet and Oldmixon.

Bolingbroke had little excuse for abdicating his duty to write history. Clarendon also had justifiable complaints about inadequate sources, but he used the sources he possessed to compose something worthy of Bolingbroke's emulation. Nor could Bolingbroke claim to be distracted by family affairs and the need to play the part of family historian, as Roger North had been. Bolingbroke was estranged from his father, his two wives predeceased him, he had no children.[92] In fact, Bolingbroke was seemingly immune from those aspects of English modernity that had frustrated eighteenth-century pretenders to Clarendon's mantle. He was a defeated statesman with the sources and the leisure to construct a Thucydidean history. While family obligations, improper social credentials, debts to political patrons, and the attractions of erudite and antiquarian modes of clerical scholarship might excuse or explain the assorted failures of Kennett or Swift or North or Burnet as historians, none of these circumstances applied to Bolingbroke. An outspoken critic of antiquarian scholarship as incompatible with a gentleman's pursuit of state service and polite letters, Bolingbroke stood little chance of being drawn into the clerical style of modern scholarship. The ecclesiastical backbiting and partisanship of Burnet and Kennett were repulsive to him. Although he made a career for himself defending 'the church in danger,' Bolingbroke was a deist who admired the heathen historians and scoffed at Christian historiography, ancient and modern. Nor did modern political bigotry imperil his classical role-playing. Because his opposition campaign depended on convincing disaffected whigs to put party labels aside and join tories in pursuit of the common good under the reign of a 'patriot king,' he might have written a relatively impartial, polite history showing how anachronistic party ideologies were, as David Hume was to do in the 1750s. He might have employed the disinterested tone of neoclassical historiography to vindicate his career, as Clarendon had his. The assorted treasons he committed, both with the Pretender, against the Pretender, and then with the French, and his adoption of whig political principles to outflank court whigs,[93] demonstrated Bolingbroke held no narrow allegiance to his own political party or even his own country.

Political ambitions rather than political parties *per se* ruined his chances as a neoclassical historian. Bolingbroke never turned his rough draft into a full-scale history or played the part of retired statesman well, because he could not accept political defeat. Re-entering the political fray remained a possibility for him, because Bolingbroke received a second chance after his dalliance with the Pretender in 1715, a pardon, not execution. Never cut off irrevocably from politics as Clarendon had been in 1667, Bolingbroke never experienced the unforgiving exile Clarendon endured in a political culture that was more vindictive than Bolingbroke's and for that reason more conducive to playing the part of Thucydides. In the end, Bolingbroke did not want to do it, or at least could not bring himself to finish the history if that meant having to set aside political ambition. The failure to bridle his political passions, to settle down to work on his history, represented just another episode in a life of brilliant failures.

Even if he and his friends did not work assiduously at such a history, toying with the possibility, inquiring about the necessary documents, making outlines, or vowing one day to complete the project furnished immediate benefits by raising low spirits. Talking up the examples of the classical historians took little effort, came as second-nature, and acted as a balm. Even if only in a brief flight of fancy, imagining themselves as Cicero or Thucydides helped to restore self-esteem. Perhaps their failure to provide an adequate riposte to Burnet and Oldmixon should not come as a surprise. The successful composition of classical-style history, in ancient as well as modern times, took place more rarely than did events in history worthy of a place in such a work. Cicero, with whom contemporaries sometimes compared Bolingbroke as a statesman and orator, provided one signal example of failure. This best-known theorist of history in the ancient world confessed his duty to write the history of Rome, but put it off, despite his enforced leisure and the importuning of his friend Atticus.[94] In Bolingbroke's case, the loss of nerve ought to be seen in the context of other failed neoclassical literary projects. Dryden, attempting epic, had also been daunted by his classical models, had also realized he was qualified to imitate them, had also crumbled under the pressure.[95] In fact, in the predicament of abortive imitation, both Dryden and Bolingbroke responded with self-pity. In each case Swift, himself a failed historian, refused to let them off the hook. Could it be that another of Bolingbroke's prompters, Pope, pleaded all the more achingly for a Bolingbrokean history, because Pope was simultaneously renouncing his own duty to compose a neoclassical epic?

Although contemporaries had good reason to expect a Thucydidean history from Bolingbroke, they had no reason to expect one from Sir Robert Walpole, Bolingbroke's arch-rival. Poor health and a reluctance to retire prevented him from enjoying his leisure, once he fell from power in 1742. In the interval between resigning and dying in 1745, he managed to read but a single book. Literature had not been a pastime for 40 years.[96] Although he was both ridiculed and eulogized as 'the Great Man' and served for two decades as first minister, he had no great deeds to glorify. In fact there would be no neoclassical history of the Walpolean era written by Walpole or by anyone else, for that matter. As the literary critic Felton had foretold decades earlier, a 'Series of

barren Times' doomed any historical project.[97] There was nothing noble about the Excise Crisis. From 1714 the whig regime
faced no internal or external threat serious enough to call forth
words or actions of virtue or vice deserving a place in history
for all time. The '15, the South Sea Bubble, the '45 did not qualify.
Farcical and cynical politics inspired satire, not classical history
or epic. The last illustrious events of English history occurred in
the war and peace of Anne's reign, and survivors from that heroic generation were dying out. Bolingbroke's circle had missed
its chance to imitate Thucydides, and the succeeding generation,
however classically motivated it might be, failed to act on a par
with his, and so it lacked a necessary prerequisite for creating
noble history. Even when the Seven Years' War (1756–63) looked
as if it might furnish the perfect analogy with the Peloponnesian
War, casting Britain as Athens, France as Sparta, and the coloni-
zation of North America as an ill-fated Sicilian Expedition, and
might have produced its own Thucydides to describe these events,
most contemporaries were struck by the historical parallels with
Roman rather than Greek imperialism[98] and none stepped forward to play Thucydides. Once there had been calls for a neoclassical history of Anne's reign and of the Civil War,[99] because
those times were as worthy of a great historian as almost any
period in antiquity. Now there was silence. The noble history of
one's own times was obsolete in England, for the time being at
least. The flame of Thucydidean history, which Bolingbroke's circle
had lit anew out of admiration for Clarendon, died out.

Even Clarendon, the bridge between Bolingbroke and Thucydides,
was losing some of his shine. In the 1750s, the noble historian's
syntax was falling from favor, his text's authenticity was challenged,
and his autobiography was published in undignified circumstances.
The gem of the Hyde archives, Clarendon's *Life* – the continuation of the *History* covering the Lord Chancellor's administration at the Restoration plus the early and more personal parts of
Clarendon's autobiography, left over from his plundering of the
original for inclusion in the *History* – had not been published
when its owner, Cornbury, died childless in 1753. The Hydes
fought over Cornbury's estate until a manuscript *Life*, lent out
20 years before, became the basis of a pirate edition in 1758. Just
as Clarendon's *History*, in 1702, had been published for partisan
purposes, so was this unauthorized *Life* tainted by a polemical
preface. In court the Hydes succeeded in suppressing the edi-

tion, then, in 1759, they printed their own.[100] The *Life* disappointed many readers on account of its lack of new revelations, its repetition of matter already in the *History*, and its archaic style.[101]

The reputation of the *History* remained high, although Oldmixon's strictures about its syntax were increasingly repeated. Swift and, before him, Sprat, had wished to fix and purify the English language, to halt changes in syntax and vocabulary, so that writers like Clarendon deserving to be read by distant posterity would not appear unintelligible to posthumous readers. Swift asked,

> How then shall any Man who hath a Genius for History, equal to the best of the Antients, be able to undertake such a Work with Spirit and Chearfulness, when he considers, that he will be read with Pleasure but a few Years, and in an Age or two shall hardly be understood without an Interpreter?

By the mid-eighteenth century, seventeenth-century writers indeed became victims of a rapidly changing language. In 1753 Hobbes' translation of Thucydides was criticized for lacking the polish English was now capable of, 'that neatness, precision, and dignity, to which the polite and refined writers within the last century have habituated our ears.' English prose had become simpler, and the preferred historical style lacked the many parentheses and long periods typical of Clarendon. According to the 5th Earl of Orrery,

> Lord Clarendon, is an historian whose dignity of expression has justly given him the preference to any of our biographical authors. But his periods are the *periods of a mile*. His parentheses embarrass the sense of his narration, and certain inaccuracies, appearing throughout his works, are delivered with a formality that renders them still more conspicuous.[102]

In 1759 Horace Walpole came to Clarendon's defense, arguing it was only because literary style had improved so much since the time Clarendon was published that his style did not seem so impressive as it had in 1702. Walpole's correspondent, Henry Zouch, thought Clarendon superior to Polybius: 'His periods, though *the periods of a mile*, show a compass of thought and a command of style superior to any other writer, upon any subject, or in any other language I ever read.'[103]

Despite mild irritation with its style, readers praised Clarendon's *History* in many of the same terms used a half century earlier, singling out the dignity and the impartiality of the narrative, and its characters. The philosopher David Hume commended the work for its impartiality, for the 'probity and goodness' of the *History* and its author, ranking it 'among the classics of our language.' He followed the fashion in referring to Clarendon as 'the noble historian.' Although he thought Clarendon's work was far from definitive, Hume and other general historians of England did rely on Clarendon as an indispensable source for their own work, and Clarendon's authority proved sturdy enough for opponents of Hume's *History of England* to fight back with citations from him.[104] William Warburton, Bishop of Gloucester, defended Clarendon's standing as a peer of the ancient historians:

> This noble historian understood his task incomparably well. Yet has party so blinded the understanding of some who most pretend to taste, that because they dislike his political principles, they will not or cannot see, that in the knowledge of human nature (the noblest qualification of the historian) this great author excels all the Greek and Latin historians put together.[105]

But Warburton had to admit he noticed Clarendon apologizing for digressions that did not in fact appear in the printed text, which led Warburton to suspect the *History*'s manuscript had indeed been tampered with. The controversy over the *History*'s authenticity continued to simmer through the 1750s, especially since Oxford failed to produce the original manuscript for purposes of comparison. Two hundred years later, as late as 1960, Christ Church was still defending itself from the charges of textual infidelity.[106]

Although many Englishmen at mid-century still regarded Clarendon as the greatest English historian, his reputation was now a little tarnished. Indeed, the relevance of Clarendon's Thucydidean role came into doubt, as other neoclassical histories of one's own times never materialized in the wake of his great achievement. With Bolingbroke's failure to imitate Clarendon and indeed without events worthy of a noble historian, the role of Thucydides appeared to belong to another age. It remained to be seen whether Livian history had also died in the eighteenth century.

6

General History in an Age of Party

While Thucydidean history suffered a lingering death in Bolingbroke's hands, in the 1720s, '30s, and '40s, Englishmen wondered whether Livian history, too, might represent an unattainable ideal. The English party system continued to cripple histories of England, and the chance that an Englishman would write a neoclassical general history seemed ever more remote. During the second quarter of the eighteenth century the weakness in English historiography became even more acute, as prominent French men of letters such as Voltaire and Montesquieu called attention to it. Montesquieu explained it as an unexpected and unfortunate by-product of the liberty in the English constitution. Voltaire savored the irony that the best historian of England was a Frenchman, Paul Rapin de Thoyras.[1] Indeed, because native Englishmen failed to supply a general history, foreigners stepped in to write it. In this period, besides Rapin,[2] William Guthrie, a Scot, and James Ralph, an American, also tried to meet the demands for a satisfactory English history. The only native Englishmen to write general histories were the jacobite Thomas Carte and the Grub Street hack John Oldmixon. That such a motley, ill-suited collection of writers undertook to glorify the English past in the noblest prose genre seemed to suggest that something was very wrong indeed with that genre, with this political culture, or with both.

Instead of the traditional patrons of elite historical writing, church and crown, an expanding press nourished the aspirations of many of these historians. The royal court and the Church of England had endorsed the modern scholarly style with its partisanship and heavy documentation, a clerical historiography much at odds with neoclassical ideals. However, as early as the 1710s the institutional sponsors of this sort of history began to lose their grip on historical culture. Although Echard had received royal aid and Queen Caroline took an interest in Carte's work, the Hanoverian court gave less official backing to elite historical projects than the Stuarts had given. Taking the jacobite threats to their throne very seriously, George I and George II lacked the dynastic confidence to construct a cult of monarchy. They were diffident about commissioning works of propaganda or participating in elaborate royal ritual.[3] Besides, the first two Georges took a greater interest in opera than in English letters. The major, though largely unsuccessful, royal initiative in historical culture was the establishment, in 1724, of the Regius Chairs of Modern History. Sir Robert Walpole and Edmund Gibson, Bishop of London – even now we find a clergyman at the heart of court projects, as Sancroft was in the previous century – sponsored this scheme to consolidate the new dynasty and, with it, whig power. Court whigs aimed to increase the loyalty as well as the competence of public servants trained in the universities.[4] They emphasized modern history because they did not want tories, and especially jacobites, continually looking over their shoulders for precedents in the Civil War or medieval periods to disturb their hold on power. The Revolution of 1688–9 had so transformed England, according to whigs, that its prehistory mattered little for the conduct of present politics.

These modernist arguments were more likely spread by the London press of the 1730s than by the Regius Professors. Abuses crept in and, after the first few holders of the chairs, the institution languished. The whole point of the project might simply have been to counter the influence of Clarendon's *History* in the tory stronghold of Oxford. However, the *History* continued to be published there until 1732, and the Regius Professors produced no establishment history of their own. On the other hand, the university was under a growing pall since the change of dynasty in 1714 and the advent of whig rule. Enrollment declined as parents, looking ahead to whig patronage for their sons' careers, searched for avenues of education unsullied by high church, jacobite, and tory associations. The university took on a lower profile, fearing government reprisals restricting its independence and privileges, a fear that must account, at least in part, for the absence of eighteenth-century print runs of Clarendon's *History* after 1732. The Delegates of the Press presumably saw such editions as risky.[5]

From 1688 to 1715 Anglo-Saxon scholarship had thrived at Oxford, nourishing the curiosity and interest of country gentlemen, clergymen, and peers. However, from about 1715 this spring began drying up. Whig modernists instigated no purge of existing Anglo-Saxon scholars. Rather, leaders of the movement were simply not replaced. By the year 1715, Edward Thwaites and George Hickes were dead. This loss of leadership and scholarly continuity proved devastating, and the movement did not revive until the nineteenth century.[6] These changes at Oxford were tied to new attitudes in the Church of England, which directed the university, and which no longer sponsored clergymen such as Echard and Kennett writing civil history on a grand scale. Bishops Hoadly and Warburton, members of the episcopal generation that succeeded Gibson, found little of interest in medieval church history. To Anglican loyalists, mining arguments from scripture and from the recent English past seemed more useful than Anglo-Saxon studies. After all, Bishop Burnet had focused on contemporary history during the last years of his life, *The History of His Own Time*. When whigs suppressed Convocation in 1717, they closed down a forum for high church opinion and, with it, another impetus to research into medieval history. Nor did new areas of dispute such as the Bangorian Controversy or the challenge of deism depend upon medieval erudition for solutions. By the 1730s the Church had in fact been pushed from the forefront of political struggle. Though it remained an institution of the highest importance, the church was becoming subordinate to ministers of the crown, no longer partners with them.[7]

As elite historical writing became less institutionalized, less dependent on church and crown, history increasingly became the domain of the marketplace and noblemen, the reading public and aristocratic patronage. Innovations in the book trade provided new financial incentives to authors, and many historians wrote for the money the new market could offer. Before this period, one's politics, one's patron, or one's literary ambition might animate one to write in the grand manner, but purely commercial motives were rare. Certainly Clarendon did not write for money. Elite history was supposed to be written by gentlemen and noblemen, who by definition enjoyed independent incomes and freedom from the need to labor for a living. We shall see, however, that English historiography increasingly drew upon the new journalists, mercenary writers whose incompetent efforts simply compounded the weakness in historiography. In the second quarter of the eighteenth century, some aspirant general historians began to find succor in a burgeoning reading public.

Historical works played a key role in the new procedures used by publishers to reach their audiences. Sales by subscription shored up the elite market for history by sharing risks among publishers. The boom in subscription publication began in the 1720s and lasted until mid-century, when the gross commerciality involved in peddling the most elevated literature finally tarnished the practice. Its province was the well-to-do buying expensive, limited-edition, prestigious works, poetry and history especially. At the other end of the market, in the same second quarter of the century that witnessed the increase in book subscriptions, serial publication enticed less affluent readers to buy history. Selling books piecemeal, in weekly or monthly installments, had the effect of spreading out payments and making history more affordable to the middling sort.[8] Publishers generally used serialization to expand the audience for a historical work, subscription to solidify a well-defined elite public. Rapin's history was issued in the former fashion, Oldmixon's in the latter, with utterly different results. Oldmixon, a Londoner of declining fortunes who delighted in 'secret history' and partisan invective, was firmly rebuffed as subversive of the social order. Rapin, a cosmopolitan Huguenot writing on the continent for foreigners, found acclaim as an impartial historian, the writer who had come closest to taming the English party system and solving the riddle of Livian historiography.

RAPIN'S POPULAR WHIGGISM

After the Revocation of the Edict of Nantes in 1685 forced him to flee France, Rapin moved between Holland and England as a writer and tutor. In 1707 he settled in Cleves where he spent the rest of his life writing the history of England. He met encouragement from the publication of Rymer's *Foedera*, which made available a huge trove of historical sources, and of which he published his own abridgement, and from his highly successful *Dissertation sur les whigs et les tories* (1717), which explained the English party system to foreigners. Rapin recognized Echard as his competition. He admired Echard's work so greatly that he considered simply translating it into French, except that too much of Echard's work, he believed, was just an abridgement, especially the Anglo-Saxon segment, and Echard had written for Englishmen with an Englishman's party spirit. Rapin thought himself immune from English partisanship and had already begun writing his own history to explain English affairs to Europeans. He died before finishing his history, but by 1724 eight quarto volumes of the *Histoire d'Angleterre* had appeared in the Hague, carrying the story to 1648. In 1725, the year of Rapin's death, Nicholas Tindal's translation began to be published in London.[9]

Rapin's publishers serialized this and most succeeding editions of *The History of England*, which in fact became England's most successful book serialization, the groundbreaking one for the entire industry. Three decades after Tindal's translation began appearing, print runs were a little better than Clarendon's 16 000 for a comparable period, possibly 18 000 copies.[10] Rapin reached the middling and lower orders, but more through vulgarization in epitomes and the London press than through serial editions. Duodecimo history catechisms mined Rapin for dates, characters, and basic constitutional information. Abridged for a mass audience, Rapin's work became almost unrecognizable, just a list of officeholders, a present-tense description of historical episodes, and a journalistic updating of events to the present.[11] More significantly, Bolingbroke's opposition used him in its press campaign against Walpole in the 1730s. Rapin replaced Tyrrell as the authoritative exponent of the traditional whig view that English liberty was ancient, an interpretation Bolingbroke used to show that, far from founding English liberty in 1688, the ministry had corrupted it. Bolingbroke's *Oldcastle's Remarks on the History of England*, published weekly in *The Craftsman* in 1730–1, made these points through free and extensive use of Rapin. Ministerialist writers in *The London Journal*, on the other hand, contended that liberty was modern, as Robert Brady's work made clear, and charged that Bolingbroke had misrepresented Rapin. Propagandists both for and against Walpole's ministry exploited Rapin. Bolingbroke simply concentrated on the free constitution Rapin described in antiquity, while court whigs focused on Rapin's continuators genuflecting before the Glorious Revolution as the holy source of the present constitution. However, some readers interpreted Rapin's *History* as a hymn to republican government originating in the Saxon aristocracy and a call for the abolition of episcopacy in favor of Saxon presbyterianism. '[A] Satire upon Kings' thundered jacobites, 'an Help to Nursery Chat, where our Children are to be instructed in Rebellion to God and his Vice-gerents.'[12]

Political controversy alone cannot account for Rapin's popularity. His factualness and impartiality enchanted Englishmen, who were so accustomed to the distortions and invectives of party history. Rapin's work lacked the self-destructive polemical fire of Tyrrell or Brady[13] and brought a refreshing semblance of detachment compared to the most recent work in the same genre – Echard's general history. A smirking Voltaire observed, 'As for good [English] historians, I have not met any so far; their history has had to be written by a Frenchman.' Repeating the commonplace complaint about English historiography, Voltaire continued:

> Possibly the English genius, which is either cool or impetuous, has not yet mastered the unaffected eloquence and noble, simple style of history; possibly, also, party spirit, which distorts the vision, has discredited all their historians: one half the nation is always the enemy of the other ... Thus in England there are polemics and not history.[14]

Even if continental and English observers alike saw Rapin as an improvement over previous English historians, the *History* was found wanting as a literary performance. Clarendon 'vastly excells him in Dignity of Sentiment, Majesty of Language, and the most beautiful Variety of Characters,' *The London Journal* noticed. Rapin lacked the polish of 'a finished and complete Historian' such as Polybius, Thucydides, Livy, or Tacitus, it continued. '[W]e have, in him, more Truth, tho' less Delicacy ... Majesty ... Dignity.' *The Daily Gazetteer* questioned Rapin's qualifications for writing the history of 'a great People,' citing Addison's demand that a 'compleat Historian' have both a poetic style and an instructive power comparable to Livy's. Despite the immense popularity of Rapin, despite the fact that 'no Book in our Language had ever more Buyers or Readers,'[15] Rapin failed to live up to the model for general history Livy created.

The Daily Gazetteer had good reason to challenge Rapin's qualifications. Rapin possessed some experience of war and politics, and lived for over a decade in England, but he was a foreigner, after all, and not a very socially-elevated one at that. He played only a minor role in accompanying William of Orange to England in 1688 and fighting for him in Ireland in 1689. After the Glorious Revolution, Rapin served as tutor for the son of a royal favorite, the Earl of Portland,[16] not a position of genteel independence. Rapin had in fact no real intention of imitating the classical historians. He complained to readers about the vagueness of classical rules for writing history. Everyone could recognize a good historian, he argued, but it was no use trying to imitate him, since the good taste which distinguished his work was innate. The best historians followed no rules other than maintaining their honesty and common sense. Like some other historians of England, Rapin thus denied the necessity of following received opinion regarding the writing of history. He did list Caesar, Livy, and Tacitus as having the sort of taste historians required, and he did find Mézeray's method of incorporating church history helpful, but Rapin decided to press on according to his own lights.[17]

Possessing neither the interest nor the best qualifications for writing a neoclassical history, Rapin in fact ended up following in the footsteps of his clericalist predecessors in England. He took Echard's work as his point of departure, so it is not surprising to find Rapin conforming to Echard's genre. Rapin interrupted his story with dissertations on constitutional matters and mixed brilliant explanatory digressions with disconnected facts and short, simple characters of leading history-makers. His narrative pacing deteriorated as his subject became more contemporary. And the staples of popular history were everywhere: providential, genealogical, martyrological passages interspersed with pious maxims ('But see how blind and short-sighted is *Human Wisdom!*').[18] Unlike most predecessors, Rapin did employ something like the classical invented speech as a way to detach himself from partisanship, using his own words to describe the reasoning that went on between opposing parties, rather than favoring one party explicitly. Since Rapin's original audience of continental readers cared less about the relation of the English past to contemporary English politics, he did not feel compelled to settle every historical controversy he met. Rapin usually withdrew from the fracas, after making the case for two sides and sometimes giving qualified support to one.[19] Although this maneuver helped secure his reputation for impartiality, it had serious drawbacks as well. Transcribing the evidence on every side of a historical event took more time than simply narrating the event itself, thus ballooning the text out of proportion.

HACK HISTORY AND POLITE SOCIETY

John Oldmixon's *History of England* (1729–39) amounted to nearly a million words in just the first of his three volumes, but for all his pains it was seen as a step backwards in historiography, less impartial than Rapin, grotesque in its size, unwieldy physically as well as intellectually. Oldmixon, like White Kennett before and James Ralph after him, wrote anonymously. He had good reason to hide, for his reputation was terrible. What was known or at least rumored about Oldmixon, largely publicized in Pope's *Dunciad*, was that Oldmixon hailed from the provinces, lacked a university education, and was immersed in the sordid world of London commercial publishing, a hack in Walpole's stable of writers, an informer, a virulent critic of Clarendon's *History*. Like other men failing in the role of professional man of letters, Oldmixon became one of Pope's 'dunces' because he had taken on elite genres and butchered them.[20] Historical composition was supposed to crown a life of public accomplishment, not serve as a safety net for shadowy figures falling into ignominy, but Oldmixon began his career at the top of the literary hierarchy with lyric and history, then, in the face of mounting criticism, he steadily descended to compiling and indexing at the bottom.

In 1724 Oldmixon began writing the *History* to glorify the present regime and to counter Clarendon and Echard, whose histories were 'manifestly intended to bring Disgrace on the Principles and Practices, which are the Foundation of our present happy Constitution.' His *History* commenced with the Reformation, culminated in the heroic defense of liberty in the teeth of Stuart subversion, and ended with the beneficent reign of the first Hanoverian king. It was not Kennett's temperate whiggism but instead a hard-line reiteration of revolution principles.[21] In the event, much of Oldmixon's argument was lost in a patchwork of documents and invective, and the sheer length of his work. Only a few hundred people bought copies, fewer for each successive volume. A successful subscription required an industrious promoter with clout, but Oldmixon was an outsider without connections, and while most histories sold by subscription listed several peers of the realm, Oldmixon's did not. The top of the social pyramid was lopped off, and in its place were less prominent persons of quality, including merchants and some whig MPs. The literary establishment ridiculed Oldmixon's *History* or, more often, simply ignored it.[22]

Because printed historical sources were becoming increasingly available, the hack could try patching them together to make a history. In his *Critical History of England* (1724–6), a survey of English historiography, Oldmixon himself had recognized in Kennett and Echard

Copiers, Collectors, and Compilers, who have lately usurp'd the Name of Historians. Men of small Learning and Parts, and less Knowledge of Persons and Things, have set up for Writers of History, and think there's no other Qualification necessary than a smooth Stile . . . Far from having Opportunities or Credit enough to procure authentick Manuscripts, most of our Modern History-Writers content themselves with the Copies of Common Records, Gazettes, News-Papers, and Pamphlets; stuffing their Pieces with long Speeches in Parliament, Votes of the House of Commons, and even Proclamations.

Oldmixon went further than Echard and Kennett in realizing this caricature of the unqualified historian. Oldmixon himself relied on commonly accessible historical sources rather than his own behind-the-scenes experience of history or his own collection of one-of-a-kind documents. Oldmixon himself lacked the credibility necessary 'to procure authentick Manuscripts.' His was the hack history par excellence, and it consolidated his place in the pantheon of literary upstarts enshrined in the *Dunciad*. Oldmixon was not properly an author but a plagiary who took other people's words and retailed them as his own. Because the hack's enterprise was not an honest pursuit of truth for the moral edification of his readers but a simple commercial transaction, he had no scruples about copying out extraneous material to puff up the size of his work to make more money, paid, as he often was, by the page. Oldmixon's *History of England* took the practice to extremes.[23]

In his biographies, secret histories, and journalism Oldmixon became the object of further contempt, because he took on taboo subjects unknown in respectable historical writing and threatening to the social order. The elite valued protocols of neoclassical history that protected its own privacy and that Oldmixon violated. The elite code dictated against self-revelation of private experience beyond one's own social circle. This long-cherished sense of exclusiveness and privacy was heightened in the late seventeenth and early eighteenth century, as the nobility and upper gentry distanced themselves from the lesser gentry and freeholders. George I and George II kept the peerage from expanding, noble status from dilution. As the designs of country houses showed, while among themselves they were becoming more sociable and reinforcing a sense of caste, members of the elite dismissed servants from view. The surrounding village they sometimes razed and rebuilt at a more seemly distance from themselves.[24]

Just as servants were discouraged from peeping through keyholes, and villagers from spying upon goings-on at his lordship's house, so were historians without social position expected to keep a respectful distance from the inner workings of government. Failure to do so could threaten social stability, according to elite theories of society. Echard, who knew his own modest place in the social hierarchy, condemned historians for 'vilifying their Superiors; . . . [B]y making bold with crown'd Heads, they bring all upon the Level, and turn Liberty into Licentiousness.' Le Moyne, the French neoclassical critic, emphasized the political responsibility required of the historian:

> Since the Perfection of a Civil Life is the end where [the historian's] Labours [tend], he must expose nothing to the publick View that has not regard to it, must therefore abstain from all sorts of Scandalous Relations, as are those that serve but to make People lose the Respect they owe their Prelates and Princes, the Hierarchy, Church and publick Government; and gives way to Heresies, Revolts and Schisms, both in Church and State.

Although this advice might be more germane to absolutist France than to England, English observers spoke in similar terms. The historian, whether nobleman or commoner, owed special respect to royal persons and to the public, which should not be demoralized by revelations about royal wrongdoing in private. Roger North believed that 'the Gospel, as well as moral Duty' forbade him from speaking 'Evil of Dignities.' He promised a balanced account of Charles II's 'public Character' but refused to dwell on his 'personal Failings,' even if kings, like 'private Men' were not beyond reproach. Out of simple decency and respect for the dignity of Charles II's and James II's royal offices, Echard vowed to expose 'publick Errors' such as James' 'frequent Breach of his Royal Word,' but not to ferret out 'private Vices. . . . To search far into their dark and secret Recesses, is presumptuous in the Writer, and dangerous to the Reader.' Defenders of the *status quo* also objected to the methods employed in exposés of the court. The existence of Stuart mistresses might be sound public knowledge, but much information about royal private life had only scanty foundation in 'secret histories' based on unsubstantiated gossip from court servants, sometimes third- or fourth-hand.[25]

Oldmixon, the most infamous practitioner of this genre, labeled as flattery 'Echard's Decencies and Decorums,' and criticized his passing over the Stuarts' 'private Vices and Extravagancies.' Roger North argued that a true history of the immediate past was one thing, a valued enterprise, but to turn such an enquiry into 'a monstrous Height of Lying and Defaming of Kings and Potentates' was another. 'Secret' historians had found 'an unhappy Pattern in Procopius' and exploited this classical precedent to justify searching into court secrets, political as well as sexual.[26] Although secret history had an ancient pedigree, establishment critics frowned on it. Tacitus enjoyed a considerable reputation as a historian, but many readers cited his scrutiny of the secret crimes of the imperial court as a failing, whatever his many virtues were. The salacious revelations of secret history strayed from war and politics, the subject of respectable history. Besides, it was considered impolite to uncover the family secrets of high-born Englishmen.

Politeness was a species of neoclassicism and an attribute of gentility and nobility; as a political and philosophical program it avoided controversy and encouraged sociability. Rather than question the social order, polite history focused on the public character of history-makers. It only alluded to the private vices of public figures when that behavior impinged directly on public events,[27] and only then in the most decorous, often circumlocutious, terms. According to Le Moyne, Christian historians could learn much from the pagans Sallust, Livy, and even

Tacitus, because their method of polite criticism succeeded in preserving 'the publick Vertue.' As a general principle, the historian ought to expose vices 'in such general Terms that cannot cause a Blush or evil Thought, and . . . touch them but in passing, and make hast[e] away as from an infected place, where his own and others Modesty are in danger.'[28]

Oldmixon had violated all standards of polite history. Seeing a market for sensationalized accounts of recently deceased public figures, he wrote the 'memoirs' of Wharton, Somers, and others. Addison was sickened.

[O]ur Grub-Street Biographers . . . watch for the Death of a Great Man, like so many Undertakers, on purpose to make a Penny of him. . . . They fetch their only authentick Records out of *Doctors Commons*; and when they have got a Copy of his last Will and Testament, they fancy Themselves furnished with sufficient Materials for his History. . . . This manner of exposing the private Concerns of Families, and sacrificing the Secrets of the Dead to the curiosity of the Living, is one of those licentious Practices which might well deserve the Animadversion of our Government . . .[29]

In 1721 the House of Lords indeed acted, declaring that the unauthorized publication of a deceased peer's biography or correspondence constituted a breach of privilege.[30] Oldmixon, however, continued to delight in aristocratic and royal scandal. Despite the strictures of polite society, his personal abuse, invective, and libel sold pamphlets and books; they were Oldmixon's stock-in-trade even though they discredited him in genteel society.

Oldmixon found that the freshest gossip of contemporary history had the best sales, so most of his historical and biographical works were a kind of instant history or mere journalism. It was a subject a true gentleman would not touch, for in general terms no reputable writer, certainly no noble historian, would publish a work of contemporary history so soon after the events he described had taken place. The closer a history intruded on the present, the less likely it was that its author had status or power to lose. A member of the elite would write near-contemporary history but then delay its publication or break off a few decades early, letting the dust settle, and not describing contemporary events, the real evidence for which was still in a family's embrace. He was writing for the benefit of distant posterity and also considered the sensibilities of the current generation of families like his own, the royal family in particular. It was the hack who took advantage of substantial historiographical achievements such as Rapin's and who wrote continuations or updates for a popular audience, picking up at the point where a respectable historian decided it was wrong to continue. Oldmixon was not part of the elite; his socially elevated victims did not belong to his circle of acquaintances. He thus had little to lose once his reputation with polite society was in tatters and he was earning a living off another reading public. Anonymous publication usually kept him out of the criminal dock, but he did not escape literary trial and conviction by the likes of Swift, Pope, and Addison, who effectively deprived him of artistic respectability and an elite audience. He faded into oblivion.

WRITERS BY PROFESSION: GUTHRIE AND RALPH

The general historians writing in the wake of Oldmixon's varied assaults on neoclassical history chose to ignore him and look instead upon Rapin as their chief competitor. Although they paid lip service to neoclassical ideals, their histories adhered to a clerical style of historical writing just as Rapin's had done. Their partisanship, their cumbersome erudition, and their occupation as journalists illustrated the difficulties English historiography continued to face in the 1740s. William Guthrie published *A General History of England from the Invasion of the Romans . . . to the late Revolution* [1688–9], 1744–51, in four volumes. James Ralph published a companion piece, *The History of England during the Reigns of K. William, Q. Anne, and K. George I . . .*, 1744–6, in two volumes. Despite serialization for less affluent readers, their folio volumes did not sell very well. Ralph was a transplanted American hack, whose *History* was subsidized by Bubb Dodington. Guthrie was a Scot, whose *History* was underwritten by Lord Chesterfield. Both aspired to be professional men of letters but came up short, never quite shaking off a desperate, Grub Street look about themselves. Pelham eventually bought both men off with pensions.[31]

Guthrie began his *History* by faulting Rapin for 'inaccuracy' and 'want of genius,' and for duping the public into believing that a foreigner was best qualified to write England's history. Some of Guthrie's readers might have considered him, a Scot, as much an outsider as Rapin, a Frenchman. Like Boyer before him, Guthrie was not a true-born Englishman but argued that as a collector and re-writer of parliamentary speeches he enjoyed a valuable vantage point for writing history. A parliamentary reporter who revelled in the freedom of the press, Guthrie professed his dependence on no patron but the new reading public. In his view, history had been poorly served at the time of the Reformation, when it was written by churchmen on orders from ecclesiastical patrons. Succeeding laymen did no better, writing as they did in the name of their own narrow political programs, not truth. Yet in the 1740s, in England, the truth could be told, according to Guthrie, because clerical and aristocratic patronage, and court censorship, had declined.[32] Guthrie promised to employ as his models 'the greatest of the ancients' to tell the truth. He rejected the dry narratives of his contemporaries, preferring the precedents of Livy's 'poetical' language, Sallust's characters, and Tacitus' ornaments. As part of this classical agenda, he wished to praise and blame the 'great scenes' of the English past. He transcribed one of Tacitus' invented speeches and defended this ancient practice, even if he did not invent any of his own.[33]

An establishment history that reaffirmed 'our happy constitution in church and state,' Guthrie's *History* had an air of moderation. Guthrie despised Oldmixon, a 'rebel or republican' whose work was as 'contemptible' for its extremism as the work of royalist historians was. A mild whig, Guthrie offered a sympathetic character of Charles I, even conceding the king was 'a martyr to the church of England.'[34] He castigated the 'ill-laboured volumes' of Tyrrell and Brady, but his work resembled theirs more than he knew. He lacked their open partisanship but shared their difficulties in sustaining a coherent narrative. He appended dissertations in the manner of Brady, and at the close of reigns he listed 'Remarkable occurrences' such as the exhumation of a 175-year-old corpse intact. Massive footnotes covered, on average, a quarter of every page. Hoping to demonstrate his objectivity, Guthrie transcribed evidence from both sides of every historical controversy, thereby increasing the size of the *History* beyond all expectation to include 'the many quotations, references and reasonings.' His work became so huge that his themes, like the very thread of his story, got lost.[35]

These failings were hardly unique in modern English historiography,[36] but Guthrie did depart from neoclassical protocols in some atypical ways, too. Classical historiography centered upon the deeds of great men, but Guthrie shifted attention away from individual heroes to less tangible, less personal forces at work in history. Ascribing political change to economic change was certainly not a novel idea, for, to take but one of many examples, Bolingbroke had traced the corruption of public life in the 1730s to the new method of public finance, which increased the power of the crown, the City of London, and a new 'moneyed interest' that endangered post-revolutionary liberty.[37] However, such analyses commonly appeared in political pamphlets or treatises, not in narrative histories focused on the deeds of men. To a greater degree than previous general historians, Guthrie tried to combine *res gestae* with economic and sociological interpretation. He analyzed politics during the time of Richard II in terms of power blocs organized according to social and economic interest and adhering to a law of history devised by Guthrie:

> in a state where a middle order presses too hard upon the inferior, the latter naturally starts out and seeks relief from the higher. The barons or great nobility of England, at this time, were extremely uneasy at the many advantages which the commons had lately acquired, as well from the countenance of the king and clergy, as from the encrease of trade, and they therefore sought to depress them. For this purpose they endeavoured not only to keep them from the knowledge of their own importance, but to bring them back to that state of villainage under which they had lived during the severest reigns of the Norman race. The crown, on the other hand, grew every day more and more sensible that the encouraging the commons, by suffering them to extend not only their property, but their rights to enjoy it, was the only means of breaking that dependance they had upon the baronetage, which had made it, perhaps, an overmatch for sovereignty.[38]

As part of this investigation of the impersonal aspects of historical causation, Guthrie posited that manners constituted a legitimate topic of historical narrative. Guthrie went beyond simply mentioning the manners of the ancient Britons, and paraphrasing what 'that noble historian,' Tacitus, had to say about them, as previous general historians had done. For example, he explained the outbreak of the Civil War in terms of a gulf in manners between London merchants and the royal court that rendered the two interests mutually antagonistic.[39] He challenged a basic tenet of neoclassical historiography when he argued that manners superseded warfare as the proper subject of history, that the manners of the ancient Britons presented 'a more profitable instruction to [Tacitus'] posterity than the most pompous details of battles and bloodshed.'[40] Indeed, when English enemies succeeded in introducing luxury and vice to England, their victory was far more effectual than any achieved by mere force of arms. The Roman conquest, the Norman Conquest, the Hundred Years' War all proved that manners, more than warriors and statesmen, exercised decisive influence over the rise and fall of states.[41] Hume, too, would bring manners onto the stage of history and challenge neoclassical assumptions about historical causation. However, for reasons to be discussed in Chapter 7, the modern, often Scottish, introduction of explicit social and economic theories into historical discourse[42] bore more fruit in his work than Guthrie's.

James Ralph was less deeply engaged than Guthrie or Hume in exploring the tensions between modern social theory and classical historiography. He wrote in the hack tradition of Oldmixon and indeed had shared a place with him in Pope's literary pillory. Like Oldmixon, Ralph was more concerned with his own commercial success than with the privacy of history-makers or their descendants, so he embarked upon a continuation of Guthrie, an updating of his history to the year 1727. As it happened, Ralph's near-contemporary history only covered the reign of William III. Ralph wrote anonymously, betting that he could flaunt elite protocols and still write a superior history, asking the public to evaluate the finished product only, not the author. Recognizing that he lacked the preferred qualifications of a historian, high social status and political experience, Ralph knew he would be raising eyebrows. If you wonder, he assured his readers, why I, 'undistinguish'd with a Title, or undignify'd with a great Office, should be able to sit in Judgment on Actions of Ministers, Kings, and States,' then I simply appeal to posterity to judge my work for what it is, 'whether made by the Image and Superscription of Caesar or not.'[43] Ralph thus argued that someone could write comparably to the ancient historians without possessing their particular careers. He did not follow up another of his observations that the figures in English history were not as impressive as the great heroes in Greek and Roman history[44] by arguing that English historians likewise lacked the stature of classical historians, although this was one implication of his argument, and his own example showed how woeful the state of English historiography had become, how far below classical standards it had descended.

Political partisanship and excessive documentation destroyed Ralph's work. He justified his project by the need to revise Rapin in the light of historical sources becoming available since Rapin wrote, but Ralph's *History* did not displace Rapin's. Like Guthrie, Ralph drowned his own occasional insights in heavy documentation and transcriptions from other historians. A skilled Grub Street practitioner, he swelled the size of his volumes by copying out large portions of North's *Examen* (usually approvingly) and Burnet's *History of His Own Time* (so as to refute it). On the last pages of his massive work, he transformed what had hitherto been a temperate, often balanced, history into a Bolingbrokean indictment of the new political system. He concentrated on the unintended evils of William's wars and the founding of the Bank of England, the alliance of creditors and politicians corrupting elections and debasing public life generally. Cinching its place in the hack book stalls, the *History's* finale betrayed the polemical point of the whole project: to provide deep background for the opposition's post-mortem on the Walpole regime, *The Critical History of the Administration of Sir Robert Walpole*, which Ralph had published three years before.[45]

JACOBITE PUBLICIST: THOMAS CARTE

After Ralph's lackluster performance and after the failure of the jacobite rebellion in 1745, and with Rapin's whig *History* still ascendant, tories and especially jacobites could hold out little hope of political or historiographical restoration. However, in 1747 Thomas Carte began to publish his four-volume *General History of England*, the culmination of a long career of jacobite scheming and scholarship. Carte (1686–1754) was an ordained, nonjuring jacobite who lived as a layman after 1714. Briefly serving as Atterbury's secretary, he escaped to France in 1722 following his patron's arrest. Through the intercession of Queen Caroline, he returned to England in 1728. In the following year he used the 2nd Duke of Ormonde's request to write the 1st Duke's life in order to buttress Carte's own defense of Charles I, which Carte had set forth in a controversial sermon in 1714 clearing the king of having instigated the Irish rebellion and massacre in 1641.

Carte published *An History of the Life of James Duke of Ormonde* in 1735 and 1736, inaugurating a publicity campaign that expropriated family papers in the service of jacobitism. In 1715 Bolingbroke and the 2nd Duke of Ormonde had joined the Pretender, and acts of attainder were passed against them. Twenty years later Carte was helping the 2nd Duke restore the reputation of the 1st Duke of Ormonde, cavalier military commander and Clarendon's colleague. Meanwhile, Bolingbroke was helping Lord Cornbury with his great-grandfather Clarendon's papers in constructing a tory and possibly jacobite pedigree for the opposition to Sir Robert Walpole. In 1715 the 3rd Earl of Strafford had chosen not to flee, and instead faced impeachment proceedings for his negotiation, with Bolingbroke, of the Treaty of Utrecht. In 1739, Strafford, a committed jacobite, published family papers rehabilitating the 1st Earl of Strafford, royalist martyr.[46] In 1742, the 5th Earl of Orrery, another jacobite peer, hesitated in the family muniment room. After a valiant royalist career, the 1st Earl of Orrery had joined Cromwell, only returning to the Stuart fold on the eve of the Restoration. The 5th Earl's edition of family letters overlooked the embarrassing Cromwellian episode and instead played up his ancestor's association with Ormonde from 1660 to 1668. Marginalized figures, Orrery, Strafford, Ormonde, and Cornbury found inspiration and solace in the lives of eminent forebears, principals in the Civil War period. As family historians they tried publicizing that past, still relevant to resuscitating a desperate jacobite cause in the 1730s and '40s.

In 1739, foreseeing no imminent foreign assistance or native initiative, Carte told the Pretender that the best course of action was 'by some publick writing to prepare the mind's of your subjects' for a future restoration. The principle of hereditary monarchy, the reputation of the Stuarts, especially that of Charles I, required a defense in the face of whig detraction. Carte argued that 'the great men in England' most needed instruction on these points. The opposition newspaper *The Craftsman*

has been unhappily successfull in poysoning the sentiments of young Gentlemen just entering into the world + destroying all manner of principle in them. It has not indeed infected the middle + common people of the kingdom, because that paper's continual railing against K. Charles I whose memory they adore, soon prejudiced them so much against it, that they left off reading it . . .[47]

Lesser landowners, the middling sort, and common laborers could be counted on to support James' restoration, because they rejected *The Craftsman*'s anti-Stuart propaganda and had less property to wager on the Stuarts' return to power.[48] The landed elite, however, still remained to be convinced of the worthiness of the jacobite cause, and so it was to it that Carte directed his major historical writings, including the *Life of Ormonde*.

Unlike his fellow nonjuror, Roger North, Carte did not abandon political activism and public history to pursue in intimate psychological detail the private life of his subject, for the high politics of the past still impinged on jacobitism's present prospects, or so Carte believed. Carte's family history took the form not of a biography but a political history of Britain, especially Ireland, chiefly from Ormonde's perspective, covering the years 1633 to 1668 and based on a huge collection of letters published as an appendix. Carte's *Life* was a landmark in the jacobites' campaign to set the Civil War record straight by publishing the lives and correspondence of their cavalier forebears. In 1742 Orrery's edition of his ancestor's letters ceded pride of place to Carte's pioneering publication, and portrayed the jacobite publicity machine as offering a partial solution to the ongoing weakness in English historiography. The lack both of qualified historians and source materials meant that Britain could not yet

boast a Livy, a Thucydides, or a Tacitus [since] the proper materials for a history of these kingdoms are either entirely lost, or warily preserved in such secret repositories, that the treasure (which perhaps is more the hoard of ignorance than avarice) can be of no use, not even to the owner. . . . There are so many qualifications necessary to form an historian, that they seldom are found to centre in one person. . . . When such a genius shall arise, the history of England may be compiled with that impartiality and elegance, which so noble a work requires. In the mean time it is the duty of every man, who wishes well to his country, or has a view to the information and improvement of posterity, to contribute all the materials in his power towards the foundation of this future edifice. In this light the following letters are presented to the publick ... [O]f late years a series of litterary anecdotes have appeared, greatly contributing towards an insight and digestion of that rude chaos, wherein the history of Ireland, and particularly the rebellion of 1641 lay involved. Mr. Carte's Life of the duke of Ormond, and the Appendix to it, led the way. They were followed by the publication of Thomas Earl of Strafford's letters; to which now succeed the large collection of Mr. Thurloe's letters, and these of Roger earl of Orrery.[49]

Immediately upon completion of his *Life of Ormonde* in 1736, Carte began collecting subscriptions for a vast, new undertaking, a general history of England calculated to push the jacobite program even further along. However, Carte came to this task with an extremist political platform and an obsession with amassing source materials, a combination of partisanship and erudition that, as we have seen in the case of so many other historians, doomed any potential piece of neoclassical historiography. Carte's object was to supplant the whig historian Rapin by incorporating, then continuing, the work of his royalist hero, Robert Brady. Carte told potential subscribers that the only real attempt to write 'The *Civil History* of this Nation' was Brady's; Rapin was a foreigner and lacked the requisite sources. English history, as handed down by Rapin and others, was murky and confusing, according to Carte, so he proposed to clarify it once and for all through a search and organization of public and private record depositories, foreign and native. All of this travel and transcribing would be costly: he estimated expenses of £1000 a year. Because Carte lacked the finances for such a project, he turned to a group of nobles and gentlemen whose money gave him leisure and whose contacts opened up archives (the Duke of Rutland getting Pelham's key to the Exchequer, Sir John Hynde Cotton securing Gower's for the Office of Privy Seal). Publicity for the project induced peers to share family records, just as the *Life of Ormonde* had induced them.[50] The *History*, in this light, may be seen as an attempt to systematize the haphazard publication of jacobite historical documents in the years 1736 to 1742, initiated by the *Life*, in that effervescence of family history just discussed. Indeed, Carte presented himself as an archivist-for-hire. Researching in the Exchequer and elsewhere,

Carte promised to look out for whatever surveys or records individual subscribers needed in order to assert their rights to family manors unlawfully seized by the crown.[51] With the financial and political backing he enjoyed, Carte had more access to sources than Hume would, the most since Bolingbroke's half-hearted attempt to write a neoclassical history.

In his preface, Carte acted as if his access to these papers guaranteed his success as a historian. It was on this basis that he criticized previous general histories and justified his own. Carte himself had never been an independent political player, only chaplain, secretary, or publicist for greater men such as Ormonde and Atterbury. Nor did he possess the political judgment advantageous to playing the part of historian. Naively seeing Walpole lean toward jacobitism in 1739, for example, Carte was hoodwinked into sharing with Sir Robert his advice to the Pretender on ecclesiastical reforms required in the event of a Stuart restoration. Despite his limitations, Carte's powerful acquaintances certainly did give him some credibility with the elite. His friend Orrery was only one of the jacobite presidents of a company of subscribers dominated by tory, sometimes jacobite, peers, MPs, colleges, and London guilds.[52] However, Carte's crass entrepreneurship was at odds with the idea of noble history. The monumental scale and folio format of his *History* bespoke a pretension to neoclassical achievement, but contemporaries recognized a huge chasm between this lofty genre and some of Carte's patrons. Horace Walpole laughed at the incongruity:

> The good City of London, who, from long dictating to the government, are now come to preside over taste and letters, have given one Carte, a Jacobite parson, fifty pounds a year for seven years, to write the history of England; and four aldermen and six Common council men are to inspect his materials and the progress of the work. Surveyors of common sewers turned supervisors of literature![53]

By appealing to the City of London, Carte tried to take advantage of a literary nationalism that was coming to a head at mid-century. He argued that public bodies, not just nobles and gentlemen, had to support his history, just as their counterparts were doing in France and Holland. Only such institutions' 'public Spirit' could sustain his national history, which would 'clear up & support the most valuable of our Rights, Liberties & privileges as English Men.'[54] Emphasizing this point and possibly suggesting that English history had for too long a time been left to foreigners – Guthrie, Ralph, Rapin, Burnet – he styled himself 'Thomas Carte, an Englishman,' on the title page. His subscribers, 'the Society of the History of England upon Mr. Carte's plan,' might thus be seen as constituting one of the many patriotic societies[55] engaged in cultural competition with France. Samuel Johnson portrayed his *Dictionary* not only as a monument to the English language, lately polluted by gallicisms, but also as a specimen of philology comparable to continental achievements in that science. Promoters of a royal academy for British artists composed their charter in terms similar to those of Johnson's preface, hoping to make amends for the poor state of native painting.[56] Both documents defended their cause with a formula identical to the one used to describe the weakness in historiography, one referring, as Bolingbroke had, to the longstanding humiliation of having to 'yield the palm' to the continent in their respective disciplines. Both took inspiration from an existing pantheon of English geniuses. Using Locke, Newton, and Dryden as icons, the Earl of Orrery bemoaned the lack of a historical genius; Johnson referred to Bacon, Hooker, Milton, and Boyle; the painters named Shakespeare, Bacon, Milton, and Newton. The canon of cultural heroes might differ according to individual taste, but the stylized complaint about English cultural achievement, a mixture of self-pity, national pride, and international competition, maintained a high degree of consistency, no matter which scholarly or artistic community employed it for purposes of justification or inspiration.

Carte's nationalistic appeals might have won him numerous subscribers, but once the *History* began to be published, many of them deserted him after seeing the first fruits of his expensive labors.[57] It became all too apparent that Carte's partisanship had ruined his chance to equal the modern French peers of classical historiography. The elitism of Carte's analysis might have pleased his socially elevated subscribers, but the tory and jacobite conclusions he drew from it placed his reputation as a historian seriously at risk. Carte took a page from Bolingbroke and bore the standard of the landed gentry and nobility against social newcomers of all kinds, especially the moneyed men. His account of the Norman Conquest included an analogy with another conquering William, William III, another 'foreign prince' disturbing the island's peace and prosperity by entangling it with foreign military ventures. William of Orange put continental interests above English ones, leaving an obvious legacy: 'every body feels the insupportable load of debts and taxes, which have ruined most of the ancient families of our gentry, and sees the general corruption, with an infinity of other evils, which they have occasioned.'[58] The wicked William, then, not only cast out the legitimate royal line of Stuarts, but also decimated the natural rulers of England, the landed elite. And just as the peaceful, simple, honest Saxons were transformed by the cunning, bloodthirsty, restless Normans, he implied, so did the Glorious Revolution effect 'an unhappy change in the customs, manners, and temper of the commonalty.' The Norman Conquest was a portent of things to come and a lesson unheeded. Carte dated the more calamitous moment of English decline in the late sixteenth century. The power-hungry Leicester, Elizabeth's favorite, packed parliament with Puritans, who would not only bring about the Civil War but also dramatically change forever the basis of representation, so that now

> whilst all the landed interest is represented by ninety-two members, and the trading or moneyed interest by about an hundred deputies of cities and great towns, there are above 300 representatives of small, inconsiderable, and many of these beggarly, burroughs, who, by a majority of three to two, are able to dispose of the property of all landed and opulent men in the kingdom, in despite of their unanimous dissent. These have been long considered as the rotten part of our constitution; and, being venal as well as poor, they have been the chief source of the corruption complained of in modern parliaments...

The survival of the constitution depended on electoral changes redressing disproportionate representation. Carte cited Machiavelli's maxim about reform through a return to first principles, and argued that in the case of the English constitution this meant limiting the franchise to gentry and freeholders with estates worth £40 or £50 a year: 'As freeholders of that substance retain more of the old *English* spirit, than any other set of men in the nation, and are the least corruptible, this would cut off at once all the scandalous bargains now made by brokers for burroughs.'[59] Carte's proposal echoed the frequent tory and jacobite contention that if the true sentiments of responsible Englishmen were permitted free exercise in an uncorrupt state, England would have a tory administration and a Stuart king.[60] As for the other house of parliament, the Tudors had nearly snuffed out 'the old heroic race of nobility' slaughtered in the struggle between York and Lancaster. Filling its place were men without ancient lineage picking on church spoils at the time of the Reformation.

> [S]ectaries, lawyers, and all that acquired fortunes in any other manner, began to fancy themselves entitled to a peerage, as if honours were of course to follow riches . . . [Z]eal for the publick good and the glory of their country, gave way to private interest . . . [The lust for power, office, and money] got the better of those generous sentiments, which a course of military service, and an emulation of the glory of great ancestors, seldom failed to inspire.[61]

Carte, again indebted to Machiavelli, appeared to be on the verge of prescribing a civic humanist antidote for corruption – arms bearing and reverence for familial glory. The fatal blow to the crown and the nobility in fact came when James I, foolishly fearing the power of the nobles, debased them further by discouraging their defining virtue, military spirit, and ennobling in their place 'favourites and moneyed men.' The Civil War destroyed James' son Charles as well as the crippled nobility, because the crown had deprived itself of a natural and powerful ally.[62]

Carte's searing analysis of the modern political order in terms of the corruption of 'the old English spirit' by new financial and social interests was indebted to Bolingbroke's *Letters on History* and *Oldcastle's Remarks on the History of England*. But Carte was an older, purer tory, averse to Bolingbroke's strategic adoption of whig theory to embarrass unwhiggish court whigs, and Bolingbroke's 'support of old Whig papers stuffed with quotations out of Rapin, a violent enemy to the Ch[urc]h [and] Monarchy.'[62] Carte was instead a disciple of Brady and used the master's work to question whig dogma such as the antiquity of the House of Commons. He replayed the 'Brady Controversy,' defending the institution of monarchy as 'more agreeable than any other' form of government, and beating down all notions of popular and republican government. Carte used Filmerian arguments that monarchy was divinely and naturally instituted and not based on a compact between the king and the people. Contractarian theorists could not discover any

historical precedent for their seditious ideas, Carte claimed, because they were only dreamt up comparatively recently by Calvin
and the popes to advance their own schemes of aggrandizement.
Tragically, English Puritans adopted Calvinist doctrines to overthrow church and state.[64]

In the midst of this Bradyesque project, Carte died, breaking off
the *History* at 1654. He had succeeded, however, in making a
number of jacobite points, even in the first volume, where a footnote alleged that in 1716 the Pretender had successfully touched
for the King's Evil. If volume four was not jacobite, it represented
the most staunch defense of the early Stuarts since Echard. Carte
made liberal use of recently published jacobite source materials
and gave spirited support to James I, Strafford, Charles I, and the
Eikon. He believed Charles' execution was 'not to be paralleled in
all the histories of nations since the creation,' and asked his reader
to consider present-day calamities as divine judgment for it, to

> reflect upon the want of virtue, and publick spirit, the irreligion,
> immorality, and corruption, which reign too generally throughout
> these nations, with the heats, animosities, divisions, burdens,
> grievances, and calamities, under which they at present groan:
> let him examine coolly into the original and causes of these evils,
> and he will see reason to think it asserted upon just grounds,
> that the worst and most irremediable of them, may be traced
> up to the execrable murther of K. Charles, and the subversion
> of the constitution at that time, as naturally and as surely, as a
> stream may to its fountain.[65]

To most readers all this was unmistakable. Carte's was yet another
partisan general history, even a dangerous jacobite one, and this
perception accounted for a sharp drop in sales.

Trained as a clergyman and linked to Brady-era historiography,
Carte produced a clericalist history with heavy documentation and
party bias. He promised to improve on Brady's 'dry performance'
with all its records but so little 'entertainment.' He vowed not to
enter the lists of historical controversy or mindlessly to transcribe
documents without incorporating them into the narrative.[66] He did
in fact take an interest in manners, the economic and social facts
affecting them, and the relation of these matters to political history, just as Guthrie had.[67] Ultimately, however, he did adhere to
much of Brady's model. He had difficulty integrating into his

narrative antiquarian material concerning manners, commerce, and
religion, and he eschewed 'reflections' in favor of the raw data of
the past. Characteristically, he attacked the 'polite' Sir William
Temple for writing 'rather out of his own imagination, than upon
a careful examination of historical facts.'[68] Carte kept his own
obsession with documents under control in the first two volumes,
but he lost his grasp covering the sixteenth century and especially
the prelude to the Civil War. Even his patrons, perusing even the
more flowing early volumes, got bogged down. Orrery confided
to a friend, 'how shall I wade through Tom Carte's first volume?
I believe it must stand like a wooden book, unmolested but well
ornamented in my library.'[69] For all these reasons Carte was never
deemed the English Livy.

Like previous general historians, those writing in the 1740s and
'50s lacked independence. Ramsay of Ochtertyre observed that
Guthrie's sales suffered 'from the personal character of the author,
who was a dissipated man, ready to write for anybody that would
pay him.'[70] Carte's willingness to write, his lack of independence,
also harmed his bid for the office of historian. Samuel Squire, a
party writer based in Cambridge, acknowledged the need England
had for a Livy, but added that 'Livys are not the Growth of
every Age and Clime; and some thing more is required in a good
Historian, than mere Zeal for a Faction, and an Assiduity in collecting and transcribing antient Records' – he required discernment,
honesty, judgment, eloquence, truthfulness. By these standards,
Carte failed to pass inspection, according to Squire. He wrote for
money and wrote as his aristocratic patrons bade him to write.
Squire finished off Carte with a stinging prediction:

> For tho' I don't doubt but the Books themselves will soon be
> as cheap, and as little regarded, as the voluminous Labours of
> his Friend Brady, yet may the Collections, as such, be of the
> greatest Service to some future Livy, who shall do Honour to
> the History of his Country.[71]

Squire proved prophetic on every count. Carte very quickly lost
his audience, and the English instead turned to the work of that
future Livy, David Hume, who indeed relied on the source collections of Carte and his predecessors. The work of Carte and his
forebears indeed went crashing into the dustbin of history, becoming, in the words of Ramsay of Ochtertyre, 'much neglected ever

since the new fashion of writing history was introduced by Voltaire, Hume, and their imitators,[72] the philosophical historians. Carte's work became as outdated and unappreciated as the general histories by Guthrie and Brady became soon after Hume's neoclassical and philosophical history appeared in the year of Carte's death, 1754. It is now to Hume, to 'the new fashion of writing history,' that we must turn.

7

David Hume as a Neoclassical Historian

A rich secondary literature has developed around Hume's *History of England*. In the role of historian, Hume has been described as a reformer of British political culture,[1] a Baconian natural historian of morals,[2] a failed scientific historian,[3] a reactionary struggling with the liberalism of his early career,[4] a 'scientific' whig who transcended political parties,[5] a student of the 'science of man,'[6] a 'practical' moralist.[7] While most recent studies of Hume have focused on his central place in the history of modern philosophy and his *History* as somehow a part of that philosophy, they have tended to lose sight of Hume's ties to classical historiography,[8] ties Hume as well as his original readers readily acknowledged. It is the contention of this Chapter that Hume and his audience saw the *History* as a neoclassical work intended to solve the weakness in English historiography. Perhaps above all other ambitions, Hume's most ardent wish was to construct such a work. It is the task of this Chapter to show how the various philosophical and political projects just mentioned could be subsumed in a neoclassical narrative that would earn a European reputation as a literary masterpiece.

Although the *History* was indeed revolutionary in its treatment of many religious and constitutional issues, and we would not want to deny how 'modern' the work is in so many respects, Hume went to great lengths to observe ancient protocols for historical writing. In a famous passage that could be read as the philosophical prospectus for a revolutionary work of modern historiography, Hume, in the *Enquiry Concerning Human Understanding* (1748), wrote that history's

> chief use is only to discover the constant and universal principles of human nature, by showing men in all varieties of circum-

stances and situations, and furnishing us with materials from which we may form our observations and become acquainted with the regular springs of human action and behaviour. These records of wars, intrigues, factions, and revolutions, are so many collections of experiments, by which the politician or moral philosopher fixes the principles of his science, in the same manner as the physician or natural philosopher becomes acquainted with the nature of plants, minerals, and other external objects, by the experiments which he forms concerning them. Nor are the earth, water, and other elements, examined by Aristotle, and Hippocrates, more like to those which at present lie under our observation than the men described by Polybius and Tacitus are to those who now govern the world.[9]

The ideas that historians seek the causes of war and politics and that by examining men in the past, statesmen in particular, we understand them in the present and the future were classical commonplaces, as Hume's references to Polybius and Tacitus might have tipped us off. What at first glance appears to be a manifesto for the new science of man turns out to be a truism operating in the ancient historians, perhaps most explicitly in Thucydides. Even the analogy of the historian as physician, which Voltaire would use to praise Hume, can be traced back to Thucydides, whose description of the plague in Athens has been called Hippocratic.[10] Familiarity with the classical tradition reveals in fact that significant parts of Hume's historical thinking and style are actually neoclassical, and we shall see, paradoxically, how neoclassical historiography could be so useful to one of the most modern and revolutionary philosophers of his time. The *History* represents a profound encounter between the modern world and this ancient literary genre, demonstrating both the versatility and durability of neoclassicism.

THE POLITE MAN OF LETTERS AND HIS PUBLIC

Hume could be dramatized as the Scot arriving out of a clear blue sky to mend the weakness in English historical culture, giving the English their general history written to classical standards, just as William Robertson, who earned a reputation as the 'Livy' of Scottish history, was simultaneously doing. The story of Hume as savior could be told in tandem with that of Robertson, who began writing in 1753 and publishing in 1759. However, this would be more properly the history of Scottish historiography, and we have been tracing the fortunes of histories of England. Hume did not actually appear quite out of the blue; in the decades before publication of his *History*, England had helped to furnish him with the role of professional man of letters, with the requisite source materials, and with an audience more inclined to his polite, neoclassical performance.

The progress of politeness – of refinement, sociability, and aesthetic excellence in opposition to crudity, pedantry, and controversy – was an uneven affair, difficult to map out. In the late seventeenth and early eighteenth century, many impolite historical projects found substantial backing from the royal court, the universities, and the Church of England. However, as we saw in Chapter 6, the part played by these institutional foes of politeness began to diminish. By about 1730 the tide was turning against clericalist histories and antiquarian works, and the wits were winning the day. The cultural establishment gravitated toward polite study of the past. While party conflict and religious dispute continued to flare up in the 1750s and beyond, Protestantism, parliament, and the royal family were all much more secure than they had been in the late seventeenth and early eighteenth century, when the specters of Catholicism, royal absolutism, and dynastic crisis had fueled polemical historical scholarship and had challenged, at the same time that it gave birth to, the cause of politeness. The decline of the Inns of Court must also have had a role in the rise of politeness. This great support of antiquarian culture had trained generations of Englishmen to discuss historical and political questions in a legal idiom but was now in retreat.[11] In these changed circumstances, polite learning flourished. Polite scholarship was meant to be more socially useful than etymological and antiquarian studies. Directly relevant to the education of a gentleman, polite learning helped him acquire political knowledge and social refinement through conversation and reading classical texts. Historical study was useful to the man of taste if it assisted in polishing his manners, cultivating his aesthetic capacity, and educating him for public life.

Politically, politeness aimed to stabilize the community by uniting its members in the common enterprise of protecting the rules of justice.[12] For his part, Hume exploited the political dimension of politeness in an attempt to end lingering party and dynastic strife. One of his principal objects in writing the *History* was to promote political moderation at a time when he believed political and religious turmoil meant that Britain was sliding towards revolution. Hume wished to modernize political philosophy, on which he believed all government rested, by convincing each political party, tory as well as whig, that it could only focus on the public good in the present and the future if it abandoned anachronistic party platforms of the past. He hoped to disabuse jacobite-leaning tories of outdated notions of passive obedience, and whigs of their views contrasting English liberty and French slavery, championing ancient constitutionalism, and decrying the evils of Stuart kingship.[13] To root out faction, Hume turned to politeness, which had a tendency to lower political temperatures and to prime social interaction. He wrote polite essays and polite history to encourage sociable, 'conversible' people to furnish their conversation with worthy subjects such as poetry, history, and philosophy, which 'learned' but often anti-social men had produced. By the same token, these somewhat monkish writers could only acquire manners, taste, and style through interaction with other human beings – the 'conversible World.'[14]

Hume somewhat ironically anointed women 'the Sovereigns of the Empire of Conversation.' Whether as readers or writers of history, however, women had little part in the neoclassical historical culture we have been studying. History was supposed to be written for, by, and about men, the makers of political and military deeds worthy of a place in history. But from the early 1740s, with essays 'Of the Study of History' and 'Of Essay Writing,'[15] Hume provided a political and philosophical sanction for women, if not as the writers, then at least as the readers of history, and as important influences upon a new political culture whose history would one day be recorded. According to Hume, women were essential to polite conversation, which moderated and enlightened politics by promoting mutual refinement and edification. Since women had such a salutary influence on polite politics, they became fit for political literature, historical literature in particular. Hume wrote his own *History* for women and they read it. One such reader, Catharine Macaulay, became perhaps Hume's most celebrated critic: in 1763 she began publishing a history of her own, an eight-volume refutation of Hume's history of the Stuarts, a decidedly impolite, republican narrative that won the respect of male and female readers alike,[16] and broke the near monopoly men had held over English historiography.

Although the spread of politeness might have piqued men's and women's interest in Hume's polite history, Hume also benefited from impolite learning. Polite historians actually valued the work of the collector, the compiler, the indexer. The ungentlemanly products of full-time historical drudgery saved time and labor for the genteel historian, for whom historical composition was only a part-time or part-career occupation. Indeed, clericalist historians and antiquarians had paved the way for Hume's career as a polite historian. Because of family historians who had published many important historical papers, and general historians, from Brady to Carte, who had done the legwork to collect and assemble key documents of English history, Hume could persevere in the role of professional man of letters without turning into a mere scholar or pedant.

He wanted literary fame, his self-confessed 'ruling Passion,' and we can see how this philosopher's quest for literary acceptance brought him to history and to classical models. Unlike John Oldmixon, who had recklessly begun at the top of the literary hierarchy, only to descend it, Hume began, more modestly, in the middle of the hierarchy and ascended it, moving from treatise to essay to history. He responded to literary setbacks by climbing rungs on the ladder, never looking down. His first literary undertaking, the *Treatise of Human Nature*, published in 1738, did not sell very well, and it was from this time that Hume first conceived of writing history. He had a keen sense of genre and realized that the *Treatise*'s poor showing 'had proceeded more from the manner than the matter.' Recasting part of it into the *Enquiry Concerning Human Understanding* (1748) helped gain him more attention, but he only acquired a real reputation with polite society by writing in a less scholastic genre, the essay. Hume remained dissatisfied even with the reception of his philosophical essays, and turned decisively to history, the noblest of prose genres, as the literary form best suited to his high ambition. Like any Briton living in the 1740s and '50s, Hume would have been hard pressed to find contemporary subject matter noble enough to treat in a Thucydidean history. Besides, a Scot, and a gentleman only – a younger son, at that – not a noble statesman or warrior, Hume realized that he lacked the political and social stature to become an English Thucydides. He lacked the clout to collect materials in England for contemporary history, and understood he could not simply write 'in my Closet, but must apply to the Great for Papers & Intelligence, a thing I mortally abhor.' Although the Scottish philosopher expected the English elite to turn him away at the door, an unofficial competition for the title of English Livy still remained open, and nothing could stop Hume from writing a general history of England covering the period from Caesar's invasion to the Glorious Revolution. Hume gratefully accepted a diplomatic post at Turin in 1748, since 'some greater experience of the Operations of the Field, & Intrigues of the Cabinet, will be requisite, in order to enable me to speak with judgement upon these subjects' in a projected history of England.[17]

The career pattern of the Livian historian had always been less specific than the career pattern of the Thucydidean historian. One did not have to be a teacher of rhetoric relying on imperial patronage, as Livy was, to write a general history; one only required sufficient independence of mind, political awareness, social status, leisure, and education, all of which Hume managed to secure. Hume would reap no psychological or political benefits from imitating Livy's nebulous career, as Bolingbroke and Clarendon had sought by casting themselves in the role of Thucydides. Instead, Hume wrote history in the role of professional man of letters. He saw himself as 'a man of letters,' and so he was. His plan of life and ambition to write a general history owed less to the example of Livy, or to English essayists-turned-historians William Temple and Francis Bacon, than to his admiration for polite writers such as Swift and Pope, and to the new and astute breed of Scottish writers and booksellers in London, the poet and dramatist David Mallet, for example, Hume's acquaintance, Bolingbroke's friend and literary executor.[18] In his essays Hume continued the program to reform political culture initiated by Addison, Steele, and Defoe, but he was more independent than they. By 1752, before embarking on his historical project, Hume was firmly established in the role of professional man of letters; by 1757, after completing the first two volumes of his *History*, Hume had mastered it, becoming the most respected man of letters in England as well as Scotland.[19]

He did so by appealing to an elite and international readership, the only one that could bestow the literary glory he coveted. A cosmopolitan Scot, a Francophile, Hume realized the weakness in English historiography was not just a parochial concern of the English but also of interest to the Europeans who had for decades needled the English about the shortcomings of their historiography. Hume considered the central themes of his *History*, liberty and civilization, to be Europe-wide phenomena, not the unique products of English experience, and so he analyzed the English past in the larger context of continental civilization.[20] He wrote for his fellow Scots because in one sense English history had become Scotland's history, too. Many Scottish literati interpreted the liberty eighteenth-century Scots enjoyed as the product of the 1707 Union with England rather than the outcome of native political and social developments. The general history of England therefore had more explanatory power for contemporary Scots than their own pre-Union history had,[21] and so the Scottish intelligentsia had come to take a real interest in the fate of English historiography, as Hume's historical writing and the Scottish reception to it would reveal.

Hume did not write for Britons ranked below the upper reaches of the middling sort, below Edinburgh professionals, for example. Unlike the classical historian, he was more interested in an immediate audience reached by the printing press than in anonymous posterity or in the set of close friends with whom he shared heretical works in manuscript. But when Hume said the *History* 'was calculated to be popular,' he meant popular compared with his philosophical writings, which were 'calculated for so few Readers.' He meant the *History* was intended to sell at least as well, probably better, than the essays, which were being reprinted every few years in editions of 1000 to 1500 copies.[22] If Hume had truly wanted to be popular, if he had written for a Rapinesque audience, he might have serialized his work, but instead he dismissed the practice as having 'somewhat of a quackish Air.' He might have published in octavo, but instead he and his publishers chose quarto, revealing their joint calculations about the most likely audience for the book – the affluent clientele widely recognized as purchasers of quarto and folio books. Hume might have published his essays and *History* not in book form but in widely-circulated journals, much as Bolingbroke had done with his *Oldcastle's Remarks on the History of England*. But Hume's plans in 1739 and 1740 to launch a *Craftsman*-like periodical never came to fruition.[23]

A NEOCLASSICAL PROGRAM

In 1753, shortly before publishing his first volume of history, Hume told a friend:

> You know that there is no post of honour in the English Parnassus more vacant than that of History. Style, judgement, impartiality, care – everything is wanting to our historians; and even Rapin, during this latter period, is extremely deficient. I make my work very concise, after the manner of the Ancients.[24]

For good measure he threw in the Thucydidean tag, in Greek, about his work being 'a possession for all time.' Clarendon, of course, had filled the Thucydidean role, so Hume's allusion to the vacant 'English Parnassus' chiefly referred to the lack of a general history of England comparable to those of the ancients or the best of the moderns. Hume made it plain that he would repair this longstanding weakness in English historiography by writing a successful history in imitation of the ancient historians. It was becoming clearer and clearer to him how radical a break he would have to make from the historians who preceded him. In two private letters written in 1754, Hume distinguished his own work from theirs:

> The more I advance in my undertaking, the more I am convinced that the History of England has never yet been written, not only for style, which is notorious to all the world, but also for matter; such is the ignorance and partiality of all our historians. Rapin, whom I had an esteem for, is totally despicable ...

> If you consider the vast Variety of Events, with which these two Reigns [James I and Charles I], particularly the last, are crowded, you will conclude that my Narration is rapid, and that I have more propos'd as my Model the concise manner of the antient Historians, than the prolix, tedious Style of some modern Compilers. I have inserted no original Papers, and enter'd into no Detail of minute, uninteresting Facts. The philosophical Spirit, which I have so much indulg'd in all my Writings, finds here ample Materials to work upon.[25]

Hume rejected the modern manner of English historians in favor of a philosophical and neoclassical approach to the past. His targets were not learning or criticism but the antiquarian form they took and the polemical use made of them by most historians. Strewn with documents, pedantic notes, and trite arguments and stories, the work of Rapin and the others had no precedents in the finest ancient historians. Hume's epitaph for Carte reinforced this indictment of English historians: 'A late author of great industry and learning, but full of prejudices, and of no penetration.'[26] Instead of a partisan and documentary history of England, Hume wished to write a polished, detached neoclassical narrative embodying a moderate political philosophy stylistically as well as substantively.

Hume decided to remove the cancer of party by cutting at its source in the early-Stuart period. He wrote his *History* backwards, beginning with the Stuarts, then covering the Tudors, and finally narrating the history of medieval England. Volume one, covering the reigns of James I and Charles I, appeared in Edinburgh in 1754. Volume two, dated 1757 and published in London, took the story to 1689. By late 1761 Hume published in London four further volumes that completed his history of England from Roman times to the Glorious Revolution, a history that bore the marks of neoclassical historiography.

Hume appears to have written the *History* in the belief that he was being as truthful as he could be, and, like the classical historians, he saw nothing incompatible with so writing and with his function as a moralist. To make value judgments in praise of such themes as liberty and civilization was a historian's high duty, not a breach of impartiality or a lapse of good taste. Hume took seriously this classical conception of history as teacher, as *magister vitae*. Before deducing a 'useful lesson' from the experience of Charles I in the Civil War, 'that it is dangerous for princes, even from the appearance of necessity, to assume more authority, than the laws have allowed them,' Hume reaffirmed the commonplace humanist view of history as the teacher of morals and politics by example: 'History, the great mistress of wisdom, furnishes examples of all kinds; and every prudential, as well as moral precept, may be authorized by those events, which her enlarged mirror is able to present to us.'[27] Hume filled the *History* with examples of behavior and policy to be imitated or avoided. His narrative was studded with aphorisms about human nature and public policy that applied not simply to the event being commented upon but to the present as well as the future, cast as they were in the present tense. Hume damned a tenth-century dispute between monks and secular clergy by concluding, 'it is a just remark, that the more affinity there is between theological parties, the greater commonly is their animosity.'[28] To insert maxims such as this one into a historical narrative was nothing new; by doing so, Hume drew upon the techniques of the classical historians. .

This last 'remark' about clerical in-fighting showed Hume to be very much a man of his time, and it is customary as well as proper to place Hume's work in the context of Enlightenment historio-graphy. The neoclassical historian was a teacher of moral and political lessons, and many of Hume's particular lessons were those commonly associated with the program of Enlightenment. He extolled the advantages of liberty of conscience and religious toleration, while he condemned their opposites. In criticism that was as Protestant as it was enlightened, he denounced the Roman Catholic Church, particularly the tyranny the pontiff had exercised over the English church, and more generally the deceitful and power-hungry priests who extended sacred and secular author-ity over prince and people. Ignorance, superstition, frivolous theology alike he inveighed against.[29] His philosophical mind advised him to distrust the miracles a credulous populace at-tributed to Joan of Arc, and he reminded readers, 'It is the busi-ness of history to distinguish between the *miraculous* and the *marvellous*; to reject the first in all narrations merely profane and human; to doubt the second. . . .'[30] Elsewhere in the *History* Hume excoriated judicial torture for its injustice and inhumanity, war for its futility and barbarity.[31] All told, it was a performance worthy of Voltaire, as his contemporaries were to notice.

On the issue of war, Hume's enlightened values came into con-flict with his obligations as a historian. Clearly he could not stomach the violence and senselessness of war, and yet he was duty-bound as a historian to record the military battles he came upon in English history, for war and politics constituted the tra-ditional subject matter of history. Hume took an interest in the latter but rarely the former. He wrote of the early Stuarts: 'The great ornament of history, during these reigns, are the civil, not the mili-tary transactions.'[32] Like Roger North and William Guthrie, Hume occasionally called into question the significance and heroism of martial events,[33] even parodying them, as one of his neoclassical models, Machiavelli, had once done: 'The whole amount of the exploits on both sides is, the taking of a castle, the surprise of a straggling party, a rencounter of horse, which resembles more a rout than a battle.'[34] Although he belittled this chivalric contest between Richard I and the French as too 'frivolous' to dwell upon, Hume did muster his literary skills to narrate a military exploit truly worthy of history. His account of the Battle of Hastings was a classical set piece: Hume gave the political background and motives for William's invasion, his preparations for the voyage, his setting sail and his landing, the doomed scene in England, where Harold ignored warnings of impending catastrophe, the speech William delivered to his troops on the eve of battle, the technical description of the fighting itself, the formal summing up of the significance of the event, and finally the piteous reaction of the English to the tragedy that had befallen them.[35] This drama and its aftermath were reminiscent of Thucydides' Sicilian Expedition, although Hume's account was truncated and his Norman invaders succeeded whereas the Athenians failed to conquer Sicily. Despite his distaste for both war and the middle ages, Hume had to admit the significance of this battle and so he adorned it with eloquence and drama comparable to his classical models.

Not only did the war and politics and didacticism of the classical historian find a place in the *History*, so did the invented speeches, or at least something that looked very much like them. Neoclassicists had disagreed about the propriety of putting words in the mouths of protagonists in order to dramatize and clarify issues at hand, but Hume found the device to be useful, whether in setting out opposing arguments of York and Lancaster in the Wars of the Roses or of the House of Commons and the court over the Petition of Right.[36] He made no pretence that the speeches were actually delivered in the words he presented, even in cases where transcripts of genuine speeches were available to him. Instead, Hume pieced together the best arguments *he* could think of, above and beyond what contemporaries managed to devise, and put them in his own style, not that of contemporaries. 'We shall relate, in a few words,' Hume wrote, 'the topics, by which each side supported, or *might* have supported, their scheme of policy.'[37] It was remarkable that this telltale conceit of classical historiography survived into the third quarter of the eighteenth century, but Hume did modify the invented speech to serve his own goals. In keeping with the chaste style of the *History*, Hume excised from the speeches the drama and rhetorical flash common to classical historiography, the bite and the directness. He did not attribute speeches to specific historical actors, only to parties, and so the 'speeches' functioned primarily as rhetorical exercises stating the pros and cons of policy. To avoid the hot-tempered example of party historians, Hume eschewed long, direct quotations of impassioned partisans and replaced them with brief, polite, reasoned discourses.

Throughout his narrative Hume wrote with the utmost solemnity and used the commonplace language of the classical historian to remind readers of this fact. Over and over again, he wrote of addressing 'posterity,' of recording only 'memorable' events according to the dual criteria of their capacity to 'instruct and entertain.' He frequently asserted that this subject matter was 'worthy' of anything in 'ancient or modern history.'[38] He disdained whatever was 'trivial' or 'frivolous,' and maintained a strict decorum regarding events which were base, unseemly, or ignoble, which he relegated to footnotes or disguised in euphemisms.[39] His language was suitably polite, dignified, and formal. Each principal character, each 'great' man or rare woman whose deeds constituted history, he assessed in a set-piece character sketch, yet another classical literary device. Carefully, systematically, he weighed the virtues and vices, successes and failures, of monarchs and ministers. Hume's characters, like Clarendon's, were destined to enshrine their subjects as historical figures, and their author as a literary figure, for all time.

In many ways, then, Hume's narrative showed a striking resemblance to the work of the classical historians and their imitators. However, we have already seen how, in minor ways, he departed from a strict adherence to his models, how his repugnance for war undermined his battle narratives, and how his commitment to political moderation minimized the drama and passion of his invented speeches. In fact, Hume was fully aware that his models, however worthy of imitation, needed to be adapted in some measure to modern circumstances. In the *History* Hume criticized the neoclassicism of Ben Jonson: 'A servile copyist of the ancients, Johnson translated into bad English the beautiful passages of the Greek and Roman authors, without accommodating them to the manners of his age and country.'[40] Here Hume touched upon a central issue of imitation: just how far should a model be reworked to take account of present-day concerns? Like earlier neoclassical historians, Hume had to decide just how modern or how ancient his work of history would be. Like his predecessors, he faced certain phenomena of the modern world that could call for compromises with his neoclassical project. Every neoclassical historian had his own dragons to slay, his own accommodations 'to the manners of his age and country' to make.

Britain during the age of Enlightenment presented numerous challenges to Hume's enterprise. Writing a complete history of England required that he describe the Christian middle ages, so Hume had to devise a way to deal with an era unworthy of a civilized history, a period so barbarous and so poorly chronicled that it could hardly afford either instruction or entertainment to a polite readership. Hume also aimed to conquer the partisanship which had capsized so many general histories. The issue of party haunted Hume. His philosophical spirit might help him to dissect those party histories, but even if Hume could write impartially – and he conceded that even he was susceptible to political prejudice[41] – could he convince his partisan readership to bury ancient differences in historical interpretation and indeed to lay aside party affiliation altogether? Besides modern political parties, Hume had to struggle with other modern subjects which either did not exist in antiquity or in which, as non-political matter, the ancient historians had taken little interest. One of his central themes was the progress of civilization, a far-ranging subject that included not just traditional political and military matters but also topics that went beyond the worthy deeds of individual heros to commerce, manners, and arts. As a philosophical historian Hume wished to discuss these cultural matters, indeed to expand his definition of 'political' to welcome them into his story. His challenge was to convince readers that the history of civilization was vitally linked to that of politics, and somehow to incorporate that cultural history into the form of a neoclassical narrative without the dissertations, lists, and documents that had torn apart the narratives of the antiquarians and clerical historians on whom he relied as sources.

A CULTURAL HISTORY OF LIBERTY AND CIVILIZATION

Let us look now at how Hume went about meeting these multiple challenges to his project, beginning with an examination of the interplay between the twin pillars of his *History*, liberty and civilization. From the earliest pages of the *History* his readers discovered Hume's interest in the history of liberty and of civilization,[42] his approbation of both, and his belief that both were fragile creations that had to be cherished if they were to survive. Hume constructed his narrative in such a manner that the events of the past pointed toward the present, the age which the historian inhabited and in which he believed both liberty and civilization flourished to an almost unprecedented extent. Before 1688, it was impossible for English governments even to approach the mature system of politics under which Hume lived. English civilization, like English liberty, grew slowly and irregularly until at last it too blossomed in Hume's own day. Hume came to learn that, far from marching steadily and triumphantly arm in arm, liberty and civilization parted ways at decisive points in their history.

Hume believed that barbarism and religious zealotry proved destructive of liberty, but he had to admit that the English people owed their precious liberty in part to the German barbarians and more especially to the Puritans of the seventeenth century. The overriding thesis of the *History* was that true liberty was a very modern, seventeenth-century achievement, not a medieval one, so it is not surprising that Hume's reference to barbarian liberty is only vague and fleeting. Hume contended that Europeans, Britons included, owed their 'sentiments of liberty, honor, equity, and valor' to 'those generous barbarians' who overrode the 'military despotism' of the Roman Empire.[43] And yet, in such a violent, unsettled age, true political liberty had little chance to bloom. To be sure, a certain few, premature shoots on the tree of liberty sprouted. Hume idolized Alfred the Great as a man whose virtues, talents, and learning, and whose concern for liberty and justice, suggested that the king had been placed by 'Fortune' in the wrong historical epoch.[44] Hume admired the independent spirit of the Saxon barbarians, but concluded that their excessive freedom resulted in lawlessness and rule by aristocratic faction.[45] The next wave of barbarian conquerors brought little succor to the conquered. The Normans, out of military necessity, instituted a feudal system of government which tended to exalt the power of the nobility; the barons oppressed the people and even threatened the authority of the monarch.[46] Rare were the bright spots in this dark age without liberty. During the reign of Henry II, the crown relaxed its arbitrary hold on the nation, and the barons likewise eased their grip on the people.[47] Another very modest step toward true liberty, indeed toward true government, came with the granting of Magna Carta: 'The barbarous licence of the kings, and perhaps of the nobles, was thenceforth somewhat more restrained,'[48] wrote Hume, although the limitations on royal power did not actually take effect until the reign of Edward III. Hume went on to clarify just how little liberty existed even then, insisting that 'the government, at best, was only a barbarous monarchy.'[49] England suffered under this yoke until the seventeenth century. Henry VII did make a change in the feudal law permitting the alienation of estates, which would contribute to a gradual shift in power from the nobles to the commonalty.[50] However, Henry's family proved in some ways to be even more averse to liberty than its predecessors. The Tudors were 'arbitrary' and 'despotic,' comparable to the sultans of Turkey.[51]

A crucial turning point in the history of liberty took place during the reign of James I, when the House of Commons began successfully to challenge the swollen authority of the crown. Motivated largely by religious principles, the Commons eventually seized control of the church and the monarchy itself. Hume deplored the fanaticism, bigotry, and barbarity by which the Puritans triumphed in the Civil War and murdered King Charles, but he confessed that 'it was to this sect, whose principles appear so frivolous and habits so ridiculous, that the English owe the whole freedom of their constitution.'[52] After locating this 'epoch of true liberty,' Hume neatly summed up the further progress of liberty by stating that it was 'confirmed by the Restoration, and enlarged and secured by the Revolution.'[53] Indeed, Hume's story reached a crescendo and conclusion in the years 1688 and 1689, when the Prince of Orange restored to England the liberty and religion James II had wrongfully seized. The Glorious Revolution established once and for all the respective powers of the prince and the people, and Hume concluded his *History* on a celebratory note: 'we, in this island, have ever since enjoyed, if not the best system of government, at least the most entire system of liberty, that ever was known amongst mankind.'[54]

This story of liberty's success was a political one; as such it enjoyed an undisputed place in a neoclassical history whose subject matter was supposed to be martial and political. Yet this first reading of the *History* leaves much unsaid. The great historians, whether classical or neoclassical, were deemed great in part because of their explanatory power, and Hume's portrayal of

English liberty, as summarized above, did not explain why liberty came so late and so suddenly to England. A second look at the *History* reveals that Hume did indeed furnish an explanation for this phenomenon; however, his analysis was not only political but also cultural. In modern history, the only way to account fully for political events was to provide the cultural context for the deeds of men, Hume came to argue. In fact, the depression as well as the rise of liberty could only he explained by reference to Hume's other principal theme, civilization. To Hume, the political movements of the past – as well as the present – remained incomprehensible without an understanding of trade, learning, manners, and law. Hume defended this methodological proposition in his famous finale to the medieval volumes:

> The rise, progress, perfection, and decline of art and science, are curious objects of contemplation, and intimately connected with a narration of civil transactions. The events of no particular period can be fully accounted for, but by considering the degrees of advancement, which men have reached in those particulars.[55]

Cultural analysis, not just political narrative, helped Hume understand both the frustration of liberty before the seventeenth century and its wondrous maturation during it. The Saxons loved liberty but they lacked the requisite level of civilization to sustain it. They did not cultivate 'the refined arts of life,' or even attend to agricultural improvement.[56] The Normans also proved to be too 'licentious' for liberty. '[T]rue or regular liberty,' with which Hume was concerned and which did not take root in England until the time of the Stuarts, required 'such improvement in knowledge and morals, as can only be the result of reflection and experience, and must grow to perfection during several ages of settled and established government.'[57] All these prerequisites Hume found lacking in Saxon and Norman societies, and he mocked the earliest parliaments as filled with 'barbarians' unfit for government. Hume fixed the eleventh century as the darkest era of ignorance, but then noticed a very gradual improvement in human knowledge, highlighted by the re-discovery of Roman law, and a shift in interest from military to civil matters. Although advantageous to liberty, none of these salutary developments alone could secure the full measure of liberty England was ultimately to achieve. Hume added a Baconian and Harringtonian economic theorem to this cultural interpretation, when he identified 'arts and commerce' as 'the necessary attendants of liberty and equality.' The House of Commons, which played such a decisive role in the eventual attainment of true liberty, came into existence in the time of Edward I, when the growth of trade, arts, and manufacturing, coupled with the growing disparity of wealth between the greater and lesser nobility, brought together the gentry and the burgesses in a lower house of parliament distinct from that of the peers.[58]

The House of Commons emerged as a force to be reckoned with, but it was not until a subsequent 'revolution in manners' took place that a revolution in politics could occur. The late fifteenth century marked a watershed in European affairs, Hume observed. The discovery of the New World, of classical literature, of movable type, of gunpowder, of an alternative to Roman Christianity amounted to a 'general revolution' that created the modern world 'with regard to commerce, arts, science, government, police, and cultivation.'[59] The changed manners of the barons had momentous and unforeseen consequences. The nobility's newfound taste for luxury items cost it a good deal of treasure, which made its way to the 'mechanics and merchants' who satisfied the demand for such goods. These suppliers thereby gained some independence from their overlords, breaking the feudal ties between lord and vassal. At the same time, the nobles strove to turn a profit from their land, so they released redundant field hands from service, dissolving feudal relationships even further. 'By all these means,' Hume explained, 'the cities encreased; the middle rank of men began to be rich and powerful' and finally this new order, represented in the House of Commons, successfully challenged the nobles and the crown to establish 'a new plan of liberty.' Hume took pains to minimize the contribution of Henry VII's legislation to the dissolution of the feudal system, claiming the law to alienate tenures only helped to sanction a practice long since common.[60] It was not a political act by a great man that effected 'the secret revolution of government.' Rather, a slow and impersonal cultural movement gave birth to the modern English constitution.

Although Hume offered a political and military narrative of the seventeenth century, as might any neoclassical historian, the epoch-breaking events of that century were grounded in phenomena hitherto not regarded strictly political by English writers of narrative history but which Hume wished to elevate to the political plane. Hume described the rise of the Puritans, the battle between parliament and the Stuarts, the course of the Civil War, but his interpretation of those events involved more literary, artistic, and economic analysis than had appeared in previous accounts. Hume traced the spread of these altered 'manners' from their origin in the fifteenth to their political eruption in the seventeenth century. The struggle for limited government, born of changes in attitudes, property, and power, never succeeded so long as the Tudor tyrants held sway, but once the new Scottish royal dynasty was installed, the passion for liberty proved irresistible. James I could not comprehend these historic changes, nor could he overcome their consequences. The discovery of West Indian gold, as well as the general growth of commerce, increased the price of goods, and the court expected the king to support it in a manner more magnificent than before, all at a time when crown income was nearly stagnant. The resolve of the people to resist the imposition of taxes on its new wealth, combined with the example of classical heroes resisting unlimited political authority, spread by broadened appreciation of classical literature, roused the House of Commons to action.[61] The century of liberty was inaugurated.

Thus, civilization and liberty triumphed, but only after a valiant struggle against barbarism and despotism. Hume argued that a high level of civilization had to exist before liberty could take hold; on the other hand, civilization's opposite, barbarism, commonly led to despotism. He believed liberty existed in his own day because the stable, polite character of British civilization allowed it to flourish. In the *History*, as well as in other writings, he encouraged these aspects of society. Even in what was generally a barbarous expanse of history, Hume singled out for praise any part of medieval life that encouraged peaceable social intercourse, while decrying whatever detracted from it. In the otherwise dark passages of history predating the reign of James I, he called attention to the administration of justice, the pursuit of peaceful arts, and the obedience to law. He saw redeeming social value in the growth of cities as well as commerce, which removed men from rustic isolation and forced them to practice politeness and tolerance. Because they usually evinced so little regard for such features of civilized life, the Saxons could not escape Hume's blanket condemnation: 'Among that military and turbulent people, so averse to commerce and the arts, and so little enured to industry, justice was commonly very ill administered, and great oppression and violence seem to have prevailed.'[62] The contrast with early seventeenth-century England could not have been greater. For a brief time commerce, liberty, and the arts mutually encouraged each other, until 'the wretched fanaticism, which so much infected the parliamentary party, [proved] no less destructive of taste and science, than of all law and order.'[63] Indeed, perhaps besides war itself, religious fanaticism above every other agent of barbarism turned out to be the most potent solvent of everything which civilization – and Hume – had so painstakingly worked to unite. The zealot's solipsistic world, a nightmarish combination of divine inspiration and an overheated imagination, showed a contemptible disregard for others. To Hume, the outbreak of the Civil War demonstrated the pernicious effects of such an asocial outlook: 'The fanatical spirit, let loose, confounded all regard to ease, safety, interest; and dissolved every moral and civil obligation.'[64] As detrimental as Christianity had often been to the progress of civilization, however, it had its redemptive moments as well, helping to rid the Saxons of their idolatry and to mitigate the militarism and anarchy of the middle ages. Protestantism introduced a more comprehensive system of justice, and the Civil War independents rejected the idea of religious persecution.[65] Finally and most ironically, the Puritans helped to bring about English liberty. As we have already noted, Hume was convinced that as absurd a sect as the Puritans were, their political leadership in the Civil War laid the groundwork for England's constitutional freedom. For a moment, an unlikely moment, freedom and fanaticism walked hand in hand.

A POLITE NARRATIVE

By making a comparative analysis of liberty and civilization, Hume tried to meet the challenge of legitimizing the union of cultural history with modern political history. However, a further challenge to his success as a neoclassical historian remained. By some literary sleight of hand, could Hume incorporate his cultural analysis into a polite narrative of deeds? He needed to take the content of his sources – the collections regarding law, commerce, and the arts – and somehow fit them into the form of a connected story. His *History* was overwhelmingly a political narrative, but in those places it was not he did in fact manage to work in his cultural theses and evidence regarding civilization. For example, he sometimes employed formal digressions in the body of the narrative itself, a practice which had precedents in classical historiography.[66] At the end of each reign he also took the opportunity to insert a 'character' of the monarch and a section on 'Miscellaneous transactions,' where he could also write about matters not strictly political. On occasion he did no better than his predecessors, simply listing the names of officeholders for little apparent reason other than commemoration.[67] Usually, however, his remarks about coinage, trade, and law referred implicitly to larger themes about liberty and civilization, and were not merely random antiquarian details.[68] His survey of literature, for example, served as an index of the progress of the peaceable arts. Even outside the history proper, in footnotes, endnotes, and appendices, where he also placed relevant but non-traditional matter, Hume tried to be as concise, polite, and non-technical as possible: foreign languages, documents, philological details he all but banished. The appendix of an essayist and philosopher, Hume, bore little resemblance to that of a polemicist and philologist, Brady, although the former relied heavily on the latter for the content of his medieval volumes.

Hume was aware of the need to preserve the integrity of his narrative against the continual threat of erudition, which had spoiled the literary quality of Brady and other predecessors. Hume, Robertson, Gibbon, Edmund Burke, and Adam Smith, among others, debated the proper placement of citations, explanations, and digressions in endnotes, footnotes, marginal notes, appendices, or the narrative itself. Taking the classical historians as his standard, Smith rejected notes of every sort as revealing either the author's ostentation or literary incompetence.[69] In his Stuart volumes as originally published, Hume used appendices but was a purist regarding the citation of his sources, which he refused to do because the ancients and their modern imitators eschewed the practice. Although he eventually retreated,[70] and supplied the citations, Hume never gave up attempting to improve the quality of his narrative. In over 20 years of revising the *History* Hume weeded out anything that seemed to mar the literary quality of his story, and either removed it to the notes or appendices or dispensed with it altogether. At one point he transferred to the notes a digression on the progress of liberty 'in order to avoid, as much as possible, the style of dissertation in the body of [the author's] history.'[71] The works of most general historians had been inundated – many readers, including Hume, thought – by dissertations, translations, transcripts, footnotes, the stock-in-trade of the modern scholar. However, Hume made sure that endnotes and appendices accounted for a mere fraction, about 7 per cent, of his *History*.[72] Whereas many historians had copied out pages of original documents into their works, Hume never inserted a document of any length, and very rarely even quoted anything directly. Instead, he paraphrased or summarized.[73] It was Hume's history, Hume's narration, and he tried to prevent his sources from overtaking him. He understood that since history was 'a collection of facts which are multiplying without end,' the historian had to abridge his materials or risk being drowned by them.[74] A sign Hume knew he was winning the battle to transform antiquarian information into narrative, to weave cultural history into the fabric of a political work, appeared in revisions to his appendix to the reign of James I, where he deleted the apologetic introductory clause 'departing a little from the historical style' and simply asserted: 'It may not be improper, at this period, to make a pause: and to take a survey of the state of the kingdom, with regard to government, manners, finances, arms, trade, learning.'[75] Hume had the confidence to see that this integration of cultural and political matters, which he helped to pioneer, had become the new 'historical style,' though one, we have been arguing, that did not on that account depart significantly from neoclassical conceptions of history.

Hume might thus have met the challenges to the integrity of his narrative and the legitimacy of his subject matter; however, he also had to find a way of dealing with the middle ages, a period almost entirely bereft of the liberty and civilization he championed and one that, by no coincidence, had left behind poor records. Hume distrusted the writings of monks, who by their very nature were prone to superstition and credulity, most unfit eyewitnesses for Hume's enlightened history. To Hume, moreover, 'the adventures of barbarous nations, even if they were recorded, could afford little or no entertainment to men born in a more cultivated age.'[76] Hume's solution was to reject all 'fables' and 'tales,' do a comparative study of 'language, manners, and customs,' then move as quickly as possible to periods later in the middle ages but especially to the modern age in the sixteenth and seventeenth century, when records as well as events became more civilized.[77] Rather than struggle to reconstruct early British history by the ingenious yet fruitless 'dark industry of antiquaries,' Hume chose to discuss only the most material events of those uncultivated times, informing the reader on occasion that 'nothing memorable' had taken place during a particular period. In a criticism of the chroniclers, Hume asked, 'What instruction or entertainment can it give the reader to hear a long bead-roll of barbarous names . . . who successively murdered, expelled, or inherited from each other, and obscurely filled the throne of [the East Angles]?'[78] Hume in effect answered his own question later in the *History*, when he advised readers that a knowledge of this epoch provided examples of uncivilized behavior that made them grateful for the system of government they enjoyed at present.[79] Tested by Hume's neoclassical criteria of selection – what was worthy, instructive, or entertaining – the middle ages nearly evaporated as subject matter. But by abridging the medieval past, by adhering to his themes of liberty and civilization, or more typically their opposites, Hume tried to rescue medieval history in order to fill out a 'complete' history of England. Perversely, he had catalogued counter-examples of events, manners, and men that Britons had to refrain from ever imitating, and he did so with enough literary polish and withering irony, he hoped, to render the dark ages palatable to a cultivated readership.

To Hume, perhaps the most important ideological task of his medieval history was putting to rest many of the historical controversies regarding that era. Part of his campaign to modernize contemporary political life necessitated burying the disputes over the origin of parliament, the impact of the Norman Conquest, and the existence of the ancient constitution, because these scholarly debates kept alive an outdated party system. To succeed in demolishing cherished opinions, Hume would have to use great tact. Hume resolved to destroy the whig myth of the ancient constitution, for example, but he went about it in a way calculated to give as little offense to whigs as possible. Tory historians had argued that the Anglo-Saxon assembly, the Wittenagemot, had been composed of judges, while whigs claimed commoners sat there. Like Rapin, Hume acted as if he had no personal stake in the outcome of this point of political contention. However, the Scot went even further than the Huguenot to defuse the issue

and adopt an impartial stance. First he claimed that not enough
evidence remained to settle the issue beyond all doubt. Next he
refused to dignify the partisan debate by even referring to the
parties by name, instead labeling them contemptuously the
'monarchical faction' and the 'popular faction.' Then he inserted
a matter-of-fact paragraph, based on Brady, making the case for
aristocratic membership in the council, followed by a paragraph
qualifying this conclusion. Finally, he drew back even more politely
from a definitive interpretation, by reaffirming the possibility
that commoners might indeed have gained membership in the
council. For good measure, Hume placed these thoughts in an
appendix, not the body of the *History*.[80] By similar devices, he
tried elsewhere in the *History* to smooth the ruffled feathers of
political controversy, even ridiculing it out of existence. As to
the game of semantics over whether William I deserved his title,
'Conqueror,' Hume concluded that 'the present rights and
privileges of the people . . . can never be affected by a transaction,
which passed seven hundred years ago.'[81] Indeed, Hume believed
that any historical event predating 1688 should not impinge upon
modern-day politics, as the revolution 'has put the nature of the
English constitution beyond all controversy.'[82]

Still, Hume was dismayed to find that certain controversial
figures of modern history acted as lightning rods for political
debate: Elizabeth I, Charles I, and Civil War parliamentarian John
Hampden proved too hot to write about, even in the third quarter
of the eighteenth century. Of the last's motives, Hume observed:
'even at present, (such is the force of party prejudices,) there are
few people who have coolness enough to see these matters in a
proper light .'[83] Although Hume's *History* employed the standard
historical agents of neoclassical historiography – individual great
men – we have also seen him attribute agency to such impersonal
phenomena as 'manners.' One such agent, almost a character in
the *History*, was the constitution itself, and Hume tended to blame
it rather than individual monarchs and ministers for some of
the disasters suffered by the English state. In the disputes between
the early Stuarts and their parliaments, Hume pointed out how
irregular and unintelligible the constitution then was, how wrong-
headed it would therefore be to place complete blame upon one
side or the other in that calamity.[84] The constitution, in each of
its sundry manifestations, was at least partly to blame for the
English defeat at Hastings, for the overthrow of Edward II, for

the tyranny of Queen Elizabeth's rule.[85] Hume was in some measure depersonalizing the past, making it more difficult for party writers to mine history for inflammatory arguments in support of contemporary policies. An economy, a constitution, an invention such as printing, each had a role to play in the historical causation of political events, and yet each could not be attacked or defended with the same visceral fervor as Charles the Martyr or Good Queen Bess could be. Although various impersonal agents of change had roused the English people in the modern age – paper credit, for example – Hume wished his readers to abandon any emotional attachment to the pre-1688 past, and reserve it completely for the event, the revolution, by which their liberty had been secured. In many ways the constitution, unsettled and contradictory, was a villain in English history until the Glorious Revolution made it a hero, settled and perfect.

HUME'S RECEPTION IN BRITAIN

Hume died in a faction-ridden Britain, in 1776, never having deleted references to the evils of the party system.[86] To his last days he worked to exorcise controversy from the past in order to rid the present of the political rancor which had proven so harmful both to civil society and the writing of history. Hume acknowledged some benefits to whig rule but none to whig history, which he thought was a blemish on civilized society: 'Compositions the most despicable, both for style and matter [including Rapin's], have been extolled, and propagated, and read; as if they had equalled the most celebrated remains of antiquity.'[87] Hume himself, by implication, had composed a history worthy of a civilized nation, one that might be read as the peer of the celebrated remains of ancient historiography. But when the *History* first began to be published in the 1750s, Hume was gravely disappointed to find that political and religious bigotry still threatened English civilization, so hostile a reception did he encounter. As late as 1773 Hume complained that Englishmen still clung to myths his *History* had exploded – the glories of the Elizabethan age, for example[88] – and still rejected his central claim about the superiority of post-1688 England to pre-revolutionary times. He asked the medievalist Thomas Percy, why still complain of the present times, which, in every respect, so far surpass all the past? I am only sorry to see, that the great Decline, if we ought not rather to say, the total Extinction of Literature in England, prognosticates a very short Duration of all our other Improvements, and threatens a new and a sudden Inroad of Ignorance, Superstition and Barbarism. There cannot be a stronger Symptom of this miserabl[e] Degeneracy, than the Treatment which I have met with for telling [Englishmen] Truth in these particulars.[89]

Although to Hume rejection of his historical truths bespoke cultural decline, by the 1770s English treatment of the *History* had improved dramatically over what it had originally been. Many believed that Hume had solved the chronic weakness in English historiography, having composed the best history of England ever written. Even on its first appearance, the volumes on the Stuarts prompted some readers, especially in France, to compare Hume with the ancient historians, Tacitus in particular. Hume succeeded in uniting history and philosophy in a neoclassical narrative, although not in rendering English politics polite.

The most crippling criticism ever directed against Hume's *History* concerned political partisanship. Hume himself blamed the poverty of English historiography on the party system, and now his *History* appeared to be a victim of that very system, gaining a reputation as a party history, not the impartial work of Livian history at which he had aimed. The furor erupting over the Stuart volumes left Hume wounded and perplexed.

I thought, that, I was the only Historian, that had at once neglected present Power, Interest, and Authority, and the Cry of popular Prejudices; and as the Subject was suited to every Capacity, I expected proportional Applause: But miserable was my Disappointment: I was assailed by one Cry of Reproach, Disapprobation, and even Detestation: English, Scotch, and Irish; Whig and Tory; Churchman and Sectary, Free-thinker and Religionist; Patriot and Courtier united in their Rage against the Man, who had presumed to shed a generous Tear for the Fate of Charles I, and the Earl of Strafford.[90]

That tear, perhaps more than anything else, stained Hume's reputation for impartiality. According to David McQueen, Hume's portrait of the Stuarts betrayed an attempt to apologize 'for the principles and acts of arbitrary power.' McQueen rebuked Hume for apportioning blame on an ambiguous English constitution: the rights and privileges of parliament were perfectly clear, as was the violation of them by Charles I and Charles II.[91] A tory, and possibly a jacobite, Hume lacked the essential qualification for a historian, a regard for truth and impartiality.[92] Richard Hurd and others argued Hume's partisanship extended to religious matters, for he lacked a proper regard for Protestantism: half of Hume's Tudor history exposed 'the absurdities of reformed religion, the other half . . . discredit[ed] the cause of civil liberty.'[93] *The Monthly Review* castigated Hume for his 'indecent reflections on the Protestant religion' as the 'effect of enthusiasm and fanaticism' rather than 'free enquiry, and rational conviction.' McQueen defended Protestants, the first reformers in particular, from the charge of fanaticism which Hume brought against them.[94] 'I am as great an atheist as Bolingbroke; as great a Jacobite as Carte,'[95] declared Hume on his early reputation as a historian. Even he, it appeared, had underestimated the political and religious passions that could be stirred by a history of England.

At least one reviewer appreciated the difficulties a moderate historian faced in addressing a nation where the embers of ancient discord still glowed. Owen Ruffhead, writing in *The Monthly Review*, explained Hume's reception this way:

> The reformation in religion, which took place under the Tudors, the frequent and important revolutions in government, which happened under the Stuarts, were events which have bred endless divisions and animosities among religious and political zealots: and Mr. Hume's free and liberal cast of mind, was ill adapted to reconcile their discordant principles. Little biassed by prejudice, a slave to no sect or party, he attacked both Papists and Protestants, Royalists and Republicans, who, each in their turns, suffered from the acuteness of his reflections, and the severity of his censures. Consequently, he has given frequent, and sometimes reasonable, cause of disgust to both sides . . .[96]

So some reviewers did in fact commend Hume for his impartiality,[97] but even after Hume's death the tory epithet stuck to him. In 1778 Joseph Towers called Hume an enemy to freedom and to Christianity. According to *The Monthly Review*, Hume had been taken in by Dr Brady. Like Brady, Hume was prepared 'to vindicate tyranny, and to destroy the rights of his nation.'[98]

As much as Hume tried to write off the 'Brady Controversy' and downplay the relevance of medieval antiquities to present politics, some readers criticized him for doing so. Ruffhead had to chastise Hume for calling Saxon history 'uninteresting,' and for relying too heavily on Brady as an authority on the middle ages. Ruffhead granted Hume's larger point, that the distant past cannot 'affect present rights, and privileges,' but he took issue with Hume's interpretation of the Norman Conquest and dating of the House of Commons.[99] While Hume found the medieval period to be devoid of much instruction or interest, medievalists objected to the way he glossed over the controversies and details of early English history. Horace Walpole praised the Tudor and Stuart volumes of the *History* in generous terms, but criticized the medieval volumes as skimpy and inaccurate, fit only for novices, not factual enough.[100] Readers had become accustomed to the inclusion of new historical sources in their general histories of England, a practice of little interest to Hume. Brady, Tyrrell, Rapin, Guthrie, Ralph, and Carte had portrayed themselves as industrious researchers rather than as elegant writers. Hume's reliance on them instead of his own original researches occasioned some criticism.[101] Thomas Warton concluded: 'You may read Hume for his eloquence, but Carte is the historian for facts.'[102]

The tory label rather than his alleged deficiencies as a scholar appeared to retard Hume's success in the book trade. Hume's Edinburgh publisher produced 2000 copies of volume one, sold 450 in five weeks, took the rest to London, only to be shut out by an English book-selling monopoly, before relinquishing control of the work to Andrew Millar in London. Millar only managed to sell 45 books in a year. The 1750 copies of volume two had better, but still weak, sales. With some further editions, Millar, by 1762, had published but not entirely sold 3500 two-volume sets on the Stuarts, 3000 on the Tudors, and 2750 on the middle ages.[103] It was a comparatively slow start: the booksellers had conspired against it and party madness had prevented it from looking as impartial as it actually was. Only in the 1770s did sales and new editions pick up, which Hume attributed, in part, to the gradual subsidence of factious party strife. His oft-quoted remark, 'this is the historical Age and this the historical Nation,' came only in 1770. From that date followed 17 eighteenth-century editions, including numerous abridgements in periodicals.[104]

Even before Hume's *History* turned into a publishing phenomenon, it was clear to most readers, even those who denigrated Hume's political and religious views and assailed his scholarly shortcomings, that Hume had produced a remarkable narrative of English history, unlike any general history of England ever written.. While an old guard might still hanker after documents and antiquarian details, most readers hailed Hume's dramatic improvement over previous historical narratives. *The Monthly Review* compared previous histories with Hume's:

> He does not perplex the minds, nor overload the memories of his Readers, with a circumstantial detail of minute incidents, or eternal references to dates and authorities; but presents them with comprehensive, and, in general, distinct views of things, interspersed with lively descriptions, and acute reflections. . . . [The] narrative [is] animated, his materials well arranged.[105]

The rhetorician Hugh Blair, a member of Hume's circle, contrasted the great triumvirate of British historians with what preceded them: 'During a long period, English Historical Authors seemed to aim at nothing higher than an exact relation of facts; till of late the distinguished names of Hume, Robertson, and Gibbon, have raised the British character, in this species of Writing, to high reputation and dignity.'[106] It was a classic work, an achievement for the ages. Lord Chesterfield called it 'The only History of England that will go down to Posterity.'[107] Ruffhead concluded his review of the medieval volumes by singling out the magisterial quality of Hume's *History*: 'Upon the whole, we do not scruple to commend these Volumes, as containing the most just and masterly account of the reigns of our early Kings, that has hitherto been penned.'[108] He compared the 'inaccuracies' of the *History* with the 'blemishes' in Milton,[109] perhaps suggesting that just as Milton had written a near-perfect work of neoclassical poetry, the epic *Paradise Lost*, so too had Hume composed a worthy neoclassical work of history. In fact Edmund Burke declared the chronic weakness in English historiography at an end:

> Our writers had commonly so ill succeeded in history, the Italians, and even the French, had so long continued our acknowledged superiors, that it was almost feared that the British

genius, which had so happily displayed itself in every other kind of writing, and gained the prize in most, yet could not enter in this. The historical work Mr. Hume has published discharged our country from this opprobrium.[110]

The Critical Review called the volumes on the Stuarts 'one of the best histories which modern times have produced.'[111] Indeed, some reviewers were prepared to grant Hume canonical status simply on the basis of the first two volumes published, on the Stuarts, and to claim his history of the seventeenth century, just a portion of the general history that would eventually be written, had already solved the weakness in English historiography. So long had the English awaited their savior, so patent was Hume's historical genius, that they slipped the toga on him before he was finished writing. Edward Gibbon observed: 'The old reproach, that no British altars had been raised to the Muse of history, was recently disproved by the first performances of Robertson and Hume, the histories of Scotland and of the Stuarts.'[112] Before becoming disenchanted with the medieval volumes, Horace Walpole called Hume 'the author of the best history of England' and asked Sir David Dalrymple, 'can I think we want writers of history while Mr. Hume and Mr. Robertson are living?'[113] It became commonplace to say that the best histories of Scotland and of England had been written contemporaneously by Robertson and Hume, whose masterpieces rivalled those of classical antiquity. Gibbon referred to Hume and Robertson as 'the Tacitus and the Livy of Scotland.'[114] 'Their peculiar excellences,' Dugald Stewart recalled,

were of a kind so different, that they might be justly said (in the language which a Roman critic employs in speaking of Livy and Sallust) to be *pares magis quam similes*. They divide between them the honour of having supplied an important blank in English literature, by enabling their countrymen to dispute the palm of historical writing with the other nations of Europe. . . . I may with confidence apply to them the panegyric which Quinctilian pronounces on the two great historians of ancient Greece; – and, perhaps, if I were inclined to characterize the beauties most prominent in each, I might, without much impropriety, avail myself of the contrast with which that panegyric concludes. 'If we turn to history, we shall find a number of distinguished writers; but there are two who must undoubtedly be set far above all their rivals: their excellences are different in kind, but have won almost equal praise. Thucydides is compact in texture, terse and ever eager to press forward: Herodotus is pleasant, lucid and diffuse: the former excels in vigour, speeches and the expression of the stronger passions; the latter in charm, conversations and the delineation of the gentler emotions.'[115]

Hume's friend, Adam Smith, was reported to have regarded Livy superior 'to all other historians, ancient and modern. He knew of no other who had even a pretence to rival him, if David Hume could not claim that honour.'[116]

Not only did contemporaries explicitly compare Hume to the classical historians, but they also singled out for praise many of those elements in the *History* most closely associated with classical and neoclassical historiography, the style, the speeches, the characters, the maxims or 'reflections.' Ruffhead praised Hume's 'judicious and manly reflections on the murder of Beckett,' declaring that '[t]hese bold, and at the same time, just sentiments are worthy the pen of a Livy or a Tacitus.'[117] Towers, along with other reviewers, commended Hume's 'many remarks equally just and acute.'[118] Towers admired Hume's style, whatever defects the *History* contained in terms of bias and inaccuracy. Hume deserved more applause 'as an ingenious, elegant, and polished writer' than 'as an exact, faithful, and impartial historian.'[119] Walpole wrote of the *History*: 'though more decried than ever book was, and certainly with faults, I cannot help liking much,' both for its 'manner' and its 'style, which is the best we have in history.'[120] Although Hume was occasionally faulted for infelicitous phrasing, the literary quality of his work was universally recognized. Ruffhead was tired of discussing it: 'As to our Historian's style, it is so well known and so deservedly approved, that it is almost needless to say, it is close, nervous, and correct.'[121] Hume drew criticism for the scoticisms which sometimes marred his English, but these might be excused in a neoclassical narrative because many of them, ironically, could be ascribed to the latinate Scots diction derived from the classical foundation for Scottish law and education.[122] Hume had modeled himself after the 'rapid' and 'concise' style of the ancient historians, so different from the style of existing histories of England, and in this he appeared to have succeeded. Two of the adjectives commonly employed to describe Hume's narrative were 'rapid' and 'succinct.'[123] On occasion Hume had put in his own words the arguments of contending parties, and this device was noted and admired for its ingenuity.[124] However, the classical set piece that drew most attention and praise was not the invented speech but rather the character sketch.[125] Many reviews of Hume's *History* reprinted these 'characters' in the same way that publishers had ransacked another neoclassical history, Clarendon's *History of the Rebellion*, for its scintillating characters, which they sold in collections separately from Clarendon's colossal narrative. Hume's characters, like his style generally, were a major selling point. To Hume's contemporaries in Britain, then, the *History* represented a great neoclassical literary achievement.

What most impressed Hume's original readers was the *History*'s artistic quality, its resemblance to the masterpieces of ancient and modern historiography, and its solving of the weakness in English historical writing, not its novelty as a 'philosophical history,' the tag we most often attach to the *History* today. It is true that some readers pointed out that Hume wrote history in a new manner, one pioneered by Voltaire, but Hume's rendition of this so-called 'philosophical' history turned out to fit within the framework of neoclassical historiography. Indeed, it may be that what most united the historical style and outlook of Hume and Voltaire was their common literary training in French classicism.[126] Contemporaries, at least, did not object to whatever innovations Hume might have introduced into British historiography as inconsistent with neoclassical standards for history.

Voltaire's *Siècle de Louis XIV* (1751) and *Essai sur les moeurs* (1756) focused on manners as an important object of historical study, and Voltairean philosophical history gained a reputation in England for its avoidance of trivial detail, its smooth, unbroken narrative, and its abundant reflections.[127] Some critics lampooned the new history for its long digressions, its emphasis on wit, novelty, and entertainment at the expense of accuracy and documentation. Even Hume determined that Voltaire 'cannot be depended on with regard to Facts.'[128] Some of Hume's readers considered him a disciple of Voltaire,[129] but Hume denied this was so. '[T]hey call me his Pupil,' Hume told a correspondent, 'and think that my History is an Imitation of his Siecle de Louis XIV. This Opinion flatters very much my Vanity; but the Truth is, that my History was plan'd, & in a great measure compos'd, before the Appearance of that agreeable Work.'[130] Despite such protestations, the link between Hume and Voltaire remained strong in some minds.

When Dugald Stewart praised Robertson's mastery of Voltairean history, he explained that while philosophical history was a worthy enrichment of the genre of history, it presented new challenges to the integrity of neoclassical narrative:

> [I]t became fashionable, after the example of Voltaire, to connect with the view of political transactions, an examination of their effects on the manners and condition of mankind, and to blend the lights of philosophy with the appropriate beauties of historical composition. In consequence of this innovation, while the province of the historian has been enlarged and dignified, the difficulty of his task has increased in the same proportion; reduced, as he must frequently be, to the alternative, either of interrupting unseasonably the chain of events, or, by interweaving disquisition and narrative together, of sacrificing clearness to brevity.[131]

Stewart believed Robertson triumphed over the technical difficulties of writing 'this combination of philosophy with history,' preserving the 'distinctness and perspicuity, so conspicuous in the great models of antiquity,' by his skilful use of transitions and deployment of notes.[132] Hume also garnered praise from readers, both for the new subjects he introduced and for the way he incorporated them unobtrusively into his narrative. His decision to minimize military affairs, which, along with politics, had been at the heart of classical historiography, met with some resistance from critics who considered battle scenes to be a rich source of entertainment and national glory.[133] However, readers generally approved of the way Hume had reshuffled the subjects of history. Ruffhead's estimation of Hume concurred with Stewart's of Robertson: the topics discussed by the philosophical historians did indeed enhance the subject matter of history. Manners constituted a legitimate, even necessary, topic of historical narrative, because they illuminated politics, a fundamental subject of history. 'We are here presented,' Ruffhead wrote of late medieval England, 'with a very just and lively picture of the manners of these times, and this may serve as a key for the more perfect understanding of the disorderly and violent transactions of these reigns. Such comments display the true characteristics of an Historian.'[134] Far from judging that a philosopher had no business writing history, Ruffhead insisted on the advantages Hume had as a philosopher narrating history: 'As it is essentially necessary for an historian, among other requisites, to be a philosopher; so philosophers only are capable of forming a right judgment of history.'[135] This estimation was congruent with traditional notions of history as philosophy teaching by examples, and with the idea that the 'perfect' historian was such a rarity because he had to master so many diverse roles in order to succeed – poet, statesman, scholar, churchman, soldier, lawyer, and philosopher.[136]

Ruffhead praised the manner in which 'philosophy and jurisprudence constantly go hand in hand with History.'[137] Hume in fact blended political philosophy, law, and manners so smoothly into his narrative that he did not break the customary form of history. *The Critical Review* took notice of Hume's singular achievement: 'we must, upon the whole, applaud the skill with which our author has involved the reflections of a philosophical historian in the detail of his facts, in a manner which throws a light upon every subject, without sensibly interrupting the course of the narration.'[138] Such classical devices as reflections, digressions, and characters gave Hume ample opportunity to insert his philosophical insights, indeed had always served classical and neoclassical historians as stopping points in the narrative of deeds where deeper analysis of men and events could be undertaken. By taking full advantage of these elements in the genre of history, and by his judicious placement of notes and attention to narrative pace, Hume succeeded in keeping his cultural analysis of English history within the bounds of neoclassical historiography, or at least contemporaries thought so. In the *History* civilization and liberty triumphed over barbarism and despotism, and Hume overcame the technical challenge of interlarding history with philosophy.

LE BON DAVID

Europeans proved to be even more effusive in their praise of 'le bon David' than Britons had been. With great enthusiasm, the Italians[139] and especially the French pronounced the weakness in English historiography finally ended. An unabashed Francophile, Hume cared very much about the reception of his works in France, and his literary ambition to write the history of England stemmed in part from a desire to satisfy the French critics who mocked English historiography. In his *Letters on England* (1733), Voltaire had penned what was, together with Montesquieu's allusion to it in the *Spirit of the Laws* (1748), perhaps the most famous French indictment of English historical writing.[140] Montesquieu died before Hume published the *History*, but Voltaire lived to see his criticism answered by Hume. In *La Gazette Littéraire* for 2 May 1764, Voltaire declared: 'Nothing can be added to the fame of this History, perhaps the best written in any language.' He repeated his old complaint that the 'fureur des partis' had deprived England both of good historians and good government, and that only a foreigner, Rapin, had written English history impartially. Yet Rapin appeared prejudiced compared with 'le nouvel historien,' Hume, whose 'mind [is] superior to his materials, who treats weaknesses, errors, and barbarities as a doctor treats epidemic diseases.'[141]

French readers put Hume on a plane with the ancient Greek and Roman historians, and compared him to Tacitus in particular.[142] Exactly why Hume should earn the appellation 'le Tacite de l'Angleterre'[143] requires some explanation. On both sides of the English Channel Tacitus enjoyed a reputation as the most philosophical of the ancient historians, and for this reason alone the Scottish philosopher could be viewed as a Tacitean figure. Tacitus enjoyed a considerable vogue in France,[144] and Adam Smith likened the political tranquility of contemporary France to that of the period in which Tacitus wrote. Not faced with pressing public matters, the French took an interest in less overtly political subjects such as manners, sentiment, and 'the motions of the human mind,' just as they believed Tacitus had done.[145] Comparing Hume to Tacitus was therefore the highest compliment Frenchmen could give a historian, especially another historian of manners.

Some readers challenged the prevailing truism that equated Hume with Tacitus, but did so only to praise Hume more extravagantly as Tacitus' superior. Charles de Brosses, an elder statesman and man of letters, admired Hume for rejecting the Tacitean manner of displaying his own cleverness and uncovering secret causes. Hume was 'more natural, more judicious' than Tacitus, and truly understood the effect of national character on

the individual.[146] Hume scored an important victory for the
moderns over the ancients, concluded Voltaire. The 'new historian,'
Hume, was a philosopher, and the public understood how
appropriate it was for philosophers to compose history. The
philosopher writing history would never rely on marvels to
support his work, as Livy had done, or ascribe secret crimes to
princes, as Tacitus had done, or set down popular rumors, as
Suetonius had done.[147] Of course, in thus praising Hume Voltaire
praised himself, since Voltaire claimed to have invented the new
history. As much as Hume attempted to shake off the association
with Voltairean historiography, the French *philosophes* widely
regarded Hume as Voltaire's disciple, and they relished in
particular Hume's portrayal of the Catholic Church and the middle
ages in acid tones.[148]

In general, French readers applauded Hume's *History* for the
same qualities Englishmen had commended. They cited its style,
its reflections, its philosophical spirit.[149] However, Hume's acclaim
in France was immediate and lavish, not late and grudging as
it had been in England. The French could not wait for a personal
visit from Hume and for the translation of his *History* into French.
Chastellux learned English for the express purpose of reading
Hume's *History*. Turgot made a personal translation of it. The
Abbé André Morellet, a prisoner in the Bastille, asked for copies
of it and of Tacitus[150] – both the ancient and the modern Tacitus,
the Roman and the British. In October 1763, at the conclusion of
the Seven Years' War between France and Britain, Hume went
to France as the private secretary of the British Ambassador, the
Earl of Hertford. He was lionized as a literary genius during his
26-month stay, the darling of French society. Hume met the king;
Madame de Pompadour showered favors upon him. Three young
princes, the future Kings Louis XVI, Louis XVIII, and Charles X,
the last a mere four-year-old, pronounced encomiums on his
History. Court society was smitten with this unlikely socialite, a
large, awkward man who spoke poor French and could not even
pronounce English properly. 'I eat nothing but ambrosia, drink
nothing but nectar, breathe nothing but incense, and tread on
nothing but flowers,' Hume wrote Robertson. 'Every man I meet,
and still more every lady, would think they were wanting in the
most indispensable duty, if they did not make me a long and
elaborate harangue in my praise.'[151] Not since Clarendon's
politically-charged history of his own times was published had

a work of English history caused such a commotion.

Englishmen had qualms about acknowledging the works of Clarendon and Hume as neoclassical masterpieces on account of their political bias. In 1778 Towers was still fuming over Hume's treatment of the Civil War, 'more partial than the celebrated history of lord Clarendon, though that nobleman was an avowed partizan of Charles.'[152] However, on the continent Hume was praised precisely for his fair-mindedness. To Voltaire, Grimm, and others, factious party politics was contemptible, and being a philosopher had helped Hume achieve a laudable detachment from all sects and parties.[153] Frenchmen, Englishmen, and, most acutely, Hume himself could not help but notice how differently the historian had been greeted in France compared with Britain, where he was commonly snubbed as a mere man of letters and persecuted for his religious views.[154] Foreigners had been tricked into their admiration for Hume, argued Towers. Ignorant of English history, they could not know how inaccurate and biased he was; they could only 'judge of his eloquence as a writer, and of the beauty of his work as a literary composition.'[155]

Beyond perceptions of Hume's literary virtuosity and neutrality, there were other ways to account for his renown in France. Towers criticized the *History* for belittling England's national character, its literary and scientific geniuses, love of freedom, and military exploits.[156] But the French had less interest than the English in the minutiae, the politics, or the reputed glory of English history. Moreover, the prevailing mania for all things English, the vogue for history and philosophy, the dramatic character of English, especially Stuart, history, Hume's personal charm and reputation as Britain's leading man of letters all added to the celebrity attending the *History*'s reception. And while some Englishmen accused the *History* of being jacobite, absolutist, anti-Protestant, and impious, these very pejoratives redounded to Hume's benefit in France, the Catholic and absolutist ally of the jacobites, and home of the *philosophes*.[157] Whatever differences existed between French and English responses to Hume, both English and French readers could agree that Hume had written one of the greatest histories of modern times, comparable to the classic works of antiquity.

Clearly, Hume was a literary genius, and yet this circumstance alone cannot fully explain his success as a historian. Other eminent writers had attempted to solve the weakness in English historiography but had failed. The fact that he was a Francophile gave Hume an incentive to end the complaint against English historiography, an incentive few compatriots shared. When Hume defended his decision to re-write English history, he told Horace Walpole that doing so would benefit posterity, polite Britons, and foreigners.[158] He had his eye on France all along, knowing his literary ambition could only be satisfied if he pleased the French literati.[159] His cosmopolitanism impelled him to look beyond Britain for acceptance and esteem. Unlike most aspirant Livian historians, Hume not only embraced the tenets of French neoclassicism but he also enjoyed the status and the leisure advantageous to filling the role of neoclassical historian. Hume could resist the temptation to write party history for money and could maintain his political independence. Beholden neither to an aristocratic patron, nor a list of subscribers, nor a mass reading public, Hume sought out instead a Franco-British literary elite more interested in neoclassical virtuosity than in making political capital. Resenting the way 'Great men in England' condescended to 'Men of Letters,' Hume defiantly asserted: 'I attatch myself to no great Man, and visit none of them but such as happen to be my Friends, and particular Acquaintance. I wish they woud consider me as equally independant with themselves or more so.'[160] In a fit of bitter exasperation at the slighting treatment he had received from the Hon. Charles Townshend, Hume equated his own independence with that of the greatest men in the realm, perhaps a hyperbolic comparison but one he could make more legitimately than previous general historians. Hume did receive a royal pension after finishing his *History*,[161] but he remained his own man and refused to comply with George III's request that he continue the *History*. Still, he did not have stature sufficient to approach men like Townshend, his social superior and English, for the archival materials on which a contemporary history would rely. Hume enjoyed enough independence to write impartial general history but still not enough social standing to prosper as a historian of his own times. He had done much to advance the social prestige of men of letters, but unless neoclassical history was transformed into the exclusive story of cultural achievements rather than political and military ones, Hume could never be a 'great man' fit to narrate Thucydidean history as statesmen and warriors had traditionally been qualified to do.

Many failed Livian historians found themselves drawn to the

example of ecclesiastical history as a model for historical writing. However, 'the infidel' Hume found no such attraction, and did not let the Christian subject matter or Christian historical genre impede his engagement with a pre-Christian literary form. In fact, he delighted in exposing the incompetence of monks as historians and presenting an utterly secular account of a nation which had the misfortune of adopting religions that tended to superstition and fanaticism. In a draft preface to his second volume, prepared as a defense of his religious skepticism but never published, Hume argued that 'the beneficent Influence of Religion is not to be sought for in History' because it did not figure 'in those Annals of Wars, & Politics, Intrigues, & Revolutions, Quarrels & Convulsions, which it is the Business of an Historian to record & transmit to Posterity.'[162] A good deal of Hume's *History* necessarily dealt with religion, but only insofar as it affected his classical subject matter of war and politics and the cultural dimensions of both. By focusing rigorously on this criterion, and his classical models, Hume avoided the clerical historical style of his predecessors. His goal had always been 'to make a tolerable smooth, well told Tale of the History of England,' to find materials worthy of philosophical reflection and of eloquence, to transform existing documents and works of scholarship into a neoclassical narrative for the benefit of those 'who have neither leizure nor inclination for such a laborious and disagreeable study,'[163] not to unearth new historical sources and put new facts on display. Hume's admission to the State Paper Office by George III in the 1760s was for revising his *History*, not writing it afresh.[164] He took an interest in new manuscript sources but relied almost entirely on the printed sources of his predecessors and even on their historical interpretations.[165] The chief problem with English historiography at the time Hume wrote was not the poverty of fact or analysis but the absence of a neoclassical narrative in the grand manner.

Hume showed an awareness of the pitfalls facing a modern writer modeling himself after the classical historians, and this insight helped him to triumph where other historians of England had failed. Modern trade, manners, print, warfare, scholarship, political parties never had to be taken account of by the ancient historians,[166] but Hume had to consider how they could be contained within the genre invented by those historians. As we have seen, he wrestled with these elements of modernity, one by one. Hume inserted accounts of trade and manners as part of the history of civilization in order to explain modern politics more fully. As an 'enlightened' historian he condensed military affairs rather than glorify them. Although print had created new agents of historical causation and audiences for history, he refused to pander to a mass audience with stories of wonders or marvels, and he did not copy printed propaganda into his narrative. Writing medieval history proved a bleak undertaking but Hume waded through it to develop his themes concerning civilization and liberty, barbarism and despotism. His sources for medieval as well as more modern history were often antiquarian or clerical works filled with partisan dissertations and source collections, but Hume rejected this modern mode of scholarship and preserved his narrative of deeds intact. Political parties poisoned modern public life in Britain and made the writing of impartial history almost impossible, but Hume was fortunate to embark on his *History* at a time, in the 1750s, when parties were beginning to waste away.

Hume's English readers sometimes quarreled with his modern accommodations to classical historiography, his discounting of military transactions, for example, and they attacked him as a tory and an atheist. However, many eventually saw past his perceived partiality and acclaimed his work the best history of England ever written. The characters, speeches, reflections, narrative pace, the style generally, succeeded in vindicating English historiography from its detractors, foreign and domestic. Some readers commented on the *History*'s success as a philosophical history, with its Voltairean emphasis on narrative, on manners, on religious skepticism. However, they saw nothing improper about a philosopher writing history, and did not criticize Hume for sometimes deviating from the traditional genre of history. While scholars today often read the *History* for the light it might shed on Hume's philosophy, as a rule Hume's contemporaries did not comment on links between his philosophy and his history, did not see the *History* as being underpinned by a system of ethics and epistemology. They admired his insights into the events of English history but were more interested in putting political labels on them or praising the way he had incorporated them into his narrative than in remarking on their novelty or philosophical coherence. Hume's original audience saw the *History* foremost as a literary achievement, as a source of national honor for having solved the chronic problem in English historiography, and as a work of political and religious controversy, not as a new form of history but as a modern peer of ancient historiography.

After Hume's *History* was published, the complaints about historiography ceased, and so the story of historiographical weakness in England must also come to an end. That these strictures had persisted even after the appearance of Clarendon's *History* suggested that most Englishmen perceived this weakness to concern the lack of a general history of England, not the history of one's own times. Clarendon's Thucydidean history of the Civil War indeed brought honor to England but it was not as satisfying as the Livian history of the entire English past supplied by Hume. With Hume's success, the tables were turned on England's former critics; now men of letters on the continent complained *their* history failed to match Hume's masterpiece.[167] In 1787 Sénac de Meilhan argued that the only historians of modern times who could rival Thucydides, Xenophon, Sallust, Livy, and Tacitus were Hume and Robertson.[168] Hume's triumph did not mark the end of neoclassical historiography in Britain by any means, as the case of Gibbon, for example, should make clear; but it does help to explain why some eminent writers chose not to compose a general history of England. Hume's formidable achievement figured in the calculations of William Robertson and Edmund Burke not to proceed as historians of England.[169] One reason why Edward Gibbon did not write the history of his native land, besides wishing to avoid a partisan reception and a provincial subject,[170] was that the role of English Livy had already been filled by Hume, and Gibbon readily admitted as much. In his *Decline and Fall of the Roman Empire* Gibbon self-consciously imitated Hume's *History*, and adopted his role as man of letters writing history in imitation of the ancients. Gibbon's readers compared him to Livy and Tacitus, just as Gibbon had once compared Hume and Robertson to them. Gibbon admired Tacitus as the most 'philosophical' classical historian and opened his *History* with a studied imitation of him.[171] To the great triumvirate of British historians, Gibbon, Robertson, and Hume, it was clear that modern philosophy could be married to ancient historiography.

Conclusion

In *The History of the Adventures of Joseph Andrews* (1742), Henry Fielding wrote:

> [B]etween my Lord Clarendon and Mr. Whitlock, between Mr. Echard and Rapin, and many others; where Facts being set forth in a different Light, every Reader believes as he pleases, and indeed the more judicious and suspicious very justly esteem the whole as no other than a Romance, in which the Writer hath indulged a happy and fertile Invention.[1]

In Fielding's view, English historical writing had been metamorphosed into little more than fairy tales made up of widely divergent historical data and interpretation–royalist and parliamentarian, tory and whig. Because political bickering had spoiled history, Fielding could minimize the differences between two forms of didactic narrative, history and the novel, and argue that the novel, badly in need of legitimization, could now challenge history as a source of moral truth. Whether the English public accepted Fielding's arguments, it surely accepted his premise that historical writing had been terribly discredited. In fact, during the eighteenth century the rise of the novel took place at the same time that the noble genre of history declined into an embarrassing condition. In the 1750s David Hume finally reversed the fortunes of English historiography and solved a longstanding problem in English letters, a problem that, as we have seen, illustrated the tensions between classical historiography and early-modern English society.

Our study of historical writing suggests that neoclassicism ought to be moved from the background to the foreground as a context for reading English histories in this period. Once we shift our emphasis from uncovering the origins of twentieth-century ideas of history to probing contemporary understandings of history, the centrality of neoclassicism becomes clear. This move allows us to explain both why contemporaries considered their histories to be so mediocre – they failed to match demanding, somewhat outdated classical models – as well as why the two most acclaimed

210

historians of the period wrote as they did and achieved the success they did – Clarendon and Hume explicitly imitated the ancient historians and were applauded for having done so. Early-modern Englishmen invoked classical comparisons to analyze their historical writing, because the ancient historians truly did remain the most revered models for writing history. Whether a treatise on history, a casual remark in a letter, a preface to a historical work, or a review of a history, the evidence leaves little doubt who the greatest historians were: they were a rather uniformly defined canon of classical historians and modern, continental historians of the sixteenth and seventeenth century inspired by their example. The most celebrated narrative histories of this era actually did resemble ancient historiography in many respects, in terms of their scale, tone, political and moral reflections, subject matter, characters, and on occasion even their invented speeches. Although this genre was showing signs of wear, increasingly anachronistic in the modernizing political culture of eighteenth-century England, it showed remarkable resiliency. Neoclassical history survived in the early-modern period, because the humanism from which it sprang continued to enjoy a strong presence in English culture, because it proved elastic enough to accommodate many changes wrought by 'modern' society, and because the English elite still found it useful as a way of analyzing and understanding its own political and military activity.

While this endorsement of the age's neoclassicism must play a part in the conclusion to any study of early-modern English historical writing, some important qualifications must also be made. As noble an ambition as it was to preserve from oblivion the greatest moral and political truths of the past for the impartial edification of posterity, in a stately style and on a grand scale, there were still those who criticized the ancient historians as inappropriate to the modern age. Indeed, many English historians simply wrote as their patrons bade them, played politics, or exploited the classical program as a pose or an expedient. Readers, too, sometimes lacked high-minded motives for purchasing and reading works of history. Many tried to demonstrate their social competence rather than discover the truths the neoclassical historian aspired to communicate. They bought historical works in order to point out their names on subscription lists or gesture towards impressive folios in their library. History, the noblest prose genre, history, *magister vitae*, was to a certain extent trivialized. While Englishmen lauded classical theories about how history was supposed to be written, in practice they often turned away from neoclassical history. Many were perfectly contented with their historiography: document-laden, partisan histories were just what they wanted to fight their political battles. When the history of their high ideals *was* finally approximated, many rejected Clarendon and especially Hume, because they disagreed with their politics. When Clarendon and Hume called the elite's bluff about wanting a Livy or a Thucydides, it turned out that many Englishmen did not appreciate neoclassical historians after all, or at least found their literary achievement less important than their political affiliation. They refused to recognize the messiah in their midst.

It is difficult not to harbor the suspicion that the French cared more about the state of English history than the English themselves did. Englishmen only seemed to become fully aware of the weakness in their historiography when they compared their histories to those of other nations, or when foreign critics, scoring points in a game of literary nationalism, brought it to their attention. Many of the key players in our story looked across the English Channel for inspiration without fully considering that France's constitutional arrangements differed so profoundly from Britain's that French neoclassicism might not be a suitable model for British historiography. Hume and Bolingbroke each lived for years at a time in France, befriended eminent French men of letters, and imbibed French historical thinking. Sprat took the French Academy as a model for English literary life. After reading French history and criticism, Temple initiated grand schemes to solve the weakness in historiography. The idea of writing a neoclassical history of England thus appeared to be in some measure alien to Englishmen. A foreigner, Polydore Vergil, first took up the project, and another foreigner of sorts, Hume, a Scot, completed it.

The somewhat reluctant acceptance of neoclassical history might best be understood in terms of a general tendency in English historiography since the sixteenth century. Many of the major developments in historiography originated on the continent and arrived late to England. Humanism and humanist historiography, for example, made a belated landing in England, and English efforts to write in a neoclassical fashion bore comparatively little fruit in the sixteenth and seventeenth century, with the exception of Clarendon's achievement. Legal antiquarianism, too, came of age on the continent long before it blossomed in England, a scholarly import that prospered sooner and more abundantly than narrative history in the grand manner did. In the nineteenth century, English historians only tentatively adopted the German professionalization of history, and in the twentieth century they have remained wary of French structuralism. English culture's qualified adoption of neoclassical historiography in the early-modern period may thus represent another episode in the long history of a society guarding against undue continental influence over its affairs.

Although the methods and aims of classical historiography appeared to be bearing up comparatively well under the strain of many early-modern phenomena, Christianity, antiquarian erudition, the printing press, and party politics all represented threats to any English historian who took classicism to heart. Ancient protocols stipulated that history had to be as truthful as possible, and yet English partisanship made this commonplace rule for history nearly impossible to obey. Party historians adopted an ecclesiastical mode of historiography to wage their political battles. Reformation controversialists had written overtly partisan works that reprinted key documents for tactical advantage, and Englishmen grafted antiquarianism onto this clerical style of historical disputation. When civil history came to be narrated for party purposes, the fact that much of English political history could only be told in tandem with church history, and that the learned culture of seventeenth-century England was so highly clerical, meant that ostensibly civil or secular historians wrote in the clericalist manner. Robert Brady was among the first English historians to compose a general history of England in such a style. Collectors of documents, copiers of chronicles, composers of antiquarian treatises, Brady and many of his successors conceded that what they were writing was not truly 'history' but a preparation for what a 'perfect' historian might one day write.

That ideal historian, the neoclassical historian, was supposed to emerge from the ranks of the leisured elite. Only a man with sufficient political experience and social standing could possess the leisure, education, connections, and insight necessary to researching and writing the history of war and politics, and being taken seriously by his peers, who as present-day makers of history alone had the interest, the time, the learning necessary to act upon the political instruction contained in neoclassical history. Few Englishmen were equipped to write either contemporary or general history, and many of the best qualified candidates had competing political, familial, and literary responsibilities. By looking at the circumstances accompanying elite historical projects in this period, we have furnished a social history of historiography that reveals both the high social credentials contemporaries expected, and, by contrast, the lowly status of many of those who actually did write history. Mere clergymen, journalists, and foreigners dared to desecrate the elite preserve of neoclassical historiography. Most of them lost all sense of political independence and adopted clericalist historiography to pursue their partisan aims.

The English elite snubbed these outsiders trying to write its history; they thereby underscored the exclusive, even familial, nature of neoclassical historical culture. The member of a powerful family would compose history for his and other families, relying on the reminiscences and opened archives of those families. Defending an ancestor's besmirched reputation became a matter of family honor, and it was usually within the family's power not just to defend itself in parliament or in a pamphlet but also to fight back by disclosing unpublished letters or histories entrusted to it. In fact, a prime ingredient of jacobite propaganda involved publication of papers inherited from royalist ancestors in the seventeenth century. As a general rule, however, highborn Englishmen were circumspect about surrendering historical sources. By shielding sensitive family documents from prying historians, family members put into operation an unofficial version of the Official Secrets Act to keep the machinations of recent politics out of view. There is little evidence that a primary or even secondary purpose of writing history was to exert social control over political and social subordinates. However, the neoclassical paradigm did serve to reinforce the elite's privacy and sense of caste, to keep its secrets.

The adoption of a neoclassical definition of history that put great men and ennobling events on center stage and possessed exacting rules of evidence and decorum undermined attempts at 'secret history,' exposés of a public man's private life. The elite denounced John Oldmixon's secret histories as subversive. To insinuate himself into historical culture was to trespass on political turf, given the extensive use the political class made of historical argument, and the elite fought off such challengers by withdrawing purses and by supporting satirists in a counter-attack. Oldmixon was spawned by a socially inferior reading public, not the elite public championing neoclassical history. However, so long as writers such as Oldmixon succeeded in convincing publishers and subscribers that they could solve the weakness in historiography or simply write a work that would appeal to partisan readers of a particular political stripe, hack histories would continue to be published with pretensions to noble history, in an expensive format, on a multi-volume scale.

The market, not the institutions of church and crown, now supported history. In the 1640s Clarendon, and in the 1680s Brady, depended on royal favor to pursue their historical projects, but at the end of our period Carte and Hume had only tangential ties to the crown. Before the second quarter of the eighteenth century, many historians relied on courtly or ecclesiastical patronage or both, but after that time the historians we have examined looked instead to various reading publics or aristocratic patrons for support. Despite comparable press runs of about 16 000 copies after the first 30 years in print, Clarendon and Hume had very different conceptions of audience. Clarendon wrote in a purposely arcane way for a tiny political cadre comprised of his own family, some like-minded bishops, the royal family, and other key political leaders. Only when the posthumously published *History* became a general sensation did his sons allow London booksellers to turn it into a commercial venture. Hume had commercial sales in mind from the start. As a cosmopolitan man of letters, Hume reached out not only to the gentry and nobility but also to urban professionals and others ranked just below the landed elite, as well as to continental literati. Hume managed to write in such a way that won him an audience of women, too, even though classical historiography was designed primarily for men. To Hume, politics is and was tied to the progress of civilization, which women had a role in as proponents of politeness and sociability. Hume, then, created a market for neoclassical history more diverse in terms of gender, nationality, and even class than Clarendon had addressed, a market Gibbon and Robertson helped to expand in the last quarter of the eighteenth century, when neoclassical history became firmly ensconced among the middling sort.

Despite differences in genre and audience, both Clarendon's

contemporary and Hume's general history demonstrated the versatility of neoclassical historiography. Hume helped to invent an 'enlightened' brand of history, a philosophical history that incorporated cultural history into an account of war and politics. Yet he managed to write this history of 'manners' with such attention to the integrity of his narrative and to several classical literary devices that his contemporaries, while acknowledging his innovations, nonetheless put him on a plane with the ancient historians. Hume understood the political uses of neoclassicism. The neoclassical historian was supposed to adopt a polite style that avoided controversy and partisanship, but this style, in turn, was so authoritative that it enhanced whatever political message he concealed beneath the surface of the text. For his part, Hume promoted a program of political moderation by deploying politeness to snuff out time-honored political divisions. Paradoxically, he found that the best way to modernize and moderate the political philosophies of whigs and tories was to write in the manner of the most ancient, not modern, historians, using the polite style of the classical historians. Clarendon, like Hume, played the part of a polite inquirer after truth, someone above politics, looking solely to the public good, when in fact his moderate royalist interpretation had undeniable political repercussions, as he well knew. His editors, too, recognized the political value of neoclassicism, and edited Clarendon's work in such a way as to fortify that quality in the text, casting him as the English Thucydides. Examining the historiography in the half century following publication of the *History of the Rebellion* makes clear the enormous impact of Clarendon on his posthumous readers. Clarendon's influence went beyond his magisterial contribution to historical interpretation and data. He showed how classicism could triumph in the modern world.

Notes

CHAPTER 1

1. Contemporary comments on the weakness in historiography include: John Dryden, 'The Life of Plutarch,' *The Works of John Dryden*, 2nd ed., 18 vols (Edinburgh, 1821), 17:58; Clarendon, *Essays Moral and Entertaining ... by the Right Honourable Edward, Earl of Clarendon*, ed. James Stanier Clark, 2 vols (London, 1815), 1:249–51; [James Hampton], *Reflections on Ancient and Modern History* (Oxford, 1746), p. 24; William Nicolson, *The English Historical Library: or, A Short View and Character of most of the Writers ... which may be Serviceable to the Undertakers of a General History of this Kingdom*, 3 vols (London, 1696–9), 1: title page, Preface; David Hume, *The History of England from the Invasion of Julius Caesar to The Revolution in 1688*, 6 vols, Foreword by William B. Todd (Indianapolis, Ind.: Liberty Classics, 1983), 5:154; [Edmund Burke], *The Annual Register* (1761), 4:301–4; Henry Felton, *A Dissertation on Reading the Classics, and Forming a Just Style* (Menston, Yorks.: Scolar Press, 1977), pp. 196–7; *The Spectator*, ed. Donald F. Bond, 5 vols (Oxford: Clarendon Press, 1965), no. 136 (2:38–9); Bolingbroke: 'I believe England has produced as much Genius first as any Country. Why then [are] Eloquence and History ... at their lowest ebb imaginable among us [?] ... [O]ur Historys are Gazettes ill digested, & worse writ. The case is far otherwise in France and in Italy [Guicciardini and Davila, for example] ...' (*Pope Corr.*, 2:220, 18 Feb. 1724). Modern, scholarly treatments of the weakness in English historiography include: Joseph M. Levine, *Humanism and History: Origins of Modern British Historiography* (Ithaca, N. Y.: Cornell Univ. Press, 1987), pp. 102, 164, 252; Nicholas von Maltzahn, *Milton's History of Britain: Republican Historiography in the English Revolution* (Oxford: Clarendon Press, 1991), pp. 49–59; James W. Johnson, *The Formation of English Neo-Classical Thought* (Princeton: Princeton Univ. Press, 1967), pp. 39–41; F. Smith Fussner, *The Historical Revolution: English Historical Writing and Thought 1580–1640* (New York: Columbia Univ. Press, 1962), p. 163; Barbara J. Shapiro, *Probability and Certainty in Seventeenth-Century England* (Princeton: Princeton Univ. Press, 1983), pp. 132–3; Irvin Ehrenpreis, *Swift: The Man, His Works, and the Age*, 3 vols (London: Methuen; Cambridge, Mass.: Harvard Univ. Press, 1962–83), 2:59–65.
2. Contemporary evidence for this canon of ancient historians comes from: Felton, p. 180; William Wotton, *Reflections upon Ancient and Modern Learning. To which is now added A Defense Thereof ...*, 3rd ed. (London, 1705), pp. 40–1; James Burgh, *The Dignity of Human Nature, or A Brief Account of the certain and established Means for attaining the*

true End of our Existence (London, 1754), pp. 125–31; *Gentleman's Magazine* (1732), 2:1023; Abel Boyer, *The History of the Life & Reign of Queen Anne*... (London, 1722), Preface (p. viii). The literary establishment thus accepted the ancients' own consensus regarding the canon of their greatest historians: Arnaldo Momigliano, *Essays in Ancient and Modern Historiography* (Middletown, Conn.: Wesleyan Univ. Press, 1977), p. 161.

3. [John Boyle, 5th Earl of Orrery (presumed author)], *A Collection of the State Letters Of the Right Honourable Roger Boyle, The first Earl of Orrery*... (London, 1742), Preface (p. i).

4. See Chapter 6 for Voltaire and Montesquieu; note 1, above, for the others.

5. Contemporary evidence for this canon comes from: Clarendon, *Essays*, 1:245–8; 2:118; Gilbert Burnet, *The Memoires of the Lives and Actions of James and William Dukes of Hamilton*... (London, 1677), Preface; Chesterfield, *The Letters of Philip Dormer Stanhope, 4th Earl of Chesterfield*, ed. Bonamy Dobrée, 6 vols (London: Eyre & Spottiswoode, 1932), pp. 1598, 2348; Wotton, *Reflections*, pp. 37–41; Boyer, *Life of Anne*, Preface (p. viii); Burgh, pp. 125–31; [René de Rapin], *The Modest Critick: Or Remarks upon the most Eminent Historians, Antient and Modern*... (London, 1689), pp. 139–51; Pierre Le Moyne, *Of the Art Both of Writing & Judging of History* (London, 1695), pp. 10–11; John Oldmixon, *The Critical History of England, Ecclesiastical and Civil*..., 2 vols (London, 1724–6), 1:170–1; *Pope Corr.*, 2:187; Greig, 1:284; James Tyrrell, *The General History of England, both ecclesiastical and civil*..., 3 vols (London, 1696–1704), 2:vii; Bolingbroke, *Letters*, VI. Bentivoglio, Grotius, Sleidan, Strada, and Vertot also sometimes found a place in the canon.

6. As Chapter 2 will demonstrate, although the moderns made important qualifications to classical history, enough continuities existed between modern works of history modeled after the ancient historians and ancient historiography itself that 'neoclassical' remains a useful term, despite the inherent anachronism and over-simplification involved in using it.

7. Bolingbroke, *Letters*, VI. Laurence Echard, *The History of England, From the First Entrance of Julius Caesar*..., 3 vols (London, 1707–18), 1: Preface, 910, 969. Hume, *History*, 3:465; 5:154. Orrery, *Collection*, Preface. Felton, pp. 197–201. *Gentleman's Magazine* (1732), 2:1023. [White Kennett], *A Complete History of England; With the Lives of All the Kings and Queens*... *Containing A Faithful Relation of all Affairs of State Ecclesiastical and Civil*..., 3 vols (London, 1706), 1: Preface. The anonymous editors of this last work wrote its preface, but because we are primarily concerned with Kennett's contribution to *The Complete History*, it will be identified with his name for purposes of convenience.

8. J. C. D. Clark, *Samuel Johnson: Literature, Religion and English Cultural Politics from the Restoration to Romanticism* (Cambridge: Cambridge Univ. Press, 1994), pp. 25–30.

9. Joseph M. Levine, *The Battle of the Books: History and Literature in*

the Augustan Age (Ithaca, N. Y.: Cornell Univ. Press, 1991), pp. 250–2.
Gerald Newman, *The Rise of English Nationalism: A Cultural History
1740–1830* (New York: St Martin's Press, 1987), pp. 126–8. Hume,
History, 6:151. For Milton's defenders, see Howard D. Weinbrot,
Britannia's Issue: The Rise of British Literature from Dryden to Ossian
(Cambridge: Cambridge Univ. Press, 1993), pp. 115–20.

10. Claude Rawson, 'Poet Squab,' *London Review of Books*, 3 March 1988,
pp. 16–17.

11. Weinbrot, *Britannia's Issue*, esp. Part I. Shelley Burtt, *Virtue
Transformed: Political Argument in England, 1688–1740* (Cambridge:
Cambridge Univ. Press, 1992), pp. 155–64. Peter N. Miller, *Defining
the Common Good: Empire, Religion and Philosophy in Eighteenth-Century
Britain* (Cambridge: Cambridge Univ. Press, 1994), pp. 119–23.

12. The most notable exception is Joseph M. Levine, *Battle of the Books;
Humanism and History;* 'Ancients and Moderns Reconsidered,'
Eighteenth-Century Studies, 15 (1981), pp. 72–89. Other scholars who
recognize, at least in passing, the importance of classical models
include Duncan Forbes, 'Introduction,' David Hume, *The History of
Great Britain*, ed. Duncan Forbes (Harmondsworth: Pelican Books,
1970), pp. 7–54; J. G. A. Pocock, *The Ancient Constitution and the
Feudal Law: A Study of English Historical Thought in the Seventeenth
Century* (Cambridge: Cambridge Univ. Press, 1957; 1987, 'A Reissue
with a Retrospect'), pp. 255–6; J. A. I. Champion, *The Pillars of
Priestcraft Shaken: The Church of England and its Enemies, 1660–1730*
(Cambridge: Cambridge Univ. Press, 1992), pp. 35–9; Herbert Davis,
Jonathan Swift: Essays on his Satire and Other Studies (New York: Oxford
Univ. Press, 1964), pp. 277–92; George H. Nadel, 'Philosophy of
History before Historicism,' *Studies in the Philosophy of History: Selected
Essays from History and Theory* (New York: Harper & Row, 1965),
pp. 49–73; Johnson, *Formation of English Neo-Classical Thought*, p. 40.

13. See, for example, Roger Schmidt, 'Roger North's *Examen*: A Crisis
in Historiography,' *Eighteenth-Century Studies*, 26 (1992), pp. 57–75;
D. R. Woolf, *The Idea of History in Early Stuart England: Erudition,
Ideology and 'The Light of Truth' from the Accession of James I to the
Civil War* (Toronto: Univ. of Toronto Press, 1990); Laird Okie, *Augustan
Historical Writing: Histories of England in the English Enlightenment*
(Lanham, Maryland: University Press of America, 1991); R. J. Smith,
The Gothic Bequest: Medieval Institutions in British Thought, 1688–1863
(Cambridge: Cambridge Univ. Press, 1987); Royce MacGillivray,
Restoration Historians and the English Civil War (The Hague: Martinus
Nijhoff, 1974); R. N. Stromberg, 'History in the Eighteenth Century,'
Journal of the History of Ideas, 12 (1951), pp. 295–304; D. J. Womersley,
'Lord Bolingbroke and Eighteenth-Century Historiography,' *The
Eighteenth Century: Theory and Interpretation*, 28 (1987), pp. 217–34;
John Kenyon, *The History Men: The Historical Profession in England
since the Renaissance* (Pittsburgh: Univ. of Pittsburgh Press, 1984);
D. W. L. Earl, 'Procrustean Feudalism: An Interpretative Dilemma
in English Historical Narration, 1700–1725,' *Historical Journal*, 19 (1976),
pp. 33–51; William Smith, Jr, *The History of the Province of New York,*

ed., intro. Michael Kammen (Cambridge, Mass.: Harvard Univ. Press, 1972), pp. xxxviii–xlv; David C. Douglas, *English Scholars* (London: Jonathan Cape, 1939); Martine Watson Brownley, *Clarendon and the Rhetoric of Historical Form* (Philadelphia: Univ. of Pennsylvania Press, 1985). For a fuller survey of eighteenth-century historiography, also see my appraisal in 'Bolingbroke, Clarendon, and the Role of Classical Historian,' *Eighteenth-Century Studies*, 20 (1987), pp. 445–71, at p. 446. The secondary literature on Hume's *History* will be considered separately, in Chapter 7.

14. Arthur B. Ferguson, *Clio Unbound: Perceptions of the Social and Cultural Past in Renaissance England* (Durham, N. C.: Duke Univ. Press, 1979). Donald R. Kelley, *Foundations of Modern Historical Scholarship: Language, Law, and History in the French Renaissance* (New York: Columbia Univ. Press, 1970). Levine, *Humanism and History.* Fussner, *Historical Revolution.* Douglas, *English Scholars.* Joyce Appleby, Lynn Hunt, Margaret Jacob, *Telling the Truth About History* (New York: Norton, 1994), chap. 1.

15. The sources listed above, in note 1, should make clear the elite character of this challenge to write neoclassical history.

16. *The Whig Interpretation of History* (London: G. Bell and Sons, 1931).

17. David Cannadine, *The Decline and Fall of the British Aristocracy* (New Haven, Conn.: Yale Univ. Press, 1990). J. C. D. Clark, *English Society 1688–1832: Ideology, Social Structure and Political Practice during the Ancien Regime* (Cambridge: Cambridge Univ. Press, 1985), pp. 95, 102, 421.

18. For this definition of elite, see Peter Laslett, *The World We Have Lost* (New York: Charles Scribner's Sons, 1965), pp. 26–43.

19. A sampling of contemporary opinion establishes the importance of most of these historians: Zachary Grey, *A Defence of our Antient and Modern Historians* (London, 1725), Preface; [Anon.], *A Letter to A Friend in the Country, On the Publication of Thurloe's State Papers* ..., 2nd ed. (London, 1742); William L. Sachse, *Lord Somers: A Political Portrait* (Madison: Univ. of Wisconsin Press, 1975), chap. 10; *London Journal*, no. 582, 26 Sept. 1730; [John Oldmixon], *The History of England* ..., 3 vols (London, 1730–9), Preface; James Ralph, *The History of England during the Reigns of K. William, Q. Anne and K. George I* ..., 2 vols (London, 1744–6), 1: The Author to his Subscribers, pp. i–iv; Hume, *History*, 1:470n, 493, 494; 2:122, 530–1; 6:154, 337, 534, 549.

20. Boyer (*Life of Anne*), Echard (*History of England*), and Kennett's editors (*Complete History of England*) all referred to these manuals in their prefaces. For a detailed review of the most prominent *artes historicae* see Levine, *Battle of the Books*, chap. 9; Nadel, pp. 49–73.

21. Charles Rollin (*The Method of Teaching and Studying the Belles Lettres* ... *Designed more particularly for Students in the Universities*, 4 vols [London, 1734]) and René de Rapin (*The Modest Critick*) were French. Hearne's *Ductor* (Thomas Hearne, *Ductor Historicus: or a short System of Universal History, and an Introduction to the Study of that Science* ... [London, 1698]) was largely a translation of a French work, as was Rawlinson's (Richard Rawlinson, *A New Method of Studying History:*

Recommending more Easy and Complete Instructions for Improvements in that Science . . ., 2 vols [London, 1728]). Le Clerc was a Huguenot (Jean Le Clerc, *Parrhasiana: Or, Thoughts upon Several Subjects; as Criticism, History, Morality, and Politics* [London, 1700]). Two of the rare, native English works were: Degory Wheare, *The Method and Order of Reading both Civil and Ecclesiastical Histories*, 3rd ed. (London, 1698); Nicolson, *English Historical Library*. The latter was not, properly speaking, an *ars historica*, but a survey of the primary and secondary sources a general historian of England would need to take notice of.

22. Newman, pp. 6, 63–7, 109–20. A. F. B. Clark, *Boileau and the French Classical Critics in England (1660–1830)* (Paris, 1925; rpt New York: Russell & Russell, 1965). Paul Hammond, *John Oldham and the Renewal of Classical Culture* (Cambridge: Cambridge Univ. Press, 1983). J. W. H. Atkins, *English Literary Criticism: 17th and 18th Centuries* (London: Methuen, 1951; rpt 1959).

23. Le Moyne, pp. 53–5, 92–6. Expanding his definition, Le Moyne emphasized history's roots, the fact that it had originally been 'invented for the Instruction of the Great' and therefore should have suitably instructive subject matter, what is 'Great and Illustrious,' not the examples of mere 'Puppets' or stories of 'Drunken Bouts.' Another description of 'the strict and severe Laws of History . . .: besides Truth, which is Essential to all Accounts of Actions and Things, (to distinguish them from Romances) [the laws] require also Political Reflections, Genuine Characters of Persons, and a Free and Faithful Representation of the Motives and Principles upon which those Persons act' (Abel Boyer, *History of the Reign of Queen Anne, Digested into Annals*, 11 vols [London, 1703–13], 1: To the Reader).

24. For example, Boyer, *Life of Anne*, Preface (p. viii).

25. History was a grave literary form that demanded the reader's concentration and patience, as Clarendon recognized (*Clarendon State Papers*, 2:333–5).

26. Burgh, pp. 125–31. Rollin, 3:1–8. *Gentleman's Magazine* (1732), 2:889–91. Hearne, *Ductor Historicus*, Dedication, pp. 112–17. Le Moyne, pp. 29–32. History was 'an impartial and fair Relation . . . of the publick Errors and Miscarriages of Men who have acted on the high Stage of Life, in order to admonish Posterity by such Examples, and to teach their Children Wisdom' ([Anon.], *A Vindication of the late Bishop Burnet from the Calumnies and Aspersions of a Libel . . . by John Cockburn, D.D.* [London, 1724], p. 40).

27. For the mirror-of-princes in England, see Philip Styles, in Levi Fox, ed., *English Historical Scholarship in the Sixteenth and Seventeenth Centuries* (London: Dugdale Society, Oxford Univ. Press, 1956), pp. 49–72.

28. Abel Boyer, *The Royal Dictionary* (London, 1699). Laurence Echard, *The Roman History, from the Building of the City, To the Perfect Settlement of the Empire by Augustus Caesar . . .*, 3rd ed., 2 vols (London, 1695), advertised in Echard's *Abridgment of Sir Walter Raleigh's History* (London, 1700) as 'For the use of his Highness the Duke of Gloucester.' William Wotton, *The History of Rome from the Death of Antoninus Pius to the Death of Severus Alexander* (London, 1701). Graham C.

Gibbs, 'Abel Boyer Gallo-Anglus Glossographus et Historicus, 1667–1729: From Tutor to Author, 1689–1699,' *Proceedings of the Huguenot Society of London*, 24 (1983), pp. 46–59. Tragically, Gloucester died in the year 1700, his education gone for naught.

29. Gilbert Burnet, *History of His Own Time* (London, 1838), p. 648. Christine Gerrard, *The Patriot Opposition to Walpole: Politics, Poetry, and National Myth, 1725–1742* (Oxford: Clarendon Press, 1994), p. 199. T. E. S. Clarke and H. C. Foxcroft, *A Life of Gilbert Burnet, Bishop of Salisbury* (Cambridge: Cambridge Univ. Press, 1907), pp. 351–5. J. C. D. Clark, intro., ed., *The Memoirs and Speeches of James, 2nd Earl Waldegrave, 1742–1763* (Cambridge: Cambridge Univ. Press, 1988), pp. 13–16, 52–8.

30. Bolingbroke adds, 'the study of history seems to me, of all other, the most proper to train us up to private and public virtue' (*Letters*, II). David Hume, *Essays Moral, Political, and Literary*, ed. Eugene F. Miller (Indianapolis, Ind.: Liberty Classics, 1985), pp. 567–8. ['A True Briton'], *Remarks on Bishop Burnet's History of his own Time . . .* (London, 1723), pp. 1–2. Hampton, p. 6. Oldmixon, *Critical History*, 1:161–3. Rawlinson, 1:23–6. *London Journal*, no. 696, 28 October 1732 ('We have Sense and Experience for our Guides, which generally conduct us safer to our Journey's End, than cool and abstract Reason. So, that History well wrote is the easiest and most effectual Teacher of Moral Science').

31. Boyer, *History of Anne*, Preface (pp. viii–x). Rapin, *Modest Critick*, pp. 4–5. Greig, 1:210.

32. For the historian's handling of other historians, see Ronald Syme, *Tacitus*, 2 vols (Oxford: Oxford Univ. Press, 1958; rpt 1963), 1:146. Polybius named names but other ancients did so without the frequency or ferocity of later times: Polybius, *The Rise of the Roman Empire*, trans. Ian Scott-Kilvert, intro. F. W. Walbank (Harmondsworth: Penguin, 1979), Book 12. In the composition of a preface, Le Moyne advised: 'The Historian must begin then with Modesty, and double it when he speaks himself; do it in such a manner, the Ink and Paper, if it were possible, should blush with him' (p. 193).

33. Thomas Hobbes, *Hobbes's Thucydides* (New Brunswick, New Jersey: Rutgers Univ. Press, 1975), ed., intro., Richard Schlatter, pp. 6–9.

34. For politeness, see Lawrence E. Klein, *Shaftesbury and the Culture of Politeness: Moral Discourse and Cultural Politics in Early Eighteenth-Century England* (Cambridge: Cambridge Univ. Press, 1994). Before proceeding to break strictures about polite history, Gilbert Burnet revealed a good grasp of them: 'it is not the work of an Historian to refute the Lies of others, but rather to deliver such a plain account as will be a more effectual confutation, than any thing can be that is said by way of Argument, which belongs to other Writers' (*The History of the Reformation of the Church of England*, 3 vols [London, 1679–1715], 1:41–2).

35. Joseph Addison, *The Freeholder*, ed. James Leheny (Oxford: Clarendon Press, 1979), no. 34, p. 193. Hume agreed with Addison, adding that ecclesiastical erudition and dispute also undermined politeness

(*History*, 4:188; 5:155; 6:540). Clarendon attacked scholasticism's 'profound and insignificant definitions and distinctions,' which he opposed to 'polite learning' (*Essays*, 1:253–5).

36. Thomas Salmon refers to the 'polite Romans' (*The History of Great Britain and Ireland . . . to the Norman Conquest*, 2nd ed. [London, 1725], Preface). Le Moyne praised Caesar's *Commentaries* as 'so Polite, so Advised, so Modest' (pp. 12–15). Addison, discussing 'Writings of the most Polite Authors,' recommended reading ancient historians as a means of acquiring 'Taste' (*The Spectator*, no. 409; 3:527–31). Also see Clarendon, *The Life of Edward Earl of Clarendon . . . in which is Included, A Continuation of His History of the Grand Rebellion*, 2 vols (Oxford: Oxford Univ. Press, 1857), 1:8–9; Hume, *History*, 5:304.

37. James Ralph claimed he was not writing 'Panegyric' or 'Invective' because he was telling the truth, thus writing a 'history' (*A Critical History of the Administration of Sir Robert Walpole* [London, 1743], Preface). Gilbert Burnet variously styled his opponent's untruthful 'histories' as 'Plays,' 'Romances,' 'Nouvelles,' and 'Fiction' (*A Defence of the Reflections On the Ninth Book . . . of Mr. Varillas's History of Heresies* [Amsterdam, 1687], pp. 15–16). Burnet's *History of His Own Time* was 'not so properly to be call'd a History' but a 'Satyr' on Charles 1 and a 'Panegyrick' on Cromwell, according to 'A True Briton' (*Remarks*, p. 44).

38. Marc Fumaroli, 'Les Mémoires du XVIIe siècle au carrefour des genres en prose,' *XVIIe Siècle*, no. 94/5 (1971), pp. 7–37. Burnet, *Memoires*, Preface. Hobbes's *Thucydides*, p. 14. Le Moyne, p. 189. Although Defoe is poking fun at Clarendon, he shows an awareness of this distinction between history and memoir: Daniel Defoe, *Memoirs of a Cavalier*, ed., intro. James T. Boulton (London: Oxford Univ. Press, 1972), pp. 11, 270.

39. Le Moyne, pp. 12–15. Echard, *Roman History*, 1: Preface. [Jean Le Clerc], *Mr. Le Clerc's Account of the Earl of Clarendon's History of the Civil Wars* (London, 1710), pp. 4–5. *Pope Corr.*, 2:249.

40. Le Clerc, *Parrhasiana*, pp. 97–107. *Pope Corr.*, 2:249. Rawlinson, 1:223. *The Spectator*, 4:520. Swift contrasted Englishmen, like his correspondent (Bolingbroke) exiled in France, unable or unwilling to write history, with Frenchmen too willing to oblige: 'It is this laziness, pride, or incapacity of great men [in England], that has given way to the impertinents of the nation where you are, to pester us with memoirs full of trifling and romance. Let a Frenchman talk twice with a minister of state, he desires no more to furnish out a volume . . .' (*Swift Corr.*, 2:320–1).

41. Roger North, *Examen, or an enquiry into the credit and veracity of a pretended complete history . . .* (London, 1740), pp. viii–xi. Burnet, *Memoires*, Preface. Momigliano, *Essays*, pp. 190–1. Oldmixon, *Critical History*, 1:170–1.

42. For references to Caesar as a historian, see *Swift Corr.*, 2:321; Felton, pp. 77–8; Ralph, *History of England*, 1:1, The Author to his Subscribers.

43. Le Clerc, *Mr. Le Clerc's Account*, pp. 4–7.

44. Echard, *Roman History*, Preface; *History of England*, 2:v, 371–9.

45. 'Biography is a species of history, with this peculiarity, that it exhibits more minutely the characters, and sets forth to view some, which are too private for history, but which are not on that account less worthy of being known [as examples of virtue or vice]' (Burgh, pp. 131–2).
46. Boyer, *Life of Anne*, Preface (p. vii).
47. Charles W. Fornara, *The Nature of History in Ancient Greece and Rome* (Berkeley: Univ. of California Press, 1983), pp. 184–90.
48. Clarendon, *Essays*, 2:135. J. Paul Hunter, 'Biography and the Novel,' *Modern Language Studies*, 9 (1979), pp. 68–84.
49. Rawlinson, 1:39. Le Moyne, pp. 48–9. Guido Abbattista, 'The Business of Paternoster Row: Towards a Publishing History of the *Universal History* (1736–1765),' *Publishing History*, 17 (1985), pp. 5–50. Fornara, pp. 42–6. Polybius, 1:3–4, 3:32.
50. Hugh Blair, *Lectures on Rhetoric and Belles Lettres*, 2nd ed., 3 vols (London, 1785), 3:20–1. Bolingbroke, *Letters*, VI.
51. The historian of one's own times Thucydides was less polite than the general historian Livy, for example. Rapin, *Works*, 1:317.
52. *Walpole Corr.*, 29:115.
53. [Kennett], *Complete History of England*, 1: Preface.
54. Thomas Hobbes, *Behemoth or The Long Parliament*, ed. Ferdinand Tönnies, intro. M. M. Goldsmith (London: Frank Cass, 1969), 2nd ed., pp. 23, 43, 155, 158. Hampton, pp. 6–24. Also see *The Freeholder*, no. 51; pp. 256–8; Howard D. Weinbrot, *Augustus Caesar in 'Augustan' England* (Princeton: Princeton Univ. Press, 1978), *Britannia's Issue*, pp. 386–7; Bolingbroke, *Letters*, III: 'Now, to improve by examples is to improve by imitation. We must catch the spirit, if we can, and conform ourselves to the reason of them; but we must not affect to translate servilely into our conduct . . . the particular conduct of those good and great men.'
55. *Pope Corr.*, 2:220, 252. Wotton, *Reflections*, pp. 37–41, 495–501. Roger North, *General Preface & Life of Dr. John North*, ed. Peter Millard (Toronto: Univ. of Toronto Press, 1984), sec. 10 ('General Preface').
56. Oldmixon, *Critical History*, 1:170–1.
57. *Hobbes's Thucydides*, pp. 12–17. Also see Polybius, 12.28; Cicero, *de Oratore*, 2.13; Fornara, pp. 49–51.
58. It was 'impossible,' wrote Abel Boyer, 'for any Writer of General History, to be Eye-Witness of all the Passages he relates . . .' (*Life of Anne*, p. 318).
59. This sketch of Livy's public career comes from the French critic René de Rapin, who relies primarily on Suetonius and Pliny: 'The Comparison of Thucydides and Livy,' *The Whole Critical Works of Monsieur Rapin*, 2 vols (London, 1706), 1:215–319, esp. 224–32.
60. For Tacitus' reputation in the seventeenth and eighteenth century, see Peter Burke, 'A Survey of the Popularity of Ancient Historians, 1450–1700,' *History and Theory*, 5 (1966), pp. 135–52; Howard Erskine-Hill, *The Augustan Idea in English Literature* (London: Edward Arnold, 1983), pp. 249–66; R. Malcolm Smuts, *Court Culture and the Origins of a Royalist Tradition in Early Stuart England* (Philadelphia: Univ. of Pennsylvania Press, 1987), pp. 26, 79.

61. J. H. M. Salmon, 'Cicero and Tacitus in Sixteenth-Century France,' *American Historical Review*, 85 (1980), pp. 307–31. Richard Tuck, *Philosophy and Government, 1572–1651* (Cambridge: Cambridge Univ. Press, 1993), pp. 40, 105. F. J. Levy, *Tudor Historical Thought* (San Marino, Calif.: The Huntington Library, 1967), pp. 237–41, 249–53.
62. Miller, *Defining the Common Good*, p. 104. Bolingbroke, *Letters*, V. Brownley, p. 136.
63. Clarendon, *Essays*, 1:249, 251.
64. Clarendon, *Essays*, 1:244–5.
65. Orest Ranum, *Artisans of Glory: Writers and Historical Thought in Seventeenth-Century France* (Chapel Hill: Univ. of North Carolina Press, 1980), pp. 98, 200–2. Mark Phillips, *Francesco Guicciardini: The Historian's Craft* (Toronto: Univ. of Toronto Press, 1977), p. 3. Peter Burke, *The Renaissance Sense of the Past* (London: Edward Arnold, 1969), pp. 92–3 (where Davila is quoted), 128. William J. Bouwsma, 'The Politics of Commynes,' *Journal of Modern History*, 23 (1951), pp. 315–28.
66. The broad outline of these careers is based on the *DNB*.
67. Addison, *The Freeholder*, no. 35, p. 194. Also see Levy, p. 254; Maltzahn, p. 62.
68. *The Adventurer*, no. 127, 22 Jan. 1754.
69. Of course, there were exceptions: Claudius wrote a history (Suetonius, *The Twelve Caesars*, trans. Robert Graves; intro. Michael Grant [Harmondsworth: Penguin Books, 1979], p. 210).
70. *DNB*. James II, King of England, *The Memoirs of James II: His Campaigns as Duke of York 1652–1660*, trans. A. Lytton Sells; pref. P. Muir, D. Randall (Bloomington: Indiana Univ. Press, 1962), Preface.
71. These historians are all examined in Chapters 2 and 3, with the exception of George, Lord Lyttelton, *The History of the Life of King Henry the Second*, 4 vols (London, 1767–71).

CHAPTER 2

1. *The Freeholder*, no. 35, p. 194.
2. For further evidence of the complaint against English historiography, see Chapter 1, note 1.
3. Burke, *Renaissance Sense of the Past*, pp. 1–20. Levy, pp. ix, 3–18, 168–9. Kenyon, *History Men*, p. 4. Levine, *Humanism and History*, pp. 11, 19–53.
4. Woolf, p. 65.
5. Paul Oskar Kristeller, *Renaissance Thought II: Papers on Humanism and the Arts* (New York: Harper & Row, 1965), pp. 10–11. Myron P. Gilmore, *Humanists and Jurists: Six Studies in the Renaissance* (Cambridge, Mass.: Harvard Univ. Press, 1963), chaps 1–2.
6. [Thomas Burnet], *Remarks Upon the Right Honourable Lord Lansdowne's Letter to the Author of the Reflections Historical and Political . . .* (London, 1732), p. 20.
7. Bolingbroke, *Letters*, V.

8. Levy, p. 282. Fussner, p. 154. LeMoyne, pp. 194–9. See, for example, Abel Boyer, *The History of the Reign of Queen Anne, Digested into Annals* (London, 1703–13), 11 vols; 1: To the Reader.
9. Donald J. Wilcox, *The Development of Florentine Humanist Historiography in the Fifteenth Century* (Cambridge, Mass.: Harvard Univ. Press, 1969). Eric Cochrane, *Historians and Historiography in the Italian Renaissance* (Chicago: Univ. of Chicago Press, 1981), pp. 3–17.
10. Thomas M. Greene, *The Light in Troy: Imitation and Discovery in Renaissance Poetry* (New Haven, Conn.: Yale Univ. Press, 1982), pp. 29–31, 38–45, 171–5, 264–7. Cochrane, pp 3–4. Ferguson, *Clio Unbound*, p. 313. Kelley, p. 84.
11. *Machiavelli: The Chief Works and Others*, ed., trans. Allan Gilbert (Durham, N. C.: Duke Univ. Press, 1965), 3:1027ff., Preface. Felix Gilbert, *History: Commitment and Choice* (Cambridge, Mass.: Harvard Univ. Press, 1977), pp. 135–53. Wilcox, chap. 4. Burke, *Renaissance Sense of the Past*, p. 123.
12. Mark Phillips, 'Machiavelli, Guicciardini, and the Tradition of Vernacular Historiography in Florence,' *American Historical Review*, 84 (1979), pp. 86–105; *Guicciardini*, pp. 114–20, 180–3.
13. Ranum, *Artisans of Glory*, chap. 7. Bouwsma, pp. 315–28. Burke, *Renaissance Sense of the Past*, p. 107, 128. H. R. Trevor-Roper, *Queen Elizabeth's First Historian: William Camden and the Beginnings of English 'Civil History,'* The Second Neale Lecture in English History (London: Jonathan Cape, 1971).
14. Levy, pp. 53–63, 173. Kenyon, *History Men*, pp. 3–4. Maltzahn, pp. 50, 180–1. Levine, *Battle of the Books*, p. 291. Ranum, *Artisans of Glory*, pp. 91, 146–7, 203.
15. Woolf, pp. 22, 116–19. Tuck, pp. 106–7. Trevor-Roper, *Queen Elizabeth's First Historian*. Burke, *Renaissance Sense of the Past*, pp. 127–8. Levy, pp. 53, 68–72, 258–62, 279–85.
16. Kenyon, *History Men*, pp. 12–13. Fussner, pp. 262–73. Levy, pp. 256–8. Brownley, p. 10. Woolf, pp. 154–5. [Kennett], *Complete History*, 1: Preface.
17. Woolf, pp. 137–9. Fussner, pp. 158–9. Levy, p. 271. *DNB*.
18. Levy, pp. 273–9. Ferguson, *Clio Unbound*, pp. 342–3.
19. Maltzahn, pp. 22–7, 73–9, 166–78, 221–2. Tyrrell, *History of England*, 1:vi. Nicolson, *English Historical Library*, 1: Preface.
20. See Chapter 7; Ferguson, *Clio Unbound*, pp. 390–2.
21. *Walpole Corr.*, 15:49.
22. Hume, *History*, 2:230.
23. Arnaldo Momigliano, *Studies in Historiography* (London: Weidenfeld and Nicolson, 1966), pp. 1–39. Joseph Addison, *Dialogue Upon the Usefullness of Ancient Medals* (New York: Garland Publishing, 1976), pp. 20–1. Levine, 'Ancients and Moderns Reconsidered,' pp. 82–3. Clarendon, *Essays*, 2:131–2.
24. Levy, pp. 129–30, 146–54. Levine, *Humanism and History*, pp. 79–88.
25. Ferguson, *Clio Unbound*, pp. 117–22, 225, 259–60. Woolf, chap. 7. Pocock, *Ancient Constitution*, chap. 5. Kelley, pp. 46–80, 102–11. Levy, pp. 165–6. Burke, *Renaissance Sense of the Past*, pp. 33–7.

26. Anthony Grafton, 'On the Scholarship of Politian and its Context,' *Journal of the Warburg and Courtauld Institutes*, 40 (1977), pp. 150–88.
27. Levine, *Humanism and History*, pp. 86, 99–103. Woolf, pp. 24–5.
28. Bolingbroke, *Letters*, III.
29. By Fussner and Ferguson, respectively. See the latter's thesis at pp. x, 228–9, 421–5.
30. For Leland, see Woolf, p. 19.
31. Hume, *History*, 1:25.
32. Peter Burke, 'The Politics of Reformation History: Burnet and Brandt,' *Clio's Mirror: Historiography in Britain and the Netherlands*, ed. A. C. Duke, C. A. Tamse (Zutphen: Walburg Press, 1985), p. 75. Momigliano, *Studies*, pp. 215–17; *Essays*, pp. 107–24, 161–5, 190–7. R. A. Markus, 'Church History and Early Church Historians,' *The Materials, Sources, and Methods of Ecclesiastical History*, ed. Derek Baker (Oxford: Ecclesiastical History Society, 1975), pp. 1–17.
33. A. E. Nobbs, 'Digressions in the Ecclesiastical Histories of Socrates, Sozomen, and Theodoret,' *Journal of Religious History*, 14 (1986), pp. 1–11. Markus, pp. 1–17.
34. Shapiro, *Probability and Certainty*, p. 155. The subtitles appear in the histories by Kennett, Tyrrell, and Rapin de Thoyras.
35. Paolo Sarpi, *The Historie of the Councel of Trent*, trans. Nathaniel Brent, 3rd ed. (London, 1640), pp. 1–2, 269, 583–4. David Wootton, *Paolo Sarpi: Between Renaissance and Enlightenment* (Cambridge: Cambridge Univ. Press, 1983), pp. 8–11, 69, 74, 104–7. Bolingbroke used Sarpi to justify dense detail in his projected history of England, promising Swift to 'render my Relation more full, or piu magra, the word is Father Paul's' (*Swift Corr.*, 3:488). For Sarpi's place in the canon of neoclassical historians, see Chapter 1.
36. Wotton, *Reflections*, pp. 495–501.
37. For the compatibility of Christian and pagan history in eighteenth-century England, see Johnson, *Formation*, pp. 44–5. For the perceived incompatibility of the pagan classics and Christian England, see Weinbrot, *Britannia's Issue*, chap. 2.
38. Momigliano, *Essays*, pp. 117–18.
39. Levy, pp. 79–83, 98–105. Woolf, pp. 36–7. Centuries before Foxe, Bede, too, had used ecclesiastical history to forge an English identity. See Patrick Wormald, '*Engla Lond*: the Making of an Allegiance,' *Journal of Historical Sociology*, 7 (1994), pp. 1–24.
40. Ferguson, *Clio Unbound*, pp. 114–15. Levy, pp. 114–23, 137. Levine, *Humanism and History*, pp. 88–9.
41. Levy, p. 104.
42. Greig, 1:284–5. Also see Le Clerc, *Parrhasiana*, pp. 107–11.
43. Hume, *History*, 5:154.
44. For the varieties of popular history and their audiences, see Robert Mayer, 'Nathaniel Crouch, Bookseller and Historian: Popular Historiography and Cultural Power in Late Seventeenth-Century England,' *Eighteenth-Century Studies*, 27 (1994), pp. 391–419.
45. Annual income figures are from Roy Porter (*English Society in the Eighteenth Century* [Harmondsworth: Penguin Books, 1982], pp. 28,

81–5, 386–7), based on Gregory King. Tyrrell, *General History*, 1:vi; 3:xxiii–xxiv. Mark Goldie, 'The Revolution of 1689 and the Structure of Political Argument,' *Bulletin of Research in the Humanities*, 83 (1980), pp. 473–564, at p. 482. Philip Gaskell, *A New Introduction to Bibliography* (Oxford: Clarendon Press, 1972), p. 177. D. F. Foxon, ed. *English Bibliographical Sources Series I* (London: Gregg, 1964), no. 4, *Bibliotheca Annua 1699–1703*.

46. For journalistic uses of Rapin, see Chapter 6. For the excerpting of Clarendon and Hume, see Chapters 3 and 7.

47. Paul Rapin de Thoyras, *Dissertation sur les Whigs & les Torys . . .* (London, 1717), p. 21; *The History of England . . .*, trans. Nicholas Tindal, 15 vols (London, 1725–31), 9:236–7, 377. Greig, 1:4.

48. Tim Harris, *Politics Under the Later Stuarts: Party Conflict in a Divided Society 1660–1715* (London and New York: Longman, 1993), pp. 1, 6, 26, 98–100, 140–1, 160, 234–6.

49. Clyve Jones, ed., *Britain in the First Age of Party 1680–1750: Essays Presented to Geoffrey Holmes* (London: Hambledon Press, 1987). J. C. D. Clark, *Revolution and Rebellion: State and Society in England in the Seventeenth and Eighteenth Centuries* (Cambridge: Cambridge Univ. Press, 1986), pp. 132–6, 144–9.

50. Hume, *Essays*, pp. 60, 62.

51. Adam Smith, *Lectures on Rhetoric and Belles Lettres*, ed. J. C. Bryce (Oxford: Clarendon Press, 1983), p. 102.

52. Montesquieu, *The Spirit of the Laws*, trans. Thomas Nugent; intro. Franz Neumann, 2 vols (New York: Hafner Press, 1949), 1:315 (bk 19, chap. 27).

53. Hampton, pp. 27–9.

CHAPTER 3

1. Clarendon, *Life*, 2:520–3. B. H. G. Wormald, *Clarendon: Politics, History and Religion, 1640–1660* (Cambridge: Cambridge Univ. Press, 1951; rpt Chicago: Univ. of Chicago Press, 1976). C. H. Firth, 'Clarendon's "History of the Rebellion,"' *English Historical Review*, 19 (1904), pp. 26–54, 246–62, 464–83. Hyde was Sir Edward Hyde previous to 1660, when he was made Baron Hyde of Hindon and then Earl of Clarendon (1661). For purposes of convenience, he will be referred to as 'Clarendon' throughout.

2. Sprat, *History of the Royal Society* [London, 1667], ed., intro. Jackson I. Cope, Harold W. Jones (St Louis, Mo.: Washington Univ. Studies, 1958), pp. 40–5 (text); p. 7 (notes).

3. *Essays*, 2:131–2.

4. *Essays*, 1:249–51.

5. *Essays*, 2:38–9.

6. Lawrence and Jeanne C. Fawtier Stone, *An Open Elite? England 1540–1880* (Oxford: Oxford Univ. Press, 1984), pp. 315–17. J. P. Kenyon, *Robert Spencer Earl of Sunderland 1641–1702* (London: Longmans, 1958), pp. 9–10, 227. Henry Horwitz, *Revolution Politicks: The Career of Daniel*

Finch Second Earl of Nottingham, 1647–1730 (Cambridge: Cambridge Univ. Press, 1968), chap. 8. David L. Smith, *Constitutional Royalism and the Search for Settlement, c. 1640–1649* (Cambridge: Cambridge Univ. Press, 1994), chap. 8.

7. Stone and Stone, pp. 78–9, 104. Douglas, pp. 332–3. Michael Maclagan, in Fox, ed., pp. 31–48. Fussner, pp. 26–32. Anthony R. Wagner, *English Genealogy*, 2nd ed. (Oxford: Clarendon Press, 1972), pp. 377–8, 398–9.

8. See the example of Roger North (Chapter 5).

9. Philip Styles, 'The Social Structure of the Kineton Hundred in the Reign of Charles II,' *Proceedings of the Birmingham Archaeological Society*, 78 (1962).

10. See Halifax, for example, in H. C. Foxcroft, ed., 'Some Unpublished Letters of Gilbert Burnet the Historian,' *Camden Miscellany*, 11, Camden 3rd ser., vol. 13 (London: Royal Historical Soc., 1907), p. 13. Also see Klein, *Shaftesbury*, pp. 15–17, 79.

11. *Clarendon State Papers*, 2:288–9.

12. *Clarendon State Papers*, 2:293.

13. Clarendon, *Life*, 2:588–9, 608. Also see the dedication to *A Brief View and Survey of . . . Mr. Hobbes's Book, Entitled Leviathan . . .* (Oxford, 1676), where Clarendon describes writing the *History* in terms of service to the crown.

14. Clarendon, *Essays*, 1:268–9; 2:4–8.

15. *Essays*, 2:16–45. *Life*, 2:588–9, 608. *Clarendon State Papers*, 2:288–9, 293.

16. *Essays*, 1:251.

17. *Essays*, 2:16, 17, 27, 34. *Clarendon State Papers*, 2:330–1.

18. *Essays*, 2:32.

19. *Essays*, 2:34–7.

20. Orrery, *Collection*, Preface (p. i).

21. Clarendon, *Essays*, 2:38–40. J. R. Jones, *Country and Court: England, 1658–1714* (Cambridge, Mass.: Harvard Univ. Press, 1978), pp. 16–20, 155–63. MacGillivray, chap. 5, p. 224. J. H. Grainger, *Character and Style in English Politics* (Cambridge: Cambridge Univ. Press, 1969), pp. 46–9, 64. Unless otherwise indicated, the source for the careers sketched in this Chapter is the *DNB*.

22. K. H. D. Haley, *The First Earl of Shaftesbury* (Oxford: Clarendon Press, 1968), pp. 662, 705–7. Jones, *Country and Court*, pp. 1–2, 19–20. Geoffrey Holmes, *British Politics in the Age of Anne* (London: Macmillan, 1967), pp. 113ff.

23. For political vengeance, see Lawrence Stone, 'The Results of the English Revolutions of the Seventeenth Century,' *Three British Revolutions: 1641, 1688, 1776*, ed. J. G. A. Pocock (Princeton: Princeton Univ. Press, 1980), pp. 96–8.

24. Kenyon, *Sunderland*, chaps. 3, 7, 10. Horwitz, *Revolution Politicks*, chap. 8. Jones, *Country and Court*, pp. 1–3. Gordon S. Wood, 'Conspiracy and the Paranoid Style: Causality and Deceit in the Eighteenth Century,' *William and Mary Quarterly*, 3rd ser., 39 (1982), pp. 401–41.

25. See Chapter 2.

26. On the dating of Clarendon's entry, see Brownley, p. 215.

27. *Hobbes's Thucydides*, pp. 12–17, 305.
28. Bodl. MS. Clarendon 127, fols 50–4.
29. *Clarendon State Papers*, 2:386, 288–9, 357.
30. *Clarendon State Papers*, 2:288–9, 375. In Thucydides Clarendon could see a man like himself, too good for his own times and finding dignity in historical composition: 'Thucydides . . . had no desire at all to meddle in the government: because in those days it was impossible for any man to give good and profitable counsel for the commonwealth, and not incur the displeasure of the people. . . . Thucydides therefore, that he might not be either of them that committed or of them that suffered the evil, forbore to come into the assemblies; and propounded to himself a private life, as far as the eminency of so wealthy a person, and the writing of the history he had undertaken, would permit' (*Hobbes's Thucydides*, pp. 12–13).
31. Examples of these classical concerns may be found in Clarendon, *The History of the Rebellion and Civil Wars in England*, ed. W. Dunn Macray, 6 vols (Oxford: Clarendon Press, 1888), 1:3, 260–1; 4: 2–4, 22, 184, 490. Clarendon justified the length of his 'character' of Falkland by citing a precedent in Livy (*Clarendon State Papers*, 2:386).
32. *History*, 1:1, xiii–xiv, 56–82, 378; 3:178–90; 4:488–9. *Clarendon State Papers*, 2:246, 383.
33. Brownley, pp. 61–2, 148.
34. *History*, 1:260–1; 4:4. Clarendon realized that Charles I would 'not find himself flattered' in the *History* (*Clarendon State Papers*, 2:288–9). In the *Life* he expanded his criticisms of the Stuarts (2:264, 307). Wormald, *Clarendon*, pp. 230–1. MacGillivray, p. 223.
35. For the perception of the *History* as 'polite,' see for example William Warburton, in Clarendon, *The History of the Rebellion . . . To Which Are Subjoined the Notes of Bishop Warburton*, 7 vols (Oxford: Clarendon Press, 1849), 6:567. In an atypically impolite passage, Clarendon characterized 1648 as 'a year of the highest dissimulation and hypocrisy, of the deepest villainy and most bloody treasons, that any nation was ever cursed with or under' (*History* [1888], 4:511). Typically, however, Clarendon used a classical historian to justify himself, quoting what Tacitus had said of Domitian's reign. Examples of Clarendon's references to himself are 2:527; 4:146–51.
36. See Chapter 2.
37. The variety of opinion concerning speeches is represented by: Rapin, *Modest Critick*, pp. 80–5; Burnet, *Memoires*, Preface; Le Moyne, pp. 169–72; Boyer, *Life of Anne*, Preface (p. x); MacGillivray, p. 6. King James II's perspective on classical speeches came from his own experience in 1654 as Duke of York on the eve of battle, when the great Turenne spoke to his officers 'in common talk' about the upcoming need for the men to be disciplined. 'And I am apt to beleeve,' observed James, 'that from this manner of conversation, historians ha[v]e made speeches for many Generalls who never made any to their Armys when they were upon the point of giving battell; for such ordinary discourses as I have mentioned, appear to me to be much more usefull th[a]n set formall speeches, which can not be

heard but by very few, in an open field, where they are commonly feign'd by writers to ha[v]e been spoken . . .' (*The Memoirs of James II*, p. 171).

38. For example, *History*, 2:88–106, 119–64.
39. While Clarendon apologized for narrative digressions, he rarely felt the need to justify his transcriptions: *History*, 1:323, 424, 472, 479, 503, 526, 536–41, 548. In his *History of the Parliament of England* (London, 1647), Thomas May had referred readers to a contemporary anthology of documents instead of reprinting them in the body of his *History*. May preferred to summarize declarations, remonstrances, petitions, messages: *History of the Parliament of England*, pp. 139, 159–75, 197, 197n.
40. Clarendon, *Essays*, 1:245. *Clarendon State Papers*, 2:333–5. Davila, *The Histoire of the Civill Warres of France* (London: Lee, Pakeman, Bedell, 1647), pp. 2–3, 528–35, 539–48, 876.
41. See Brownley, pp. 21, 131–2.
42. *Clarendon State Papers*, 2:333–5.
43. Woolf, pp. 206–7. Clarendon, *Essays*, 2:131–2.
44. *Essays*, 1:244–5.
45. For Clarendon's moderate royalism, see Smith, *Constitutional Royalism*, pp. 64–81, 297; Harris, *Politics Under the Later Stuarts*, pp. 34–5.
46. Clarendon, *Life*, 1:205–8; 2:594; *History*, 4:4, 254. H. R. Trevor-Roper, *Edward Hyde, Earl of Clarendon* (Oxford: Clarendon Press, 1975), p. 11.
47. Clarendon, *A Brief View*, Epistle Dedicatory. *Clarendon State Papers*, 3: supplement, xl, xliv–xlv.
48. Richard Ollard, *Clarendon and his Friends* (London: Hamish Hamilton, 1987), pp. 226–7. Hume, *History*, 6:164.
49. *History*, 1:xiii–xiv, 2–3; 4:2–4. Brownley, pp. 20–1. George Watson, 'The Reader in Clarendon's *History of the Rebellion*,' *The Review of English Studies*, 25 (1974), pp. 396–409. Clarendon postponed publication because he claimed his work was so honest and impartial that 'it will make mad work among friends and foes, if it were published' (*Clarendon State Papers*, 2:288–9, 357).
50. *Clarendon State Papers*, 2:288–9, 357; 3: supplement, xlvi.
51. The nonjurors were Archbishop Sancroft and Bishop Turner. Other readers included Sir John Nicholas and Bishop Sprat. John Burton, *The Genuineness of Ld. Clarendon's History of the Rebellion Printed at Oxford Vindicated. Mr. Oldmixon's Slander Confuted* (Oxford, 1744), pp. 86–7. Harry Carter, *A History of Oxford University Press to the Year 1780*, 2 vols (Oxford: Clarendon Press, 1975), 1:231. Clarendon, *History*, 1:xi–xiii.
52. G. V. Bennett, *The Tory Crisis in Church and State 1688–1730: The Career of Francis Atterbury Bishop of Rochester* (Oxford: Clarendon Press, 1975), pp. 26–31. L. S. Sutherland and L. G. Mitchell, eds, *The Eighteenth Century* (Oxford: Clarendon Press, 1986), vol. 5 of *The History of the University of Oxford*, T. H. Aston, gen. ed., pp. 9–14, 889.
53. For example, Klein, *Shaftesbury*, pp. 8–9.
54. Sutherland and Mitchell, pp. 10–14, 40–2, 309–17, 360–7, 526. G. V. Bennett contributed pp. 31–97, 359–400 to this volume.

55. Bennett, *Tory Crisis*, pp. 38–43. Levine, *Battle of the Books*, chaps. 2–3.

56. For a polemic against pedantry as socially unuseful, see the chapter on 'Learning' in *The Gentleman's Library: Containing Rules for Conduct in all Parts of Life*, 4th ed. (London, 1744).

57. MacGillivray, pp. 2–3, 10–11, 64–5. Burnet, *Memoires*, Epistle Dedicatory to the King, where Burnet, writing in 1673, is still conscious of the advantages in heeding the Act of Oblivion. James Sutherland, *The Restoration Newspaper and its Development* (New York: Cambridge Univ. Press, 1986), pp. 12–25. J. P. Kenyon, ed., *The Stuart Constitution 1603–1688*, 2nd ed. (Cambridge: Cambridge Univ. Press, 1986), p. 342; *History Men*, pp. 27–8.

58. J. G. A. Pocock, *Virtue, Commerce, and History: Essays on Political Thought and History, Chiefly in the Eighteenth Century* (Cambridge: Cambridge Univ. Press, 1985), p. 233. J. P. Kenyon, *Revolution Principles: The Politics of Party 1689–1720* (Cambridge: Cambridge Univ. Press, 1977), p. 66. A. B. Worden, ed., intro., *Edmund Ludlow; A Voyce from the Watch Tower*, Camden, 4th ser., 21 (London: Royal Historical Society, 1978), pp. 48–51.

59. Francis Madan, *A New Bibliography of the Eikon Basilike*, Oxford Bibliographical Society Publications, new ser., 3 (Oxford: The Society, 1950), pp. 1–5, 139–46. *Eikon Basilike: The Portraiture of His Sacred Majesty in His Solitudes and Sufferings*, ed. Philip A. Knachel (Ithaca, N. Y.: Cornell Univ. Press, 1966). MacGillivray, chap. 7, pp. 226–7.

60. MacGillivray, pp. 2–3, 59–61. Worden, *Edmund Ludlow*, pp. 1–2. Mark Goldie, 'The Roots of True Whiggism 1688–94,' *History of Political Thought*, 1 (1980), pp. 195–236.

61. The Christ Church editors functioned as Sprat had hoped his projected English academy would, helping to revise a neoclassical history of the Civil War (*History of the Royal Society*, p. 44).

62. H. G. Hiscock, *Henry Aldrich of Christ Church 1648–1710* (Oxford: Christ Church, 1960), chap. 8.

63. Carter, 1: 231. Sutherland and Mitchell, pp. 60–2.

64. Edmund Calamy, *An Historical Account of my own Life . . . (1671–1731)*, ed. J. T. Rutt, 2 vols (London, 1829), 1:442–52. Bodl. MS. Rawl. letters 14, fols 381–9. I. G. Philip, 'The Genesis of Thomas Hearne's *Ductor Historicus*,' *Bodleian Library Record*, 7 (1966), pp. 251–64. Hearne's project never came to fruition.

65. The total number of sets published by 1732 was c. 15 950. Publication in folio was c. 2500 in 1702–4, c. 900 in 1707, 500 in 1732; in octavo, 2500 in 1705, 2500 in 1707, 1500 in 1712, 1950 in 1717, 2000 in 1720–1, and 1600 in 1731–2. These figures are pieced together from the following incomplete and sometimes contradictory sources: Carter, 1: Appendix; *Delegates of the Press: Minute Book 1668–1758* (typescript), Oxford Univ. Archives; *The New Cambridge Bibliography of English Literature*, ed. George Watson, 5 vols (Cambridge: Cambridge Univ. Press, 1971), vol. 2; N. Hodgson, C. Blagden, *The Notebook of Thomas Bennet and Henry Clements*, Oxford Bibliographical Society Publications, new ser., 6 (Oxford: The Society, 1956), appendix 9. My count does not include the unauthorized Dublin ed. of 1719.

66. Bodl. MS. Ballard 10, fol. 64. Carter, 1:165–6. *Delegates of the Press.*
67. *The Wentworth Papers 1705–1739*, ed. James J. Cartwright (London: Wyman & Sons, 1883), p. 101. Hodgson, Blagden, appendix 9.
68. Nicolas Barker, ed., *The Oxford University Press and the Spread of Learning 1478–1978* (Oxford: Clarendon Press, 1978), pp. 27–8.
69. For the classical editions of Aldrich and Fell, see Levine, *Humanism and History*, p. 101.
70. Carter, 1:231–6. Hiscock, chap. 8. Barker, pp. 27–8.
71. *De Orat.*, 2.15. Barker reproduces the title page, which is not found in Macray's edition of the *History*.
72. *History*, 1:xviii, xix, xxv, xl, xli, xlv, xlvi.
73. Jonathan Swift, *Miscellaneous and Autobiographical Pieces, Fragments and Marginalia*, ed. Herbert Davis, *The Prose Works of Jonathan Swift*, vol. 5 (Oxford: Basil Blackwell, 1962), p. xxxvii. R. W. Harris, *Clarendon and the English Revolution* (Stanford, Calif.: Stanford Univ. Press, 1983), pp. 416–17.
74. Edward Gregg, *Queen Anne* (London: Routledge & Kegan Paul, 1980), pp. 157–8, 166. David Green, *Queen Anne* (New York: Charles Scribner's Sons, 1970), pp. 115–20, where Anne's comments are quoted. On the other hand, the Electress Sophia of Hanover, next in line to the throne, appears to have been pleased by the *History*. See Levine, *Battle of the Books*, p. 317n.
75. For the royal patronage afforded Robert Brady, James Tyrrell, and Laurence Echard, see Chapter 4.
76. Woolf, p. 247.
77. [Anon.], *An Antidote against Rebellion : Or, The Principles of the Modern Politician, Examin'd and Compar'd with the Description of the Last Age by . . . Clarendon* (London, 1704), pp. 3–5, 15–16. Sutherland and Mitchell, pp. 60–2. Kenyon, *Revolution Principles*, pp. 80–2. HMC *Portland*, 4:73 (St John to Harley, 16 Oct. 1703).
78. For example, see Calamy, 2:10.
79. Le Clerc, *Mr. Le Clerc's Account*, p. 3.
80. Le Clerc, *Mr. Le Clerc's Account*, p. 4.
81. Le Clerc, *Mr. Le Clerc's Account*, p. 4.
82. John Oldmixon, *Clarendon and Whitlock Compar'd . . .* (London, 1727), Preface.
83. Oldmixon, *Clarendon and Whitlock Compar'd*, Preface.
84. Oldmixon, *Clarendon and Whitlock Compar'd*, pp. 172–3.
85. Felton, pp. 203–5.
86. Quoted in Harris, *Clarendon and the English Revolution*, pp. 416–17.
87. Le Clerc, *Mr. Le Clerc's Account*, pp. 7–8.
88. Quoted in Harris, *Clarendon and the English Revolution*, pp. 416–17.
89. Oldmixon, *Critical History*, 2:184. Felton, pp. 203–5. *The Spectator*, 4:45.
90. Quoted in Harris, *Clarendon and the English Revolution*, pp. 416–17.
91. Quoted in J. W. Gough, 'James Tyrrell, Whig Historian and Friend of John Locke,' *Historical Journal*, 19 (1976), pp. 581–610, at p. 604n.
92. Le Clerc, *Mr. Le Clerc's Account*, p. 8. [Kennett], *Complete History*, 3:62–3, 125–32.

93. For this particular listing of ancients and moderns comparable to Clarendon, see René de Rapin, *Works*, 1: The Preface of the Publisher.
94. Wotton, *Reflections*, pp. 495–501. Levine, *Battle of the Books*, pp. 40–1.
95. Wotton, *Reflections*, pp. 500–1.
96. References to 'the noble Historian' or to Clarendon's social or aesthetic nobility: Echard, *History of England*, 2:69, 215; Clarendon, *History*, 1:xlv; Oldmixon, *Clarendon and Whitlock*, Preface; Warburton, in Clarendon, *History* (1849), 6:495, 508.
97. Felton, pp. 203–5.
98. *An Antidote against Rebellion*, p. 4.

CHAPTER 4

1. See Chapter 2.
2. J. G. A. Pocock, 'Robert Brady, 1627–1700: A Cambridge Historian of the Restoration,' *The Cambridge Historical Journal*, 10 (1951), pp. 186–204.
3. J. H. Plumb, *The Growth of Political Stability in England, 1675–1725* (London: Macmillan, 1967), pp. 14–17. Ranum, *Artisans of Glory*, p. 153.
4. R. O. Bucholz, *The Augustan Court: Queen Anne and the Decline of Court Culture* (Stanford, Calif.: Stanford Univ. Press, 1993), pp. 11–26.
5. Denys Hay, 'The Historiographers Royal in England and Scotland,' *Scottish Historical Review*, 30 (1951), pp. 15–29. Douglas, chap. 11. Paul Seaward, 'A Restoration Publicist: James Howell and the Earl of Clarendon, 1661–6,' *Historical Research*, 61 (1988), pp. 123–31.
6. Roswell G. Ham, 'Dryden as Historiographer-Royal,' *Review of English Studies*, 11 (1935), pp. 284–98. Hay, pp. 25–7.
7. Burke, 'Politics of Reformation History,' pp. 80, 84.
8. Harris, *Politics Under the Later Stuarts*, pp. 96–7, 121–2.
9. Pocock, *Ancient Constitution*, chap. 2, pp. 189–91, 261, 274–5.
10. Pocock, *Ancient Constitution*, pp. 148–9, 151–5, 187–91, 343–9; 'English Historical Thought in the Age of Harrington and Locke,' *Topoi*, 2 (1983), pp. 149–62, at p. 154. John Locke, *Two Treatises of Government: A Critical Edition*, ed., intro. Peter Laslett (Cambridge: Cambridge Univ. Press, 1960), pp. 51, 57.
11. Pocock, 'Robert Brady,' pp. 190–4; *Ancient Constitution*, pp. 64, 152, 206.
12. Robert Brady, *An Introduction to the Old English History, Comprehended in Three Several Tracts . . .* (London, 1684), Epistle to the Candid Reader, pp. 325–6; *A Complete History of England, From the First Entrance of the Romans under the Conduct of Julius Caesar, Unto the End of the Reign of King Henry III . . .* (London, 1685), Dedication, Preface to the Reader; *A Continuation of the Complete History of England containing the Lives and Reigns of Edward I, II, & III and Richard the Second* (London, 1700), Advertisements to the Candid Reader.
13. Brady, *Introduction*, Epistle to the Candid Reader.
14. Pocock, *Ancient Constitution*, pp. 194–5, 212–13. In composing the *Complete History*, Brady did not necessarily execute the plan of 1675.

However, the words on the title page of the *History* resembled those he used in his advertisement to Secretary of State Sir Joseph Williamson: *A Complete History of England . . . Delivered in plain Matter of Fact, without any Reflections . . .* (title page); 'a complete impartial history, written without reflections'(*Calendar of State Papers, Domestic* [London, 1907] for 3 April 1675 [SPD Car. II. 369:155]).

15. *Complete History*, The Preface to the Reader.
16. For example, *Complete History*, pp. 94, 505.
17. For example, *Complete History*, pp. 22, 41–50, 97–100, 185–216.
18. Pocock, *Ancient Constitution*, pp. 218–21, 224–5. For example, Brady offered no explanation for the decline of feudalism (*Complete History*, General Preface, pp. xxvi–xxviii).
19. *Complete History*, The Preface to the Reader.
20. *Complete History*, pp. 21, 57.
21. *Complete History*, p. 51.
22. See Chapter 7.
23. *Complete History*, 1: Dedication to James II.
24. *Complete History*, 1: The Preface to the Reader.
25. *Complete History*, 1: The Preface to the Reader.
26. Oldmixon, *Critical History*, 1: chap. 4. Also see William Guthrie, *A General History of England from the Invasion of the Romans . . . to the late Revolution*, 4 vols (London, 1744–51), 1: Preface.
27. The neoclassical complaint against English historiography persisted after Brady's death, as eighteenth-century reiterations of the complaint make clear. See Chapter 1, note 1.
28. See Chapter 2.
29. For Selden, see Woolf, pp. 220, 224, 233–4, 240–1.
30. See Chapter 2.
31. Burnet, *History of the Reformation*, 1: Epistle Dedicatory, Preface, 41–3; 2: title page, Preface, Appendix (p. 410); 3: Introduction, i–ii, 331–2. Low language and details, which could be found in Foxe as well, appear in Burnet's portrait of the 'bloody' Bishop Bonner, who liked eating puddings and pears (2:128). Burke, 'Politics of Reformation History,' pp. 78–82.
32. For Brady's erastianism, see *Continuation*, Advertisements to the Candid Reader; *Introduction*, Epistle to the Candid Reader.
33. G. V. Bennett, *White Kennett, 1660–1728, Bishop of Peterborough: A Study in the Political and Ecclesiastical History of the Early Eighteenth Century* (London: SPCK, 1957), pp. 13–14, 166, chap. 7; *Tory Crisis*, p. 4. Douglas, pp. 20–1, 249–51, 266–9, 320–1.
34. Geoffrey Holmes, *Augustan England: Professions, State and Society, 1680–1730* (London: Allen & Unwin, 1982), pp. 34 ff. John Gascoigne, *Cambridge in the Age of the Enlightenment: Science, Religion and Politics from the Restoration to the French Revolution* (Cambridge: Cambridge Univ. Press, 1989), pp. 10–15, 17, 21, 57–8. Douglas, pp. 66–79, 319, 329. Sutherland and Mitchell, pp. 355–7, 386, 807–29.
35. James Tyrrell, *Bibliotheca Politica: Or An Enquiry into the Ancient Constitution of the English Government . . .* (London, 1692–1702).
36. Tyrrell, *General History*, 2:xx, xxv.

37. Tyrrell, *General History*, 3: Preface to the Appendix, ii.
38. Tyrrell, *General History*, 1:iii, cxxvii.
39. Tyrrell, *General History*, 2:xxx.
40. Tyrrell, *General History*, 1:xli, xlv–lviii, lxxxvi, cv–cvii.
41. Tyrrell, *General History*, 1:lxix–lxxii, 18.
42. Tyrrell, *General History*, 1:lxviii.
43. Tyrrell, *General History*, 1:v–vi, xxiv, 37.
44. Tyrrell, *General History*, 2:xxxi.
45. Tyrrell, *General History*, 1:cxxviii, 1, 116, 150; 3:xxiii–xxiv.
46. Tyrrell, *General History*, 2:xxiv; 3:xiii–xiv.
47. See, for example, the confrontation between Henry II and Beckett (Tyrrell, *General History*, 2:310–65) and the reign of William I (2:1–72).
48. Tyrrell, *General History*, 1:xxiii, 86–7, 109, 111–114; 2:495.
49. Tyrrell, *General History*, 1:vii. Tyrrell follows his classical sources very closely as well. See, for example, 1:21–66.
50. For example, Tyrrell, *General History*, 1:188–95.
51. Tyrrell, *General History*, 1:248.
52. Tyrrell, *General History*, 2:vii, xxii; 3: xiii.
53. Tyrrell, *General History*, 1:78, 328; 2:xxiii, 112, 180–1, 432; 3:xv, 1021.
54. Tyrrell, *General History*, 1:v; 2:vii, xxiii.
55. An exception is the citation from Cicero: Tyrrell, *General History*, 2:xxii.
56. Tyrrell, *General History*, 2:vii, xxii; 3:xiv. For these historians, see Chapter 2.
57. Tyrrell, *General History*, 2:v.
58. Tyrrell, *General History*, 2:v–vii.
59. Gough, pp. 581, 584–7. Richard Ashcraft, *Revolutionary Politics & Locke's Two Treatises of Government* (Princeton: Princeton Univ. Press, 1986), p. 464.
60. Bucholz, pp. 91, 117, 134.
61. '[I]t hath been a general Complaint of the most Learned and Judicious Men of this Nation, that we have extreamly wanted an exact Body of *English* History in our own Language, for the Instruction and Benefit of our Nobility and Gentry . . .' Tyrrell, *General History*, 1:v.
62. Tyrrell, *General History*, 1:ii.
63. Tyrrell, *General History*, 2:xv–xvi.
64. Tyrrell, *General History*, 2:xxv.
65. Hampton, p. 5.
66. Tyrrell, *General History*, 2:xv–xvi; 3:xiii–xiv; 1:xxiii–xxiv, 106–11, bk 4. The history planned by Timothy Childe and Thomas Hearne in 1703 was calculated to attract readers by its inclusion of genealogy, legal texts, and a rehashing of the 'Brady Controversy' (Bodl. MS. Rawl. letters 14, fols 383–4).
67. Tyrrell, *General History*, 3:xxiii–xxiv.
68. My account of the Battle relies on Levine, *Battle of the Books*, especially pp. 1–46.
69. William Temple, 'Introduction to the History of England,' *The Works of Sir William Temple*, 4 vols (London, 1757), 3:67–194.
70. For Swift's project, see Levine, *Battle of the Books*, pp. 306–9; A. C.

Elias, *Swift at Moor Park: Problems in Biography and Criticism* (Philadelphia: Univ. of Pennsylvania Press, 1982), pp. 55–9; Swift, *Miscellaneous*, pp. ix–x, 3–7, 13–78.

71. Swift, *Miscellaneous*, pp. 11–12.
72. J. A. Downie, *Jonathan Swift: Political Writer* (London: Routledge & Kegan Paul, 1984), pp. 33–5, 43–6, 52–61, 65–8, 73–8, 81–2.
73. For the relation of Echard to Temple, see Deborah Stephan, 'Laurence Echard – Whig Historian,' *Historical Journal*, 32 (1989), pp. 846–50.
74. Laurence Echard, *An Appendix to the Three Volumes of Mr. Archdeacon Echard's History of England* . . . (London, 1720), p. 30; *History of England*, 1: Preface.
75. Echard, *Appendix*, pp. 36, 30.
76. Calamy, 2:395–401.
77. Echard, *Appendix*, pp. 30, 36; *History of England*, 2: Preface.
78. Echard, *Appendix*, p. 36.
79. Calamy, 2:395–401. Echard, *History of England*, 2: Dedication, i. *DNB*. Richard W. Goulding, *Laurence Echard, M.A., F.S.A., Author and Archdeacon* (London: n. p., 1927).
80. Echard, *History*, 1:45, 164, 250.
81. The case for Echard as 'church whig' is made by Stephan, pp. 843–66.
82. Echard, *History*, 2:1–2, 5, 566–7, 585–645; 3: Preface, 667–78, 981.
83. Tyrrell, *General History*, 3: Preface to the Appendix, iv–v.
84. Echard, *History*, 2:v.
85. Echard was frank about appropriating Clarendon for his own purposes: 'I have made bold with that great Man . . . as well to skreen and vindicate, as to enrich and ennoble my own Work . . . As I have sometimes copy'd, so I have oftner abridg'd him: I have sometimes new-modell'd and methodiz'd him . . . clear'd . . . explain'd . . . confirmed . . . vindicated him; and a few Times deserted and contradicted him'(*History*, 2:v–vi).
86. Echard, *History*, 2:644–5. For other borrowings from Clarendon, including the 'peace and plenty' thesis, various 'characters,' and the systematic analysis of Charles' councilors, see 2:1–2, 69, 81–7, 215, 443–4, 512.
87. Echard, *History*, 2:v.
88. Echard, *History*, 2:v.
89. Laurence Echard, *A General Ecclesiastical History, from the Nativity of our Blessed Saviour* . . . (London, 1702), Preface; *Roman History*, 1: Preface.
90. Echard, *History of England*, 1:412, Preface; 2:iii–iv.
91. Echard, *History*, 1: Preface, 62–3.
92. For example, see Echard's insertion of documents and extensive quotations: *History*, 2:565, 637; 3: chap. 1. Frequently, Echard simply listed random facts at the end of each reign (1:434).
93. Echard, *History*, 2:714–27.
94. Calamy, 2:395–401.
95. Echard, *Appendix*, pp. 32, 22, 31. Some examples of providentialism: *History*, 1:9, 44, 213, 577, 716–17; 2:714.
96. But see Clarendon, *History* (1849), 6:545, 562, 593, for Warburton's strictures.

97. Douglas, p. 169.
98. Post-Echardian complaints about history include those by Hume, Burke, Hampton, Bolingbroke (see Chapter 1, note 1), Voltaire, Montesquieu, and Squire (see Chapter 6).

CHAPTER 5

1. *Complete History*, 1: Preface. Levine, *Battle of the Books*, pp. 292–316.
2. Isaac Kramnick, 'Augustan Politics and English Historiography: The Debate on the English Past, 1730–35,' *History and Theory*, 6 (1967), pp. 33–56. Bennett, *Tory Crisis*, pp. 20–2; *Kennett*, chaps. 2, 7. Douglas, pp. 260–3. Harris, *Politics Under the Later Stuarts*, p. 153.
3. Bennett, *Kennett*, chap. 2, pp. 24–6, 86, 89, 96, 103–5. Bodl. MS. Eng. hist. b. 2, fol. 198. Kennett's eulogistic depiction of Burnet suggests the extent of his patron's influence over the project (*Complete History*, 3:488).
4. '[N]o prudent Writer would set a Name to the History of his own Times; for it is impossible to please, or to be thought impartial, till Posterity find out his plain and honest Dealing' ([Kennett], *Complete History*, 1: Preface [To the Reader]).
5. Kennett, *Complete History*, 1: Preface (To the Reader); 3: 53, 62–3, 79, 83–4, 90, 96, 125–32.
6. Bennett, *Kennett*, pp. 87–8, 90–5, chap. 7.
7. [Roger North], *Reflections Upon Some Passages in Mr. Le Clerc's Life of Mr. John Locke . . .* (London, 1711), pp. 6, 7, 9, 10.
8. *Complete History*, 3:849. Examples of his defective narrative are found at 3:369–71, 401–7. An example of his antiquarian detail: the Bishop of Winchester was 'Buried in a little Vault at the foot of the Steps ascending to the Choir on the North-side' (3:429).
9. *Pope Corr.*, 2:249–51. Abel Boyer, *The History of King William the Third*, 3 vols (London, 1702–3), 3:518.
10. On the difficulty of characterizing Swift's complex political outlook, see Ian Higgins, *Swift's Politics: A Study in Disaffection* (Cambridge: Cambridge Univ. Press, 1994), chap. 1.
11. Ehrenpreis, 3:864.
12. Ehrenpreis, 2:597–8.
13. Jonathan Swift, *The History of the Four Last Years of the Queen*, intro. Harold Williams, *The Prose Works of Jonathan Swift*, ed. Herbert Davis, vol. 7 (Oxford: Basil Blackwell, 1951), pp. 121–4.
14. Swift, *History*, pp. 5–12.
15. Swift, *History*, pp, 68–78, 2–3.
16. Swift, *History*, p. 166.
17. Swift, *History*, p. 1.
18. [Anon.], *A Whig's Remark's on the Tory History of the Four last Years of Queen Anne, By Dr. Jonathan Swift* (London, 1758), Dedication; pp. 3–9, 58–63. Since Oxford and Bolingbroke had had a falling out, there were two sides of the story, not a unified vision of the four last years. This pamphlet pointed out the fallacy of a single,

tory interpretation of events, by setting Bolingbroke's writings against Swift's *History* to show the discrepancies between their characters of Oxford and of Marlborough. See Bolingbroke (*Letters*, VIII) for the counterpoint to Swift's sketch of the duke.

19. *Monthly Review* (March, April, 1758), 18:258–60, 381–90.
20. *The Orrery Papers*, ed. Emily C. Boyle, Countess of Cork and Orrery, 2 vols (London: Duckworth, 1903), 2:88.
21. John Boyle, 5th Earl of Orrery, *Remarks on the Life and Writings of Dr. Jonathan Swift . . .* (London, 1752), Letter XXIV.
22. *Walpole Corr.*, 21:184–5.
23. Chesterfield, *Letters*, pp. 2297, 2303–4.
24. Swift often made extracts of important documents, especially treaties, sometimes quoting them at length; for example, *History*, pp. 36–7, 42–3, 47–51, 130.
25. Ehrenpreis, 2:600.
26. Swift, *History*, p. 80.
27. Swift, *History*, p. 80.
28. See Chapter 4.
29. Swift, *History*, Preface, p. xxxiii.
30. Downie, *Jonathan Swift*, pp. 178–9.
31. Ehrenpreis, 2:746.
32. *Swift Corr.*, 2:321.
33. *Monthly Review* (March, April, 1758), 18: 258–60, 381–90.
34. Felton, pp. 77–8.
35. Frederick S. Siebert, *Freedom of the Press in England 1476–1776: The Rise and Decline of Government Controls* (Urbana: Univ. of Illinois Press, 1952), pp. 346–52. Boyer, *Life of Anne*, pp. iii–v, viii.
36. Siebert, *Freedom of the Press*, chaps. 12, 13, 17.
37. *Pope Corr.*, 3:372–3. *Swift Corr.*, 2:320.
38. *DNB*. Sachse, pp. 15–20, 321–3, chaps. 10, 15.
39. F. J. M. Korsten, *Roger North (1651–1734): Virtuoso and Essayist* (Amsterdam: Holland Univ. Press, 1981), pp. 3–28, 65, 76, 97.
40. North, *General Preface*, Millard, ed., sec. 45. Thomas Carte, *An History of the Life of James Duke of Ormonde . . .*, 3 vols (London, 1735–6), 1:1–3. James Boswell, *The Life of Samuel Johnson, LL.D.* (Chicago: Encyclopaedia Britannica, 1952), p. 506.
41. Clarendon, *History*, 1:xl. North, *Examen*, pp. 32–3. *Wentworth Papers*, p. 101. Burton, *Genuineness*, p. 105. *A Whig's Remarks*, Dedication. George Granville, *A Letter to the Author of Reflections Historical and Political* (London, 1732), *passim*. Dr Edmund Calamy's attack on Echard's *History* was a defense of Calamy's grandfather (Goulding, *Echard*). *Walpole Corr.*, 31:293–4. Greig, 2:268.
42. North, *Reflections Upon Some Passages; The Life of the Honourable Sir Dudley North . . . And of the Honourable and Reverend Dr. John North* (London, 1744), Dedication; *The Life of the Right Honourable Francis North . . .* (London, 1742), pp. 7–8; *General Preface*, ed. Millard, 'General Preface,' sec. 42, 'John' (Life), sec. 2. Korsten, pp. 23–5, 268, 284.
43. North, *Examen*, p. ii; *Life of Francis*, pp. 7–8.

44. North, *Examen*, p. 350; *Reflections upon some Passages*, p. 11; *General Preface*, ed. Millard, 'General Preface,' sec. 29. Korsten, pp. 93–4.

45. Schmidt, pp. 62–5.

46. Korsten, pp. 79–80, 160–5, 24. North, *Examen*, p. 77; *General Preface*, ed. Millard, 'John' (introduction), sec. 3.

47. *General Preface*, ed. Millard, 'General Preface,' sec. 23, 10–12, 16. Oldmixon was familiar with this kind of reasoning, although he ultimately rejected it: 'What to us, the Stratagems of War, and the Arts of Government? What can we learn from the *History of Alexander*, or the Life of *Caesar*? 'Tis enough for us to mind our Business, and take Care of our selves and Families. Are we like to be Emperors and Kings, Consuls and Generals?' (*Critical History*, 1:2).

48. North, *Life of Francis North*, pp. 9, 11; *General Preface*, ed. Millard, 'General Preface,' sec. 12, 27.

49. Hunter, 'Biography and the Novel,' pp. 68–84. Attacking 'the great Abuse of Novels,' Samuel Croxall located the novel's origins in 'Imitations of History' and argued that the novel, like history, aimed 'only for Instruction and entertainment' and 'the Rewarding of Honour and Virtue, and the Punishing of Dishonour and Vice' (*A Select Collection of Novels*, 6 vols [London, 1720–2], 1: Preface). Appropriations of the title were fooling nobody. The *Gentleman's Magazine*'s listing of books for February 1749 puts *The History of Tom Jones* under the heading of 'Plays, Poetry, and Entertainment,' not under 'Historical and Miscellaneous.' *Joseph Andrews* had also been put in its place in the August 1742 issue.

50. Henry Fielding, *The History of the Adventures of Joseph Andrews*, ed. Douglas Brooks (Oxford: Oxford Univ. Press, 1970), Preface, book 3 (chap. 1). Leo Braudy, *Narrative Form in History and Fiction: Hume, Fielding & Gibbon* (Princeton: Princeton Univ. Press, 1970), esp. pp. 91–4, 211.

51. North, *General Preface*, ed. Millard, pp. 38–44 (editor's intro.).

52. Burton, *Genuineness*, pp. 14–15. Swift, *History*, Advertisement to Millar's edition, pp. 171–7; *Miscellaneous*, p. 184. HMC *Downshire*, 1:879. [A. Campbell], *An Examination of Lord Bolingbroke . . .* (London, 1753), pp. 93n–9n. HMC *Portland*, 7:367–8. Worden, *Edmund Ludlow*, pp. 1–5. Curll's unauthorized translation of *Bishop Parker's History of His Own Time* (London, 1728) has a preface hostile to Parker and his son's authorized translation, 'a Monument of Infamy to his Father's Ashes.' Gilbert Burnet, *A Supplement to Burnet's History of My Own Times*, ed. H. C. Foxcroft (Oxford: Clarendon Press, 1902), pp. xxviii–xxix.

53. Burnet, *Supplement*, pp. xxiv–xxv.

54. BL Add. MS. 11404, fols 51–63. Bodl. MS. Add. D. 23, fols 151–6. Calamy, 1:44–5.

55. Clarke and Foxcroft, p. 403. Burnet, *Supplement*, pp. viii–xvii, xxii–xxix; *History of His Own Time*, p. 20.

56. Burnet, *History*, p. 903.

57. *Swift Corr.*, 3:358–9.

58. Burton, *Genuineness*, Preface, pp. 9–15, 59–62, 113–14. Oldmixon,

Critical History, 1:170–1; *Clarendon and Whitlock*, Advertisement, Preface. Francis Atterbury, *The Late Bishop of Rochester's Vindication of Bishop Smalridge, Dr. Aldrich, and Himself, from the Scandalous Reflections of Oldmixon* (London, 1731). [Anon.], *Mr. Oldmixon's Reply to the Late Bishop of Rochester's Vindication . . .* (London, 1732).

59. Calamy, 1:44–5. Critics mentioned Burnet's ignoble use of the first person singular and his dedication of the work to God. See Philalethes [Matthias Earberry], *Impartial Reflections upon Dr. Burnet's Posthumous History* (London, 1724), Preface, p. 109; 'A Gentleman,' *A Review of Bishop Burnet's History . . .* (London, 1724), pp. 2, 67–9. Swift gave examples of Burnet's indecorous language: '*Clapt up, Left in the lurch, The Mob, Outed, A great beauty, Went roundly to work*: All these phrases used by the vulgar, shew him to have kept mean or illiterate company in his youth' (Swift, *Miscellaneous*, pp. 183–4).

60. Stratford to Edward Harley, 15 Nov. 1723, *HMC Portland*, 7:367–8.

61. Swift, *Miscellaneous*, pp. 183–4.

62. Blair, *Lectures*, 3:51.

63. Smith, *Lectures*, p. 116.

64. Burnet, *History of His Own Time*, pp. 1, 4–9, 30, 60–9, 199–200, 253, 397, 554, 648, 669, 702–3, 804, 903–24; *Supplement*, pp. 451–2.

65. When Burnet's *History* mentioned Clarendon's, Swift commented on the latter and implied a judgment on the former: 'Writ with the spirit of an historian, not of (a raker) into scandal' (Swift, *Miscellaneous*, p. 267). Thomas Burnet, *Remarks*, pp. 20–1. 'A True Briton,' *Remarks*, pp. 18–19. Philalethes, *Impartial Reflections*, p. 53.

66. Burnet, *History*, pp. 199–200, 247, 648, 853; *Supplement*, pp. xix– xx. Clarke and Foxcroft, p. 405.

67. Burnet, *History*, pp. 924, 30, 253, 554; *Supplement*, p. 452. Addison, *Freeholder*, no. 35, p. 194.

68. J. A. Downie, 'Walpole, "the Poet's Foe,"' in Jeremy Black, ed., *Britain in the Age of Walpole* (London: Macmillan, 1984), pp. 185–6. J. H. Plumb, *Sir Robert Walpole*, 2 vols (London: Cresset Press, 1956– 60), 1:xi–xii. *DNB*. Tom Woodman, 'Pope and the Polite,' *Essays in Criticism*, 28 (1978), pp. 19–37. Isaac Kramnick, *Bolingbroke and his Circle: The Politics of Nostalgia in the Age of Walpole* (Cambridge, Mass.: Harvard Univ. Press, 1968), pp. 7, 56–83, 205–35.

69. For an appreciation of Walpole's 'hack' writers, see Simon Targett, 'Government and Ideology during the Age of Whig Supremacy: The Political Argument of Sir Robert Walpole's Newspaper Propagandists,' *Historical Journal*, 37 (1994), pp. 289–317; Burtt, chap. 6.

70. Miller, *Defining the Common Good*, p. 89. H. T. Dickinson, *Liberty and Property: Political Ideology in Eighteenth Century Britain* (London: Holmes and Meier, 1977), p. 176. J. G. A. Pocock, *The Machiavellian Moment: Florentine Political Thought and the Atlantic Republican Tradition* (Princeton: Princeton Univ. Press, 1975), p. 483. Holmes, *British Politics*, p. 47.

71. Bennett, *Tory Crisis*, pp. 200–2. Maynard Mack, *The Garden and the City: Retirement and Politics in the Later Poetry of Pope 1731–1743*

(Toronto: Univ. of Toronto Press, 1969), p. 62. Bertrand Goldgar, *Walpole and the Wits: The Relation of Politics to Literature, 1722–1742* (Lincoln: Univ. of Nebraska Press, 1976).

72. Linda Colley, *In Defiance of Oligarchy: The Tory Party 1714–60* (Cambridge: Cambridge Univ. Press, 1982), p. 290. Pat Rogers, 'Book Subscriptions Among the Augustans,' *TLS*, 15 Dec. 1972, pp. 1539–40.

73. Burton, *Genuineness*, Preface. Bennett, *Tory Crisis*, p. 120. Eveline Cruickshanks, 'Lord Cornbury, Bolingbroke, and a Plan to Restore the Stuarts, 1731–1735,' *Royal Stuart Papers*, 27 (1986). H. T. Dickinson, *Bolingbroke* (London: Constable, 1970), p. 29.

74. *HMC Portland*, 7:465–6.

75. *Pope Corr.*, 2:107. Bennett, *Tory Crisis*, pp. 200–2, 295–310.

76. *Pope Corr.*, 2:166–70, 78–79. Francis Atterbury, 'Of Religious Retirement,' *Sermons and Discourses on Several Subjects and Occasions*, 5th ed., 4 vols (London, 1740–5), 1:347–75. Just as Clarendon justified retirement with classical precedents, and consoled himself that in retirement he might better serve the public than he had while holding office, so Pope assured Atterbury: 'Remember it was at such a time, that the greatest lights of antiquity dazled and blazed the most; in their retreat, in their exile, or in their death . . . it was then that they did good, and they gave light, and that they became Guides to mankind' (*Pope Corr.*, 2:166–70).

77. Aram Bakshian, Jr, '"A Hangdog Whom I dearly Love:" The Third Earl of Peterborough,' *History Today*, 31 (Oct. 1981), pp. 14–19. *Pope Corr.*, 3:188, 487–9; 4:35–6.

78. *DNB*. Horwitz, *Revolution Politicks*, chap. 12.

79. Private correspondence with Dr J. C. D. Clark, 22 August 1989.

80. *Pope Corr.*, 3:372–3.

81. Ehrenpreis, 2:597. Swift, *History*, intro. Harold Williams, pp. x–xi.

82. *Swift Corr.*, 5:66. Ehrenpreis, 3:863–4.

83. Swift, *History*, p. xxxiii.

84. Swift, *History*, p. xxxvi.

85. Swift, *History*, p. xxxvi.

86. Ehrenpreis, 3:864.

87. The phrase comes from J. H. Plumb, *The Death of the Past* (Boston: Houghton Mifflin, 1970).

88. For the full story of Bolingbroke's neoclassical history, see Philip Hicks, 'Bolingbroke, Clarendon, and the Role of Classical Historian,' *Eighteenth-Century Studies*, 20 (1987), pp. 445–71.

89. Bolingbroke, *Letters*, VI.

90. Bolingbroke to Sir William Wyndham, 16 March 1738, Petworth House Archives, vol. 19, fols 108–10.

91. This work is not extant. In a series of letters to Marchmont in the early 1740s, Bolingbroke discussed the change of plan: 'I have been forced by many disappointments . . . to lay aside all thoughts of writing a continued history . . . I must content myself to throw upon paper such notes, anecdotes, and observations, as I have the means of collecting, and the opportunity of making in this retreat.

They will be rather memorials for history, than history' (*A Selection from the Papers of the Earls of Marchmont*, ed. George Henry Rose, 3 vols [London, 1831], 2:213–16, 253–8, 286). George Harris, *The Life of Lord Chancellor Hardwicke*, 3 vols (London, 1847), 2:439–40.

92. Dickinson, *Bolingbroke*, pp. 7, 156, 247, 278, 294–5.
93. For this ideological maneuver, see Chapter 6.
94. Syme, *Tacitus*, p. 133. Philologus Cantabrigiensis, *The Freethinker's Criteria Exemplified, in a Vindication of the Characters of M. Tullius Cicero and the Late Duke of Marlborough . . .* (London, 1755), pp. 14, 23. Reed Browning, *Political and Constitutional Ideas of the Court Whigs* (Baton Rouge: Louisiana State Univ. Press, 1982), pp. 223–5, 256.
95. For Dryden, see Chapter 1, and Rawson, 'Poet Squab.'
96. *DNB*.
97. Felton, pp. 173–5. This idea was also articulated in Renaissance Italy (Cochrane, *Historians and Historiography*, p. 163).
98. For the Seven Years' War, see Miller, *Defining the Common Good*, pp. 192–4.
99. See, for example, Sprat (Chapter 3) and Felton (above).
100. Bodl. MS. Top. Oxon. d. 387, fols 49–50. Ian Green, 'The Publication of Clarendon's Autobiography and the Acquisition of his Papers by the Bodleian Library,' *The Bodleian Library Record*, 10 (1982), pp. 347–67. [Francis Gwyn, ed., John Shebbeare, intro.], *The History of the Reign of King Charles the Second from the Restoration To the End of the Year 1667. Written by Edward Earl of Clarendon . . .* (London, 1758), 1:i–lv. Also see the manuscript note in the British Library's copy of the pirate edition (shelfmark 806.e.13–14).
101. For example, *Walpole Corr.*, 15:32, 34; Raymond Klibansky, Ernest C. Mossner, eds, *New Letters of David Hume* (Oxford: Clarendon Press, 1954), p. 50.
102. Orrery, *Remarks*, p. 236. *Hobbes's Thucydides*, p. xiv. Swift, *A Proposal for Correcting, Improving and Ascertaining the English Tongue* (London, 1712), p. 42. Another history suffering from changes in English prose was Cherbury's *Henry VIII*: *Gentleman's Magazine* (1732), 2:1023.
103. 'Periods of a mile' is Pope's phrase. *Walpole Corr.*, 15:32–4n; 16:18. Also see 18:480; 21:14; 31:138.
104. David McQueen, *Letters on Mr. Hume's History of Great Britain* (Edinburgh, 1756), pp. 246–55, 273–85. William Guthrie called Clarendon 'more blameless than any writer I know, who has composed the history of his own times . . . [C]onsidering what he acted, and what he suffered, we may truly say, that his candour is the gift of God, and his mistakes are the infirmities of nature' (Guthrie, *General History*, 4:903, 1225). Hume's judgment came in his *History of England*, 5:232, 548n; 6:154, 215. Dr Johnson agreed that the narration was not fast enough, but admitted Clarendon's 'ignorance or carelessness of the art of writing is amply compensated by his knowledge of nature and of policy, the wisdom of his maxims, the justness of his reasonings, and the variety, distinctness, and strength of his characters' (*The Rambler*, no. 122, 18 May 1751).

105. Warburton's comments are printed in Clarendon, *History* (1849), 6:475–600.
106. This is how I interpret H. G. Hiscock, *Henry Aldrich of Christ Church 1648–1710* (Oxford: Christ Church, 1960). Also see Warburton in Clarendon, *History* (1849), 6:489, 495, 503, 505; Samuel Johnson, *The Idler*, no. 65, 14 July 1759; Bodl. MS. Top. Oxon. d. 387, fols 49–50, where Sir William Blackstone, Delegate of the Press, Oxford University, drafts a letter to the Hydes describing the difficulty in any edition of Clarendon's *Life* with 'unacknowledged Omission of any historical Passages,' since this might 'give a handle to revive those Clamours, which have been thoroughly refuted & are now pretty well subsided, in regard to [the] genuineness of [the] former History.'

CHAPTER 6

1. For Montesquieu, see Chapter 2; for Voltaire, below.
2. For the remainder of this study, 'Rapin' will refer to the Huguenot historian Rapin de Thoyras and not to the literary critic quoted in Chapter 1 and elsewhere, René de Rapin.
3. Linda Colley, *Britons: Forging the Nation, 1707–1837* (New Haven, Conn.: Yale Univ. Press, 1992), pp. 202–3, 229.
4. Sutherland and Mitchell, p. 474. Douglas, p. 328. Downie, 'Walpole, "the Poet's Foe,"' p. 187.
5. H. R. Trevor-Roper, *History: Professional and Lay* (Oxford: Clarendon Press, 1957). Sutherland and Mitchell, pp. 97, 309–17, 752– 4. Carter, 1:271–2, 334.
6. David Fairer, 'Anglo-Saxon Studies,' in Sutherland and Mitchell, pp. 807–29. Douglas, p. 339, chap. 13. I. G. Philip, 'Thomas Hearne as a Publisher,' *Bodleian Library Record*, 3 (1951), pp. 146–55.
7. Bennett, *Tory Crisis*, pp. 308–10; *Kennett*, chap. 7. W. A. Speck, *Stability and Strife: England, 1714–60* (Cambridge, Mass.: Harvard Univ. Press, 1977), pp. 93–5. Douglas, pp. 356–7, 363–4. Smith, *Gothic Bequest*, p. 45.
8. R. M. Wiles, *Serial Publication in England Before 1750* (Cambridge: Cambridge Univ. Press, 1957), pp. ix, 4–11, chap. 7. J. W. Saunders, *The Profession of English Letters* (London: Routledge & Kegan Paul, 1964), pp. 132–4. Abbattista, pp. 9–12. P. J. Wallis, 'Book Subscription Lists,' *The Library*, 5th ser., 29 (1974), pp. 255–86. W. A. Speck, in Isabel Rivers, ed., *Books and their Readers in Eighteenth-Century England* (New York: St Martin's Press, 1982), pp. 47–68. Rogers, 'Book Subscriptions.'
9. Paul Rapin de Thoyras, *Histoire d'Angleterre*, 10 vols (The Hague, 1723–7), 1:xix. D. W. L. Earl, 'Paul Rapin de Thoyras and the English Historiography of his Time 1700–1730,' Cambridge Univ. M. Litt. dissertation, 1961, pp. 20–5, 39–43. H. R. Trevor-Roper, 'A Huguenot Historian: Paul Rapin,' *Huguenots in Britain and their French Background, 1550–1800* (London: Macmillan, 1987), ed. Irene Scouloudi, pp. 3–19.
10. Total copies in the 30 years after 1725 = c. 17 750: 1725–31 Knapton ed. in 15 vols (2000 copies); 1729–31 Roberts ed. in French (1500);

1732 Knapton reprint in folio (5000); 1732 Kelly translation in folio (1000); further editions including Tindal's continuation of Rapin, 1735–1750s (2500, 2000, 2000, 1750). My estimate is based on the following sources: Wiles, pp. 5, 10–11, 44–6, 61, 246, 305, chap. 7, Appendix B; *London Journal*, 11 Nov. 1732; Bodl. MS. Grolier 19471, fols xiv, xvi, 81, 120; Bodl. MS. don. b. 4, fol. 103; Earl, 'Paul Rapin de Thoyras,' p. 47, Bibliography (pp. v–vi).

11. [Anon.], *An Abridgement of the History of England, Being a Summary of Mr. Rapin's History and Mr. Tindal's Continuation ... to the Death of King George I ...*, 3 vols (London, 1747). [John Lockman], *A New History of England, By Question and Answer. Extracted from the most celebrated English Historians; particularly M. de Rapin Thoyras ...*, 2nd ed. (London, 1735).

12. [Anon.], *A Defence of English History Against the Misrepresentations of M. de Rapin Thoyras ...* (London, 1734), p. 105. Salmon, *History of Great Britain*, Preface. *Gentleman's Magazine*, 2:1023; 6:138–40. *London Journal*, 24 Oct. 1730, 20 Nov. 1731, 16 March 1734.

13. See, for example, how he handled the 'Brady Controversy,' *History*, 2:159–64.

14. Voltaire, *Letters on England* (1733), trans. Leonard Tancock (Harmondsworth: Penguin Books, 1980), pp. 109–10.

15. *The London Journal* and *The Daily Gazetteer* are reprinted in *The Gentleman's Magazine*, 2:1023; 6:138–40.

16. Earl, 'Paul Rapin de Thoyras,' pp. 20–9.

17. Rapin, *Histoire*, 1:ii–iii; *History*, 1:xi–xii.

18. Rapin, *History*, 1:77, 134, 222, 282–92, 424–8; 2:135–210; 3:90–1; 4:342; 7:704; 10:455–575; 11:193–9, 517–25, 558–61.

19. Rapin, *History*, 1:348; 2:118–20, 159–94; 3:491–2; 4:186; 9:498–502; 11:14–15; 12:571–6.

20. Pat Rogers, *Grub Street: Studies in a Subculture* (London: Methuen, 1972), pp. 185–95.

21. Oldmixon, *The History of England*, 1:781; 3: Preface; *Clarendon and Whitlock*, Advertisement.

22. Pat Rogers, 'The Printing of Oldmixon's Histories,' *The Library*, 5th ser., 24 (1969), pp. 150–4; 'Book Subscriptions.' According to F. J. G. Robinson, P. J. Wallis, *Book Subscription Lists: A Revised Guide* (Newcastle upon Tyne: Book Subscription Lists Project, 1975), 740 copies of vol. 1 were subscribed to, 371 of vol. 2, and 253 of vol. 3.

23. Addison, *The Freeholder*, no. 35, p. 195. Rapin, *Histoire*, 1:xxxiii–xxxiv. Oldmixon, *Critical History*, 1:161–3.

24. Plumb, *Walpole*, 1:12–13; 2:81–91. Mark Girouard, *Life in the English Country House: A Social and Architectural History* (New Haven, Conn.: Yale Univ. Press, 1978), pp. 11, 184–94. Stone and Stone, p. 329. Wagner, pp. 106–24.

25. Echard, *History of England*, 1:904; 3: Preface, 766. Le Moyne, pp. 92–6, 104–16. Rawlinson, 1:230–5. North, *Examen*, p. 656. Seconding such views, an anonymous respondent to Rapin maintained that 'The use of History is to keep Mankind in Decorum ...' (*A Defence of English History*, p. 122).

26. North, *Examen*, pp. ix–xi. Oldmixon, *Critical History*, 2: Introduction.
27. 'It is the duty of history to draw a veil over the failings of princes where they have no great public consequences; but she cannot place in too striking a view the sources of public calamity' (Guthrie, *History*, 4:825–6).
28. Le Moyne, pp. 110–16. *The Gentleman's Library*, pp. 306–14, 328–40.
29. *The Freeholder*, no. 35, pp. 195–6. Addison continued: 'as the Lives of Great Men cannot be written with any tolerable Degree of Elegance or Exactness, within a short Space after their Decease; so neither is it fit that the History of a Person, who has acted among us in a publick Character, should appear till Envy and Friendship are laid asleep, and the Prejudice both of his Antagonists and Adherents be, in some Degree, softned and subdued.'
30. For the Lords' action, see the *DNB* entry for Thomas Carte.
31. Duncan Forbes, *Hume's Philosophical Politics* (Cambridge: Cambridge Univ. Press, 1975), pp. 253–7. Robert W. Kenny, 'James Ralph: An Eighteenth-Century Philadelphian in Grub Street,' *Pennsylvania Magazine of History and Biography*, 64 (1940), pp. 218–30. HMC Laing, 2:410–14, 452. Wiles, appendix B. *Gentleman's Magazine* (Feb. 1744, Feb. 1749).
32. Guthrie, 1: Preface. In the time of Charles II and James II it was 'dangerous for a writer to have attempted a fair and impartial history of England. The castrations which Bacon's discourses suffered in the year 1682, and the many prosecutions carried on, in that reign, against the liberty of the press, are so many melancholy proofs of this. Dr. Brady's history was a shameful attempt to support the schemes of his patron king James II; and Mr. Tyrrel's an ill-judged one, to weaken the principles of hereditary right.'
33. Guthrie, *History*, 1: Preface, 43–4; 4:821, 895.
34. Guthrie, *History*, 4:1221–3, 1225; 1: Preface.
35. Guthrie, *History*, 1:46, 114, 117–19, 317–25; 2:11, 391–2, 854n; 4:819–21, 1064–71, 1370–96.
36. Supplying the full context for documentary quotations, Brady admitted, accounted for the 'tedious' length of his own quotations (*An Introduction to the Old English History*, Advertisement to the Impartial and Judicious Reader). Gilbert Burnet also explained how the charge of partisanship had forced historians to pack their works with documents: '[The] common failings of Historians have in this last Age made people desire to see Papers, Records, and Letters published at their full length' (Burnet, *Memoires*, Preface).
37. Bolingbroke, *Letters*, II.
38. Guthrie, *History*, 2:390–1.
39. Guthrie, *History*, 4:1064–5, 1071. Also see 1:117–23; 2:170–1.
40. Guthrie, *History*, 1:43–4.
41. Guthrie, *History*, 1:37, 40, 317–25; 2:731.
42. For the development of Scottish historical sociology, see Colin Kidd, *Subverting Scotland's Past: Scottish Whig Historians and the Creation of an Anglo-British Identity, 1689–c. 1830* (Cambridge: Cambridge Univ. Press, 1993), pp. 108–20.

43. Ralph, *History of England*, 1:1, The Author to his Subscribers.
44. Ralph, *History of England*, 1: The Author to his Subscribers.
45. Ralph, *History of England,*, 1: The Author to his Subscribers, 1–9, 125, 696, 707, 839–44; 2:1–20, 480–1, 1023–4n.
46. [William Knowler, ed.], *The Earl of Strafforde's Letters and Dispatches . . .*, 2 vols (London, 1739), 1: Dedication, where the chaplain-editor Knowler describes the 3rd Earl's intentions in these volumes 'to vindicate [the 1st Earl's] Memory from those Aspersions, which it is grown too fashionable to cast upon him, of acting upon Arbitrary Principles, and being a Friend to the Roman Catholics.'
47. Carte to the Pretender, July 1739. Stuart Papers, Royal Archives, RA SP(M) 216/111B.
48. Stuart Papers, RA SP(M) 216/111C; Box 1/299.
49. [John Boyle, 5th Earl of Orrery (presumed editor)], *A Collection of the State Letters*, Preface (p. ii). Carte, *Life of Ormonde*, 1: Dedication, 54; 3: Preface. *Orrery Papers*, 1:193.
50. Bodl. MS. Carte 175 (fol. 6), 240 (fols 241–2). BL Add. MS. 21500 (fols 115–16), 32691 (fols 382–3). *Swift Corr.*, 4:524.
51. Carte to Newcastle, 28 Sept. 1738, BL Add. MS. 32691, fols 382–3.
52. Bodl. MS. Carte 175, fols 22–3, 61, 75–6. Colley, *In Defiance of Oligarchy*, p. 32. R. W. Greaves, 'Fathers and Heretics in Leicester,' in Anne Whiteman, *et al*, eds, *Statesmen, Scholars and Merchants: Essays in Eighteenth-Century History Presented to Dame Lucy Sutherland* (Oxford: Clarendon Press, 1973), pp. 68–9.
53. *Walpole Corr.*, 18:480.
54. Bodl. MS. Carte 175, fols, 75–6.
55. For these societies, see Colley, *Britons*, pp. 88–95.
56. For the *Dictionary* as well as the charter, see the texts reproduced in Newman, pp. 112–13.
57. Carte's first volume came out in an edition of 3000; 750 for succeeding volumes: Bodl. MS. don. b. 4., fols 117, 119, 122, 131, 144.
58. Thomas Carte, *A General History of England*, 4 vols (London, 1747–55), 1:450–2.
59. Carte, *General History*, 4:4–6.
60. For this kind of populism, see Clark, *English Society*, pp. 291–2.
61. Carte, *General History*, 4:301–2.
62. Carte, *General History*, 4:301–2.
63. BL Add. MS. 21500, fols 115–17.
64. Carte, *General History*, 4:3–4.
65. Carte, *General History*, 4:605–610; 1:291–2; 4:4–6, 126–30, Book XXII, 301–32, 325–55. *Gentleman's Magazine*, 18 (1748), pp. 13–14.
66. Carte, *General History*, 1: Preface, 2. Bodl. MS. Carte 240, fols 241–2.
67. Besides the examples of this interest already discussed, see *General History*, 1: Preface, 1–2; 2:866–7. Carte actually used Guthrie in vol. 4, Book XXII, of the *General History*.
68. Carte, *General History*, 1:450, Preface. An example of the failure to integrate antiquarian data is 1:71–80.
69. *Orrery Papers*, 2:45.
70. Alexander Allardyce, ed., *Scotland and Scotsmen in the Eighteenth*

Century, 2 vols (Edinburgh and London, 1888), 2:547–9.

71. [Samuel Squire], *Remarks upon Mr. Carte's Specimen of his General History...* (London, 1748), Advertisement to the Reader, pp. 9–11, 47.

72. Quoted in Allardyce, ed., 2:548.

CHAPTER 7

1. Nicholas Phillipson, *Hume* (London: Weidenfeld & Nicolson, 1989).

2. Craig Walton, 'Hume's *England* as a Natural History of Morals,' *Liberty in Hume's History of England*, ed. Nicholas Capaldi, Donald W. Livingston (Dordrecht: Kluwer, 1990), pp. 25–52.

3. David Fate Norton, 'History and Philosophy in Hume's Thought,' *David Hume: Philosophical Historian*, ed. David Fate Norton, Richard H. Popkin (Indianapolis, Ind.: Bobbs-Merrill, 1965), pp. xlvii–l.

4. Giuseppe Giarrizzo, *David Hume politico e storico* (Turin: Einaudi, 1962), reviewed by Duncan Forbes in *Historical Journal*, 6 (1963), pp. 280–94.

5. Forbes, *Philosophical Politics*, chap. 5, p. 263.

6. Victor G. Wexler, *David Hume and the History of England*, Memoirs of the American Philosophical Society, vol. 131 (Philadelphia: The Society, 1979), Preface. Constant Noble Stockton, 'Economics and the Mechanism of Historical Progress in Hume's *History*,' *Hume: A Re-evaluation*, ed. Donald W. Livingston, James T. King (New York: Fordham Univ. Press, 1976), pp. 296–320.

7. Donald T. Siebert, *The Moral Animus of David Hume* (Newark: Univ. of Delaware Press, 1990), pp. 9, 19.

8. The classical or humanist dimension of the *History* has been mentioned, but not pursued, by Phillipson, *Hume*, p. 80; Wexler, p. 17; Forbes, 'Introduction,' *History of Great Britain*, p. 9, *Philosophical Politics*, p. 121; David Allan, *Virtue, Learning and the Scottish Enlightenment: Ideas of Scholarship in Early Modern History* (Edinburgh: Edinburgh Univ. Press, 1993), pp. 170–5.

9. *Enquiries Concerning the Human Understanding and Concerning the Principles of Morals*, ed. L. A. Selby-Bigge, 2nd ed. (Oxford: Clarendon Press, 1902), pp. 83–4. S. K. Wertz shows how this passage has been misconstrued as a declaration of the uniformity of human nature: 'Hume, History, and Human Nature,' *Hume as Philosopher of Society, Politics and History*, ed. Donald Livingston, Marie Martin (Rochester, N. Y.: Univ. of Rochester Press, 1991), pp. 77–92. Also see Forbes, *Philosophical Politics*, chap. 4, esp. p. 121.

10. For Hippocrates, see M. I. Finley, 'Introduction,' Thucydides, *History of the Peloponnesian War* (Harmondsworth: Penguin Books, 1972), trans. Rex Warner, p. 20. For human nature, see Thucydides: 'It will be enough for me ... if these words of mine are judged useful by those who want to understand clearly the events which happened in the past and which (human nature being what it is) will, at some time or other and in much the same ways, be repeated in the future' (1.22).

11. Douglas, pp. 16, 357. Pocock, *Ancient Constitution*, pp. 240–1, 363. John Spurr, *The Restoration Church of England, 1646–1689* (New Haven: Yale Univ. Press, 1991), p. 383. Levine, *Humanism and History*, pp. 95–6.

12. Nicholas Phillipson, 'Politics and Politeness in the Philosophy of David Hume,' *Politics, Politeness, and Patriotism*, ed. Gordon J. Schochet, Proceedings of the Folger Institute, Center for the Study of British Political Thought, vol. 5, (Washington, D. C.: The Folger Shakespeare Library, 1993), pp. 305–18, esp. pp. 314–16.

13. Greig, 1:4, 168, 237. Phillipson, *Hume*, p. 18. Forbes, *Philosophical Politics*, pp. 121, 136–9, 206–7; 'Introduction,' *History of Great Britain*, pp. 10–11, 16, 21.

14. Hume, *Essays*, pp. 533–7.

15. Hume, *Essays*, pp. 533–7, 563–8.

16. Catharine Macaulay, *The History of England from the Accession of James I to that of the Brunswick Line*, 8 vols (London, 1763–83). Bridget Hill, *The Republican Virago: The Life and Times of Catharine Macaulay, Historian* (Oxford: Clarendon Press, 1992). I intend to pursue the Macaulay-Hume relationship in a separate study of eighteenth-century historiography. For Hume and women, see Jerome Christensen, *Practicing Enlightenment: Hume and the Formation of a Literary Career* (Madison: Univ. of Wisconsin Press, 1987).

17. Greig, 1:1–7, 17, 26–7, 99, 109, 233, 359, 378, 380. Ernest C. Mossner, *The Life of David Hume*, 2nd ed. (Oxford: Clarendon Press, 1980), pp. 6–19, 138–40, 176.

18. Greig, 1:109, 233, 236, 385–7. Mossner, *Life*, pp. 4, 107, 223–5, 234.

19. Mossner, *Life*, pp. 4, 225–7. Phillipson, *Hume*, pp. 24–9. Greig, 1:109.

20. Forbes, *Philosophical Politics*, pp. 140–1.

21. Kidd, pp. 209–10, 270.

22. BL Add. MS. 48800, fols 83, 93, 96. [John Brown], *An Estimate of the Manners and Principles of the Times*, 2 vols (London, 1757–8), 1:57–8. Greig, 1:34, 37n, 180, 189, 198, 217–19, 237, 249, 251, 264, 278; 2:106, 233.

23. Mossner, *Life*, pp. 138–40. Greig, 1:232, 236, 359, 377; 2:125. The decision about quarto had been made more than a year before publication of volume one, or at least Hume was then writing with quarto in mind (Greig, 1:180). For the audience implied by the format, see Brown, *Estimate*, 1:55–8. Quarto reached the same sort of readers as folio, or so Andrew Millar, Hume's publisher, thought. In the first edition of volume two of the *History*, Millar chose to advertise his folio products only, which included works by Burnet (*Reformation* and *Own Time*), Bacon, Sidney, Locke, Ludlow, de Thou, and Harrington. Millar thus judged Hume's first readers to be interested in other serious, limited-edition works of philosophy and history.

24. Greig, 1:170–1.

25. Greig, 1:179, 193.

26. Hume, *History of England*, 2:527.

27. *History*, 5:545.

28. *History*, 1:93. For further examples, see 1:27, 79, 80, 103, 203, 311; 2:262, 525; 3:436, 437; 5:276, 330; 6:395.
29. *History*, 1:52–4, 56, 60–1, 90–3, 104–6, 205–7, 237, 333–4; 3:136–8, 5:125, 474.
30. *History*, 2:398.
31. *History*, 1:46, 95–6; 4:358–9; 5:49. Hume was not alone. For earlier criticisms of Roman civilization as violent and rapacious, hence inappropriate as a cultural model for modern Britons, see Weinbrot, *Britannia's Issue*, chap. 7.
32. *History*, 5:469.
33. *History*, 1:400–2; 2:266, 5:469.
34. *History*, 1:400.
35. *History*, 1:148–59, 186–8.
36. *History*, 5:192–4; 2:436–8; 1:156–7; 5:273–5, 352–6; 6:388–91, 454–6, 524–5.
37. *History*, 3:431–4 (my italics).
38. For example, *History*, 1:xvi, 39, 74–5, 287–8; 2:40, 271, 518; 6:142.
39. For example, *History*, 1:31, 94–5, 100–2, 244, 400; 2:513; 5:53. For possible exceptions to this decorum, see Siebert, *Moral Animus*, pp. 156–7.
40. *History*, 5:151.
41. Greig, 1:237, 379.
42. *History*, 1:3–16.
43. *History*, 1:160–1
44. *History*, 1:74–81.
45. *History*, 1:160–1, 168–9, 174.
46. *History*, 1:460–4, 254; 4:355n.
47. *History*, 1:370–2.
48. *History*, 1:487–8.
49. *History*, 2:284, 277, 283.
50. *History*, 3:77–80.
51. *History*, 2:277; 3:74, 220, 261, 285–6; 4:124, 360, 370; 5: 557–8.
52. *History*, 4:145–6; 5:550, 558–60.
53. *History*, 2:536.
54. *History*, 6:531, 475–6, 481, 504, 520, 530.
55. *History*, 2:519.
56. *History*, 1:15–16.
57. *History*, 1:254.
58. *History*, 2:104–9, 519–24; 5:556–7.
59. *History*, 3:80–2.
60. *History*, 4:384–5.
61. *History*, 5:18–19, 39–40; 4:384.
62. *History*, 1:166, 15–16, 23, 46, 50, 70, 75, 146, 185, 296–7, 340, 350, 463; 5:142.
63. *History*, 6:150, 148–19.
64. *History*, 5:380, 493–4; 6:4, 25, 142–3; 1:95–6, 237–9. Also see Hume's 'Of Superstition and Enthusiasm,' *Essays*, pp. 73–9.
65. *History*, 1:32, 33, 37; 2:14; 3:324; 5:443.
66. For example, Hume, *History*, (3:134–7; 2:99–110); Tacitus, *Annals*

(11.14), *History* (2.2–3; 5.2–10); Thucydides (6.1–5, 54–9).
67. *History*, 5:122–3.
68. For example, *History*, 1:404–6; 2:65–72.
69. Dugald Stewart, 'Account of the Life and Writings of William Robertson, D. D.,' in William Robertson, *The Works of William Robertson, D. D.* (London, 1831), pp. xxi–xxii. Burke, writing in *The Annual Register* (1761, pp. 301–4), argued that Hume had placed in the appendix discussions of the feudal law that more properly belonged in the text.
70. See Chapter 2; Greig, 1:284–5.
71. *History*, 5:559. Hume's original words were italicized.
72. The modern edition, used in the present study, runs to 3044 pages, of which 220 are comprised of endnotes and appendices.
73. Hume referred readers to 'several collections' – including Tyrrell's *History* – for details of charges against Richard II's ministers, because '[i]t would be tedious to recite the whole charge' (*History*, 2:301).
74. *History*, 2:3–4.
75. *History*, 5:124. Compare the revised passage with the first edition, in Forbes, ed., intro., *History of Great Britain*, p. 219.
76. *History*, 1:3, 25.
77. *History*, 1:4; 2:518.
78. *History*, 1:39–40, 17, 128; 2:4–5.
79. *History*, 2:525.
80. *History*, 1:162–5.
81. *History*, 1:226–7, 467–71.
82. *History*, 6:531.
83. *History*, 5:574, 583; 4:354.
84. *History*, 5:43; 6:531. Also see Forbes, 'Introduction,' *History of Great Britain*, p. 54.
85. *History*, 1:187; 2:173–4; 4:354–5.
86. For example, *History*, 6:381. For his last revisions, made in 1776, see Todd, 'Foreword,' *History*, 1:xxi–xxii.
87. *History*, 6:533.
88. For the cult of Elizabeth in the 1730s, see Gerrard, chap. 6.
89. *New Letters of David Hume*, p. 199.
90. Greig, 1:4.
91. McQueen, *Letters*, pp. 246–55.
92. *Monthly Review* (March, 1755, Jan., 1757).
93. [Richard Hurd], *Moral and Political Dialogues between Divers Eminent Persons of the Past and Present Age* ... (London and Cambridge, 1759), Postscript.
94. McQueen, *Letters*, Letters I, II, IX. *Monthly Review* (March, 1755).
95. Greig, 1:214.
96. *Monthly Review* (Dec., 1761), pp. 401–2. Hampton prophesied as much in 1746 (*Reflections*, pp. 27–9) and in the *History* itself Hume acknowledged that 'moderate opinions' would never 'please either faction' (6:534). T. E. Jessop, (*A Bibliography of David Hume* [London: A. Brown & Sons, 1938], p. 30) attributes the unsigned review to Ruffhead.

97. Also see *Critical Review* (April, 1759).

98. The quotation is from Gilbert Stuart, cited in the *Monthly Review*'s (vol. 59 [1778], pp. 19–25) review of Towers' *Observations*. Joseph Towers, *Observations on Mr. Hume's History of England* (London, 1778), pp. 9, 145.

99. *Monthly Review* (Dec., 1761), pp. 402, 407–10. *Monthly Review* (Feb., 1762), p. 84. Hume took Ruffhead's strictures seriously. See Greig, 1: 378; J. H. Burton, ed., *Letters of Eminent Persons Addressed to David Hume* (Edinburgh and London, 1849), pp. 41–4.

100. *Walpole Corr.*, 15:75. Also see Towers, pp. 6–9.

101. McQueen, Letter I.

102. Quoted in C. H. Firth, 'The Development of the Study of Seventeenth-Century History,' *Transactions of the Royal Historical Society*, 3rd ser., vol. 7 (1913), pp. 37–8.

103. These calculations are based on the ledger of the printer William Strahan, BL Add. MS. 48800, fols 112, 119, 132, 140. They do not include the pirate octavo edition (Dublin, 1755). Also see Jessop, pp. 27–8; E. C. Mossner and Harry Ransom, 'Hume and the "Conspiracy of the Booksellers:" The Publication and Early Fortunes of the *History of England*,' *Studies in English*, 29 (1950), pp. 162–82; Greig, 1:4–5, 214, 217–19.

104. BL Add. MS. 48800, fol. 140. Jessop, p. 28. Greig, 1:244, 382, 385, 491; 2:83, 196–7, 230. For the takeoff of a new market for history beginning c. 1757 but flowering later in the century, see J. B. Black, *The Art of History: A Study of Four Great Historians of the Eighteenth Century* (New York: F. S. Crofts & Co., 1926), p. 14; Mossner and Ransom, p. 179.

105. *Monthly Review* (Jan., 1757).

106. Blair, *Lectures*, 3:51.

107. Chesterfield is quoted in a letter from Andrew Millar to Hume. Greig, 2:106n.

108. *Monthly Review* (Feb., 1762), p. 95.

109. Burton, *Letters of Eminent Persons*, p. 44.

110. [Edmund Burke], *The Annual Register*, (1761), 4:301–4.

111. *Critical Review* (Dec., 1756).

112. Edward Gibbon, *Memoirs of My Life*, ed., intro., Betty Radice (Harmondsworth: Penguin Books, 1984), p. 114.

113. *Walpole Corr.*, 15:32; 40:135.

114. 'Le Tacite et le Tite Live de l'Ecosse.' *The Letters of Edward Gibbon*, ed. J. E. Norton, 3 vols (London: Cassell, 1956), 2:107.

115. Stewart, 'Life of Robertson,' p. viii. According to the Advertisement, Stewart's memoir, though dated 1801, was written 'long' before that time. Stewart quotes Quintilian in Latin; the English translation is from *Institutio Oratoria*, X.1.73, *Quintilian*, trans. H. E. Butler, The Loeb Classical Library, vol. 4 (Cambridge, Mass.: Harvard Univ. Press, 1936).

116. Smith's opinion is relayed by an anonymous literary memoir (quoted here), dated 1780, first published in *The Bee*, 11 May 1791, and reprinted as Appendix I in Smith, *Lectures*, p. 229.

117. *Monthly Review* (Dec., 1761), p. 410.
118. Towers, p. 144. *Monthly Review* (Feb., 1762), pp. 82, 84, 92; (March, 1755), pp. 206–9; (Jan., 1757), pp. 36–50.
119. Towers, p. 151. Towers praised Hume's 'beauty of diction, harmony of periods, and acuteness and singularity of sentiment' (p. 1).
120. *Walpole Corr.*, 35:214.
121. *Monthly Review* (Dec., 1761), p. 414.
122. For scoticisms generally, see J. C. Bryce, 'Introduction,' Adam Smith, *Lectures*, p. 15.
123. For example, McQueen, Letter I; *Critical Review* (April, 1759). For an appreciation of Hume's neoclassical prose style, see Wexler, p. 17.
124. *Critical Review* (April, 1759).
125. *Monthly Review* (Feb., 1762), pp. 89, 94; (Dec., 1761), pp. 407, 412; (March, 1755); (Jan., 1757). *Critical Review* (Dec., 1756); (April, 1759). For nineteenth-century editions of *Characters from Hume . . .*, see Jessop, p. 32.
126. For French classicism, see Paul H. Meyer, 'Voltaire and Hume as Historians: A Comparative Study of the *Essai sur les Moeurs* and *The History of England*,' *PMLA*, 73 (1958), pp. 51–68.
127. McQueen, Letter I.
128. Greig, 1:326. *The World*, no. 107, 16 Jan. 1755. *Walpole Corr.*, 34:208–9.
129. *Walpole Corr.*, 35:214. *Critical Review* (Dec., 1756).
130. Greig, 1:226. Modern scholarship has confirmed 'the mutual independence of Hume and Voltaire:' Meyer, p. 53.
131. Robertson, *Works*, p. xxi.
132. Robertson, *Works*, pp. xx, xxi.
133. *Critical Review* (Dec., 1756). According to Towers, 'He could describe a theological disputation with abundantly more energy and spirit than any warlike actions, though of the most brilliant kind. His descriptions of the battles of Cressy, Poictiers, or Agincourt, are much inferior, in point of spirit, to his account of king Henry the Eighth's disputation with John Lambert' (p. 146).
134. *Monthly Review* (Feb., 1762), p. 86.
135. *Monthly Review* (Feb., 1762), p. 89.
136. For example, Oldmixon listed 'the endowments of a Divine, a Statesman, a Scholar, a Philosopher, a Gentleman' (*Critical History*, 1:170–1).
137. *Monthly Review* (Feb., 1762), p. 95.
138. *Critical Review* (April, 1759).
139. See Mossner, *Life*, pp. 228–9, 388–9; Laurence L. Bongie, *David Hume: Prophet of the Counter-revolution* (Oxford: Clarendon Press, 1965), p. 12n.
140. For the texts of these two indictments, see Chapters 2 and 6.
141. *Oeuvres Complètes de Voltaire*, ed. Émile de la Bedollière, Georges Avenel, 9 vols (Paris, 1867–73), 4:627–8.
142. Burton, *Letters of Eminent Persons*, pp. 275, 23. Bongie, p. 74.
143. Delisle de Sales, *De la philosophie de la nature . . .*, 3rd ed., 6 vols (London, 1777), 2:273n; 6:411. Bongie, pp. 1, 10, 28. Mossner, *Life*, pp. 224–5.

144. For example, see Gabriel Sénac de Meilhan, *Considérations sur l'esprit et les moeurs* (London, 1787), pp. 364–5. A case for imperial Britain's growing interest in Polybius rather than Tacitus is made by Miller, *Defining the Common Good*, pp. 104–5.
145. Smith, *Lectures*, p. 112. *The World*, no. 107, 16 Jan. 1755.
146. Burton, *Letters of Eminent Persons*, pp. 275–6.
147. Voltaire, *Oeuvres Complètes*, 4:627.
148. See Bongie, pp. 24–8.
149. Burton, *Letters of Eminent Persons*, pp. 13, 275. Friedrich Melchior Grimm, *Correspondance littéraire*, 18 vols (Paris, 1812–29), 3:330.
150. See Bongie, p. 9.
151. Greig, 1:406–11, 414–17. Mossner, *Life*, chap. 31.
152. Towers, p. 121.
153. Grimm, 3:330. Voltaire, *Oeuvres Complètes*, 4:627. Burton, *Letters of Eminent Persons*, pp. 13, 275. Bongie, pp. 10–13.
154. Greig, 1:409, 415. *Walpole Corr.*, 10:176. Burton, *Letters of Eminent Persons*, p. 23.
155. Towers, pp. 4–5.
156. Towers, pp. 6, 134–43, 146.
157. Mossner, *Life*, p. 446. Bongie, pp. 3–8, 16.
158. Greig, 1:285.
159. Mossner, *Life*, pp. 92, 176.
160. Greig, 1:355.
161. Mossner, *Life*, p. 555.
162. The draft preface is reprinted in Mossner, *Life*, p. 306.
163. Greig, 1:285, 193, 240, 262.
164. Greig, 2:151, 162.
165. Greig, 1:332–5, 355, 382. Black, *Art of History*, p. 90. Forbes, 'Introduction,' *History of Great Britain*, pp. 13, 41–2; *Philosophical Politics*, p. 256. Firth, 'Development,' pp. 33, 38. Hume, *History*, 1:374, 470n, 493–4; 2:122, 530–1; 6:337, 534, 549.
166. For example, Hume, *Essays*, pp. 88–9. Also see Chapter 2.
167. For example, see Voltaire, *Correspondance*, ed. Theodore Besterman, 10 vols (Paris: Gallimard, 1964–86), 7:744 (20 June 1764).
168. Meilhan, pp. 364–5.
169. *Walpole Corr.*, 9:407; 43:126. Stewart, 'Life of Robertson,' pp. x–xi. Besides Gibbon's work, Catharine Macaulay's *History* also has a neoclassical dimension to it, as I intend to demonstrate in a future study.
170. *Memoirs*, p. 132.
171. David Womersley, *The Transformation of The Decline and Fall of the Roman Empire* (Cambridge: Cambridge Univ. Press, 1988), pp. 54, 80–8. Patricia B. Craddock, *Edward Gibbon, Luminous Historian 1772–1794* (Baltimore: The Johns Hopkins Univ. Press, 1989), pp. 67–70, 263. J. G. A. Pocock, 'Edward Gibbon in History: Aspects of the Text in *The History of the Decline and Fall of the Roman Empire*,' The Tanner Lectures on Human Values, vol. 11, ed. G. B. Petersen (Salt Lake City: Univ. of Utah Press, 1990), pp. 291–364. Levine, *Humanism and History*, pp. 182–3.

CONCLUSION

1. Henry Fielding, *The History of the Adventures of Joseph Andrews*, ed. Douglas Brooks (Oxford: Oxford Univ. Press, 1970), Preface, book 3 (chap. 1).

Bibliography

PRIMARY SOURCES

A Manuscript Sources

Bodleian Library
  MS. Add. D. 23
  MS. Ballard 10
  MS. Carte 175, 240
  MS. Clarendon 127
  MS. don. b. 4
  MS. Eng. hist. b. 2
  MS. Grolier 19471
  MS. Rawl. letters 14
  MS. Top. Oxon. d. 387
British Library
  Additional MS. 4253
                11404
                21500
                32691
                48800
Oxford University Archives
  Delegates of the Press: Minute Book 1668–1758 [typescript]
Petworth House
  Egremont MS., vol. 19 [consulted at West Sussex Record Office]
Royal Archives
  Stuart Papers: RA SP(M) 216/111B, C; Box 1/299

B Printed Sources

1 Periodicals

The Adventurer
The Annual Register
Bibliotheca Annua [*English Bibliographical Sources Series I*. D. F. Foxon,
  ed. London: Gregg, 1964.]
The Critical Review
The Daily Gazetteer
The Freeholder [James Leheny, ed. Oxford: Clarendon Press, 1979.]
The Gentleman's Magazine
The Idler
The London Journal
The Monthly Review

The Rambler
The Spectator [Donald F. Bond, ed. 5 vols. Oxford: Clarendon Press, 1965.]
The World

2   *Books and Pamphlets*

A Defence of English History Against the Misrepresentations of M. de Rapin Thoyras .... London, 1734.
A Gentleman. *A Review of Bishop Burnet's History.* ... London, 1724.
A Letter to A Friend in the Country, On the Publication of Thurloe's State Papers .... 2nd ed. London, 1742.
A True Briton. *Remarks on Bishop Burnet's History of his own Time* .... London, 1723.
A Vindication of the late Bishop Burnet from the Calumnies and Aspersions of a Libel ... *by John Cockburn, D. D.* London, 1724.
A Whig's Remarks on the Tory History of the Four last Years of Queen Anne, By Dr. Jonathan Swift. London, 1758.
Addison, Joseph. *Dialogue Upon the Usefullness of Ancient Medals.* New York: Garland Publishing, 1976.
Allardyce, Alexander, ed. *Scotland and Scotsmen in the Eighteenth Century.* 2 vols. Edinburgh and London, 1888.
An Abridgement of the History of England, Being a Summary of Mr. Rapin's History and Mr. Tindal's Continuation ... *to the Death of King George I* .... 3 vols. London, 1747.
An Antidote against Rebellion: Or, The Principles of the Modern Politician, Examin'd and Compar'd with the Description of the Last Age by ... *Clarendon.* London, 1704.
Atterbury, Francis. *The Late Bishop of Rochester's Vindication of Bishop Smalridge, Dr. Aldrich, and Himself, from the Scandalous Reflections of Oldmixon.* London, 1731.
Atterbury, Francis. *Sermons and Discourses on Several Subjects and Occasions.* 5th ed. 4 vols. London, 1740–5.
Blair, Hugh. *Lectures on Rhetoric and Belles Lettres.* 2nd. ed. 3 vols. London, 1785.
Bolingbroke, Henry St John, 1st Viscount. *Letters on the Study and Use of History.* 2 vols. London, 1752.
Boswell, James. *The Life of Samuel Johnson, LL. D.* Chicago: Encyclopaedia Britannica, 1952.
Boyer, Abel. *The History of King William the Third.* ... 3 vols. London, 1702–3.
Boyer, Abel. *The History of the Life & Reign of Queen Anne.* ... London, 1722.
Boyer, Abel. *History of the Reign of Queen Anne, Digested into Annals.* 11 vols. London, 1703–13.
Boyer, Abel. *The Royal Dictionary.* ... London, 1699.
Brady, Robert. *A Complete History of England, From the First Entrance of the Romans under the Conduct of Julius Caesar, Unto the End of the Reign of King Henry III.* ... London, 1685.
Brady, Robert. *A Continuation of the Complete History of England containing the Lives and Reigns of Edward I, II, & III and Richard the Second.* London, 1700.

Brady, Robert. *An Introduction to the Old English History, Comprehended in Three Several Tracts. . . .* London, 1684.

[Brown, John]. *An Estimate of the Manners and Principles of the Times.* 2 vols. London, 1757–8.

Burgh, James. *The Dignity of Human Nature, or A Brief Account of the certain and established Means for attaining the true End of our Existence.* London, 1754.

Burnet, Gilbert. *A Defence of the Reflections On the Ninth Book . . . of Mr. Varillas's History of Heresies.* Amsterdam, 1687.

Burnet, Gilbert. *History of His Own Time.* London, 1838.

Burnet, Gilbert. *The History of the Reformation of the Church of England.* 3 vols. London, 1679–1715.

Burnet, Gilbert. *The Memoires of the Lives and Actions of James and William Dukes of Hamilton. . . .* London, 1677.

Burnet, Gilbert. *A Supplement to Burnet's History of My Own Times.* H. C. Foxcroft, ed. Oxford: Clarendon Press, 1902.

[Burnet, Thomas]. *Remarks Upon the Right Honourable Lord Lansdowne's Letter to the Author of the Reflections Historical and Political. . . .* London, 1732.

Burton, J. H., ed. *Letters of Eminent Persons Addressed to David Hume.* Edinburgh and London, 1849.

Burton, John. *The Genuineness of Ld. Clarendon's History of the Rebellion Printed at Oxford Vindicated. Mr. Oldmixon's Slander Confuted.* Oxford, 1744.

Calamy, Edmund. *An Historical Account of my own Life . . . (1671–1731).* J. T. Rutt, ed. 2 vols. London, 1829.

Calendar of State Papers, Domestic.

[Campbell, A.]. *An Examination of Lord Bolingbroke. . . .* London, 1753.

Carte, Thomas. *A General History of England.* 4 vols. London, 1747–55.

Carte, Thomas. *An History of the Life of James Duke of Ormonde. . . .* 3 vols. London, 1735–6.

Chesterfield, Philip Dormer Stanhope, 4th Earl. *The Letters of Philip Dormer Stanhope, 4th Earl of Chesterfield.* Bonamy Dobrée, ed. 6 vols. London: Eyre & Spottiswoode, 1932.

Clarendon, Edward Hyde, 1st Earl. *A Brief View and Survey of . . . Mr. Hobbes's Book, Entitled Leviathan . . . .* Oxford, 1676.

Clarendon, Edward Hyde, 1st Earl. *Essays Moral and Entertaining . . . by the Right Honourable Edward, Earl of Clarendon.* James Stanier Clark, ed. 2 vols. London, 1815.

Clarendon, Edward Hyde, 1st Earl. *The History of the Rebellion and Civil Wars in England.* W. Dunn Macray, ed. 6 vols. Oxford: Clarendon Press, 1888.

Clarendon, Edward Hyde, 1st Earl. *The History of the Rebellion . . . To Which Are Subjoined the Notes of Bishop Warburton.* 7 vols. Oxford: Clarendon Press, 1849.

Clarendon, Edward Hyde, 1st Earl. *The History of the Reign of King Charles the Second from the Restoration To the End of the Year 1667. Written by Edward Earl of Clarendon. . . .* London [1758].

Clarendon, Edward Hyde, 1st Earl. *The Life of Edward Earl of Clarendon . . .*

in which is Included, A Continuation of His History of the Grand Rebellion. 2 vols. Oxford: Oxford Univ. Press, 1857.

Clarendon, Edward Hyde, 1st Earl. *State Papers Collected by Edward, Earl of Clarendon*. . . . 3 vols. Oxford, 1767–86.

Croxall, Samuel, ed. *A Select Collection of Novels*. 6 vols. London, 1720–2.

Davila, E. C. *The Histoirie of the Civill Warres of France*. London: Lee, Pakeman, Bedell, 1647.

Defoe, Daniel. *Memoirs of a Cavalier*. James T. Boulton, ed., intro. London: Oxford Univ. Press, 1972.

Dryden, John. *The Works of John Dryden*. 2nd ed. 18 vols. Edinburgh, 1821.

Echard, Laurence. *Abridgment of Sir Walter Raleigh's History*. London, 1700.

Echard, Laurence. *An Appendix to the Three Volumes of Mr. Archdeacon Echard's History of England*. . . . London, 1720.

Echard, Laurence. *A General Ecclesiastical History, from the Nativity of our Blessed Saviour*. . . . London, 1702.

Echard, Laurence. *The History of England, From the First Entrance of Julius Caesar*. . . . 3 vols. London, 1707–18.

Echard, Laurence. *The Roman History, from the Building of the City, To the Perfect Settlement of the Empire by Augustus Caesar*. . . . 3rd. ed. 2 vols. London, 1695.

Eikon Basilike: The Portraiture of His Sacred Majesty in His Solitudes and Sufferings. Philip A. Knachel, ed. Ithaca, N. Y.: Cornell Univ. Press, 1966.

Felton, Henry. *A Dissertation on Reading the Classics, and Forming a Just Style*. Menston, Yorks.: Scolar Press, 1971.

Fielding, Henry. *The History of the Adventures of Joseph Andrews*. Douglas Brooks, ed. Oxford: Oxford Univ. Press, 1970.

Foxcroft, H. C., ed. 'Some Unpublished Letters of Gilbert Burnet the Historian.' *Camden Miscellany*, 11. Camden 3rd ser., 13. London: Royal Historical Society, 1907.

The Gentleman's Library: Containing Rules for Conduct in all Parts of Life. 4th ed. London, 1744.

Gibbon, Edward. *The Letters of Edward Gibbon*. J. E. Norton, ed. 3 vols. London: Cassell, 1956.

Gibbon, Edward. *Memoirs of My Life*. Betty Radice, ed., intro. Harmondsworth: Penguin Books, 1984.

Granville, George. *A Letter to the Author of Reflections Historical and Political*. London, 1732.

Grey, Zachary. *A Defence of our Ancient and Modern Historians*. . . . London, 1725.

Grimm, Friedrich Melchior. *Correspondance littéraire*. 18 vols. Paris, 1812–29.

Guthrie, William. *A General History of England from the Invasion of the Romans . . . to the late Revolution*. 4 vols. London, 1744–51.

[Hampton, James]. *Reflections on Ancient and Modern History*. Oxford, 1746.

Hearne, Thomas. *Ductor Historicus: or a short System of Universal History*, *and an Introduction to the Study of that Science.* . . . London, 1698.

Historical Manuscripts Commission

Downshire I.

Laing II.

Portland IV, VII.

Hobbes, Thomas. *Behemoth or The Long Parliament.* Ferdinand Tönnies, intro.; M. M. Goldsmith, intro. 2nd ed. London: Frank Cass, 1969.

Hobbes, Thomas. *Hobbes's Thucydides.* Richard Schlatter, ed., intro. New Brunswick, N. J.: Rutgers Univ. Press, 1975.

Hume, David. *Enquiries Concerning the Human Understanding and Concerning the Principles of Morals.* L. A. Selby-Bigge, ed. 2nd ed. Oxford: Clarendon Press, 1902.

Hume, David. *Essays Moral, Political, and Literary.* Eugene F. Miller, ed. Indianapolis, Ind.: Liberty Classics, 1985.

Hume, David. *The History of England from the Invasion of Julius Caesar to The Revolution in 1688.* Foreword by William B. Todd. 6 vols. Indianapolis, Ind.: Liberty Classics, 1983.

Hume, David. *The Letters of David Hume.* J. Y. T. Greig, ed. 2 vols. Oxford: Clarendon Press, 1932.

Hume, David. *New Letters of David Hume.* Raymond Klibansky, Ernest C. Mossner, eds. Oxford: Clarendon Press, 1954.

[Hurd, Richard]. *Moral and Political Dialogues between Divers Eminent Persons of the Past and Present Age.* . . . London and Cambridge, 1759.

James II, King of England. *The Memoirs of James II: His Campaigns as Duke of York 1652–1660.* A. Lytton Sells, trans.; P. Muir, D. Randall, pref. Bloomington: Indiana Univ. Press, 1962.

[Kennett, White]. *A Complete History of England; With the Lives of All the Kings and Queens . . . Containing A Faithful Relation of all Affairs of State Ecclesiastical and Civil.* . . . 3 vols. London, 1706.

[Knowler, William, ed.]. *The Earl of Strafforde's Letters and Dispatches.* . . . 2 vols. London, 1739.

[Le Clerc, Jean]. *Mr. Le Clerc's Account of the Earl of Clarendon's History of the Civil Wars.* London, 1710.

Le Clerc, Jean. *Parrhasiana: Or, Thoughts upon Several Subjects; as Criticism, History, Morality, and Politics.* London, 1700.

Le Moyne, Pierre. *Of the Art Both of Writing & Judging of History.* London, 1695.

Locke, John. *Two Treatises of Government: A Critical Edition.* Peter Laslett, ed., intro. Cambridge: Cambridge Univ. Press, 1960.

[Lockman, John]. *A New History of England, By Question and Answer. Extracted from the most celebrated English Historians; particularly M. de Rapin Thoyras.* . . . 2nd ed. London, 1735.

Macaulay, Catharine. *The History of England from the Accession of James I to that of the Brunswick Line.* 8 vols. London, 1763–83.

Machiavelli, Niccolò. *Machiavelli: The Chief Works and Others.* Allan Gilbert, ed., trans. Durham, N. C.: Duke Univ. Press, 1965.

May, Thomas. *History of the Parliament of England.* London, 1647.

[McQueen, David]. *Letters on Mr. Hume's History of Great Britain.* Edinburgh, 1756.

Meilhan, Gabriel Sénac de. *Considérations sur l'esprit et les moeurs*. London, 1787.

Montesquieu. *The Spirit of the Laws*. Thomas Nugent, trans.; Franz Neumann, intro. 2 vols. New York: Hafner Press, 1949.

Mr. Oldmixon's Reply to the Late Bishop of Rochester's Vindication. London, 1732.

Nicolson, William. *The English Historical Library: or, A Short View and Character of most of the Writers . . . which may be Serviceable to the Undertakers of a General History of this Kingdom*. 3 vols. London, 1696–9.

North, Roger. *Examen, or an enquiry into the credit and veracity of a pretended complete history. . . .* London, 1740.

North, Roger. *General Preface & Life of Dr. John North*. Peter Millard, ed. Toronto: Univ. of Toronto Press, 1984.

North, Roger. *The Life of the Honourable Sir Dudley North . . . And of the Honourable and Reverend Dr. John North*. London, 1744.

North, Roger. *The Life of the Right Honourable Francis North. . . .* London, 1742.

[North, Roger]. *Reflections upon some Passages in Mr. Le Clerc's Life of Mr. John Locke. . . .* London, 1711.

[Oldmixon, John]. *Clarendon and Whitlock Compar'd. . . .* London, 1727.

Oldmixon, John. *The Critical History of England, Ecclesiastical and Civil. . . .* 2 vols. London, 1724–6.

Oldmixon, John. *The History of England. . . .* 3 vols. London, 1730–9.

[Orrery, John Boyle, 5th Earl]. *A Collection of the State Letters Of the Right Honourable Roger Boyle, The first Earl of Orrery. . . .* London, 1742.

Orrery, John Boyle, 5th Earl. *Remarks on the Life and Writings of Dr. Jonathan Swift. . . .* London, 1752.

The Orrery Papers. Emily C. Boyle, Countess of Cork and Orrery, ed. 2 vols. London: Duckworth, 1903.

Parker, Samuel. *Bishop Parker's History of His Own Time*. London, 1728.

Philalethes [Matthias Earberry]. *Impartial Reflections upon Dr. Burnet's Posthumous History*. London, 1724.

Philologus Cantabrigiensis. *The Freethinker's Criteria Exemplified, in a Vindication of the Characters of M. Tullius Cicero and the Late Duke of Marlborough. . . .* London, 1755.

Polybius. *The Rise of the Roman Empire*. Ian Scott-Kilvert, trans.; F. W. Walbank, intro. Harmondsworth: Penguin Books, 1979.

Pope, Alexander. *The Correspondence of Alexander Pope*. George Sherburn, ed. 5 vols. Oxford: Clarendon Press, 1956.

Quintilian. *Institutio Oratoria*. H. E. Butler, trans. The Loeb Classical Library, vol. 4. Cambridge, Mass.: Harvard Univ. Press, 1936.

[Ralph, James]. *The Critical History of the Administration of Sir Robert Walpole*. London, 1743.

Ralph, James. *The History of England during the Reigns of K. William, Q. Anne and K. George I. . . .* 2 vols. London, 1744–6.

[Rapin, René de]. *The Modest Critick: Or Remarks upon the most Eminent Historians, Antient and Modern. . . .* London, 1689.

Rapin, René de. *The Whole Critical Works of Monsieur Rapin*. 2 vols. London, 1706.

Rapin de Thoyras, Paul. *Dissertation sur les Whigs & les Torys.* . . . London, 1717.

Rapin de Thoyras, Paul. *Histoire d'Angleterre.* 10 vols. The Hague, 1723–7.

Rapin de Thoyras, Paul. *The History of England.* . . . Nicholas Tindal, trans. 15 vols. London, 1725–31.

Rawlinson, Richard. *A New Method of Studying History: Recommending more Easy and Complete Instructions for Improvements in that Science.* . . . 2 vols. London, 1728.

Rollin, Charles. *The Method of Teaching and Studying the Belles Lettres . . . Designed more particularly for Students in the Universities.* 4 vols. London, 1734.

Rose, George Henry, ed. *A Selection from the Papers of the Earls of Marchmont.* 3 vols. London, 1831.

Sales, Delisle de. *De la philosophie de la nature.* . . . 3rd ed. 6 vols. London, 1777.

Salmon, Thomas. *The History of Great Britain and Ireland . . . to the Norman Conquest.* 2nd ed. London, 1725.

Sarpi, Paolo. *The Historie of the Councel of Trent.* Nathaniel Brent, trans. 3rd ed. London, 1640.

Smith, Adam. *Lectures on Rhetoric and Belles Lettres.* J. C. Bryce, ed. Oxford: Clarendon Press, 1983.

Smith, William, Jr. *The History of the Province of New York.* Michael Kammen, ed., intro. Cambridge, Mass.: Harvard Univ. Press, 1972.

Sprat, Thomas. *The History of the Royal Society.* Jackson I. Cope, Harold W. Jones, ed., intro. St Louis, Mo.: Washington Univ. Studies, 1958.

[Squire, Samuel]. *Remarks upon Mr. Carte's Specimen of his General History.* . . . London, 1748.

Stewart, Dugald. 'Account of the Life and Writings of William Robertson, D. D.' *The Works of William Robertson, D. D.* London, 1831.

Suetonius. *The Twelve Caesars.* Robert Graves, trans.; Michael Grant, intro. Harmondsworth: Penguin Books, 1979.

Swift, Jonathan. *The Correspondence of Jonathan Swift.* Harold Williams, ed. 5 vols. Oxford: Clarendon Press, 1963.

Swift, Jonathan. *The History of the Four Last Years of the Queen.* Harold Williams, intro. *The Prose Works of Jonathan Swift*, vol. 7. Herbert Davis, ed. Oxford: Basil Blackwell, 1951.

Swift, Jonathan. *Miscellaneous and Autobiographical Pieces, Fragments and Marginalia.* Herbert Davis, ed. *The Prose Works of Jonathan Swift*, vol. 5. Oxford: Basil Blackwell, 1962.

Swift, Jonathan. *A Proposal for Correcting, Improving and Ascertaining the English Tongue.* London, 1712.

Temple, William. *The Works of Sir William Temple.* 4 vols. London, 1757.

Thucydides. *History of the Peloponnesian War.* M. I. Finley, intro.; Rex Warner, trans. Harmondsworth: Penguin Books, 1972.

Towers, Joseph. *Observations on Mr. Hume's History of England.* London, 1778.

Tyrrell, James. *Bibliotheca Politica: Or An Enquiry into the Ancient Constitution of the English Government.* . . . London, 1692–1702.

Tyrrell, James. *The General History of England, both ecclesiastical and civil.* . . . 3 vols. London, 1696–1704.

Voltaire. *Correspondance*. Theodore Besterman, ed. 10 vols. Paris: Gallimard, 1964–86.

Voltaire. *Letters on England*. Leonard Tancock, trans. Harmondsworth: Penguin Books, 1980.

Voltaire. *Oeuvres Complètes de Voltaire*. Émile de la Bedollière, Georges Avenel, eds. 9 vols. Paris, 1867–73.

Walpole, Horace. *The Yale Edition of Horace Walpole's Correspondence*. W. S. Lewis, *et al*, ed. 48 vols. New Haven, Conn.: Yale Univ. Press, 1937–83.

The Wentworth Papers 1705–1739. James J. Cartwright, ed. London: Wyman & Sons, 1883.

Wheare, Degory. *The Method and Order of Reading both Civil and Ecclesiastical Histories*. 3rd ed. London, 1698.

Worden, A. B., ed., intro. *Edmund Ludlow; A Voyce from the Watch Tower*. Camden 4th ser., 21. London: Royal Historical Society, 1978.

Wotton, William. *The History of Rome from the Death of Antoninus Pius to the Death of Severus Alexander*. London, 1701.

Wotton, William. *Reflections upon Ancient and Modern Learning. To which is now added A Defense Thereof. . . .* 3rd ed. London, 1705.

SECONDARY SOURCES

A   Printed Books and Articles

Abbattista, Guido. 'The Business of Paternoster Row: Towards a Publishing History of the *Universal History* (1736–1765).' *Publishing History*, 17 (1985), pp. 5–50.

Allan, David. *Virtue, Learning and the Scottish Enlightenment: Ideas of Scholarship in Early Modern History*. Edinburgh: Edinburgh Univ. Press, 1993.

Appleby, Joyce; Hunt, Lynn; Jacob, Margaret. *Telling the Truth About History*. New York: Norton, 1994.

Ashcraft, Richard. *Revolutionary Politics & Locke's Two Treatises of Government*. Princeton: Princeton Univ. Press, 1986.

Atkins, J. W. H. *English Literary Criticism: 17th and 18th Centuries*. London: Methuen, 1951; rpt 1959.

Bakshian, Aram, Jr. '"A Hangdog Whom I dearly Love:" The Third Earl of Peterborough.' *History Today*, 31 (Oct. 1981), pp. 14–19.

Barker, Nicolas, ed. *The Oxford University Press and the Spread of Learning 1478–1978*. Oxford: Clarendon Press, 1978.

Bennett, G. V. *The Tory Crisis in Church and State 1688–1730: The Career of Francis Atterbury Bishop of Rochester*. Oxford: Clarendon Press, 1975.

Bennett, G. V. *White Kennett, 1660–1728, Bishop of Peterborough: A Study in the Political and Ecclesiastical History of the Early Eighteenth Century*. London: SPCK, 1957.

Black, J. B. *The Art of History: A Study of Four Great Historians of the Eighteenth Century*. New York: F. S. Crofts & Co., 1926.

Bongie, Laurence L. *David Hume: Prophet of the Counter-revolution*. Oxford: Clarendon Press, 1965.

Bouwsma, William J. 'The Politics of Commynes.' *Journal of Modern History*, 23 (1951), pp. 315–28.

Braudy, Leo. *Narrative Form in History and Fiction: Hume, Fielding & Gibbon*. Princeton: Princeton Univ. Press, 1970.

Browning, Reed. *Political and Constitutional Ideas of the Court Whigs*. Baton Rouge: Louisiana State Univ. Press, 1982.

Brownley, Martine Watson. *Clarendon and the Rhetoric of Historical Form*. Philadelphia: Univ. of Pennsylvania Press, 1985.

Bucholz, R. O. *The Augustan Court: Queen Anne and the Decline of Court Culture*. Stanford, Calif.: Stanford Univ. Press, 1993.

Burke, Peter. 'The Politics of Reformation History: Burnet and Brandt.' *Clio's Mirror: Historiography in Britain and the Netherlands*. A. C. Duke, C. A. Tamse, eds. Zutphen: Walburg Press, 1985.

Burke, Peter. *The Renaissance Sense of the Past*. London: Edward Arnold, 1969.

Burke, Peter. 'A Survey of the Popularity of Ancient Historians, 1450–1700.' *History and Theory*, 5 (1966), pp. 135–52.

Burtt, Shelley. *Virtue Transformed: Political Argument in England, 1688–1740*. Cambridge: Cambridge Univ. Press, 1992.

Butterfield, Herbert. *The Whig Interpretation of History*. London: G. Bell and Sons, 1931.

Cannadine, David. *The Decline and Fall of the British Aristocracy*. New Haven, Conn.: Yale Univ. Press, 1990.

Carter, Harry. *A History of Oxford University Press to the Year 1780*. 2 vols. Oxford: Clarendon Press, 1975.

Champion, J. A. I. *The Pillars of Priestcraft Shaken: The Church of England and its Enemies, 1660–1730*. Cambridge: Cambridge Univ. Press, 1992.

Christensen, Jerome. *Practicing Enlightenment: Hume and the Formation of a Literary Career*. Madison: Univ. of Wisconsin Press, 1987.

Clark, A. F. B. *Boileau and the French Classical Critics in England (1660–1830)*. Paris, 1925; rpt New York: Russell & Russell, 1965.

Clark, J. C. D. *English Society 1688–1832: Ideology, Social Structure and Political Practice during the Ancien Regime*. Cambridge: Cambridge Univ. Press, 1985.

Clark, J. C. D., ed., intro. *The Memoirs and Speeches of James, 2nd Earl Waldegrave, 1742–1763*. Cambridge: Cambridge Univ. Press, 1988.

Clark, J. C. D. *Revolution and Rebellion: State and Society in England in the Seventeenth and Eighteenth Centuries*. Cambridge: Cambridge Univ. Press, 1986.

Clark, J. C. D. *Samuel Johnson: Literature, Religion and English Cultural Politics from the Restoration to Romanticism*. Cambridge: Cambridge Univ. Press, 1994.

Cochrane, Eric. *Historians and Historiography in the Italian Renaissance*. Chicago: Univ. of Chicago Press, 1981.

Colley, Linda. *Britons: Forging the Nation, 1707–1837*. New Haven, Conn.: Yale Univ. Press, 1992.

Colley, Linda. *In Defiance of Oligarchy: The Tory Party 1714–60*. Cambridge: Cambridge Univ. Press, 1982.

Craddock, Patricia B. *Edward Gibbon, Luminous Historian 1772–1794*.

Baltimore: The Johns Hopkins Univ. Press, 1989.

Cruickshanks, Eveline. 'Lord Cornbury, Bolingbroke, and a Plan to Restore the Stuarts, 1731–1735.' *Royal Stuart Papers*, 27 (1986).

Davis, Herbert. *Jonathan Swift: Essays on his Satire and Other Studies.* New York: Oxford Univ. Press, 1964.

Dickinson, H. T. *Bolingbroke.* London: Constable, 1970.

Dickinson, H. T. *Liberty and Property: Political Ideology in Eighteenth Century Britain.* London: Holmes and Meier, 1977.

Dictionary of National Biography.

Douglas, David C. *English Scholars.* London: Jonathan Cape, 1939.

Downie, J. A. *Jonathan Swift: Political Writer.* London: Routledge & Kegan Paul, 1984.

Downie, J. A. 'Walpole, "the Poet's Foe."' *Britain in the Age of Walpole.* Jeremy Black, ed. London: Macmillan, 1984.

Earl, D. W. L. 'Procrustean Feudalism: An Interpretative Dilemma in English Historical Narration, 1700–1725.' *Historical Journal*, 19 (1976), pp. 33–51.

Ehrenpreis, Irvin. *Swift: The Man, His Works, and the Age.* 3 vols. Cambridge, Mass.: Harvard Univ. Press; London: Methuen, 1962–83.

Elias, A. C. *Swift at Moor Park: Problems in Biography and Criticism.* Philadelphia: Univ. of Pennsylvania Press, 1982.

Erskine-Hill, Howard. *The Augustan Idea in English Literature.* London: Edward Arnold, 1983.

Fairer, David. 'Anglo-Saxon Studies.' *The Eighteenth Century*, L. S. Sutherland, L. G. Mitchell, eds. *The History of the University of Oxford*, T. H. Aston, gen. ed., vol. 5. Oxford: Clarendon Press, 1986.

Ferguson, Arthur B. *Clio Unbound: Perceptions of the Social and Cultural Past in Renaissance England.* Durham, N. C.: Duke Univ. Press, 1979.

Firth, C. H. 'Clarendon's "History of the Rebellion."' *English Historical Review*, 19 (1904), pp. 26–54, 246–62, 464–83.

Firth, C. H. 'The Development of the Study of Seventeenth-Century History.' *Transactions of the Royal Historical Society*, 3rd. ser., vol. 7 (1913), pp. 25–48.

Forbes, Duncan. *Hume's Philosophical Politics.* Cambridge: Cambridge Univ. Press, 1975.

Forbes, Duncan. 'Introduction.' David Hume, *History of Great Britain.* Duncan Forbes, ed. Harmondsworth: Pelican Books, 1970.

Forbes, Duncan. [Review of Giarrizzo, *David Hume politico e storico*] *Historical Journal*, 6 (1963), pp. 280–94.

Fornara, Charles W. *The Nature of History in Ancient Greece and Rome.* Berkeley: Univ. of California Press, 1983.

Fox, Levi, ed. *English Historical Scholarship in the Sixteenth and Seventeenth Centuries.* London: Dugdale Society, Oxford Univ. Press, 1956.

Foxcroft, H. C., Clarke, T. E. S. *A Life of Gilbert Burnet, Bishop of Salisbury.* Cambridge: Cambridge Univ. Press, 1907.

Fumaroli, Marc. 'Les Mémoires du XVIIe siècle au carrefour des genres en prose.' *XVIIe Siècle*, 94/95 (1971), pp. 7–37.

Fussner, F. Smith. *The Historical Revolution: English Historical Writing and Thought 1580–1640.* New York: Columbia Univ. Press, 1962.

Gascoigne, John. *Cambridge in the Age of the Enlightenment: Science, Religion and Politics from the Restoration to the French Revolution*. Cambridge: Cambridge Univ. Press, 1989.

Gaskell, Philip. *A New Introduction to Bibliography*. Oxford: Clarendon Press, 1972.

Gerrard, Christine. *The Patriot Opposition to Walpole: Politics, Poetry, and National Myth, 1725–1742*. Oxford: Clarendon Press, 1994.

Giarrizzo, Giuseppe. *David Hume politico e storico*. Turin: Einaudi, 1962.

Gibbs, Graham C. 'Abel Boyer Gallo-Anglus Glossographus et Historicus, 1667–1729: From Tutor to Author, 1689–1699.' *Proceedings of the Huguenot Society of London*, 24 (1983), pp. 46–59.

Gilbert, Felix. *History: Commitment and Choice*. Cambridge, Mass.: Harvard Univ. Press, 1977.

Gilmore, Myron P. *Humanists and Jurists: Six Studies in the Renaissance*. Cambridge, Mass.: Harvard Univ. Press, 1963.

Girouard, Mark. *Life in the English Country House: A Social and Architectural History*. New Haven, Conn.: Yale Univ. Press, 1978.

Goldgar, Bertrand. *Walpole and the Wits: The Relation of Politics to Literature, 1722–1742*. Lincoln: Univ. of Nebraska Press, 1976.

Goldie, Mark. 'The Revolution of 1689 and the Structure of Political Argument.' *Bulletin of Research in the Humanities*, 83 (1980), pp. 473–564.

Goldie, Mark. 'The Roots of True Whiggism 1688–94.' *History of Political Thought*, 1 (1980), pp. 195–236.

Gough, J. W. 'James Tyrrell, Whig Historian and Friend of John Locke.' *Historical Journal*, 19 (1976), pp. 581–610.

Goulding, Richard W. *Laurence Echard, M. A., F. S. A., Author and Archdeacon*. London: [n. p.] 1927.

Grafton, Anthony. 'On the Scholarship of Politian and its Context.' *Journal of the Warburg and Courtauld Institutes*, 40 (1977), pp. 150–88.

Grainger, J. H. *Character and Style in English Politics*. Cambridge: Cambridge Univ. Press, 1969.

Greaves, R. W. 'Fathers and Heretics in Leicester.' *Statesmen, Scholars and Merchants: Essays in Eighteenth-Century History Presented to Dame Lucy Sutherland*. Anne Whiteman, *et al*, eds. Oxford: Clarendon Press, 1973.

Green, David. *Queen Anne*. New York: Charles Scribner's Sons, 1970.

Green, Ian. 'The Publication of Clarendon's Autobiography and the Acquisition of his Papers by the Bodleian Library.' *The Bodleian Library Record*, 10 (1982), pp. 347–67.

Greene, Thomas M. *The Light in Troy: Imitation and Discovery in Renaissance Poetry*. New Haven, Conn. and London: Yale Univ. Press, 1982.

Gregg, Edward. *Queen Anne*. London: Routledge & Kegan Paul, 1980.

Haley, K. H. D. *The First Earl of Shaftesbury*. Oxford: Clarendon Press, 1968.

Ham, Roswell G. 'Dryden as Historiographer-Royal.' *Review of English Studies*, 11 (1935), pp. 284–98.

Hammond, Paul. *John Oldham and the Renewal of Classical Culture*. Cambridge: Cambridge Univ. Press, 1983.

Harris, George. *The Life of Lord Chancellor Hardwicke*. 3 vols. London, 1847.

Harris, R. W. *Clarendon and the English Revolution*. Stanford, Calif.: Stanford Univ. Press, 1983.

Harris, Tim. *Politics Under the Later Stuarts: Party Conflict in a Divided Society 1660–1715*. London and New York: Longman, 1993.

Hay, Denys. 'The Historiographers Royal in England and Scotland.' *Scottish Historical Review*, 30 (1951), pp. 15–29.

Hicks, Philip. 'Bolingbroke, Clarendon, and the Role of Classical Historian.' *Eighteenth-Century Studies*, 20 (1987), pp. 445–71.

Higgins, Ian. *Swift's Politics: A Study in Disaffection*. Cambridge: Cambridge Univ. Press, 1994.

Hill, Bridget. *The Republican Virago: The Life and Times of Catharine Macaulay, Historian*. Oxford: Clarendon Press, 1992.

Hiscock, H. G. *Henry Aldrich of Christ Church 1648–1710*. Oxford: Christ Church, 1960.

Hodgson, N., Blagden, C. *The Notebook of Thomas Bennet and Henry Clements*. Oxford Bibliographical Society Publications, new ser., 6. Oxford: The Society, 1956.

Holmes, Geoffrey. *Augustan England: Professions, State and Society, 1680–1730*. London: Allen & Unwin, 1982.

Holmes, Geoffrey. *British Politics in the Age of Anne*. London: Macmillan, 1967.

Horwitz, Henry. *Revolution Politicks: The Career of Daniel Finch Second Earl of Nottingham, 1647–1730*. Cambridge: Cambridge Univ. Press, 1968.

Hunter, J. Paul. 'Biography and the Novel.' *Modern Language Studies*, 9 (1979), pp. 68–84.

Jessop, T. E. *A Bibliography of David Hume*. London: A. Brown & Sons, 1938.

Johnson, James W. *The Formation of English Neoclassical Thought*. Princeton: Princeton Univ. Press, 1967.

Jones, Clyve, ed. *Britain in the First Age of Party 1680–1750: Essays Presented to Geoffrey Holmes*. London: Hambledon Press, 1987.

Jones, J. R. *Country and Court: England, 1658–1714*. Cambridge, Mass.: Harvard Univ. Press, 1978.

Kelley, Donald R. *Foundations of Modern Historical Scholarship: Language, Law, and History in the French Renaissance*. New York: Columbia Univ. Press, 1970.

Kenny, Robert W. 'James Ralph: An Eighteenth-Century Philadelphian in Grub Street.' *Pennsylvania Magazine of History and Biography*, 64 (1940), pp. 218–30.

Kenyon, J. P. *The History Men: The Historical Profession in England since the Renaissance*. Pittsburgh: Univ. of Pittsburgh Press, 1984.

Kenyon, J. P. *Revolution Principles: The Politics of Party 1689–1720*. Cambridge: Cambridge Univ. Press, 1977.

Kenyon, J. P. *Robert Spencer Earl of Sunderland 1641–1702*. London: Longmans, 1958.

Kenyon, J. P., ed. *The Stuart Constitution 1603–1688*. 2nd ed. Cambridge: Cambridge Univ. Press, 1986.

Kidd, Colin. *Subverting Scotland's Past: Scottish Whig Historians and the Creation of an Anglo-British Identity, 1689–c. 1830*. Cambridge: Cambridge Univ. Press, 1993.

Klein, Lawrence E. *Shaftesbury and the Culture of Politeness: Moral Discourse and Cultural Politics in Early Eighteenth-Century England*. Cambridge: Cambridge Univ. Press, 1994.

Korsten, F. J. M. *Roger North (1651–1734): Virtuoso and Essayist*. Amsterdam: Holland Univ. Press, 1981.

Kramnick, Isaac. 'Augustan Politics and English Historiography: The Debate on the English Past, 1730–1735.' *History and Theory*, 6 (1967), pp. 33–56.

Kramnick, Isaac. *Bolingbroke and his Circle: The Politics of Nostalgia in the Age of Walpole*. Cambridge, Mass.: Harvard Univ. Press, 1968.

Kristeller, Paul Oskar. *Renaissance Thought II: Papers on Humanism and the Arts*. New York: Harper & Row, 1965.

Laslett, Peter. *The World We Have Lost*. New York: Charles Scribner's Sons, 1965.

Levine, Joseph M. 'Ancients and Moderns Reconsidered.' *Eighteenth-Century Studies*, 15 (1981), pp. 72–89.

Levine, Joseph M. *The Battle of the Books: History and Literature in the Augustan Age*. Ithaca, N. Y.: Cornell Univ. Press, 1991.

Levine, Joseph M. *Humanism and History: Origins of Modern British Historiography*. Ithaca, N. Y.: Cornell Univ. Press, 1987.

Levy, F. J. *Tudor Historical Thought*. San Marino, Calif.: The Huntington Library, 1967.

MacGillivray, Royce. *Restoration Historians and the English Civil War*. The Hague: Martinus Nijhoff, 1974.

Mack, Maynard. *The Garden and the City: Retirement and Politics in the Later Poetry of Pope 1731–1743*. Toronto: Univ. of Toronto Press, 1969.

Madan, Francis. *A New Bibliography of the Eikon Basilike*. Oxford Bibliographical Society Publications, new ser., 3. Oxford: The Society, 1950.

Maltzahn, Nicholas von. *Milton's History of Britain: Republican Historiography in the English Revolution*. Oxford: Clarendon Press, 1991.

Markus, R. A. 'Church History and Early Church Historians.' *The Materials, Sources, and Methods of Ecclesiastical History*. Derek Baker, ed. Oxford: Ecclesiastical History Society, 1975.

Mayer, Robert. 'Nathaniel Crouch, Bookseller and Historian: Popular Historiography and Cultural Power in Late Seventeenth-Century England.' *Eighteenth-Century Studies*, 27 (1994), pp. 391–419.

Meyer, Paul H. 'Voltaire and Hume as Historians: A Comparative Study of the *Essai sur les Moeurs* and *The History of England*.' *PMLA*, 73 (1958), pp. 51–68.

Miller, Peter N. *Defining the Common Good: Empire, Religion and Philosophy in Eighteenth-Century Britain*. Cambridge: Cambridge Univ. Press, 1994.

Momigliano, Arnaldo. *Essays in Ancient and Modern Historiography*. Middletown, Conn.: Wesleyan Univ. Press, 1977.

Momigliano, Arnaldo. *Studies in Historiography*. London: Weidenfeld and Nicolson, 1966.

Mossner, Ernest C. *The Life of David Hume.* 2nd ed. Oxford: Clarendon Press, 1980.

Mossner, Ernest C., Ransom, Harry. 'Hume and the "Conspiracy of the Booksellers:" The Publication and Early Fortunes of the *History of England.*' *Studies in English*, 29 (1950), pp. 162–82.

Nadel, George H. 'Philosophy of History before Historicism.' *Studies in the Philosophy of History: Selected Essays from History and Theory.* George H. Nadel, ed. New York: Harper & Row, 1965.

Newman, Gerald. *The Rise of English Nationalism: A Cultural History 1740–1830.* New York: St Martin's Press, 1987.

Nobbs, A. E. 'Digressions in the Ecclesiastical Histories of Socrates, Sozomen, and Theodoret.' *Journal of Religious History*, 14 (1986), pp. 1–11.

Norton, David Fate. 'History and Philosophy in Hume's Thought.' *David Hume: Philosophical Historian.* David Fate Norton, Richard H. Popkin, eds. Indianapolis, Ind.: Bobbs-Merrill, 1965.

Okie, Laird. *Augustan Historical Writing: Histories of England in the English Enlightenment.* Lanham, Maryland: Univ. Press of America, 1991.

Ollard, Richard. *Clarendon and his Friends.* London: Hamish Hamilton, 1987.

Philip, I. G. 'The Genesis of Thomas Hearne's *Ductor Historicus.*' *Bodleian Library Record*, 7 (1966), pp. 251–64.

Philip, I. G. 'Thomas Hearne as a Publisher.' *Bodleian Library Record*, 3 (1951), pp. 146–55.

Phillips, Mark. *Francesco Guicciardini: The Historian's Craft.* Toronto: Univ. of Toronto Press, 1977.

Phillips, Mark. 'Machiavelli, Guicciardini, and the Tradition of Vernacular Historiography in Florence.' *American Historical Review*, 84 (1979), pp. 86–105.

Phillipson, N. T. *Hume.* London: Weidenfeld and Nicolson, 1989.

Phillipson, N. T. 'Politics and Politeness in the Philosophy of David Hume.' *Politics, Politeness, and Patriotism.* Gordon J. Schochet, ed. Proceedings of the Folger Institute, Center for the Study of British Political Thought, vol. 5. Washington, D. C.: The Folger Shakespeare Library, 1993.

Plumb, J. H. *The Death of the Past.* Boston: Houghton Mifflin, 1970.

Plumb, J. H. *The Growth of Political Stability in England, 1675–1725.* London: Macmillan, 1967.

Plumb, J. H. *Sir Robert Walpole.* 2 vols. London: Cresset Press, 1956–60.

Pocock, J. G. A. *The Ancient Constitution and the Feudal Law: A Study of English Historical Thought in the Seventeenth Century.* Cambridge: Cambridge Univ. Press, 1957; 1987, 'A Reissue with a Retrospect.'

Pocock, J. G. A. 'Edward Gibbon in History: Aspects of the Text in *The History of the Decline and Fall of the Roman Empire,*' The Tanner Lectures on Human Values, vol. 11, ed. G. B. Petersen. Salt Lake City: Univ. of Utah Press, 1990.

Pocock, J. G. A. 'English Historical Thought in the Age of Harrington and Locke.' *Topoi*, 2 (1983), pp. 149–62.

Pocock, J. G. A. *The Machiavellian Moment: Florentine Political Thought and the Atlantic Republican Tradition*. Princeton: Princeton Univ. Press, 1975.

Pocock, J. G. A. 'Robert Brady, 1627–1700: A Cambridge Historian of the Restoration.' *The Cambridge Historical Journal*, 10 (1951), pp. 186–204.

Pocock, J. G. A. *Virtue, Commerce, and History: Essays on Political Thought and History, Chiefly in the Eighteenth Century*. Cambridge: Cambridge Univ. Press, 1985.

Porter, Roy. *English Society in the Eighteenth Century*. Harmondsworth: Penguin Books, 1982.

Ranum, Orest. *Artisans of Glory: Writers and Historical Thought in Seventeenth-Century France*. Chapel Hill: Univ. of North Carolina Press, 1980.

Rawson, Claude. 'Poet Squab.' *London Review of Books*, 3 March 1988, pp. 16–17.

Rivers, Isabel, ed. *Books and their Readers in Eighteenth-Century England*. New York: St Martin's Press, 1982.

Rogers, Pat. 'Book Subscriptions Among the Augustans.' *TLS*, 15 Dec. 1972, pp. 1539–40.

Rogers, Pat. *Grub Street: Studies in a Subculture*. London: Methuen, 1972.

Rogers, Pat. 'The Printing of Oldmixon's Histories.' *The Library*, 5th ser., 24 (1969), pp. 150–4.

Sachse, William L. *Lord Somers: A Political Portrait*. Madison: Univ. of Wisconsin Press, 1975.

Salmon, J. H. M. 'Cicero and Tacitus in Sixteenth-Century France.' *American Historical Review*, 85 (1980), pp. 307–31.

Saunders, J. W. *The Profession of English Letters*. London: Routledge & Kegan Paul, 1964.

Schmidt, Roger. 'Roger North's *Examen*: A Crisis in Historiography.' *Eighteenth-Century Studies*, 26 (1992), pp. 57–75.

Seaward, Paul. 'A Restoration Publicist: James Howell and the Earl of Clarendon, 1661–6.' *Historical Research*, 61 (1988), pp. 123–31.

Shapiro, Barbara J. *Probability and Certainty in Seventeenth-Century England*. Princeton: Princeton Univ. Press, 1983.

Siebert, Donald T. *The Moral Animus of David Hume*. Newark: Univ. of Delaware Press, 1990.

Siebert, Frederick S. *Freedom of the Press in England 1476–1776: The Rise and Decline of Government Controls*. Urbana: Univ. of Illinois Press, 1952.

Smith, David L. *Constitutional Royalism and the Search for Settlement, c. 1640–1649*. Cambridge: Cambridge Univ. Press, 1994.

Smith, R. J. *The Gothic Bequest: Medieval Institutions in British Thought, 1688–1863*. Cambridge: Cambridge Univ. Press, 1987.

Smuts, R. Malcolm. *Court Culture and the Origins of a Royalist Tradition in Early Stuart England*. Philadelphia: Univ. of Pennsylvania Press, 1987.

Speck, W. A. *Stability and Strife: England, 1714–60*. Cambridge, Mass.: Harvard Univ. Press, 1977.

Spurr, John. *The Restoration Church of England, 1646–1689*. New Haven, Conn.: Yale Univ. Press, 1991.

Stephan, Deborah. 'Laurence Echard – Whig Historian.' *Historical Journal*, 32 (1989), pp. 843–66.

Stockton, Constant Noble. 'Economics and the Mechanism of Historical Progress in Hume's *History*.' *Hume: A Re-evaluation*. Donald W. Livingston, James T. King, eds. New York: Fordham Univ. Press, 1976.

Stone, Lawrence, Stone, Jeanne C. Fawtier. *An Open Elite? England 1540–1880*. Oxford: Oxford Univ. Press, 1984.

Stone, Lawrence. 'The Results of the English Revolutions of the Seventeenth Century.' *Three British Revolutions: 1641, 1688, 1776*. J. G. A. Pocock, ed. Princeton: Princeton Univ. Press, 1980.

Stromberg, R. N. 'History in the Eighteenth Century.' *Journal of the History of Ideas*, 12 (1951), pp. 295–304.

Styles, Philip. 'The Social Structure of the Kineton Hundred in the Reign of Charles II.' *Proceedings of the Birmingham Archaeological Society*, 78 (1962).

Sutherland, James. *The Restoration Newspaper and its Development*. New York: Cambridge Univ. Press, 1986.

Sutherland, L. S., Mitchell, L. G., eds. *The Eighteenth Century*, vol. 5 of *The History of the University of Oxford*. T. H. Aston, gen. ed. Oxford: Clarendon Press, 1986.

Syme, Ronald. *Tacitus*. 2 vols. Oxford: Oxford Univ. Press, 1958; rpt 1963.

Targett, Simon. 'Government and Ideology during the Age of Whig Supremacy: The Political Argument of Sir Robert Walpole's Newspaper Propagandists.' *Historical Journal*, 37 (1994), pp. 289–317.

Trevor-Roper, H. R. *Edward Hyde, Earl of Clarendon*. Oxford: Clarendon Press, 1975.

Trevor-Roper, H. R. *History: Professional and Lay*. Oxford: Clarendon Press, 1957.

Trevor-Roper, H. R. 'A Huguenot Historian: Paul Rapin.' *Huguenots in Britain and their French Background, 1550–1800*. Irene Scouloudi, ed. London: Macmillan, 1987.

Trevor-Roper, H. R. *Queen Elizabeth's First Historian: William Camden and the Beginnings of English 'Civil History'*. The Second Neale Lecture in English History. London: Jonathan Cape, 1971.

Tuck, Richard. *Philosophy and Government, 1572–1651*. Cambridge: Cambridge Univ. Press, 1993.

Wagner, Anthony R. *English Genealogy*. 2nd ed. Oxford: Clarendon Press, 1972.

Wallis, P. J. 'Book Subscription Lists.' *The Library*, 5th ser., 29 (1974), pp. 255–86.

Wallis, P. J., Robinson, F. J. G. *Book Subscription Lists: A Revised Guide*. Newcastle upon Tyne: Book Subscriptions List Project, 1975.

Walton, Craig. 'Hume's *England* as a Natural History of Morals.' *Liberty in Hume's History of England*. Nicholas Capaldi, Donald W. Livingston, eds. Dordrecht: Kluwer, 1990.

Watson, George, ed. *The New Cambridge Bibliography of English Literature*. 5 vols. Cambridge: Cambridge Univ. Press, 1971.

Watson, George. 'The Reader in Clarendon's *History of the Rebellion*.'

Review of English Studies, 25 (1974), pp. 396–409.

Weinbrot, Howard D. *Augustus Caesar in 'Augustan' England*. Princeton: Princeton Univ. Press, 1978.

Weinbrot, Howard D. *Britannia's Issue: The Rise of British Literature from Dryden to Ossian*. Cambridge: Cambridge Univ. Press, 1993.

Wertz, S. K. 'Hume, History, and Human Nature.' *Hume as Philosopher of Society, Politics and History*. Donald Livingston, Marie Martin, eds. Rochester, N. Y.: Univ. of Rochester Press, 1991.

Wexler, Victor G. *David Hume and the History of England*. Memoirs of the American Philosophical Society, 131. Philadelphia: The Society, 1979.

Wilcox, Donald J. *The Development of Florentine Humanist Historiography in the Fifteenth Century*. Cambridge, Mass.: Harvard Univ. Press, 1969.

Wiles, R. M. *Serial Publication in England Before 1750*. Cambridge: Cambridge Univ. Press, 1957.

Womersley, D. J. 'Lord Bolingbroke and Eighteenth-Century Historiography.' *The Eighteenth Century: Theory and Interpretation*, 28 (1987), pp. 217–34.

Womersley, D. J. *The Transformation of The Decline and Fall of the Roman Empire*. Cambridge: Cambridge Univ. Press, 1988.

Wood, Gordon S. 'Conspiracy and the Paranoid Style: Causality and Deceit in the Eighteenth Century.' *William and Mary Quarterly*. 3rd ser., 39 (1982), pp. 401–41.

Woodman, Tom. 'Pope and the Polite.' *Essays in Criticism*, 28 (1978), pp. 19–37.

Woolf, D. R. *The Idea of History in Early Stuart England: Erudition, Ideology and 'The Light of Truth' from the Accession of James I to the Civil War*. Toronto: Univ. of Toronto Press, 1990.

Wootton, David. *Paolo Sarpi: Between Renaissance and Enlightenment*. Cambridge: Cambridge Univ. Press, 1983.

Wormald, B. H. G. *Clarendon: Politics, History and Religion, 1640–1660*. Cambridge: Cambridge Univ. Press, 1951; rpt Chicago: Univ. of Chicago Press, 1976.

Wormald, Patrick. '*Engla Lond*: the Making of an Allegiance.' *Journal of Historical Sociology*, 7 (1994), pp. 1–24.

B   Unpublished Dissertations

Earl, D. W. L. 'Paul Rapin de Thoyras and the English Historiography of his Time 1700–1730.' Cambridge Univ. M. Litt. dissert., 1961.

Hicks, Philip Stephen. 'Historical Culture from Clarendon to Hume: The Fortunes of Classic British History, 1671–1757.' Johns Hopkins Univ. Ph. D. dissert., 1988.

INDEX

absolute monarchy, 44, 84, 86, 94–5, 115, 152, 172, 187, 205

Act of Indemnity and Oblivion, 65, 232

Addison, Joseph, 1, 10, 21, 148, 154, 155, 175, 223, 246

Aldrich, Henry, Dean of Christ Church, 63–4, 66, 67, 68, 70–3, 74

Alfred the Great, 183

America and Americans, 140, 143, 155

ancient constitution, 33, 65, 69
  in historiography of the Exclusion Crisis, 85–7, 94, 107
  whig devotion to, 173, 191

ancient historiography and ancient historians, *see* classical historiography

Anglicanism, *see* Church of England

Anglo-Scottish Union (1707), 176

annals and annalists, 25, 38, 95, 97, 105, 119

Anne, queen, 117, 127
  as dedicatee of Clarendon's *History*, 66, 71–3, 74
  historical apologies for, 116, 136
  reign of, 43, 62, 131, 134
  reign of as a worthy historical subject, 135, 140

antiquarianism, 31–5, 39–40, 99, 122, 172
  ancient precedents for, 31
  clerical, 39, 92, 93, 133, 138
  English, 32–5, 100
  incorporated into English general histories, 107–8, 167–8, 188–90, 207, 208
  legal, 32, 49–50, 60–1, 83, 85, 89, 91, 95, 213

as a threat to neoclassical history, 4, 31, 80, 82, 111, 114, 178, 213

antiquarians, 5, 91, 97–8, 124
  Hume's debts to, 174, 182
  reputation of, 34, 191

appendices, use of in historiography, 4, 87, 161, 189, 190, 192, 251

aristocracy, 192, 215
  see also elite; nobility

Aristotle, 15, 171

Arlington, Henry Bennet, 1st Earl of, 55

artes historicae, 7

the arts as a subject in historiography, 33, 182, 186, 187, 188

atheism, 73, 195, 208

Athens, 16, 56, 140, 171, 180

Atterbury, Francis, bishop, 112, 127, 131, 132, 133–4, 159, 163

Atticus, 139

Atwood, William, 85–6

audience for history, 5–6
  implied by book format, 176, 249
  commercial expansion of reading public creates new, 41, 145–6, 151, 156, 206, 208, 215
  families as, 68, 123
  lower orders and middling sort as, 41, 105, 147, 215
  prefers clerical to neoclassical history, 97, 212
  royal, 8–9, 12, 71, 73–4, 77, 215
  theoretical, 8–9, 73–4, 221, 236
  women as, 173–4, 215
  see also Clarendon; Hume; posterity

Augustus, 17, 19, 47

autobiography, 46, 126, 140